1495

This historical anthropology of the family represents a new departure in family studies. Over the past ten years or so, the social scientific sociological analysis of the family has undergone a change, and has been obliged to reconsider its traditional view that industrialisation triggered a shift within society from the 'large family', which fulfilled all social functions from socialising the children to caring for the sick and the old, to the modern nuclear family, which was regarded solely as being the locus for emotional relationships. Historians have shown that in the past there was in fact a great variety of different family structures within a wide range of varying demographic, economic and cultural frameworks, distinctive for each society. At the same time, the interaction between sociology and social anthropology has led to a clearer conceptual analysis of that vague, polysemic term 'family'; and notions of dwelling-place, descent, marriage, the relative roles of husband and wife and parent–child relations, as well as the more general relations between generations, have in a variety of past and present social contexts been taken apart and analysed. In this book, Martine Segalen reviews and synthesises a rich wealth of often little-known European and North American historical and social anthropological material on the family. This results in a reversal of the frequently held view of the family as an institution in decline, showing it instead to be both dynamic and resistant.

Historical anthropology of the family

Themes in the Social Sciences

Editors: *Jack Goody & Geoffrey Hawthorn*

The aim of this series is to publish books that will focus on topics of general and interdisciplinary interest in the social sciences. They will be concerned with non-European cultures and with developing countries, as well as with industrial societies. The emphasis will be on comparative sociology and, initially, on sociological, anthropological, and demographic topics. These books are intended for undergraduate teaching, but not as basic introductions to the subjects they cover. Authors have been asked to write on central aspects of current interest that have a wide appeal to teachers and research students, as well as to undergraduates.

Other books in the series

Edmund Leach: *Culture and Communication: the logic by which symbols are connected: an introduction to the use of structuralist analysis in social anthropology*

Anthony Heath: *Rational Choice and Social Exchange: a critique of exchange theory*

P. Abrams and A. McCulloch: *Communes, Sociology and Society*

Jack Goody: *The Domestication of the Savage Mind*

Jean-Louis Flandrin: *Families in Former Times: kinship, household and sexuality*

John Dunn: *Western Political Theory in the Face of the Future*

David Thomas: *Naturalism and Social Science: a post-empiricist philosophy of social science*

Claude Meillassoux: *Maidens, Meal and Money: capitalism and the domestic community*

David Lane: *Leninism: a sociological interpretation*

Anthony D. Smith: *The Ethnic Revival*

Jack Goody: *Cooking, Cuisine and Class*

Roy Ellen: *Environment, Subsistence and System*

S. N. Eisenstadt and L. Roniger: *Patrons, Clients and Friends: interpersonal relations and the structure of trust in society*

John Dunn: *The Politics of Socialism*

Historical anthropology of the family

MARTINE SEGALEN

Translated by J.C. WHITEHOUSE *and* SARAH MATTHEWS

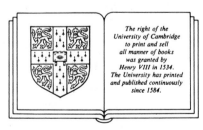

The right of the
University of Cambridge
to print and sell
all manner of books
was granted by
Henry VIII in 1534.
The University has printed
and published continuously
since 1584.

CAMBRIDGE UNIVERSITY PRESS

Cambridge

London   New York   New Rochelle
Melbourne   Sydney

Published by the Press Syndicate of the University of Cambridge
The Pitt Building, Trumpington Street, Cambridge CB2 1RP
35 East 57th Street, New York, NY 10022, USA
10 Stamford Road, Oakleigh, Melbourne 3166, Australia

© Cambridge University Press 1986

First published 1986

Printed in the United States of America

Library of Congress Cataloging-in-Publication Data
Segalen, Martine.
Historical anthropology of the family.
(Themes in the social sciences)
Translation of: Sociologie de la famille.
Includes bibliographies.
1. Family.   2. Family – History.   3. Kinship.
4. Marriage.   I. Title.   II. Series.
HQ737.S4413   1986   306.8′5   85–26975

British Library Cataloguing in Publication Data
Segalen, Martine
Historical anthropology of the family. – (Themes
in the social sciences)
1. Family
I. Title   II. Series
306.8′54   HQ728
ISBN 0 521 25704 2 hard covers
ISBN 0 521 27670 5 paperback

Contents

Foreword   *page* ix

INTRODUCTION   1
   Talking about the family: paradoxes and contradictions   1
   The sociology of the family: where history and
   anthropology meet   3
   The aim and scope of this work   6
   Suggested reading   8

Part One: The area of kinship   11

1 THE DOMESTIC GROUP   13
   The large peasant family   14
   The domestic group in the past: size and structure   20
   The instability of the old domestic group   31
   Recent developments   37
   Domestic groups and kin relationships   39
   Suggested reading   40

2 KINSHIP AND KINSHIP GROUPS   43
   The terminology of kinship   45
   Filiation   46
   Marriage   56
   Lines and kindred groups in peasant societies   61
   Suggested reading   71

3 KIN RELATIONSHIPS IN URBAN SOCIETY   73
   Social and kinship change   73
   Lines and kindred groups in contemporary society   80
   Kinship group versus nuclear family: an ideological
   position   103
   Suggested reading   103

v

Contents

Part Two: The making of the domestic group   105

4   THE HISTORICAL SOCIOLOGY OF MARRIAGE   107
From alliance to marriage   108
Towards contemporary marriage   132
Suggested reading   137

5   MARRIAGE AND DIVORCE IN CONTEMPORARY SOCIETY   139
Marriages   139
Choosing a partner: who marries whom?   143
Love, a social force of reproduction   147
Cohabitation and the younger generation   148
Divorce   151
Suggested reading   158

6   THE CHILD AND THE FAMILY   159
Towards a norm of two children   160
The diverse and changing nature of parental
relationships   173
The family life cycle   181
New kinds of parents and children?   183
Suggested reading   196

Part Three: Domestic roles and activities   199

7   ROLES WITHIN THE COUPLE IN THE NINETEENTH CENTURY   201
A complex problem   201
Peasant households   204
Artisans' and shopkeepers' households   210
Working-class households   212
Bourgeois households   218
Suggested reading   221

8   ROLES WITHIN THE PRESENT-DAY COUPLE   223
Sociological role theories   223
Factors leading to changes in roles   227
The contemporary couple   244
Suggested reading   255

9   THE DOMESTIC GROUP AND ECONOMIC ROLES   257
The domestic group as an income unit and a consumption
unit   258
The domestic group and inheritance   273
Suggested reading   285

Contents

10 FAMILY AND SOCIETY   286
    The family and social control   287
    The family and social power   293
    Women in the family and in society   298
    The family and social destiny   304
    Suggested reading   306

Notes   309
Index   323

Foreword

There is no truly comprehensive textbook on "the family" currently available. There are many works on the family in pre-industrial cultures, mostly written by social anthropologists. There are books on the past of specific European societies, mainly by historians. There are studies of contemporary western communities, largely by sociologists. But the differences between training and research methods in these disciplines result in publications of very different kinds.

In this book, Martine Segalen manages to cross these disciplinary divides in a highly constructive way. Her continental European background affords a fresh perspective from that of much Anglo-American sociological writing, which tends to take as its norms the lower-class family in Bethnal Green, the blacks of Chicago, or the middle class of Yankee City. But at the same time she is well acquainted with the work done in English-speaking areas, concerning both the present and the past. It is one of her great strengths that she not only avoids parochialisation but spans the various academic fields of anthropology, history and sociology. She is thus able to deal with the family both in pre-industrial and 'Third-World' societies, and in its urban and rural manifestations in the industrialised world.

Martine Segalen has done research in rural Normandy and Brittany, having worked as well in an urban milieu. Starting with an enquiry into the selection of marriage partners, her work later expanded into a study of the connections between domestic groups, the relations between the sexes and types of inheritance and succession, as well as of related rites and symbols. Her research is therefore truly interdisciplinary, and she is familiar with both the village and the town, the past (over two hundred years) and the present, the use of documents and that of questionnaires and participant observation, the employment of genealogical reconstruction, of computer processing and of conceptual reformulation. Although I have used the word interdisciplinary, her endeavour is more one of estab-

ix

lishing a new field that cross-cuts the earlier boundaries between anthropology, sociology and history. No mere electicism, her research is guided by the desire to test the very general distinction between elementary and complex forms of alliance made by Lévi-Strauss on the basis, essentially, of freedom of choice. But aside from that, its main strength derives from the active combination of interests of an anthropological, sociological, historical and demographic kind which enables the reader to place the concerns of the present in the context of the past and of the other.

Jack Goody

Lacapelle

Introduction

Can there be such a thing as a sociology of the family? Unlike other areas in which we may admit that we have no special competence, this particular field is, naturally enough, one we all feel we know well – we were all born into a family and, perhaps, have started one. This empirical, felt knowledge of the family makes it one of the most ideologically loaded of topics.

The family also holds some of the keys to our future as a nation. Should families cease to produce enough children as some demographers, historians and politicians have already claimed with alarm, should couples break up and teenagers harass people in the streets, then the state will look for ways and means of setting the family on a path with a less disastrous significance for the future, and at a lower social cost.

TALKING ABOUT THE FAMILY: PARADOXES AND CONTRADICTIONS

The assumptions on which we base our judgements concern the contemporary family, as compared to some mythical one that is 'felt' rather than analysed or known. The press and television echo the same clichés and talk of the 'disintegrating family', 'the weakening of the family', 'state aid for the family', 'the family at risk' and so on, stressing the link between the idea of family and the notion of crisis.

It would be useful at this point to suggest briefly the major ways in which this theme is formulated before going on to analyse them in the subsequent chapters. In our time, the family has contracted. It consists now of the couple. It is a unit of consumption rather than of production. It no longer provides the help it used to accept as its responsibility in the past, such as caring for the elderly, the sick or

1

the mentally ill, and such functions of the kind that it still carries out (the socialisation of children, for example) are now shared with other institutions. Moreover, this 'insular' family now has very few relationships with other family cells. These relationships are seen as being 'impoverished', and in making such statements we are implicitly referring to some period in the past when they were 'rich'. According to this way of seeing things, the family cell manipulated by social institutions appears weak.

But there is another way of looking at the family that sees it as formidably powerful, a refuge and the special focus for our feelings. The couple first and foremost, and the children secondarily, are seen as investing in the family all those emotions that cannot be expressed in a dehumanised society. According to this view, all the warmth of those social relations that once embraced a wide range of kinfolk, neighbours and friends is now seen as being focussed more narrowly and more intensely on the nuclear family and on close relatives.

It is clear that these two ways of seeing the family are contradictory. On the one hand, it is said to be undergoing a crisis, on the other to wield inordinate power, since it has a virtual monopoly of emotional power in an emotionally starved society. As one sociologist investigating the family in Paris was told, '*The* family is in a bad way, but *my* family is fine.'

Is the family truly in crisis? Perhaps to talk about the question in such terms misses the point and may, perhaps, gloss over the real problem, namely that *society* is in crisis.

This theme was recurrent throughout the nineteenth century. Industrialisation drew to the towns enormous numbers of workers who had lost their old cultures and been assimilated into the proletariat, and the number of abandoned children and illegitimate births and the rate of juvenile delinquency all increased. The instability of proletarian families was a source of concern to the dominant classes, who wished to restore the power of the family and that of patriarchal and monarchical authority and to use the former as an instrument to foster morality amongst the working classes.

As an institution, the family can both resist and adapt. It has lived through all the changes, both economic and social, that have brought Western societies from the stage of a peasant to that of an industrial economy. It is more than the 'basic cell' of society or a 'last bulwark' against destructive forces and, seen in historical perspective, has powers of flexibility and resistance. Instead of analysing it in terms of a 'crisis', we should try to discover how the family has lived through the economic, social and cultural upheavals of the last hundred and fifty years, how it has resisted them and how it has contributed to them.

THE SOCIOLOGY OF THE FAMILY: WHERE HISTORY AND ANTHROPOLOGY MEET

In France, although in the 1950s and 1960s the sociology of the family was not quite as formless and empty as the American historian Edward Shorter saw it, it was nevertheless a rather underdeveloped field, very much under the influence of a consciously empirical American sociology. It was unable to provide relevant conceptual frameworks or, until quite recently, exact data, and very probably this explains why there has been so much talk of 'crisis'. American sociology, because it has remained faithful to the concept of long-range social development, presents the family as a defined structure without precise references to its social and cultural environment and not as a domestic group undergoing change within a specific historical framework. The abstract nature of this position can be explained by the dominant ideology of the post-war years, that of individualism and freedom. This has meant that each family cell tended to be seen as unique and independent of cultural influences or economic and historical contingencies.

William Goode, however, in his work published in the 1960s, proposed quite a different approach. Whereas classical sociology produced more and more empirical research, Goode's innovation was to compare the American family with that in other cultures. He observed the frequently dynamic role of family systems, which sociology had often seen as passive objects, and drew a distinction between norms and practices, stressing that the ideology of the conjugal family did not necessarily imply a conjugal structure.

Goode's works, with their pioneering ideas, produced no great response in the sociological field for some time. It was left to historians interested in family structures to rediscover them in the 1970s. Sociology and history come together when exponents of both disciplines leave their traditional confines and go beyond the classic contrast of their respectively diachronic and synchronic approaches, that is, when historians refuse to concern themselves exclusively with changes and sociologists with structures. And sociology, as its knowledge of the family in bygone times increases, is gradually becoming more aware of its own limits. This increasing knowledge seems decisive, since every change is implicitly or explicitly referred to the family in the past.

Sociology is formulating this need and history is discovering or

3

rediscovering the family. The latter has been influenced in its new orientation by the current ideology of 'the crisis in the family'. Also, although it has long been exclusively concerned with the state, it has rediscovered the family under the influence of those branches of itself that are directed towards the economic, social and cultural history of the mass of the population. Similarly, demographers interested in large-scale population movements find that the family is a central factor in their investigations. In France, as a result of their anxiety about the downward trend in fertility in the years before the Second World War, demographers both looked back into the past to attempt to produce a demographic history as well as made a close study of the family cell, that mysterious place in which fertility, once a natural phenomenon, had become a controlled and limited one. The *Institut national d'études démographiques,* as a result of the impetus given by Louis Henry, introduced a *fiche de famille* that made it possible to measure the degree of fertility and variations in it. This new technique, which attracted a great deal of interest both in France and elsewhere, made available a great deal of data. However, although historical demography enables us to discern trends and developments, it proposes no answers. Through the questions it raises, though, it does provide a new perspective on the historical problems connected with the family by moving towards a psychological history that could explain why such developments might occur.

The work of Philippe Ariès on the child's place in the awareness of the family has had a considerable influence on sociologists by offering support for those ideas concerned with the contraction of the family round the conjugal couple. Although that position is much more complex nowadays, it is, after twenty years of research, widely accepted. At the same time, his hypotheses have become an integral part of the cluster of questions that demographers have raised for themselves and for others and have contributed to the new deployment of forces in historical research on the family and the history of ways of thinking. This is based on sources well known to historians (notarial, judicial and ecclesiastical archives, account books, surveys and economic and social documents) but hitherto not fully exploited in studies concerning the family.

This 'new history' of a social, economic and cultural kind has, even if it sometimes goes beyond these areas, been a fertile source of information and ideas with regard to the study of the family.

History has been illuminating in two ways with regard to the general movement of sociology. In the first place, it has shown us how naïve many of our old simplistic concepts were. Some of our theories were based on an erroneous view of life in the past, and some of our suppositions about the constancy of behaviour patterns were without foundation. A historical perspective has meant that we are now able to see the relative nature of a particular attitude towards the family or a particular aspect of the family as a characteristic of contemporary society. One example of this is our cliché of the 'shrinking' of the present-day family.

In this book we will see that kinship relations that had supposedly been overstretched by the effects of incipient industrialisation were in fact maintained and that certain forms were even strengthened. Here, the task of history is to demystify and demythologise our contemporary analyses of and statements about the family. These are still based on an implicit image of the 'good old days', of the family as the repository of every virtue and of all the harmony we have since lost. Increased knowledge of the family of former times means that we can form a fresh judgement of the family of our own day and its supposed crises and deviant behaviour.

Second, history teaches modesty. Relationships between changes taking place within the family and those taking place within society and technical, economic and social changes can never be explained in terms of simple and single models. Every study of the family in a particular social and economic context shows the wide range of different situations involved. It is not simply a question of no longer being able to claim that industrialisation alone changed the family in a fundamental way. We also have to make a more sophisticated study of the various complex relationships between the two processes.

During the earliest, artisanal stage of industrialisation, family structures remained relatively unchanged. They had, in fact, experienced some modification before industrialisation got under way, that may perhaps have facilitated the latter. Developments at the level of the domestic unit and the unit of production must therefore be examined simultaneously rather than consecutively, since both are produced by the same cultural and social changes. It follows that in other societies with different family traditions and patterns, different models of family and industrial development can be expected.

Reflecting on the family against the background of history therefore shows that there is not one single type of family and family organisation over the spectrum of time and space, but rather several. In thus perceiving the relative nature of the object of study, the historian encounters the variety of patterns that social anthropology observes.

This encounter with social anthropology is teaching historians and sociologists to take a new look at the body of knowledge and the set of theories we have built up concerning the family, and shows us that although it is a universal phenomenon the various forms it takes differ greatly in specific societies. There is a difference in degree, if not in kind, between those societies traditionally studied by anthropologists and contemporary ones. In the former, the basic matter of social categories, the framework of relationships of production, of consumption, power and so on, is provided by kinship, whereas in the latter, kinship is in competition with other social institutions, and with the state in particular. The way in which the family is currently organised in Western societies is merely one of the possible ways provided by the whole range of cultures. History enables us to re-create the family in the flow of time, and social anthropology shows us how relative it is with regard to other types of culture.

Social anthropology also proceeds in a way that greatly enriches the sociology of the family, by making considerable use of monograph studies. It stresses the need to examine the nature of the family within a carefully determined culture and in terms of its relationship with that culture. In conjunction with psychological and psychoanalytical approaches it also seeks the meaning of the symbols revealed by an analysis of behaviour patterns and rituals. This means that the family need no longer be seen simply as a passive and externally determined object, but can be envisaged as an institution capable of resistance and action.

THE AIM AND SCOPE OF THIS WORK

There are three parts to this book. The first sets out to elucidate the structural relationships between family, domestic group and kinship. It is based on anthropological concepts and attempts to show which of these are the most relevant to a better understanding of the contemporary family. The second is centred on the make-up of the family, marriage and the birth of children. The third deals with the roles and activities of the spouses. In the final chapter, the relationships between the family and society are discussed.

Each theme is introduced from both the historical and anthropological point of view. It is in this that both the orginality of the approach and its difficulty lie, for when one is dealing with the family everything is interrelated and the intersections in the range of problems related to the family are indicated by the multiplicity of cross-references.

Comparisons of this kind, involving cultures from different times and places, raise a further major difficulty. If we compare a family from another time or place with a contemporary family, we are really contrasting a rural and an urban society. Although there is a generally accepted definition of the former with regard to social relationships, the latter is highly differentiated and still inadequately conceptualised.

The family, whether considered from the point of view of kinship, affective relationships or its structural links with society, is, wherever possible and useful, allocated a place in terms of social categories seen not as classes but as cultural milieux. Thus, women and children, for example, are discussed in terms of working-class, peasant, bourgeois families and so on. The book does not pretend to present definitive theories about the family. Contemporary sociology is obliged to exercise a certain prudence, for it has no conceptual framework capable of accounting for the wide range of family phenomena. Now is not the time for a general theory, but rather for a 'medium-range' one, relating certain structural trends and certain types of families whose behaviour patterns are studied within well-defined temporal and spatial frameworks. Nor can we hope to provide a complete and exhaustive analysis of the subject itself, though perhaps the suggested reading may fill some of these gaps.

The word 'family' is a polyseme indicating both individuals and relationships. It refers both to the conjugal cell and offspring in today's society and to the household of former times. Here it is called the domestic group. Depending on the context, it can designate a very restricted group (parents or grandparents) or a wider one (uncles, aunts or cousins) of relatives. In other contexts it can be used of relationships between individuals or family units. Its meaning can be widened (as in, for example, 'the Smith family') to cover a dynasty of relatives who do not cohabit but share a joint patrimony. These are but a few of the meanings of the word.

The family not only presents lexical difficulties. The feelings centred in it are also full of snares. 'Love', 'family closeness' and 'the sense of childhood' are all vague expressions, used and judged in terms of the awareness of them that our own experience has given us. Consequently, we all too often tend to judge situations in the past (when relationships were different) by the yardstick of our present-day experience. I will try to say what is meant by such expressions, or at least to point out the difficulty inherent in the problem. Can one measure the intensity of love?

In terms of a precise vocabulary, instead of always speaking of the 'family', I will instead use whichever term seems to define most clearly that institution in the particular aspect of it under discussion,

7

Introduction

using such expressions as 'nuclear family', 'domestic group' and 'kinship relations'.

SUGGESTED READING

Works of a sociological nature

Anderson, Michael, ed. *Sociology of the Family*. London: Penguin, 1982. (Contains very useful comparative quantitative indicators of family change.)

'The Family'. *Daedalus* 106(1977): 2.

Mendras, Henri. *Eléments de Sociologie*. Paris: Colin, 1975. See in particular chapter VIII on the family.

Michel, Andrée. *La Sociologie de la famille*. Paris: Mouton, 1970.

Sociologie de la famille et du mariage. Paris: PUF, 1972; new ed., 1978.

Sociologie comparée de la famille contemporaine. International conferences of the Centre National de la Recherche Scientifique. Paris: CNRS, 1955.

Stoetzel, Jean. 'Révolution industrielle et changements dans la famille'. In *Renouveau des idées sur la famille*. Cahiers de l'INED, no. 18. Paris: PUF, 1954.

Williams, Robin M., Jr. *American Society*. 3d ed. Chapter IV, 'Kinship and the Family in the United States'. New York: Knopf, 1970.

A contemporary critique of American sociology

Elder, Glen. 'Approaches to Social Change and the Family'. In *Turning Points. Historical and Sociological Essays on the Family*, supplement to *American Journal of Sociology* 84 (1978): 1–38. Ed. John Demos and Sarane Spence Boocock.

On the contribution of history

Anderson, Michael. 'The Relevance of Family History'. In *The Sociology of the Family: New Directions for Britain*. Ed. Chris Harris. Monograph no. 28. Keele: University of Keele Press, 1979.

Burguière, André. 'Famille et société', in a special edition of *Annales Economies, Sociétés, Civilisations* 4–5 (1972): 799–801, devoted to the family.

On the contribution of social anthropology

Héritier, Françoise. 'Famille'. *Encyclopedie Einaudi*, vol. 6. Einaudi, 1978.

Lévi-Strauss, Claude. *La Famille*. Papers by and on Claude Lévi-Strauss. Collected by R. Bellour and C. Clément. Paris: Gallimard, 1979.

A pioneer sociology listening to history and social anthropology:

Goode, William. *World Revolution and Family Patterns*. Glencoe, Ill.: Free

Suggested reading

Press, 1963. Also published, with a simplified sociological presentation, as *The Family*. Englewood Cliffs, N.J.: Prentice-Hall, 1964.

Historical approaches

Anderson, Michael. *Approaches to the History of the Western Family 1500–1914.* London: Macmillan, 1980.

Ariès, Philippe. *Histoire des populations françaises et leurs attitudes devant la vie depuis le XVIIIe siècle.* Paris: Seuil, 1948. Published in the Points collection.

Flandrin, Jean-Louis. *Families in Former Times.* Cambridge: Cambridge University Press, 1979. (An essential work with up-to-date historical material relating to the subject.)

Hareven, Tamara K., ed. *The Family and the Life Course in Historical Perspective.* New York: Academic Press, 1978.

Journal of Family History: Studies in Family, Kinship and Demography, published by the National Council on Family Relations, Minneapolis.

Lebrun, François. *La Vie conjugale sous l'Ancien Régime.* Paris: Colin, 1975. A useful pedagogical work dealing with all aspects of the family in the *ancien régime*.

Mitterauer, Michael, and Reinhard Sieder. *The European Family.* Oxford: Basil Blackwell, 1982.

Shorter, Edward. *The Making of the Modern Family.* New York: Basic Books, 1975. (To be read critically in that it contains some attractive but unproved assertions and adopts an ethnocentric approach.)

Stone, Lawrence. *The Family, Sex and Marriage in England, 1500–1800.* New York: Harper & Row, 1977.

Wheaton, Robert, and Tamara K. Hareven, eds. *Family, Sexuality in French History.* Philadelphia: University of Pennsylvania Press, 1980.

PART ONE

The area of kinship

Chapter 1

vuvuvuvuvuvuvuvuvuvuvuvuvuvuvuvuvuvuvuvuvuvuvuvuvuvuvuvuvuvuvuvuvuvuvuvuvuvuvuvuvuvuvu

The domestic group

Starting from the basis of the most ordinary experience, we begin this study by examining the domestic group. By a domestic group we mean a set of people sharing the same living-space. Cohabitation and shared residence is a crucial element in our definition.

The living-space may also be a place of work and production, such as a farm, an artisan's workshop or a shop. For most modern Western families, it may be no more than a place of relaxation, of social activity and consumption. In this way, the nature of the shared space may change, as may the group sharing it.

The associated idea of the nuclear family, which is more restricted than that of the domestic group, refers essentially to the married couple and their children. Some domestic groups may consist of a single nuclear family, others of several, perhaps combining several married couples with either filial links (aged parents and married children) or collateral ones (couples of brothers and sisters). The domestic group, in addition to one or more nuclear families, might include people without kinship links either taking part in its productive activity, such as servants, journeymen or apprentices, or not, as in the case of tenants, lodgers and so forth. If the concept of the domestic group is clearly a wider one than that of the nuclear family, how does it stand in relation to that of the household (which has the advantage of referring to residence, house, hearth), an ancient term used when calculating the number of families? 'Household' is not used here, 'domestic group', which is a wider and more neutral expression, being preferred.

The main concern of this chapter is to examine the types and structures of domestic groups seen from the outside. Their internal relationships, that is the relationships existing between the members making up these groups, will be discussed in Chapter 7. This method of approaching the family from the point of view of the

13

domestic group makes it possible to draw comparisons between communities at different dates and in different locations. The type of family pattern we know in our own society then comes to be seen as simply one possible grouping in the whole range of cultures, and as neither better, more final or even necessarily really very different from other groupings in different, very varied contexts.

This approach will also lead to a refutation of certain stereotypes about the existence of 'extended families' or 'extended family communities'. This is an important point. Any assertion that changes in the family are due to a 'contraction in the family' must be questioned once it has been established that the numbers making up domestic groups in the past were not much greater than they are today.

THE LARGE PEASANT FAMILY

Historical research has shown that there was not one single type of large family, but several. These were the tacit community, the zadruga and the stem family.

Tacit communities

Family and security are often synonymous. In troubled times, during wars, epidemics and calamities of all kinds, people formed groups for mutual help and support and to work together. The development of family communities may perhaps date from the late Middle Ages, which saw the growth of the religious fraternities in which men joined together to pray, do penance and bury the dead. They also came together to make good use of uncultivated land given by a lord or an abbey to be cleared or cultivated collectively. Whole population movements sometimes occurred, with new settlers being brought in to make up for the depletion of the labour force as the result of an epidemic. Family communities might include outsiders who would join on a fraternal basis, creating a kind of blood link by means of 'contracts of brotherhood' (*affrairement*) made between individuals or, on a much more secure basis, between conjugal cells consisting of a couple and their children. They were also made up of groups of relatives who formed associations for which there was no written legal basis, hence their title of 'tacit communities'.

Who made up these communities and how did they work? Family communities were particular forms of domestic groups and had as their essential feature co-residence. The division of labour and goods alone does not provide a sufficient definition, as all the members, or

14

The large peasant family

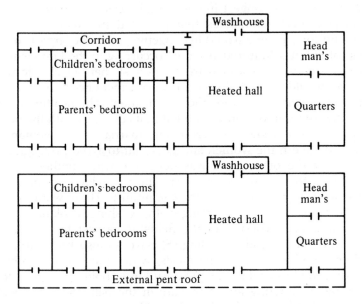

Fig. 1.1. Plan of a typical tacit community. Two types: with corridor, or covered way. (From Henriette Dussourd, *Les Communautés familiales agricoles du centre de la France* [Paris: Maisonneuve et Larose, 1978], p. 88.)

parsonniers, as they were called, not only lived under the same roof but, more important, shared the same kitchen. It was not enough simply to be sleeping in the same house. The most important binding element was the preparation and eating of food in common. It was this last alone that made it possible for the family community to take advantage of certain benefits. As Henriette Dussourd writes:

> If it was shown that members of a community living under the same roof had their own fires or a fireplace where they did their own cooking, apart from the single hearth required by law, they became once more subject to mortmain and the lord again assumed his right to inherit from serfs having no further direct descendants.[1]

In the Middle Ages, respecting the rule of such communities enabled group members to pass on an inheritance to their descendants. Thus the group remained in one place. For their part, the lords acquired a cheap supply of labour, and these family associations were encouraged by means of exemption from taxes. Although they were not the only form of family organisation, the tacit associations were found over large areas of France in the Middle Ages. They were broken up at different times in different parts of the

15

country, surviving longest in the central areas, where oral evidence concerning them illuminates that provided by archives. Between thirty and forty people would live together, with the largest communities (of about a hundred persons) occurring in the Limousin. The *parsonniers* chose a headman from amongst themselves. He would often be the eldest, and always a man of experience. These communities have been called 'republics of kinsmen'. The headman would direct the community, representing it in its dealings with the outside world, allotting tasks and arranging marriages. A woman was elected to govern the women and girls, but to avoid privileging one family over the others, she was never the wife, mother, sister or daughter of the headman. The headwoman divided up the various duties between the women of the community. These would include domestic tasks such as preparing cloth, washing, cooking and gardening and also working in the fields at harvest time, gathering fruits and certain kinds of tilling. She would also bring up all the children together, prepare the meals, which the whole community ate round the huge table, the great cauldron 'holding about a dozen bucketfuls' simmering above the fire in the hall, the only room in the house that had any heating (Fig. 1.1).

Community goods were also held in common. Each *parsonnier* was fed and clothed according to his need, but could never withdraw his 'share' in the community, as to do so would make it poorer. Strict control was therefore kept on marriages that ran the risk of breaking up the community. The headman's strategy was to keep his sons at home and settle an apanage on girls marrying outside the community. This dowry cancelled all their claim to the goods held in common. The preferred kind of marriage was an endogamous union between two members of the community, thereby strengthening it.

Such unions were of course between kinfolk, and since, within certain degrees of kinship, they were forbidden by the church, dispensations were necessary. Indeed, marriage between blood relatives was so common in some communities that they were granted permanent dispensations. Another common form of marriage was by exchange, with a group of brothers or sisters from one community marrying another group of brothers or sisters from another, thus ensuring that only people moved and goods remained within the community.

When we speak of a family community, we are referring both to a particular domestic group and to the agricultural land held jointly. The relationships between domestic groups and the ways in which land was held are complex. The equilibrium within the community

16

was precarious since it was based on a contradiction: Under Roman law each member had equal rights to jointly owned property, whilst at the same time the only way to keep such a system in existence was to forgo those rights. At any given time, there was the threat of a split as a result of internal tensions. If a member claimed his rights, the community would collapse. Indeed, many of them did disappear in the seventeenth century, when very heavy taxation forced peasants to sell their property, which was then bought back by the nobles and the bourgeoisie. Paradoxically, communities deprived of property were able to remain in existence as a result of collective share-cropping contracts granted by large landowners. Their continued existence was justified by the fact that they represented an abundant source of labour accustomed to working together.[2] Communities of this kind were dissolved for economic, demographic, social and cultural reasons arising from developments in society, but also for internal reasons such as the disagreements (often between women) inherent in life in a community, or the threat of dissolution when a member decided to leave and claim his share or his mother's apanage that had fallen into the common stock of goods. Gradually, individualism and a right to personal gain and the increasing focus of family feeling on the nuclear family induced people to reject the burden of community life, for which the need grew less as collective insecurity decreased.

The family community that, in contemporary ideology, is seen in a very generalised way as consisting in the 'extended family', can thus in fact be defined in very specific terms: It is a domestic group made up of a number of households based on a specific organisation of economics and labour, set within strict historical and geographic limits, in which it formed the way of life for a minority. The family community might well occupy an entire hamlet, but it never held sway over the totality of common land – this it shared with other, smaller domestic groups.

The Yugoslav zadruga

In his *Famille et tradition communautaire en Yougoslavie*, Jean-François Gossiaux has shown that community of residence and of meals was as fundamental as in the tacit communities in France. The zadruga did, however, have small rooms built onto the main accommodation for the use of married couples. Such rooms were not heated and had no cooking facilities, but their existence nevertheless indicated the potential for individual private life inherent in the conjugal couple. In the zadruga, the men's goods were held in common, but those of the women were excluded. This followed customary law, in which girls received no inheritance apart from a small sum of their own when they married and which gave them no scope to acquire wealth. The place of women was subordinate, and wives, daughters and daughters-in-law had virtually no power. On the other hand, the community could provide itself with adopted sons who immediately had a say in its running. An elected headman governed it and organised the men's work. His authority was even greater than in corresponding institutions in France, since here it had a religious origin, as he was responsible for the rites connected with the patron saint who protected the zadruga. The headwoman was responsible for organising the women's work, which was strictly limited to the domestic sphere. As marriages were exogamous (i.e. between different zadrugas), unlike marriages in the French tacit communities, daughters-in-law were outsiders and rivals and were jealous of the daughters of the house, who were exempt from household tasks and spent their time embroidering their bridal goods.

As with the tacit communities, the reasons for the breakup of the zadrugas were varied, with rivalry between women being one structural cause. The buildings for individual couples tended to become real houses, acquiring their own cooking facilities, and as communal living decreased, the domestic group as a single entity disappeared. Work was no longer organised on a community basis, but divided up within conjugal domestic groups. The zadrugas became increasingly open in response to the same forces that were at work in other parts of Europe. With the industrialisation of the country and the consequent demand for labour, peasants from the zadrugas migrated to the towns.

The stem family

Unlike the tacit community, which in France was significant only within a limited central region, the stem family is a recognised type of 'large family' that covered a still imprecisely defined area over much of south-western France.

The stem family was a domestic group that gathered three generations under one roof: the father and mother, one of the married sons and his wife, and that couple's children. To these might be added other unmarried children and servants. In his *Organisation de la famille*, Frédéric Le Play described one family in the Lavedan region in

1856 consisting of eighteen persons: grandfather, father and mother, the heir and his wife, nine children, two unmarried relatives and two servants.

These domestic groups are closely identified with the house (called the *oustal* in Oc, the Aquitanian dialect), which included not only the farm where the family lived and its dependencies in the form of buildings and land, but also rights over collective wealth that played a large part in the economy of the holding. Each house had the right to use particular woods, water and common pastures, and also had its own plot in the cemetery. It had to be handed on from generation to generation in its entirety, and it was a matter of honour for each successive owner to do so, maintaining both the total area of land farmed and its standing amongst the other houses comprising the village community.

This system had two consequences. The first was that the house stamped its reputation and prestige on all its members. There was no individual social position, no 'status', as we will discuss later. Every member of the settled extended family bore not only the name he had in the civil registry but also that of the house in which he lived.

The second effect was that the property could not be divided and that there could be only one heir. Although in certain regions daughters could inherit, the general rule was that over the generations son should succeed father in the type of inheritance later to be called patrilineal. The heir's residence was also patrilineal, since he was obliged to live with his father. As in the Yugoslavian zadruga, the daughter-in-law was always an outsider and subject to her mother-in-law's authority. The other children who were not heirs were provided with a dowry and hence excluded from the succession. A small cash payment removed from them any right to the undivided patrimony, and younger sons would generally try to marry an heiress from another house and become a 'son-in-law'. The other unmarried children would remain at home and tacitly give up their share to the heir. Their status was somewhere between that of servant and kinsman.

In this domestic group covering three and sometimes four generations it was the eldest who had the authority. That is why those nineteenth-century ideologues who were worried about the instability of working-class families urged a return to the settled extended family, which could ensure patriarchal authority and stress the continuity of values from generation to generation. For example, Le Play wrote:

Influenced by a community including and bringing together four generations, children adopt, from the very earliest age, the habits and ideas of
their ancestors. The customs and spirit of the race are thus maintained in
the waves of young people periodically leaving the community, under the
guidance of the experienced old man.[3]

We have looked at tacit communities, zadrugas and stem families,
and it would be possible to list other forms also. We have tried to
show that they correspond to fully defined types of domestic groups
and not to vague family patterns; that they appeared, functioned
and finally disappeared in particular social and economic contexts
and are not ahistorical phenomena; and that they are far more important as concepts concerning the family than they were in reality.
In essence, the myth of the extended family has provided food for
the collective imagination in its search for the image of a golden age
in past models of the family, an image held up in contrast against a
present fraught with all kinds of problems.

Current ideology tends to see things in terms of a simplistic contrast between two idealised types of family with, on the one hand,
an enormous gathering of kinfolk in the past and, on the other, the
small nuclear family of our day. These are viewed respectively as
being good and bad. The large, multiform domestic group is seen as
the repository of real family values, having, for example, grandparents to ensure family continuity and facilitate the care and upbringing of the children. The contemporary couple, with husband
and wife both working, is regarded as being unable to experience
'real' family life, since the children are in a crèche, at school or in the
street, and all this, it is said, leads to juvenile delinquency. There is
no such thing as family tradition any more.

Such a simplistic contrast will not stand up to any in-depth analysis. We have shown that the large tacit communities and stem families were no more than particular and relatively rare patterns in
terms of the family as a whole. Let us therefore now look at the
most common forms of family organisation.

THE DOMESTIC GROUP IN THE PAST: SIZE AND STRUCTURE

Over a period of ten years or so, an important aspect of historical and
anthropological research has been the investigation of the size and
structure of domestic groups in European societies from the fifteenth
century to the present day. This research has been, on occasion, the
subject of passionate debate between the two disciplines.

The domestic group in the past

The size of the domestic group

How many people lived together in the domestic groups of the past? Four? Fourteen? Did they all live under the same roof? Any discussion of the size of such groups entails coming to grips with the question of fertility in bygone times. Amongst the wealth of misconceptions on this topic is the notion that women married young and then produced a child every year of their fertile lives. But, as demographic research over the last twenty years has shown, nothing is further from the truth. For a long time, everything worked against such prolific childbearing. Couples married late, perinatal mortality and the numbers of women dying in childbirth were both high, and economic circumstances, such as famine, reduced female fertility. This meant that over a long period there was very little increase in population and that, indeed, it often barely reached replacement levels. Trends in fertility will be considered further in Chapter 6. Here it is sufficient to point out that it was very rare for the domestic group to produce large numbers of children.

Who lived together in the group and contributed to its size, in terms of numbers of persons? It included relatives, fathers and forefathers and collateral kin, but also non-kinfolk such as servants in noble or bourgeois houses, male and female farm-workers and journeymen in artisans' establishments. Their number clearly varied according to the socio-economic circumstances of the domestic group, and there were some enormous households including ten or more male and female servants alongside conjugal groups made up of an agricultural day-labourer, his wife and their youngest children, the elder ones having left to work elsewhere. Within one village or in the same quarter of a village, huge households and small ones might exist side by side, each corresponding to the area of the land they worked. At Sennely, in the Sologne, on large farms with holdings of between 75 and 100 hectares, the domestic group was big, and the labour force of children was strengthened by the addition of agricultural workers. On the other hand, small leaseholds, which were more common than large ones, were worked by a family of day-labourers who needed extra wages and hired themselves out on a temporary basis to large undertakings. Here the size of the holding and that of the group went hand in hand.[4]

The size of the group also varied according to the ethnic origin of the group. In Holyoke, Massachusetts, in 1800, the largest households were those of Irish or French Canadian origin, as might be expected from the traditionally high fertility of those two ethnic groups (Table 1.1).

Table 1.1 *Mean and median sizes of households by place of birth of the head*

Place of birth of head	Mean size	Median size[a]
United States	4.54[b] (± 0.46)	3.42
Ireland	5.57[b] (± 0.33)	4.83
Canada	6.78[b] (± 0.66)	6.10
All birthplaces	5.49 (± 0.28)	4.53

[a]The median household size is smaller than the mean for all groups since in Holyoke household sizes have a positive skew.   [b]Differences significant at .01 level.
Source: Myfanwy Morgan and Hilda H. Golden, "Immigrant families in an industrial city: a study of households in Holyoke, 1880," *Journal of Family History* 4(1979), p. 61.

Their make-up was also different. Over two thirds of them included non-relatives, but in the case of native American families these were servants (reflecting their higher social status) and in others chiefly boarders (Table 1.2). For Irish and Canadian households, taking in an outsider was a useful way of increasing income, and for the boarder it meant cheap lodgings.[5]

By studying parish records from the sixteenth, seventeenth and eighteenth centuries, historians have been able to establish that the size of the domestic group in England over that period was close to that shown by present-day figures and that its structure was comparatively simple. The average size remained relatively constant at perhaps just under 4.75 persons from the time of the earliest records up until 1901. From a sample of 100 English parishes, Peter Laslett and his team show in their *Household and Family in Past Time* that in England in the sixteenth, seventeenth and eighteenth centuries the average domestic group consisted of father, mother and children. This suggests that the effect of industrialisation has not been to reduce the size and modify the structure of the household.

The structure of the domestic group

Rather than the *size,* it is the *structure* of the domestic group that is significant, for it reveals a certain form of organisation governing the transmission of practices and cultural values, and linking family and work, family and power, and family and possessions. It also provides information about what sociologists call family interaction. William Goode notes in *The Family:*

The various forms of the household have a number of implications for family interaction. They help to determine, for example, the chances of

Table 1.2. *Percentage distributions of households according to presence of boarders, domestic servants and other resident employees, by place of birth of head of household*

	Place of birth of the head			
Type of Non-relative[a]	United States	Ireland	Canada	All birthplaces
Boarder	24.3	25.0	33.7	26.6
Domestic servant	15.3[b]	3.4	3.5	6.9
Other resident employee	4.5	1.4	–	2.1
Total	100.0	100.0	100.0	100.0
	(N = 111)	(N = 148)	(N = 86)	(N = 379)

[a]Categories are not mutually exclusive.   [b]Significant difference from percentage of Irish and Canadian households with domestic servants, .01 level.
Source: Myfanwy Morgan and Hilda H. Golden, "Immigrant families in an industrial city: a study of households in Holyoke, 1880," *Journal of Family History* 4(1979), p. 62.

more or less intimate social relations among members of the kinship group. Thereby, these structural patterns shape in part the processes of strain and adjustment among relatives. Various role relations may have to be spelled out in detail, if the household includes certain relatives. For example, if the household usually includes a man and his mother-in-law, there may be rules requiring much reserve or *non*interaction between the two.

Socialization patterns are also affected by who is included in the household. A mother-in-law may continue to supervise the socialization of a young daughter-in-law, or a young boy may go to his mother's brother's house to grow up. A young child in a polygynous household sees a wider range of adult models intimately than he could observe in a nuclear family. Those who share the same household are likely to share the same budget, and thus economic exchanges are partly determined by the forms of the household.[6]

Peter Laslett and the historians of the Cambridge Group for the History of Population and Social Structure suggest a typology that serves to clarify debate and organise the gathering of data. Their classification has four categories:

1. Domestic groups 'with no family structure' that do not seem to correspond very clearly to anything apart from old friends sharing the same residence. This category most often includes single persons.

2. 'Simple' domestic groups corresponding to our contemporary nuclear family, and consisting either of father, mother and children or a widow or widower with his or her children, but no other relative.

3. 'Extended' domestic groups made up of both the members of

23

the 'simple' group and their parents, descendants and collaterals, that is of the father or mother of the head of the family or of his wife, a grandson or granddaughter of the head of the family or his wife, his brother or his sister, of a nephew or great-nephew. The extension corresponds to the addition, to a central nucleus of a conjugal nature, of a more or less close relative who has to some degree been made into a satellite.

4. 'Multiple' (or 'polynuclear') domestic groups, in which several related families live together. Within this category, a further distinction is made according to the leadership within the group. If the older parental couple assumes this function, and the younger married couple consisting of their offspring and his or her spouse accept their authority, we have an archetypal settled extended family. If this type of domestic group consists only of families of married brothers and sisters of the same generation we have a 'fraternal' situation like that obtaining in the tacit communities of central France or in the Yugoslav *zadruga*. It should be noted that these communities may or may not in each case also include male and female servants and journeymen, i.e. persons who are not kinfolk. It should also be pointed out that one of the criteria for this classification is based on how the leadership of the domestic group is attributed, which sometimes introduces distinctions more of form than of substance.

One advantage of a classification of this kind is that it enables us to compare a whole range of historical data based on lists of returns or population censuses. For example, in the sixteenth, seventeenth and eighteenth centuries, 78 per cent of the households in Ealing (England), 76 per cent of those in Longuenesse (France), 67 per cent of those in Belgrade and 90 per cent of those in Bristol (in the British colonies in America) were 'simple' domestic groups (see Table 1.3). The nuclear family is therefore not just a purely contemporary phenomenon. Nevertheless, there were regions in which 'extended' or 'multiple' domestic groups (groups 3 and 4 in the preceding classification) were the most frequent. In *Families in Former Times* Jean-Louis Flandrin presented figures showing that in the central and southern areas of France under the *ancien régime,* and in Mediterranean societies, the stem family was a fairly widespread model. The figures in Table 1.4 relate to extended and multiple domestic groups in the south of France.

The dynamics of the domestic group

All domestic groups evolve over time, but systems of classification and statistics have tended to ignore the temporal dimension. This is

Table 1.3. *Structure of households, seventeenth and eighteenth centuries (in %)*

Date of census	Ealing (England) 1599	Longuenesse (France) 1778	Belgrade (Serbia) 1733–4	Nishinomiya (Japan) 1713	Bristol (American colonies) 1689
1 Solitaries and domestic groups with no family structure	14	7	4	9	7
2 Simple domestic groups	78	76	67	43	90
3 Extended domestic groups	6	14	15	27	3
4 Complex domestic groups	2	3	14	21	0
Totals	85 (100)	66 (100)	273 (100)	132 (100)	72 (100)

Source: P. Laslett and R. Wall, *Household and Family in Past Time*, Table 1.15, p. 85.

Table 1.4. *Household structures in southern France (in %)*

| Type of household | Périgord | Rouergue | | Provence | County of Nice | | Hautes-Pyrénées |
	Mont-plaisant (1644)	Mostué-jouls (1690)	Laguiole (1691)	Mirabeau (1745)	Saint-Martin-deVésubie (1718)	Péone (1787)	Bulan (1793)
1 Solitaries	11.0	3.2	7.0	6.7	11.2	NDA[a]	3.7
2 No family	1.6	2.1	3.3	0.8			
3 Simple family households	50.8	51.0	56.0	50.8	47.4	NDA	54.7
4 Extended family households	15.9	42.6	32.2	19.2	41.4	41.7	32.0
5 Multiple family households	20.6			22.5			9.4
4 + 5	36.5	42.6	32.2	41.7	41.4	41.7	41.4
Number of households	63	94	214	120	152	259	53

[a]NDA, no data available.
Source: Jean-Louis Flandrin, *Families in Former Times* (Cambridge: Cambridge University Press, 1979), p. 73.

a result of the way the data are drawn up: Lists of returns or population censuses freeze the reality of the family at the point at which they were collected. The percentages they reveal only provide us with, so to speak, a photographic still; what we really need for a satisfactory analysis of the family is a moving picture.

Without entering at this stage into a detailed discussion of the family life cycle, suffice it to say that a couple is formed by marriage, that it has children, that it may share land with the parents of one or the other spouse, which it subsequently either leaves or takes over, together with the responsibility for an old widowed parent or unmarried sister. We have seen briefly the distinctions between the simple domestic group and the complex, extended or polynuclear domestic group. All domestic groups are in transition, are processes not permanencies, and to seek to understand them by means of censuses fixes their image as a particular kind of household, whereas in fact their organisation at any one time may be only temporary. If we look at them again over an extended period we can distinguish two major types of domestic groups – the *structural* and the *non-structural*. This makes it possible to ask whether domestic groups are consistently multiple or conjugal, whether they go through a typical sequence of phases, and if so what the model is, and we can seek to explain the norm and the average in so far as any given model has been recognised as dominant in a particular society.

Two techniques can be used to examine the question over a long period. Using figures from a single census, it is possible to classify types of domestic groups according to the age of the head of the household. Using a sequence of data of this kind, covering the same population over a fairly extended period, we can observe a whole cycle in the life of a group from its inception to its disappearance. It is also important to combine such purely statistical evidence with socio-economic data concerning the way in which the land was worked and how it was inherited. There is often a gap between the establishment of a household and the point at which it gains possession of a holding, just as the breakup of a group does not necessarily coincide with the transmission of property.

With the help of documents of this kind, some historians have illustrated the dynamics of domestic groups. Agnès Fine-Souriac, in her article on the stem family in the Pyrénées, has shown how demographic developments over a period of time affected the structure of the household. Her analysis of the population returns for Bessède, a village in the Aude region of the Pyrénées, for 1846, 1851, 1856, 1861 and 1866, indicates that even in an area in which the stem family was the clear-cut norm, there were also simple domestic groups:

In 1846, Joseph Marion's household was a typical stem family and remained so until 1866, when, after the death of both parents, it had become a nuclear family. Thus, using P. Laslett's typology, its status in 1866 would be that of a simple domestic group, whereas it is quite clear that its real structure was a complex one. Joseph Marion was a well-to-do miller, and in his mill he needed hands. The household was able to feed nine people in 1846 and would probably later take another young married couple.[7]

Similarly, in those areas of western France where the conjugal group is thought to have been more typical, forms of multiple domestic groups did occur when well-to-do farmers had their children living with them for a few years before leaving to settle independently on another farm. This multiple structure would also reappear at the end of the cycle of family life when parents and children once more cohabited, the latter inheriting the lease. Although the conjugal household was the rule, in practice polynuclear households resembling stem families were found in all the censuses.[8] And in certain areas in northern Europe, where the conjugal domestic group was also the norm, it has been possible to show that at certain stages of the cycle a household would generally take the form of a stem family, as happened in the Heidenreichsstein domain in lower Austria in 1763.[9]

E. A. Hammel, studying the patterns of Serbian zadrugas over an extended historical period, shows in *Household and Family in Past Times* that the zadruga family pattern, involving many relatives, was essentially a process with structural principles that remained basically unchanged from the sixteenth century. He sees it as a set of rules regulating the maximum size of the groups by the introduction of means of continually increasing or reducing their size.[10] Each zadruga, like every domestic group, contained the optimum number of people for working its land. When cohabitation resulted in too many people, a fissionary process came into operation; when there were not enough, fusion occurred.

The likelihood of a domestic group being composed of several generations was closely linked to the number of relatives still alive and was thus subject to demographic constraints. In the *ancien régime*, the mortality rate in France was such that grandparents had often died before their grandchildren were born. In the Pyrenean villages discussed in Fine-Souriac's article, when the high mortality rate is taken into account, it would seem that between 20 per cent and 30 per cent of complex domestic groups offer sufficient statisti-

Table 1.5. *Wealth and cohabitation with parents in Saint-André-les-Alpes*

Amount of dowry (livres)	Contracts providing for cohabitation		Contracts not providing for cohabitation		Number of contracts
	(No.)	(%)	(No.)	(%)	
Under 100	0	0	2	100	2
100–199	13	28	33	72	46
200–299	17	35	31	65	48
300–699	44	65	24	35	68
700–1,000	5	100	0	0	5

Source: Collomp in Jean-Louis Flandrin, *Families in Former Times*, p. 89.

cal evidence for the predominance of the stem family. But given the mortality rate, they could never amount to 100 per cent.

The way production was organised also influenced the size and structure of the domestic group as a unit of production. Certain kinds of domestic groups may have been the result of adaptation to economic circumstances. The size of the patrimony was also a determining factor. As we have already pointed out, complex domestic groups built up around well-to-do farmers and conjugal groups associated with day-labourers existed alongside each other. The latter could support neither their aged parents nor their children, who had to be sent out to live and work as labourers on other farms when they were between ten and twelve years old. Not only was the form of the labourers' household simpler; it was also smaller in size. When the household was wealthy, young married couples continued to live with their parents all the more frequently, and the domestic group was larger. The gap between the rule and what was done in practice is explained by the size of the patrimony (Table 1.5).

As Christiane Klapisch notes in *Household and Family in Past Time:*

In urban surroundings, at least in Florence, the proportion of multiple households increases markedly with wealth. The four lower categories of assets which contain some 45% of all households, have an overwhelming proportion (about 95%) of simple households. The four categories above these, extending over the middle range between 100 and 800 florins, have about average numbers (92–93% of simple households). But in the three uppermost categories of assets in Florence, comprising about one-fifth of all the returns, the proportion of multiple households increases rapidly, climbing from 10% to 23%.[11]

Finally, there is the influence of the system of inheritance on the structure of the domestic group. Lutz Berkner considers this in *Population Patterns in the Past*, comparing two towns in Lower Saxony, Calenberg and Göttingen, in the seventeenth century. In the former, where inheritances were not divided, extended domestic groups (30 per cent) were predominant. In the latter, where property was divided amongst several heirs, they amounted to only 7 per cent (1689 census). There is clearly a model approaching that of the stem family in Calenberg, and by analysing the 1766 figures, Berkner goes on to show that population growth did not weaken it.

The relationships between all these variables are of course not simple. Demographic trends influenced inheritance customs, which in turn were likely to be affected by social and economic changes. There can never be a mechanistic relationship between these factors from which a model for a domestic group can be infallibly deduced from a demographic model, a type of agriculture or a system of inheritance. Our present state of knowledge allows us to do no more than talk of convergence. Nevertheless we should always bear in mind the need for sophisticated analyses that simultaneously take into account all the variables when we are trying to understand types of organisation of domestic groups and the causes of the changes they undergo.

There is a further danger in trying to classify domestic groups too rigidly. Under the heading of extended or multiple domestic groups, family patterns may differ considerably from one period to another. In a Breton village where family structures have been studied since 1836, there is now a fairly high percentage of complex domestic groups, but their significance is quite different from that of such groups in the nineteenth century. At that time, parents and their married children would live together on the biggest farms and the most fertile land, whereas nowadays the complex household is more an indicator of malfunction and is experienced as 'abnormal'. Poverty obliges old parents to struggle on with their farm with their daughter's help while the son-in-law brings in the major part of the income from an outside job. The fact that complex domestic groups are perpetuated in no way means that the *status quo* has been maintained. Indeed, it often indicates a state of social and economic crisis.

If the group ceased to be productive, did it necessarily become nuclear? The 'evolutionist' view tends to see a link between industrialisation and the transformation of larger domestic groups into nuclear ones. But this has little real basis. In villages where there were rural cottage industries with production geared to a market dominated by a capitalist economy, there were many extended domestic groups but, as Hans Medick writes in 'The Proto-Industrial Family Economy':

Viewed from a comparative perspective, the extended family of the rural artisans was much more the forerunner of the corresponding proletarian household configuration than a variation of the peasant stem-family. It did not function as an instrument of conservation of property, of well-being and of care for the aged, as was the case with the full peasant household, but as a private means to redistribute the poverty of the nuclear family.[12]

In towns that were undergoing industrialisation, there was no 'nu-clearisation' of the domestic group. In Preston (Lancashire), a town that was rapidly industrialised during the nineteenth century as a result of the growth of the textile industry, the 1851 census showed that 23 per cent of the domestic groups were of the extended or multiple type. In this industrial town the structure of domestic groups was actually more complex than in the English parishes studied two centuries earlier. The urban-industrial revolution seems to have gone hand in hand with a considerable *increase* in the numbers of parents and married children living together. As Michael Anderson shows in *Household and Family in Past Time*, a large number of old people lived with their children. The develop-ment of this multiple or extended domestic group can be explained by the economic constraints arising from industrial work, such as a shortage of housing, the need for the mother to work and the difficulty of minding young children. Cohabitation was therefore due to necessity rather than choice. Since there was no real social provision for illness or poverty, all the individual could do in such cases was to turn to his nearest relatives and set up wider domestic groups within which mutual help was possible. General models of the structure of American households in the nineteenth century also show that, for the same structural reasons, between 12 and 15 per cent included distant relatives and between 23 and 30 per cent boarders and lodgers.[13]

THE INSTABILITY OF THE OLD DOMESTIC GROUP

The prevailing model of the size and structure of the domestic group has been that it was stable, and the image has been of a family group with a farm, a shop, a workshop, rooted in its own space and leading its own life with one generation succeeding another. In fact, the opposite was the case, and the old domestic group was less stable than the nuclear families of today, even when divorce is taken into account. Instability was produced both by geographic mobility and the unforeseen effects of an often galloping mortality rate.

Widowhood and remarriage

In the population patterns of past times, conjugal cells were broken up by mortality more frequently than nowadays, and remarriage was common. M. Baulant has used the striking image of the 'crumbling family'.[14] If a spouse died, the survivor quickly remarried, since this was imperative if a household, which was identical with the farm and based on the mutually complementary work of a husband and wife, was to remain in existence.

That is why there are many examples of domestic groups in which, over the years, a man might have several wives one after the other (this arrangement was much more frequent than the other way around), in which children from several marriages lived together or in which orphaned older children were scattered amongst the families of kinfolk. A family consisting of father, mother and children was often unknown to a good number of our ancestors, and when we think of the attention paid today to children of divorced parents we may well wonder about the effects of such deaths and remarriages on the minds of the children affected by them. It is true that the death of a close relative was culturally more easily accepted than in our own times, when it seems less frequent and immediate and more unbearable, but references in popular literature to stepmothers and exploited stepchildren suggest the difficulties posed by death in the past. Perhaps the *ancien régime* produced whole generations of neurotics, or perhaps orphans found the psychological support they needed amongst either their own age-group or the wider nexus of relatives. It is hard to say what people in past times were like in psychological terms, but it is salient to know that the domestic group in our own day is relatively more stable.

In a nineteenth-century Breton village with demographic structures still similar to those prevailing under the *ancien régime* (i.e., both a high birth rate and a high death rate), we can see an example of the type of couple often dissolved by a death. In 1830 a tailor, Jacques Garrec, married Marie Anne Nicolas, who died on 14 March 1845 leaving three children including a son twelve days old. Three months later, Garrec married Marie Arnoult, who bore him two more children. She died at the age of thirty-two, and six months later Garrec married another woman who bore him four additional children. He thus had nine children by three different wives, and the older ones soon left home (at around the age of twelve) to take employment as apprentices or farmhands. Sometimes a widower and a widow would marry, pooling, so to speak, both their possessions and their children. If one of the two died, the other's children would be dependent on someone not related to them. Hence the need for arrangements for guardians and the importance of a system of godparents.

Table 1.6 gives some figures for remarriage in France from the seventeenth to nineteenth centuries. As indicated, these vary considerably from one region to another. The number of marriages involving a widow or a widower ranges between 5.8 and 43 per cent of the total. These figures cluster (there is no question of an 'average', as the data are sparse) around 20–22 per cent, which means that almost a quarter and sometimes almost half (as at Sennely-en-Sologne) of marriages were remarriages. These differences are probably due in part to widely varying sanitary and economic conditions in the seventeenth century, when certain regions were unhealthy, high-mortality areas, but there is nothing unusual in second marriages reaching 20 per cent of the total. During the early years of marriage, mortality was highest amongst women who died (excess female mortality rate) for reasons connected with pregnancy and childbirth. Towards the end of married life, however, the situation was reversed, and the excess male mortality rate was as marked then as it is now.

When a young man lost his wife and was left with dependent children, he had to marry again very quickly, since a widower had no one to look after the children, do the cooking or help in the fields. This explains why widowers remarried much more frequently than widows and much sooner after the death of a partner. In Crulai (Normandy), for example, one in two of all widowers remarried, but only one widow in six. In the case of women, their age when they were widowed was an important factor in terms of another marriage. Up to the age of forty, they still had a chance of remarrying, although it was less than that of a man, but after forty it was very small indeed. In three villages in the Ile-de-France, for example, three quarters of widowers remarried up to the age of sixty, whereas after forty only one widow in nine did so,[15] reflecting the truth of the old proverb, 'Let it rain, let it snow, let the wind blow haughty, a woman's fine till she reaches forty.' Widowers remarried much more quickly than widows, and in all the parishes examined there was less than a two-year interval between the death of the first wife and remarriage, with a large proportion of remarriages occurring within six months, whereas widows tended to have to wait three or four years to set up a new home.

These frequent remarriages, particularly amongst males, created a

Table 1.6. *Some examples of widowhood and remarriage, eighteenth and nineteenth centuries*

	Marriages of widow(er) & single person (%)			Marriages widow & widower (%)	Total marriages of one widow(er)	Marriages between bachelors & spinsters	Total (%)
	Widower & spinster	Widow & bachelor	Total				
Crulai 17th & 18th centuries (Orne)[a]	15.2	6.7	21.9	3.8	25.7	72.3	98
Sennely-en-Sologne, 18th & 19th centuries[b]	21	13	34	19.4	43.4	46.4	100
Meulan 1670–1739[c]	9.4	7.7	17.1	3.1	20.2	79.8	
Meulan 1790–1869	10.6	5.7	16.3	5.4	22.7	78.3	
Vraiville (Eure)[d]							
1706–1800					15.2	84.8	
1801–1900					14.9	86.1	
Saint-Jean-Trolimon (Finistère)[e]							
1831–1890	11.8	3.5	15.3	6.5	21.8	78.2	
1891–1920	8.4	2.4	10.8	2.6	13.4	86.6	
Saint-André-d'Hébertot, 17th & 18th centuries[f]	5.6	3	8.6	9	17.6	82.2	99.8
Four villages in Tonnerois 1720–1800[g]	14.6	4.4	21.0	8.5	29.5	72.5	
Coulommiers and Chailly in Brie 1557–1715[h]	20.4	10.2	30.6	11.1	41.7	58.3	

Boulay (Moselle)[i]						
Before 1720	10	6	16	3	19	81
1720–1809	12.6	5.4	18	4.4	22.4	77.6
Three villages in Ile-de-France 18th century[j]	17.5	3.7	21.2	3.9	25.1	74.7
Bilhères d'Ossau (Béarn) 1740–1859[k]	4.3	1.5	5.8	0	5.8	94.2
Bas-Quercy 18th century[l]	9.4	3.3	12.7	1.9	14.6	85.3

[a] Michel Fleury and Louis Henry, *La population de Crulai* (Paris: Presses Universitaires de France, 1958).

[b] Gérard Bouchard, *Le village immobile* (Paris: Plon, 1972).

[c] Marcel Lachiver, *La population de Meulan* (Paris: Société d'éditions et de vente des publications de l'Education Nationale, 1969).

[d] Martine Segalen, *Nuptialité et alliance, le choix du conjoint dans une commune de l'Eure* (Paris: Maisonneuve et Larose, 1972).

[e] Martine Segalen, unpublished data.

[f] Françoise Bécart, 'Saint-André-d'Hébertot', *Annales de Normandie*, (1977): 281–94.

[g] Dominique Dinet, 'Quatre paroisses du Tonnerois', *Annales de démographie historique* (1969).

[h] Jean-Claude Polton, 'Coulommiers et Chailly en Brie', *Annales de démographie historique* (1969).

[i] Jacques Houdaille, 'La population de Boulay', *Population* 6(1967): 1054–84.

[j] Jean Ganiage, *Trois villages d'Ile-de-France* (Paris: Presses Universitaires de France, 1963).

[k] Michel Frezel-Lozey, *Histoire démographique d'un village en Béarn: Bilhères d'Ossau* (Bordeaux: Biscaye Frères, 1969).

[l] Pierre Valmary, *Familles paysannes au XVIIIe siècle en Bas-Quercy* (Paris: Presses Universitaires de France, 1965).

situation of serial monogamy, the limit to the number of remarriages being social tolerance of unions that were often socially disruptive in that they sometimes involved husbands and wives of very different ages or social backgrounds, at a time when the norm tended towards homogamy, or congruity of age and status between spouses (see Chapter 4). If, for example, a widow remarried a man much younger than herself, such as her former husband's journeyman, she created a situation in which she was the dominant partner. Since it reversed the roles assigned by the social norm, a union of that kind could be socially disruptive and as such might attract vigorous adverse comment.

Thus, to maintain a domestic group identical with the unit of production, a multiplicity of unions, to some degree reminiscent of the spate of divorces and remarriages in our own time, was formed. Such remarriages affirmed the primacy of the economic over the family organisation. The domestic group was constantly threatened by the dangers of mortality, and its instability chiefly affected the children it cared for or entrusted to the kinship system. The grandparents, brothers and sisters of the deceased spouse would perhaps take them in, acting within the framework of a traditional and tightly knit group that had a place for those on the margins of society, namely the old, the mentally defective and the orphaned.

Mobility

Geographic mobility was a second, and often underestimated, cause of instability in the domestic group. Nowadays we like to contemplate a stylised image of the family of the past, rather like those groups of figures in pictures by Millet or Le Nain that depict clean, poor (but not wretched) rustic interiors in which men, women, children and animals are gathered round a frugal but satisfying meal. They seem to have been looking out at us for a century or two and never to have left the framework we see them in. It is perhaps pictures like that that have strengthened our stereotype of the old, stable domestic group. But that stereotype is often erroneous. In certain regions in which the peasants owned their own farms, the son or son-in-law could succeed the father, but that was not possible for all of them. Only one child could stay where he was, and the others had to move out, as we saw in the case of the stem family.

In regions where farms were rented or share-cropping was the norm, mobility could be enforced if economic conditions favoured the landowner (who was often a middle-class town-dweller) seeking to increase his income. It is true that there was no question of total uprooting, since the peasant stayed in his home area, but a change of residence meant a break or a loosening of tightly knit relationships with the village community, neighbours and certain relatives. Even if the distances involved were not great, they were, given slower forms of transport and fewer roads, more significant than they would be today.

In mountain regions, seasonal migration meant that the father had to leave the domestic group each year to seek temporary work elsewhere. Small farmers from the Limousin, for example, moved down to the south-west and the Landes area, where they were employed as sawyers, or up to Paris or other towns to work as joiners or masons. Sometimes they would come back to their villages to take part in the major tasks on the farm during the summer, but they were often away for longer. This meant that the wife's position in the domestic group was ambiguous. If the grandfather kept his authority, it was to him that the son sent the money he earned. Sometimes the migrant would continue to run the farm from afar, deciding how arable land was to be used and when livestock were to be sold, leaving the wife to see that all these decisions were carried out while, at the same time, she had to cope with a difficult financial situation. This frequently meant that while her husband was away she ran up accounts with the shopkeepers and craftsmen in the village and sometimes even with the schoolmaster. When the migrant, as sometimes happened, appeared to have left his household for good, she might take on a 'partner', who was in effect a second husband.[16]

Temporary emigration, which in France peaked under the Second Empire, caused upsets in family routine comparable to that brought about by emigration from Portugal, Spain and North Africa into France in the last twenty years, although the cultural systems surrounding these two sets of circumstances are totally different. This emigration drained villages of men in their prime, reorganised the yearly cycle around the summer festival, which was generally that of returning and harvesting, and left the socialisation of young children to women and old men, but with reference to the sublimated image of the absent father.

RECENT DEVELOPMENTS

The wealth of statistical data available for our own time is not strictly comparable to that from earlier periods, since the definitions used do not refer to precisely identical family patterns. The idea of the domestic group is mingled with that of the household, and thus it is not easy to outline development or even, paradoxically, to obtain the most recent figures for France.

According to the INSEE, a household is 'all the occupants of a private dwelling occupied as a main residence'. Thus, the notion of cohabitation is the basic one. The Institut National de la Statistique et des Etudes Economiques (INSEE) then goes on to distinguish between 'ordinary households' and 'the population not living in ordinary households' but in collective ones such as old people's homes, workers' hostels and religious communities, as well as 'special categories' such as psychiatric hospitals, penal establishments, barracks and educational establishments.

In France there were 14,588,941 households in 1962, 15,762,508 in 1968, and 17,743,760 in 1975. Over this period the size of households decreased slightly. There were on average 3.10 persons per household in 1962, 3.06 in 1968 and 2.88 in 1975. The number of households consisting of one person has also increased correspondingly, being 19.6 per cent in 1962, 20.3 per cent in 1968 and 22.2 per cent in 1975. This relatively high rate of single residences explains why only 39 per cent of households consisted of a married or unmarried couple with one or more children (1962 census).

Although households during this period usually had their own dwelling, there was some degree of cohabitation, involving either two married couples or a married couple and an aged parent. In over 5 per cent of households three generations were cohabiting. This was more often the case with farmers than with other socioprofessional categories, as a result of building separate houses in agricultural areas. In over 8 per cent of households a couple or surviving spouse and one or more parents were cohabiting. Thus when allowance has been made for increased life expectancy, few households included an aged parent. Old people in fact constituted a high proportion of the households consisting of one person. Once more, the cohabitation of younger couples and older parents was more frequent in agricultural groups than elsewhere.

Although cohabitation was the exception rather than the rule, it was less exceptional if the temporary sharing of a home is taken into account, since 25 per cent of young married couples lived with the parents of the husband or the wife for at least some months, although this was only a makeshift arrangement while waiting for their own home.[17]

Nowadays, the likelihood of the death of a spouse in the early stages of marriage is extremely small. What was once a situation simply to be endured whatever the grief and suffering it caused is now something our contemporary sensibility cannot accept, just as it

Table 1.7. *Probability of death of spouse as sole cause of ending of marriage (1966–70)*

Time into marriage (years)	Female	Male
10	1.8	0.7
20	5.2	2.0
30	12.6	4.6
40	26.6	8.3

Source: D. Maison and E. Millet, 'La Nuptialité', *Population*, June 1974, p. 49.

is deeply upset when children die at birth or at a very early age.[18] In our society, premature death has become so unusual that marriages have very little likelihood statistically of being terminated by the death of one of the partners. something that was common in the past.

As the marriage runs it course, the proportion of widows nowadays increases greatly as a result of excess male mortality (see Table 1.7).

DOMESTIC GROUPS AND KIN RELATIONSHIPS

At least since the eighteenth century, Western societies have been accustomed to permanent and solid housing that imposes constraints on family structures. In tropical societies, where building materials are cheap and the climate allows for flimsier housing, the idea of a domestic group in a single dwelling is less firmly rooted. Thus, Jack Goody writes in 'Domestic Groups':

Since compounds built in temporary materials constantly change their shape according to the number and nature of those who live there, it is the dwelling group that determines the size of the building, rather than vice versa. Of course, society has to make some allowance for expanding families, by moving house, by building a separate cottage, or, as in Montenegro, by adding another room to the existing ones. But with less permanent materials, the correspondence between dwelling and family is closer.[19]

The English term 'household', like the French 'groupe domestique' or 'maisonnée', refers both to a residence group and a consumer group. Although it is clear that a farm is both, as is a separate flat in a tower block, the distinction is harder to make when certain human groups occupy relatively huge dwellings such as Dyak or Iroquois long-houses. Thus the size of the unit of residence must be distinguished both from that of the unit of consumption symbolised by a 'hearth' or 'a table and a pot' and from that of the group of kinfolk or relatives by marriage co-operating in their daily work.[20] Our censuses showing grandparents as members of a household cannot tell us whether they really take their meals with their married children or what degree of co-operation and mutual help is implied by that type of arrangement. A way of life cannot be inferred from a census.

That example can be compared to the way in which a contemporary Western family (rather exceptionally, it must be admitted) might share a block of flats. Let us suppose that the members of one family line are joint owners of a building in which each flat is occupied by a household of that same line. Each home is separate, but there are many interactions between the occupants, who are all related to each other, and these relationships may be either loving and helpful or based on animosity and rivalry.

An anthropologist studying the family would be interested in *the domestic group in the kinship system* seen as one of the structuring principles in social organisation. If we are to talk in terms of family and kinship, studying the domestic group from the point of view of size and structure is not enough. The very thing we are studying cannot be contained in censuses. A sociology of the family therefore demands an analysis of the relationships between domestic groups and kinship in contemporary societies, whether they be peasant, working-class or bourgeois ones.

Putting the problem in this way means that in place of a study of the family, which is a vague term, we must put the concept of kinship. This provides us with a number of theoretical approaches, which can offer a framework within which to reformulate the questions we want to ask. We are not prepared to accept unproved the assertion that the functions of the domestic group and of kinship have been and are being eroded in contemporary society. Would it not be possible, in fact, to see kinship as continuing to perform, albeit latently, a certain number of functions in our society, though these functions are hidden at a number of different levels?

SUGGESTED READING

Tacit communities

Dussourd, Henriette. *Au même pot et au même feu. Etude sur les communautés familiales agricoles du Centre de la France.* Moulins: Pottier, 1962.
  Les Communautés familiales agricoles du centre de la France. Paris: Maisonneuve et Larose, 1978.

Suggested reading

Zadrugas

Gossiaux, Jean-François. 'Famille et tradition communautaire en Yougoslavie'. *Annales de l'Institut francais de Zagreb* 2(1976): 135–50.

Halpern, Joel M. *A Serbian Village*. New York: Harper & Row, 1967.

Halpern, Joel M., and Barbara Krewsky Halpern. *A Serbian Village in Historical Perspective*. New York: Holt, Rinehart & Winston, 1972.

Sicard, Emile. *La Zadruga sud-slave dans l'évolution du groupe domestique*. Paris: Ophrys, 1943.

The domestic group

Le Play, Frédéric. *L'Organisation de la famille suivant le vrai modèle signalé par l'histoire de toutes les races et de tous les temps*. Tours: Mame, 1871.

Laslett, Peter, and Richard Wall, eds. *Household and Family in Past Time*. Cambridge: Cambridge University Press, 1972. The French translation of the introduction to this work has produced much discussion and several critical reviews providing new information and ideas. The chief one is: Collomp, Alain. 'Ménages et famille. Etudes comparatives sur la dimension et la structure du groupe domestique.' *Annales Economies, Sociétés, Civilisations* 3(1974): 777–86.

More data and discussions in

Netting, Robert McC., Richard R. Wilk and Eric J. Arnould, eds. *Households, Comparative and Historical Studies of the Domestic Group*. Berkeley: University of California Press, 1984.

Wall, Richard, in collaboration with Jean Robin and Peter Laslett, eds. *Family Forms in Historic Europe*. Cambridge: Cambridge University Press, 1983.

Articles and books on the domestic group

Berkner, Lutz K. 'Inheritance, Land Tenure and Peasant Family Structure: A German Regional Comparison'. In *Family and Inheritance*. Ed. Jack Goody, Joan Thirsk and E. P. Thompson. Cambridge: Cambridge University Press, 1976.

'Peasant Household Organization and Demographic Change in Lower Saxony (1689–1766)'. *Population Patterns in the Past*. Ed. Ronald Demos Lee. New York: Academic Press, 1977.

Collomp, Alain. 'Famille nucléaire et famille élargie en Haute-Provence au XVIIIe siècle'. *Annales Economies, Sociétés, Civilisations* 4–5(1972): 969–75.

Demos, John. *A Little Commonwealth Family in Plymouth Colony*. New York: Oxford University Press, 1970.

Fine-Souriac, Agnès. 'La Famille-souche pyrénéenne au XIXe siècle'. *Annales Economies, Sociétés, Civilisations* 3(1977): 478–87.

Greven, Philip, Jr. *Four Generations: Population, Land and Family in Andover, Mass*. Ithaca, N.Y.: Cornell University Press, 1970.

Löfgren, Orvar. 'Family and Household among Scandinavian Peasants'. *Ethnologia Scandinavia* 2(1974): 17–52.

41

The domestic group

Medick, Hans. 'The Proto-Industrial Family Economy: The Structural Function of Household and Family during the Transition from Peasant Society to Industrial Capitalism'. *Social History* 3(1976): 291–315.

Segalen, Martine. 'Household Structure, the Family Life Cycle over Five Generations in a French Village'. *Journal of Family History* 2, 3(1977): 223–36.

'Cycle de la Vie Familiale et Transmission du Patrimoine en Bretagne. Analyse d'un cas'. *Ethnologie Française* 8(1978): 271–8.

Smith, Richard, ed. *Land, Kinship and Life-Cycle*. Cambridge: Cambridge University Press, 1985.

An anthropological approach to domestic groups

Goody, Jack. 'The Evolution of the Family'. *Household and Family in Past Time*. Ed. P. Laslett and Richard Wall. Cambridge: Cambridge University Press, 1972.

'Domestic Groups'. *Anthropology*. Addison-Wesley module 28. Reading, Mass.: Addison-Wesley, 1972.

The Structure of domestic groups in the urban milieu

Anderson, Michael. *Family Structure in XIXth Century Lancashire*. Cambridge Studies in Sociology no. 5. Cambridge: Cambridge University Press, 1971.

Modell, John, and Tamara K. Hareven. 'Urbanization and the Malleable Household'. *Journal of Marriage and the Family* 35(1973): 467–79.

Chapter 2

vwvwvwvwvwvwvwvwvwvwvwvwvwvwvwvwvwvwvwvwvwvwvwvwvwvwvwvwvwvwvwvwvwvwvwvwvwvwvw

Kinship and kinship groups

We are naturally inclined to think that our family, which is so much a part of our lives, is something universal, and it comes as a shock to find quite different patterns in other parts of the world. It is here that the concept of kinship can help us see things in a detached way. Every human group is based on the same biological fact, and the way in which it moves from that stage to the social one provides a means of understanding its real nature.

That basic biological fact, or starting point, is a man, a woman and their children. Between the children and the woman there is the tie of giving birth and descent, and the children in turn are linked to their mother and hence to each other. The brother-sister and mother-child link is biological, whereas the association of man and woman is social. Every society has to give a name to the ties that bring a whole range of relationships, feelings and obligations into these two- or three-part groupings. Having said that, it is immediately apparent that the ties between all these individuals are not of the same kind, for those between mother and children are ties of blood, whereas those between man and woman are ties of marriage.

The word 'kin' is still to be found in dictionaries, but in everyday language it is losing ground since it is not much used and is easily mixed up with 'family'. The vagueness of the former is consequently transferred to the latter. Kin indicates those persons who are related to us, i.e. father, mother, sisters, brothers, uncles, aunts and cousins, either by blood or by marriage, and kinship is an institution that to varying degrees governs the functioning of social life.

Why is kinship so important? In present-day society, it would seem, marriage partners are found by chance at the office, at a dance or on holiday, and a house or flat by means of newspaper advertisements. In many societies, marriage, work and residence depend on the individual's place in the kinship organisation and the whole of the organisation of society is governed by kinship groups, whether it be in terms of economy, politics or religion. Those sociologists studying present-day families not only have an a priori assumption that the domestic group is shrinking, but also maintain that kinship has almost disappeared as a basis of relationships. It is this proposition that we wish to discuss and to refute. It is a proposition in which one can detect more than a whiff of what can only be called evolutionism. When anthropologists and sociologists first studied the family, their view was that the kinship system had developed from a matriarchal society characterised by sexual promiscuity in which children knew only their mother to a more refined patriarchal one in which each couple recognised its own children and finally reached its completed model, that of late nineteenth-century Europe, in which the relationships imposed by kinship were supposed to be of lesser social importance. The superiority of this model of kinship within the whole range of possible models was a reflection of the technical superiority of the triumphant nineteenth century.

Theories of this kind lie behind all the earliest anthropological work. In 1871 the American lawyer Morgan published a work entitled *Systems of Consanguinity and Affinity in the Human Family* in which he used different kinship systems to attempt to trace the points along the line of development from the first 'savage' family to the 'civilised' one of his own day. Since then, anthropology has shown that there is no direct correlation between the type of economy in a society and the way in which it is organised, and that value judgements cannot be made about different kinship systems, which are neither 'better' nor 'worse' than each other. As Robin Fox, reflecting on the kinship system of the Australian Aborigines with their Stone Age hunting and gathering economy, writes in *Kinship and Marriage:*

. . . kinship systems are not subject to *cumulative* evolution in the way that, say, technology is. Kinship systems, unlike technological inventions, cannot be ranked as better or worse, higher or lower; they simply represent alternative ways of doing things. Also the evolutionists failed to see that the *whole* of mankind need not have gone through the *same* series of stages – that there were alternative possible routes.[1]

In our society, kinship is recognised and still performs certain functions, and our task is to evaluate its nature and weight compared with those of other social subsystems. It is one of the possible combinations in the whole spectrum of known arrangements.

44

THE TERMINOLOGY OF KINSHIP

As Fred Zimmerman has shown in his *La Parenté*, we are dealing with a system of social landmarks that depends on terminology, which is used to designate the whole range of relatives provided by consanguinity, marriage and, in certain cases, adoption, and which is also a system of classification of relatives indicating the attitudes – avoidance, respect, jocularity and so on – which can be adopted towards them. In our society, there are not many such terms: father, mother, uncle, aunt, cousin, brother, sister and so on. These are terms of reference. Terms of address, of which the function is easily understandable, are used when speaking to the person in question: Dad, Mum, auntie, etc. Some of these can occasionally lead to confusion. In French, for example, 'beau-père' and 'belle-mère' mean both 'stepfather' and 'father-in-law' and 'stepmother' and 'mother-in-law' respectively. Neither English nor French distinguishes between the father's sister's husband (a relative by marriage) and the father's brother (a blood relative). Both are uncles. In general, French kinship terminology makes no distinction between consanguinity and affinity, whereas English does, and logically enough uses two different terms to indicate the difference. Thus, in England relatives by marriage are called 'in-laws', a phrase that emphasises the legal aspect of the relationship. In French, the term 'beau' (beau-père, belle-mère) can be interpreted either as an attempt to endow the new member of the family with virtues as an aid to integration or, as is the case in English, as a means of stressing the distance between him and the existing kinship group.

The earliest anthropologists perceived the difference between various cultures when they examined the specific terms used by natives to refer to their relatives. As early as 1724, Lafiteau in his *Moeurs des sauvages américains* and then Morgan, the advocate of the Iroquois, observed that in Indian societies both the actual father and his brother were called 'father' and both the actual mother and her sister were called 'mother'. This is what anthropologists usually call 'classificatory terminology', as such a device means that a very large range of relatives can be put into a small number of groups. Radcliffe-Brown and Forde describe such classificatory terminology in the following manner in *African Systems of Kinship and Marriage*:

The main principle of the classificatory terminology is a simple one. If A and B are two brothers and X stands in a certain relation to A, then he is regarded as standing in a somewhat similar relation to B. Similarly if A and B are two sisters. In any particular system the principle is applied over a certain range. The similarity of the relation is indicated by applying a single term of relationship to A and B. The father's brother is called 'father' and the mother's sister is called 'mother'. The father's father's brother is regarded as similar to the father's father and therefore his son is also called 'father'. Once the principle is adopted it can be applied and extended in different ways. However the principle is used, it makes possible the recognition of a large number of relatives and their classification into a relatively few categories. Within a single category relatives are distinguished as nearer or more distant.[2]

Our society can also be analysed in terms of kinship categories. David Schneider does this in his *American Kinship, A Cultural Account:*

In sum, the cultural universe of relatives in American kinship is constructed of elements from two major cultural orders, the *order of nature* and the *order of law*. Relatives in *nature* share heredity. Relatives *in law* are bound only by law or custom, by the code for conduct, by the pattern for behavior. They are relatives by virtue of their *relationship*, not their biogenetic attributes.

Three classes of relatives are constructed from these two elements. First there is the special class of relatives in nature alone. This class contains the natural or illegitimate child, the genitor or genetrix who is not the adoptive father or mother, and so on. The second class consists of relatives in law alone. This class may be called 'by marriage' or it may be called 'in law'. It contains the husband and wife, the step-, in-law, foster- and other such relatives. The third class consists in relatives in nature *and* in law. This class of relatives is called 'blood relatives' and contains the 'father . . . daughter', 'uncle . . . granddaughter', 'cousin', sets and so on.[3]

The terminology of kinship is closely tied in with modes of filiation and of alliance, two of the other major principles of kinship. To provide any sort of simple summary of filiation and alliance is not easy, since they are theoretically highly complex and the subject of much debate amongst contemporary anthropologists. A simple summary runs the risk of caricaturing some highly productive ideas and deeply committed discussions. Nonetheless, it is worthwhile facing the challenge this poses so as to broaden the scope of studies of the contemporary family in general and, in particular, of domestic groups within the kinship network. Such groups are our special concern here.

FILIATION

Filiation implies the recognition of links between individuals arising from the fact that some are the offspring of others. It is a principle that works in both directions, both backwards and forwards between successive generations. The concept is known in all societies, but is accorded more importance in some societies than in others. Our own society is very clearly aware of it. With every year that passes more and more people are eager to establish their family trees. (It would, indeed, be worth looking into this need to return to one's roots and to find a place for oneself within a network of preferably illustrious but, if necessary, quite humble ancestors.)

There is a distinction between the *direct* line, which runs through our parents' parents and so on, and the *collateral* one, which is that of our cousins, cousins born of close relatives and relatives with whom we share a common ancestor but from whom we are not descended and for whom we have no ready name. It is difficult to designate relatives further back than grandparents since, for the most part, we do not know who they were or what they did. In our society, our genealogical memory is not far-reaching and does not go beyond three generations or so. Without knowing whether we are dealing with a cause or an effect, we must admit the poverty of our vocabulary indicating those ancestors with whom all that we share is often merely some property or name that is 'in the family'. We talk of 'branches' of the family or the family 'line', and the image of the tree starting at the ancestor we have pinpointed and growing out to the buds of the youngest generation graphically expresses the desire of the person drawing it up to get back to the 'roots'. We also recognise that from our ancestors we inherit a range of characteristics or goods, a name or perhaps family features. Our society still needs family symbols. For example, a study carried out in the Chicago area showed that specific first names were given to over 60 per cent of children and that this was expressly linked to a desire to preserve family continuity.[4]

In exotic societies, filiation is of greater importance. Depending on whether a particular person is the son of this or that man or woman or is descended from this or that mythical or real ancestor, that person will share a certain number of rights or duties with certain relatives. With them, there will be a certain prescribed mode of social and affective relationships, and a different mode for those outside the group. Such multi-functional kinship groups, known as 'descent groups', divide society into segments and are responsible for a greater or lesser share of social organisation.

What distinguishes our own industrialised societies from exotic societies is not the absence of a concept of filiation, but the fact that our social groups are formed less on kinship than on other bases (age groups, social class, friendship, factory or office, leisure activities and so on). We may be members of a PTA, the Rotary, a trade union, a sports club, or we may simply spend our spare time with our friends, whereas in an exotic society all these social subgroups would be combined and shaped in terms of membership in a kinship group. But it would be too easy to draw rigid contrasts and consequently underestimate the role of kinship, which is still important in advanced societies. Filiation is universally recognised and its importance in social organisation varies in all the widely different human societies that amongst them include all the possible variations of that system.

Where unilineal descent is concerned, only descendants in the male or female line are recognised as relatives. Recognition of an individual in his kinship group may be by reference to a given common ancestor to whom a genealogical link can be traced. This is called *lineage*. The *clan* includes kin going back further in time to a common ancestor with whom it is not possible to trace a direct link and who becomes mythical. The former could be seen as a subdivision of the latter, and belonging to a given lineage or clan completely determines the social position of an individual both within his own descent group and in relation to those outside it. Thus, he either has to marry within that group or marriage within it is forbidden to him; from the group he may inherit goods or privileges appropriate to it and so on. The lineage is more than a collection of relatives united by special links; it is also a legal entity owning indivisible property and carrying out military, political and religious functions. Sometimes, when lineages are really a subdivision of wider clans, they will assemble for various ceremonies.

Unilineal filiation thus adopts a system of classification based on sex and assigns an individual to a single group of relatives. How did such groups come into being and how do they work? In the view of certain writers, the residence pattern depends on the principle of descent, with, for example, an individual living with his father because he belongs to his paternal line. Robin Fox, however, in his *Kinship and Marriage,* expresses the view that it is rather the residence pattern that determines the principle of descent. The earliest human groups, hunting over a vast territory, would probably have been based around fixed encampments occupied by their wives and mothers, in other words, a matrilocal residence. By the very nature of things, women are obliged to lead a more settled life, since they are subject to pregnancy, to breast-feeding and the task of raising small children, whereas men, covering large areas in their hunting expeditions, would return home from time to time to bring back their catch, take part in certain ceremonies and the like. Thus a matrilineal society might well evolve. Fox gives an example of this drawn from the way in which a pattern of life developed for certain Shoshone Indians who, under pressure from the Apaches moving in from the north, moved southwards and settled on the desert plateaux of the south-western United States. The women cultivated crops and the men hunted. Matrilocal residence was the rule:

A small group consisting of perhaps an old grandmother, her daughters, and their daughters, lived in a house or group of connected houses and looked after the plots of corn. To these houses came husbands who spent most of their time away in hunting or warfare or religious activity with other males of the band. . . . The ecological and military conditions were such that large population centres were impossible or, even if marginally possible, not necessary. Now, these reformed Shoshone for some reason moved further south. They may have been forced south by marauding bands of Apaches from the north. But, in any case, they moved into larger agglomerations and either began to build for themselves, or take over from previous inhabitants, large compact villages or groups of related villages. At first, these were built in the valleys, but finally they came to rest on the tops of the great *mesas* – high flat-topped spurs of rock in the Arizona desert, not far from the Grand Canyon. They became the Hopi Indians, one of the best known tribes in anthropological literature.

Now when they moved into their larger villages, the matrilocal household remained (and remains to this day) the basic unit of their social organization. But an important consequence followed from the crowding together of the previously scattered households. The men born into the household – the natal members – had previously been lost to it on marriage. They had gone perhaps many miles away and become totally absorbed in another unit. They may have returned home from time to time – on divorce or estrangement, for example – but they cannot have been able to keep up any constant contact with their natal households. Once in the villages, however, such contact became easy and natural.[5]

In those Shoshone groups that became Hopi it is clear that mothers and daughters formed the element of stability in the household and the sons and husbands the element of mobility. Divorce was easy: The wife simply put her husband's things outside her hut. This example clearly shows the links between descent, the residence pattern and the domestic group.

In matrilineal systems, the men belong to their mother's social group, which gives women a certain pre-eminence without, however, totally denying it to men, for in a matrilineage, the important man is the mother's brother. The sole function of the father is to beget children. The men belonging to the matrilineage are the ones in the house with authority, and it is they who bring up their sister's children. Other solutions are compatible with societies with matrilineal filiation. A type of avunculocal residence found amongst the Trobriand Islanders of the West Pacific (well known in anthropological literature for their distinctive system of exchange, in which the man takes his wife to live with his mother's brother) has been described by Malinowski.

Patrilineal filiation is not a mirror image of its matrilineal equivalent, since the latter contains its own inherent contradictions of the principle on which the group functions, in particular in that it is the men who wield authority. In fact, despite the views of the earliest anthropologists, matrilineal societies are in no way identical to matriarchates, the latter being societies in which political power (in the widest sense of the term) is held by women. There is no example of this from any exotic society. Matrilineal societies thus have to resolve the contradictions between the principle of residence pattern centred on matrilineal filiation in order to make marriage possible, and the maintenance of good relations with men from other matrilineages.

Although in certain societies it is the women who own the property, in most cases it is the men who really possess it. We can consider the striking arrangement offered by the example of the Menangkabao of Sumatra, where the father-mother-children nucleus has no role. The basic unit is the *samandai,* consisting of the mother and her children. The *parui,* which includes several of these units, to which men living with a sister attach themselves, owns the land managed by the mother's brothers. A man who marries lives in the *parui* he originally came from. This is the classic example of what is known as 'furtive marriage', for when a young woman takes a husband, an extra room is built onto the house for her and he comes to visit her at night. The *parui* are grouped into *kampueng,* each under the authority of the oldest person in the longest-established *parui.* In their turn, the *kampueng* are grouped in clans that meet in halves and cut across the village unit. Thus the whole social life of the village is divided in terms of political and, above all, ritual and religious functions such as ancestor worship.

In societies with patrilineal filiation, residence is patrilocal. This means that the young couple consisting of the son and his wife goes to live in the 'neolocal' house, namely one attached to that of the husband's father but independent of it. In systems of this kind, there is no conflict over the attribution of authority as can be the case in matrilineal societies, in which women might have a right to demand it since the mode of filiation passes through them and the

Filiation

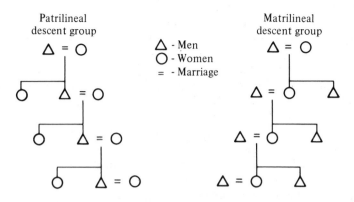

Fig. 2.1. Unilineal filiation.

residence pattern is often centred on the mother-daughter group (Fig. 2.1).

In patrilineal (also called agnatic) filiation, names, goods, privileges, rights, political, religious, economic and similar duties are passed on from father to son (*agnatus*). It is therefore crucial to establish paternity. Hence Fox's remark, 'We might expect in patrilineal societies to find a lot more fuss being made over marriage and the rights over wife and child than in matrilineal'.[6] In a matrilineal society, only the exclusively obvious child-mother relationship is of primary importance, a view that is pushed to extremes in those societies that see no link between sexual union and fertilisation.

Women occupy a subordinate place in matrilineal systems, which, as we have seen, give men the dominant role as brothers and uncles rather than as husbands and fathers. In patrilineal filiation, women may be excluded from their original lineage, and certain societies recognise them not as sisters to be got rid of by marriage but as wives. This process is followed by an amendment of the rules for allocating dowries, which are then paid into the lineage accepting the woman, enabling the husband who pays a dowry to assert his rights over his children and the lineage that accepts it to settle its rights on one of the members of the group.

It should not be assumed from these extremely brief and schematic descriptions of the two types of unilineal filiation that patrilineal or matrilineal societies function wherever this type of descent on the same model is observed. Onto these modes of social organisation, which are no more than a kind of external framework, is grafted all the broad range of cultural variations: the functions of lineage groups, typical patterns of interpersonal relationships, marriage rules, the overall aim of the society, all of which explain why the range of possible cultures is so vast.

The 'tacit communities', for example, those 'large families' mentioned earlier, present a variant of the possible ways of organising a patrilineal society. Membership in the Quittard-Pinon community in Thiers was passed from father to son over the generations, and that membership conferred rights over the collective and undivided property and a status arising from the standing of the community. Women were excluded from the lineages and the rights that went with them by virtue of the dowry they received when they married outside the community, which was a kind of compensation for giving up their share of the collective property. In addition, the lineage, in order to preserve its property and hence pay out as little as possible in ready cash, encouraged endogamy, that is, marriage within the community, unlike primitive societies, in which lineages were most frequently exogamous. The tacit communities were patrilineal in so far as there was reference to an identifiable common ancestor, but were not clans, since there was no grouping of such patrilineages collectively identifying themselves with a common mythical ancestor or performing of religious or political rituals together. Above and beyond the tacit communities, the village community also included family units of a different kind, simple or extended domestic groups. There were other principles of solidarity at work that often cut across kinship networks.

It was difficult for tacit communities to develop when demographic pressure was strong, since as in all European peasant societies, the amount of land they worked was limited. The situation was quite different in the vast underpopulated areas of Africa or Asia, where virtually unlimited space meant that when lineages became too large they grew and multiplied by a process of fission. Above a certain level of segmentation it is possible to discern a certain degree of hierarchisation. In Europe, when we can trace genealogies forwards from a common ancestor it is possible to distinguish branches with differing social futures before them, such as small peasant or large farming families in which the sons inherit either property or status from their fathers and whose sons in their turn become merchants or doctors, whilst their distant cousins remain in their villages working their small farms or migrate to swell the labour force in the towns.

Bilineal and complementary filiation

There are societies in which bilineal filiation operates with each descent group following a different path and patrilineage performing certain functions and matrilineage others. That of the Yako of Nigeria is well known. Fox describes it thus:

[Their town] is divided into wards and each ward is inhabited by a patriclan (*kepun*), which is exogamous and conducts rites in a central assembly house. The clan is composed of a number of separate lineages (*yeponama*: singular *eponama*), which own land within the clan territory and the members of which live with their wives and children in a single compound. (*Eponama* means 'urethra', thus stressing the biological link between agnates.) The *kepun* is not a segmentary clan, and lineages only trace their genealogies for a few generations. A man's rights to house, land and to some extent protection, then, lie in the patriclan and patrilineage. Umor is however also divided into matriclans (*yajima*: singular *lejima*). These are obviously dispersed because of patrilocal residence and the rule of patriclan exogamy. The matriclan is divided into lineages of shallow depth (*yajimafat*: singular *lejimafat*). Exogamy is only now enforced within these lineages although previously it operated for the matriclan as a whole. Each matriclan has a shrine to its spirit, and a priest, who is a man of great authority. But the most striking feature of matrilineal kinship is that all movable goods and inheritable wealth are passed matrilineally. Thus, for an individual man inheritance is divided; he gets his house and land and all other immovables from his father, but it is from his mother's brothers that he gets money and livestock and all movable property. Looked at another way, on a man's death his land and house go to his own sons or other close agnates, while his money and cattle will go to his sisters' sons or other close uterine relatives. . . . The matriclans are also very important as ritual groups and are expected to 'keep the peace' of the village. This can be seen as stemming from the fact that they cross-cut the territorially defined patriclans and so in a sense bring them together.[7]

Although complicated, the system works well as each lineage makes provision for a distinct principle and the structural elements of social organisation fit together harmoniously. The mobility of the women matches the mobility of their property (transmitted by their lineage) and the immobility of the men that of the land they inherit from the patrilineage. But despite the relative equilibrium the Yako had achieved when anthropologists were studying their social organisation, it is clear that a bilineal descent system is fragile as a result of the competition between the two lineages. Fox goes on to observe:

All the things that we have said about the problems and difficulties of unilineal descent-groups – matrilineal and patrilineal – remain true when these are combined in a double-descent system. If we simply take the viewpoint of the matrilineage, then it is still true that it is concerned that its women should be impregnated, and that it should have control over their children for whatever purposes it is to fulfil; the matriclan priests of the Yako, for example, are anxious to have sisters' sons to follow them in office.

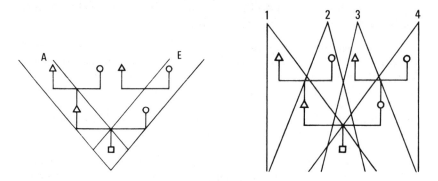

Fig. 2.2. Bilineal (*left*) and undifferentiated (*right*) filiation.

It is also still true that the patrilineages want to 'unload' their consanguine women and acquire wives in order to produce sons. To this end, they have institutionalized polygyny and brideprice – although the latter is not always effective in asserting the rights of the pater over the genitor.[8]

In addition, Meyer Fortes has established that any society with a unilineal descent also included a complementary system, which he calls 'complementary filiation' and which, he says,

all confirm the tremendous importance of the web of kinship as a counter-weight to the tendency of unilineal descent grouping to harden social barriers. Or to put it slightly differently, it seems that where the unilineal descent group is rigorously structured within the total social system there we are likely to find kinship used to define and sanction a personal field of social relations for each individual.[9]

Undifferentiated or cognatic filiation

In undifferentiated or cognatic filiation, membership of a kinship group is not based on sex, and all the descendants of a particular individual are members of his group. When the difference between bilineal filiation and cognatic filiation is shown diagrammatically, it can be seen that each individual is not a member of two lineages, but of as many for which he can trace an ancestor (Fig. 2.2). At the theoretical level, such groups seem to be of very little functional value. How, for example, can the multi-functional nature of the lineages be reconciled with residence, which demands a choice, since it is impossible to live everywhere and work all the land belonging to the various lineages? These groups are functional to the extent that they are flexible enough to adapt to major demographic fluctuations; unlike the unilineal system, which forbids an individual to move from one group of relatives to another, the cognatic system allows him to activate his relationships with a different patri- or matriline and to exercise his rights with regard to their land should those of his current lineage be inadequate, as might happen in cases of demographic pressure, for example.

French society operates under a system of undifferentiated filiation, apart from the case of the family name, which is transmitted by patrilineal filiation. It is possible to inherit from any of four grandparents and it is normal to recognise kinship with every ancestor in any line that can be traced through a family tree. The Scottish clan is also a form of cognatic filiation group. *Clann* originally signified 'child' or 'descendant' in Gaelic, and although the clan has a patrilineal shading, every true Highlander had two names, his father's and his mother's. Thus, Robert MacAlpine MacKinnon was a MacAlpine on his mother's side and a MacKinnon on his father's and could, from birth, belong to either of the clans.[10] Similarly, Spanish women always have two names, their father's and their mother's, or, more exactly, their mother's father's, the latter being replaced by their husband's when they marry.

There is another danger in an overschematic presentation of filiation systems. It is important not to enclose societies within too rigid a series of classifications. Societies change over time, as with the matrilineal Shoshone evolving towards the patrilineal Hopi, and some agnatic societies may tend towards an undifferentiated system according to particular historical, social or demographic conditions. The crucial thing is not to imprison these societies within rigid Procrustean typological frameworks that distort their social reality, but rather to identify types of organisations that make it possible to situate those changes that occur in time and from place to place.

Kindred

The kinship groups we have described briefly are based on one or more common ancestors. Kindred, however, is a concept based on the individual who recognises his blood relatives and relatives by marriage as far as the genealogical links in his memory or that of his group of relatives can take him. Unlike unifiliation groups, in which a large number of relatives see themselves as belonging to an identical filiation group, only close relatives (by which we mean groups of brothers and sisters) have an identical kindred. These groups, in contrast to filiation groups, are not legal entities, since they do not share common rights or possess undivided property.

Kindred groups are very much alive in our societies. Their size varies according to the social occasion involved. Nowadays, they normally extend as far as first cousins, but at funerals in village communities larger kindred groups gather to pay their last respects to the departed to whom they are related by blood or marriage without that tie necessarily depending on a common ancestor. This means that the whole field of social interaction is not dependent on rigidly structured groups such as paternal or maternal lineages.

Yet the kindred group is no more specific to contemporary societies than the restricted domestic group of parents and children. There are also exotic societies based on kindred groups with less constricting functions than those of lineages. An example of this is the Iban of Borneo, described by J. D. Freeman:

In much of the organization of Iban social, economic, and ritual life the *bilek* family . . . is a group of limited size – a stem family which when fully developed seldom comprises more than ten members – and it thus provides an inadequate basis for the various activities, beyond the domestic family level, in which Iban engage. It is in these circumstances, in a society lacking large-scale corporate groups, that kindred relationships become significant. The whole of Iban society is traversed by a network of interlocking kindreds, and it is this network which provides the organizational basis for the performance of tasks which, for various reasons, are beyond the capacity of the *bilek* family. Because this network of kindreds is so important, I have thought it prudent to illustrate its basic characteristics diagrammatically. . . . What regularly happens in a bilateral society like that of the Iban is that the cognatically unrelated sets [of first cousins] are brought into co-activity by Ego (or one of his siblings), and that out of this co-activity by (which had its origin in the fact that both sets were part of Ego's kindred) new relationships grow. That is, on subsequent occasions members of [these] sets may engage in co-activity that has not been initiated by their common cognate Ego.[11]

The Iban example illustrates the point of connection between the domestic group and kinship and also shows that systems often seen as necessarily linked to the industrial development of society are also found in primitive societies. It also underlines the flexibility and multi-functional nature of kindred groups in terms that, almost without transposition, could define our own societies.

MARRIAGE

Before proceeding any further, let us define exogamy, *marrying out*, a concept we have already referred to in our discussion of lineages. Exogamy is a type of marriage outside the original social group, which thus makes it possible to establish relations with other filiation groups. The prohibition of incest can thus be seen, with an exogamous framework, as being the negative expression of a system of exchange. As Claude Lévi-Strauss writes in *The Elementary Structures of Kinship*:

Sexual relations between man and woman are an aspect of the total prestations of which marriage provides both an example and the occasion. We have seen that these total prestations have to do with material goods, social values such as privileges, rights and obligations, and women. The total relationship of exchange which constitutes marriage is not established between a man and a woman, where each owes and receives something, but between two groups of men, and the woman figures only as one of the objects in the exchange.[12]

He also observes that all marriages are linked to each other, since

this cycle of reciprocity is only a secondary mode of a wider cycle of reciprocity, which pledges the union of a man and a woman who is either someone's daughter or sister, by the union of the daughter or sister of that man or another man with the first man in question.[13]

Thus all lineages and through them all domestic groups are progressively linked in marriage relationships bringing with them a certain number of behaviour patterns and values.

Elementary systems

There are two marriage systems in human societies, *elementary* and *complex*. Elementary systems are characterised by rules of marriage that prescribe for the individual both the category of women from amongst whom he must choose a wife and those that are forbidden to him.

The simplest form of marriage outside the group is the systematic exchange of sisters, a type that becomes more complex and sophisticated within the same principle. In the kinship terminology of certain societies there is a basic difference between cousins. Those who are the children of close relatives of the same sex are called 'parallel' cousins, and those who are children of close relatives of the opposite sex are called 'cross'-cousins. In the simplest system, called 'restricted exchange', a man has to marry his bilateral female cross-cousin, taking a wife where his father had taken a wife (the *Kariera* system). Starting from this basis, the system can become more complex if, for example, the rule demands that a man marry his second female cross-cousin by virtue of the fact that the tribe is organised in eight sections. This is the *Aranda* system, bearing the name of the

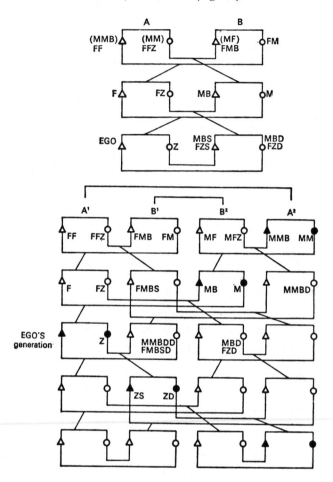

Fig. 2.3. Kariera system (*top*) and Aranda system (*bottom*). (From Robin Fox, *Kinship and Marriage* [Cambridge: Cambridge University Press, 1983], pp. 186, 196.)

human group famous for this precise arrangement, in which a man had to seek a wife where his grandfather had sought one (Fig. 2.3). A more elaborate variant of this system is that of marriage with the patrilateral female cross-cousin, which produces a direct but deferred exchange. The rule demands that a young woman take a husband from the group her mother came from. If A takes a wife from B, he has to return a wife to B in the next generation. B will be superior to A for a generation and then the situation will be reversed. This type of marriage enables an alternation of lines in

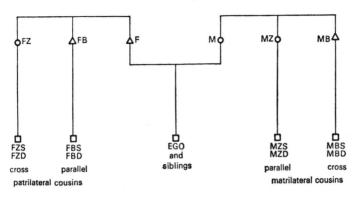

Fig. 2.4. Cross- and parallel cousins. (From Robin Fox, *Kinship and Marriage* [Cambridge: Cambridge University Press, 1983], p. 185.)

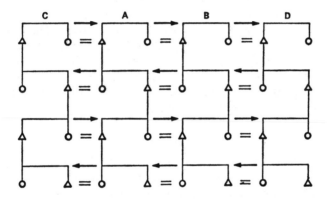

Fig. 2.5. Asymmetrical marriage system. (From Robin Fox, *Kinship and Marriage* [Cambridge: Cambridge University Press, 1983], p. 205.)

power, the balance between the giving and receiving lineage being re-established in the second generation. In this type of direct-exchange marriage, it can be seen that the tribe is based on the juxtaposition of pairs of exchanging partners and that in the long term a segmentation must occur (Fig. 2.4).

The second type of elementary marriage system is the *asymmetrical* or *generalised-exchange* system, as it mutually links all the sections of the tribe. A particular marriage rule justifies this name: marriage with the matrilateral female cross-cousin, or the daughter of the mother's brother. In this system, as Fig. 2.5 clearly shows, the line giving brides is never the same as that taking them. This rule means

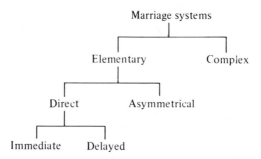

Fig. 2.6. Marriage systems classification. (After Claude Lévi-Strauss.)

that marriage unites all the lineages in a continuous *connubium* in which each both gives and takes brides.

Elementary kinship systems all have a twofold specific content. There is a category of persons one may not marry, and a second category from which one must choose one's spouse. The differences between such systems are the result of the way in which the positive rules are organised. In every unit examined, either those providing brides were the same group as those taking them or the two groups were quite distinct. Demographic considerations based on the group size are one of the variables of this system.

Complex systems

For their part, complex systems involve only negative marriage rules and do not define the categories of relatives from which brides may be obtained, but only those from which they may not (Fig. 2.6). Contemporary societies function on the complex model, but a number of exotic societies also prescribe no particular brides and demand only exogamy, marriage outside the clan. The difference, as Fox points out, is one of degree rather than principle.[14] Indeed, complex systems distribute individuals across the whole social system, whether it be founded on categories of kinship or wealth or on the criteria of profession or social class. Thus, our marriage system enforces the universal prohibition of incest, for which structurally elementary societies contain a simple 'explanation',[15] but which structurally complex ones continue to impose simply by means of negative rules. The marriage system of contemporary societies is no more a simplified or impoverished form of more elaborate ones than was the case with filiation systems. It is one of the variants or possible ways of ordering of a system of marriage along a continuum from restricted exchange to the (supposed) free choice of a spouse.

Lines and kindred groups in peasant societies

There is a relationship between the vocabulary of kinship and types of marriage. Since, given the rule against incest, it is not permissible to marry a sister, all those women an individual cannot marry are called sisters.

In the 'symmetrical' type of marriage (i.e. with cross-cousins on both sides) the terminology shows an alternation of generations and a sex distinction. In the central generations, in a given generation and sex position, all the relatives are divided into two categories. In the father's generation, he himself, his brother and the mother's sister's husband come into a category that could be called parallel, whilst the mother's brother and the sister's husband come into the 'cross'-category. In asymmetrical marriage, both types of cross-cousin and cross-relatives in general on the paternal and maternal sides are kept distinct, which corresponds to the unilateral nature of marriage and to the distinction between those who take and those who provide brides. There is also a tendency to confuse generations by putting relatives from different generations into the same category as in the case of both providers and takers.[16]

At the other end of the range of possible ways of providing a suitable lexis we find our own system of nomenclature, the Eskimo category as it is called, after the people who also use it. This is a fairly common one amongst peoples with no unifilation group or elementary type of marriage. It emphasises the nuclear family and stresses the balance between patri- and matrilateral kindred groups.[17] Our vocabulary even now has traces of former marriage systems. Concerning the word 'uncle', which comes from the Latin *avunculus*, Emile Benveniste notes that

only the rule of marriage between cousins, which when applied means that the same person is my father's father and my mother's brother, indicates that the Latin word *avunculus*, from *avus*, which means paternal grandfather, signifies 'maternal uncle'.[18]

LINES AND KINDRED GROUPS IN PEASANT SOCIETIES

Anthropology therefore suggests that the domestic group should be considered within the framework of kinship and offers us the means for an analysis of this kind. First, the concepts appropriate to exotic societies must be adapted to other peasant and urban ones. Can one speak in this latter context of unifiliation groups, lineages and clans? Are there other forms of social groupings based on ties of blood and marriage? What are their functions and their relationships with domestic groups?

Kinship and kinship groups

Over their long history, peasant societies have become increasingly subject to the control of central authority, religious, administrative and educational institutions and the like. Nevertheless, if we look at kinship within the framework of village society, our position will be rather like that of the anthropologist studying exotic societies since a village has few inhabitants and consequently they will all know each other.

In this situation, the anthropologist will immediately encounter kinship, an active principle today as in the past, which is more evident here than in an urban context and structures social relationships between domestic groups both vertically and horizontally. There are, of course, organisations within the village, such as youth clubs, guilds and various kinds of associations, whose membership is not entirely kinship based and that may separate out along political lines, but there is usually some sort of overlap between such organisations and kinship networks. As in exotic societies, although in a different manner, the place of kinship within peasant societies is linked to ways of acquiring land. We know that in the former, rights to land are collectively assigned to a lineage that works it. In addition, the territory belonging to such groups is not firmly fixed. New land can be acquired or the group can move. In peasant societies, property is owned by individuals and the land available is generally limited; consequently, once it has been cleared for cultivation, there is no possibility of finding new locations for the villages. Land is owned by domestic groups who pass it on from generation to generation and hence occupy a major place in the community.

Isac Chiva emphasises the twofold characteristics of peasant societies in which there is both family ownership of the land and the identification of the family with the farm. Kinship is defined from without and in particular by reference to the house (in large areas of central and southern Europe). The domain of alliance only partly overlaps with that of kinship, and is defined in terms of landholding and of the way in which it is passed on. Chiva also notes that despite the patrilineal ideology permeating certain societies, the system is profoundly bilateral.[19] These various characteristics differentiate lineage societies from peasant societies.

Are kinship concepts relevant to peasant societies?

Through the device of individual ownership, land, a forge or a weaving shop, or the right to a lease, can be transferred down the generations from one domestic group to another. This means that in country areas one can observe a family succession leading to the domestic group under examination.

Can this be described as a lineage? Certainly not in strict terms, in so far as ownership of land or status is an individual matter and property is not undivided and hence becomes the subject of debate and transfer from one generation to another. In this situation, however, there is a range of features characteristic of lineages. These include a family ideology going back a long time and firmly rooted in a specific land holding, of attachment to an ancestor who may be both quasi-mythical and eponymous, in the sense that he has founded a lineage and given his family name to it, and membership of a family line conferring rights and duties, such as not marrying into another particular line, assuming certain political or religious responsibilities within the village community, and so on. In village societies there are also kindred groups of the kind described for exotic societies.

The existence of lineages or lines, of more or less structured kindred groups around a domestic group, depends on a range of ecological, economic, social and cultural phenomena, such as the abundance or scarcity of land in relation to the size of the human group occupying it, its fertility and aridity, whether it is owned or rented, and whether the inheritance system protects holdings in their integrity or divides them.

If you trace a family tree with a peasant, he will immediately orient himself in relation to the vertical and horizontal kinship structures within which he functions. The line will be called a 'stem' or some similar term. This line, amongst all the other lines of descent that are an individual's biological inheritance, is the line that is singled out as of special and unique importance. At the same time both the individual and the domestic group can identify a collateral line of kin, with whom they share no direct ancestor but only a lateral link. This is the kindred group, a group that functions in a very similar way to that in Iban society, which we looked at earlier. As a result of this twofold branching, the domestic group is committed to certain prescribed forms of behaviour and enjoys particular privileged relationships, rights and duties. Through the line, the domestic group is tied in to the sequence of those preceding and succeeding it in the same place, and through the kindred group it is linked to all those relatives in whose company it is involved in all the vicissitudes of social life: quarrels, friendships and hatreds.

Peasant lines

As distinct from lineage, which distinguishes between individuals in terms of their sex, lines take a path that moves via men and women as memory, economic and social circumstances, migrations or personal factors take it. The last may be either demographic (a branch dying out without heirs) or individual (a failed marriage, unlucky speculation, illness or accident) in nature. The domestic group is inserted in the line or lines from which it has received a patrimony.

The link between filiation and patrimony is so marked in peasant societies that Pierre Lamaison noted that in Gévaudan there were real 'patrimonial lines', consisting of the successive heirs of each house or *ostal*.

Patrimonial lines, the material traces of which are the *ostals*, have a place in that society which is so pre-eminent as to be like that of patrilines or matrilines in societies in which unifiliation is the determining factor.[20]

This example is from a society (that of the stem family) in which there is a single heir and in which, in principle, the whole patrimony is left to the domestic group inheriting it.

Are things different in societies with a system of equal inheritance for all children? Let us consider Minot, in Burgundy, where each generation had to reassemble property that had been divided by inheritance, using a family strategy involving marriages, relationships between close relatives and skilful buying. The case of the Baudot-Camuzet family cited by Marie-Claude Pingaud in *Paysans en Bourgogne* provides an excellent illustration of manoeuvres of this kind. To the 27 hectares left by their ancestor Jean Baudot, the present-day descendants can now add almost a further 50 and are the largest landowners in the village as a result of the stubbornness of five generations of heirs (Fig. 2.7).

Through the patient strategies of each generation the specific effort of each domestic group appears to be linked to the more general one of the family line and ideology. These strategies also account for carefully planned marriages, for antagonism between the forces of fission linked to the inheritance system and the attempts to put together again land that has been divided, and their fight against demographic accidents (an only child or more than one child). It is not so much a question of making up a viable holding as of accumulating capital in the form of land and hence accumulating a symbolic capital with the local community. In such cases, family cohesion is so strong and the prestige of belonging to an ancient family such a vital factor that the village expresses the distance betwen such fami-

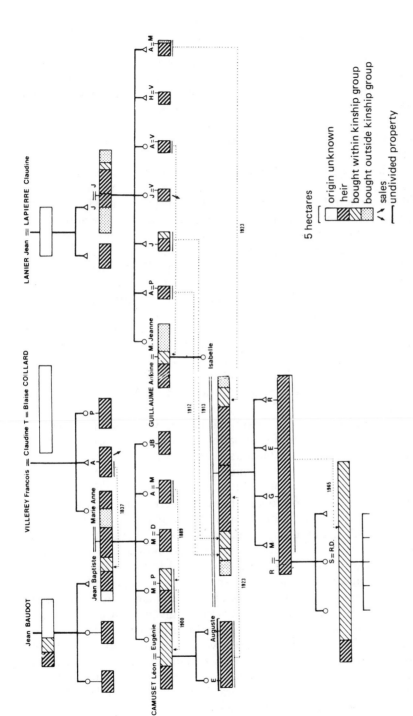

Fig. 2.7. Genealogy of the Baudot-Camuzet family. (From M.-C. Pingaud, *Paysans en Bourgogne, Les gens de Minot* [Paris: Mouton, 1970], pp. 130–1.)

lies and the general community that has grown up over the generations. The Baudot-Camuzets nowadays, for example, are said to be 'aloof in their dealings with other people'.[21] This ideology is rooted in the collective memory, and the family is spoken of as a collective plural, including all temporal and spatial relatives, and the vertical and horizontal lines and the living and the dead are all equally part of it.

The line imposes itself both on the domestic group and on the village group. The link between the line and the patrimony seems well illustrated by a study of local political power. Real family dynasties remain members of local councils, both showing their hold over the local region and completing the circle by strengthening it, and also bearing witness to the enduring nature of the economic, social and symbolic patrimony. What has been said about Minot also applies to a large number of communes within a certain context of the acquisition of land by peasants: 'The reserves of power in kinship and its hereditary transmission go hand in hand with those in patrimonies in the form of land and often of professions.'[22] A village ideology accrues around the lines of peasants who gather land or local status to themselves, and these lines represent the village at the level of local politics. Sometimes the line forms not around property but around the right to a lease, the inheritance of a status. Rented farms do not necessarily make for mobility, and here as elsewhere everything depends on the region, the times and the economic situation. If landowners are dominant, they tend to dispossess farmers when their lease expires, but in different circumstances, it is more profitable for them to give their tenant's son some sort of right to inherit the lease. This explains why one sees lines of tenant farmers succeeding each other on farms much more stable in size than those owned by peasants and which in each generation are subject to division and redistribution. The adequacy of the size of a farm in relation to that of the domestic group can thus be seen to be the major factor in stability when technical conditions remain the same. It has been possible to establish a constant ratio between size of farm and labour force throughout the nineteenth century by tracing a given farm over that period. To work the 11 hectares of one farm properly, a labour force of between five and seven people was necessary, and it could feed between seven and twelve. In that specific example, it was noted that the family line of the tenant farmers working the land was stable, matching the stability of the family lines of the landowners, who were nobles or urban bourgeois.[23]

There is also evidence of the presence of lines in families of artisans, where the domestic groups and the ownership of the means of production are one and the same. Learning the trade goes hand in hand with the socialisation of the child and is handed on from father to son, and lines of weavers, blacksmiths, cobblers and tailors can be traced. The small independent craftsman, however, was even more sensitive to external economic influences than the farmer, and when the French market was opened up to English textiles in 1861, a large proportion of the cottage weaving in the Seine Valley disappeared. Thus there was not a long enough period of time over which to observe successive generations of weavers likely to develop an original craft and family culture. As they generally owned only tiny patches of land and the tools of their trade, they were less firmly rooted to the land than peasants and were the first to migrate from villages to towns. Similarly, blacksmiths were to disappear later, in the 1920s, as mechanisation spread and the disappearance of horses made their trade superfluous, surviving only when the modernisation of old ways meant that a son or son-in-law became a garage owner or a tractor salesman. The prerequisites for a line are a certain genealogical depth, property to be passed on and a family ideology. This is surely implicit in the replies made by agricultural families who, when questioned about their strategy with regard to the patrimony, replied that they had not acquired it and it was not theirs to consume. For such people, the 'longer image' of the patrimony is thus 'the expression in material terms of the line implying the major duty of conserving property passed as an inheritance from one generation to another'.[24] This view is typical of many agricultural households (see Chapter 9).

So far, we have proceeded as if each domestic group recognised only one particular line as its kin, but there are others with an important part to play. On Tory Island, a small island off the extreme north-west coast of Ireland, Fox has observed a cognatic filiation that he studies in his book *The Tory Islanders, a People of the Celtic Fringe.* Around 1963, all four hundred islanders were descended from eighteen major and five secondary ancestors. Unlike the lineage system, in which filiation is from a single ancestor, the situation there was that each islander traced his filiation from as many as possible, which was very important as all the lines owned land. Every islander had a kind of right to the land he farmed for as long as he was capable of farming it, after which it passed to another heir who needed it.

In this case, the line was not linked to an individual property but to a collective one, and each member had both potential and real rights to the land owned by the line. Figure 2.8 depicts an example of the lineages that in Gaelic are called a *clann*. Curiously enough, however, the meaning anthropologists have given to the word clan

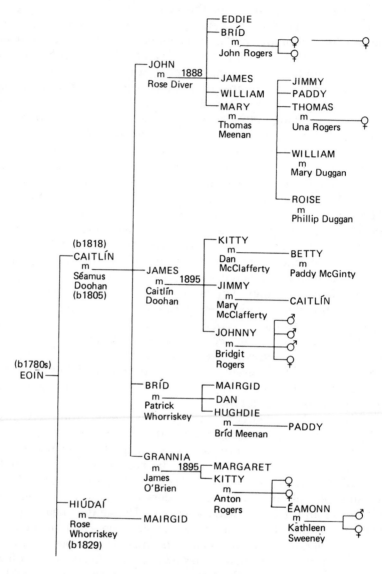

Fig. 2.8. Genealogy of the Clann Eoin (descent of two out of three children). (From Robin Fox, *The Tory Islanders: A People of the Celtic Fringe* [Cambridge: Cambridge University Press, 1978], p. 38.)

(i.e. several lines attached to a mythical ancestor) is not applicable in the case of the Tory Islanders. As has been indicated the word clan describes agnatic societies with unilineal filiation and means that each individual can belong to only one lineage and only one clan. On Tory Island, however, every individual tried to be linked – in particular by means of the ways in which names were transmitted – to as many *clanns* as possible.

Peasant kindred groups

The kindred group, that flexible cluster of relatives with whom one can decide to have or not to have relationships, determines the networks that interlink the various related domestic groups and can be seen as the channels along which news, mutual help and goods and services travel.

On Tory Island, kinship had both a vertical and a horizontal function. Crews for fishing-boats were made up on the basis of the kindred group. In Fig. 2.9, the ten members of the crew shown in capitals were related by filiation and marriage. Lines and kindred groups function complementarily, with the vertical and horizontal principles latent in all human groups predominating in this or that context for economic reasons or for reasons of inheritance. At Minot, where it was possible to trace lines, the kindred group was an active principle in social organisation: 'Awareness of genealogy is limited, being wider collaterally than retrospectively, and there is a tendency to ignore the principle of generations.'[25] In a diffuse kinship of that kind, which is quite distinct from close kinship, 'all that remains is awareness of a kinship network'.[26] It fulfils a certain number of functions and in particular offers a choice of possible marriage partners. A good few marriages are between people described as 'strangers but distant relatives'. Such marriages of this kind, which we will study later, gradually unite all the domestic groups of the same social level in the village and the microregion.

Within these kindred groups, assembling people who are remote both genealogically and geographically, there are patron groups where family honour and power are forged. Kindred groups have political functions, as families provide mayors from generation to generation. It has even been possible to demonstrate the distribution of power in one commune in Burgundy between two kindred groups 'with leaders being able to rely absolutely on the votes of their numerous children, cousins, nephews and nieces'.[27] They also have commercial functions. When Yves Canevet, a blacksmith in Pont-l'Abbé, became the agent for the Landerneau agricultural co-opera-

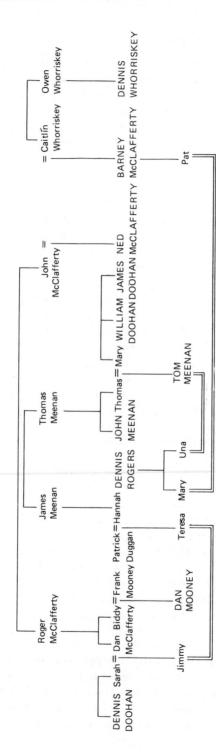

Fig. 2.9. Filiation and marriage links in the crew of one of the Tory Islanders' fishing-boats. (From Robin Fox, *The Tory Islanders: A People of the Celtic Fringe* [Cambridge: Cambridge University Press, 1978], p. 145.)

tive, the first people he approached as possible customers were his numerous near and distant relatives scattered throughout the area. Village society is now less homogeneous than it once was. Instead of peasants the French countryside is now populated with *agriculteurs*, and the town–country distinction is becoming blurred. Yet the line is still of major importance in so far as the domestic group and the farm are still seen as synonymous and kindred groups are as alive and effective as in the past.

SUGGESTED READING

Very few works offer a synthetic description of the various points of view adopted by anthropological schools of thought. Some of those that do are as follows:

Cresswell, Robert. 'La Parenté'. *Eléments d'ethnologie*, no. 1. Paris: Colin, 1975.
Dumont, Louis. *Introduction à deux théories d'anthropologie sociale. Groupes de filiation et alliance de mariage*. Paris: Mouton, 1971.
Fox, Robin. *Kinship and Marriage, an Anthropological Perspective*. London: Penguin, 1967.
Héritier, Francoise. *L'Exercice de la parenté*. Paris: Gallimard-Le Seuil, 1981.

The following provides a good commentary on anthropological texts dealing with kinship:

Zimmerman, F. *La Parenté*. Paris: PUF, 1972.

This work deals with Africa and raises general problems:

Augé, Marc, ed. *Les Domaines de la parenté*. Paris: Maspero, 1975.

The preceding preliminary reading will provide general concepts. The reader can then move on to one or two classic texts:

Lévi-Strauss, Claude. *Les Structures élémentaires de la parenté*. Paris: PUF, 1949; new ed., Mouton: 1967. Published in English as *The Elementary Structure of Kinship*. London: Eyre & Spottiswoode; Boston: Beacon Press, 1969.
Radcliffe-Brown, A. R. *Structure and Function in Primitive Society*. London: Cohen and West, 1952.
Radcliffe-Brown, A. R., and Daryl Forde. *African Systems of Kinship and Marriage*. Oxford: Oxford University Press, 1950.

Some more recent and more polemical works:

Bourdieu, Pierre. *Outline of a Theory of Practice*. Cambridge: Cambridge University Press, 1977.
Farber, Bernard. *Conceptions of Kinship*. New York: Elsevier, 1981.
Leach, Edmund. *Rethinking Anthropology*. London: Athlone Press, 1961.

Kinship and kinship groups

Needham, Rodney. *Rethinking Kinship and Marriage*. London: Tavistock, 1971.

Schneider, David M. *American Kinship: A Cultural Account*. Englewood Cliffs, N.J.: Prentice-Hall, 1968.

Peasant societies

Arensberg, Conrad, and S.-T. Kimball. *Family and Community in Ireland*. Cambridge, Mass.: Harvard University Press, 1940; 2d ed., 1968.

Collomp, Alain. *La Maison du père*. Paris: PUF, 1983.

Cuisenier, Jean. *Economie et parenté, leurs affinités de structure dans le domaine turc et le domaine arabe*. Paris: Mouton, 1975.

Fox, Robin. *The Tory Islanders: a People of the Celtic Fringe*. Cambridge: Cambridge University Press, 1978.

Habakkuk, S. 'Family Structure and Economic Change in XIXth Century Europe'. *Journal of Economic History* 15 (1955): 1–12.

Jolas, Tina, and Françoise Zonabend. 'Cousinage, voisinage'. *Echanges et communications. Mélanges offerts a Claude Lévi-Strauss à l'occasion de son 60e anniversaire*. Paris: Mouton, 1970.

Jolas, Tina, Yvonne Verdier and Françoise Zonabend. 'Parler Famille'. *L'Homme* 10(1970): 5–26.

Karnoouh, Claude. 'Le Pouvoir et la parenté'. In *Paysans, femmes et citoyens*. Ed. Hugues Lamarche, Susan Rogers and Claude Karnoouh. Le Paradou: Actes Sud, 1980.

Pingaud, Marie-Claude. *Paysans en Bourgogne. Les gens de Minot*. Paris: Flammarion, 1978.

Plakans, Andrejs. *Kinship in the Past. An Anthropology of European Family Life, 1500–1900*. Oxford: Basil Blackwell, 1984.

Segalen, Martine. *Quinze générations de bas Bretons. Parenté et société dans le pays bigouden sud, 1720–1980*. Paris: PUF, 1985.

Zonabend, Françoise. *The Enduring Memory*. Manchester: Manchester University Press, 1985.

Inheritance systems

Augustins, Georges. 'Division égalitaire des patrimoines et institution de l'héritier'. *Archives européennes de sociologie* 20(1979): 127–41.

Bouchard, Gérard. 'Les systèmes de transmission des avoirs familiaux et le cycle de la société rurale au Québec, du XVIIe au XXe siècle', *Social History* 16 (1983): 35–60.

Goody, Jack, Joan Thirsk and E. P. Thompson, eds. *Family and Inheritance*. Cambridge: Cambridge University Press, 1976.

Le Roy Ladurie, Emmanuel. 'Family Structures and Inheritance Customs in Sixteenth Century France'. In *Family and Inheritance* (see preceding work).

Yver, Jean. *Egalité entre héritiers et exclusion des enfants dotés. Essai de geographie coutumière*. Paris: Sirey, 1966.

Chapter 3

vvvvvvvvvvvvvvvvvvvvvvvvvvvvvvvvvvvvvvvvvvvvvvvvvvvvvvvvvvvvvvvvvvvvvvvvvvvvv

Kin relationships in urban society

Kin is a prime factor in the way in which exotic societies are organised and a dominant one in rural societies, but seems of secondary importance in urban, industrialised ones. Do such societies, which are dominated by an industrial mode of production and divided by social class and associations of all kinds, have a place for kinship outside the domestic groups, which has been reduced in size and 'nuclearised' in structure, as we have seen?

Let us look briefly at how ideas about kinship within the context of industrialisation have developed, and then investigate, with the help of recent research, the importance of kinship in urban societies. After that we will consider the tenacious myth of the dominance of the nuclear family that persists despite the fact that historians, sociologists and anthropologists are once again coming to see just how important kinship is.

SOCIAL AND KINSHIP CHANGE

A great deal of literature has been devoted to the study of the relationships between social changes brought about by industrialisation, urbanisation and cultural developments and changes in the family.

Talcott Parsons's thesis

One of the most influential theories has been that put forward by Talcott Parsons, which was introduced into France in the 1960s by François Bourricaud.[1] It should be noted that the title of the article that summarises Parsons's suggestions refers to the *anthropological* concept of kinship, a fact the sociologists discussing his ideas subsequently blurred. What Parsons said can be summed up in a certain number of propositions that sparked off a still-smouldering and often violent ideological debate.

Parsons's view was that the process of industrialisation fragments the family, first by cutting it off from its kinship network and then by reducing the size of the domestic group to that of a small nuclear family, which loses its productive, political and religious functions and becomes simply a unit of residence and consumption. It shares its financial and educative functions with other institutions and its major remaining function is to provide for the socialisation of children and, above all else, the psychological balance of adults. This domestic group, isolated from its kin, is based on a marriage between partners who have chosen each other freely, and its values are rational and pragmatic. Specialised male and female roles help maintain the existence of the family subsystem within the social system. The father's role is 'instrumental', in that he provides the link with society and material goods, and the wife's is 'expressive' and exercised within the family.

Parsons's view was a functionalist one to the extent that it saw this family model as well adapted to the economic features of contemporary society. In particular, social mobility, the condition for economic development and its cause, was made possible by the breaking of family ties. There was much criticism of his ideas and Parsons later clarified what he meant, pointing out that he was speaking of the isolated nuclear family in terms of 'structure'.[2] But despite these clarifications, his ideas had caused too much of a stir to remain his exclusive property. As John Mogey points out in his survey of the sociological literature dealing with the relationships between residence, family and kinship, most of what Parsons suggested has been found incorrect:

In a continuing series of researches, these critics have shown conclusively that social isolation of the nuclear family from kin, as distinct from structural isolation, has not occurred. Indeed, interaction between members of a kinship group continues in all known societies, and these contacts bring with them advice, psychological support of family identities, financial help, and assistance with child rearing and household tasks.[3]

This expresses in sociological terms what social anthropologists would call kin relationships.

Certain historians, analysing the links between the family and industrialisation, have adopted some of Parsons's views. One of them, Edward Thompson, dramatically describes the effects of the Industrial Revolution in his *The Making of the English Working Class:*

Social and kinship change

Each stage in industrial differentiation and specialisation struck also at the family economy, disturbing customary relations between man and wife, parents and children, and differentiating more sharply between 'work' and 'life'. It was to be a full hundred years before this differentiation was to bring returns, in the form of labour-saving devices, back into the working woman's home. Meanwhile, the family was roughly torn apart each morning by the factory bell.[4]

Other historians and anthropologists have diametrically opposed views. Is it not possible to observe family resistance to the destructive effects of industrialisation and even to sense a certain dynamic power in kinship that perhaps acted as a catalyst in the changes in industrial society?

Industrialisation and kinship

All the way up the social ladder, kinship networks have had an important part to play.

Working-class families. Several studies emphasise the active role played by the family in migratory processes, where it represented a factor of continuity and stability in the struggle with the pressures of the new environment. At the other end of the spectrum are studies that assert that the family did not collapse, but was able to maintain an active control over the careers of its members. As the crucial locus for the transmission of the premigratory culture, the family is seen in these studies as the repository for tradition, providing a cultural heritage that could help individuals adapt to new conditions. In France, there are the examples of the masons from the Creuse area, the Auvergne nurses, the Savoie chimneysweeps and the Cantal café keepers.[5] There are similar examples from the United States, amongst the Puerto Ricans, who maintain close ties with their relatives who have stayed on the island, and amongst Italian migrants.[6] Between those who have stayed at home and those who have moved to the towns there is a steady flow not only of letters and presents but also of a great deal of help for those having to adapt to new conditions in industry.

Tamara Hareven has studied the case of a textile factory in Manchester, New Hampshire. Observations showed a high proportion of female workers, and an intense interaction between workers of French Canadian origin and their kin remaining in Canada. This American example is quite relevant, with whatever transpositions are necessary, in accounting for what happened to English families in the mid-nineteenth century, and in France at the end of the century.[7]

The Amoskeag Manufacturing Company depended on kinship networks to recruit and socialise its workers within the framework of a paternalist ideology. Although the two sides were not equal, firm and family, in their day-to-day dealings, seem to have been two interacting institutions. The company was quite aware of the importance of kinship networks and made deliberate use of them with the aim of turning them into a means of controlling their labour force. It relied on them for recruitment, and, until the early years of the twentieth century, employed whole families. The policy was obviously of great benefit to Amoskeag, since it meant that the company could economise on transport costs and concentrate its efforts in the field of housing for its employees. Social benefits were chiefly for the families of workers and not for individuals. There were schemes for house purchase, dental care for children and so on. Benefits of this kind were part of a programme influenced by Taylorism and aimed at centralising labour policies and increasing the speed of production. Although the work mothers and children did in the factory was new to them, the traditional roles of the couple were scarcely changed, being now simply carried out in the workshop.

Family power had a multiple effect on industrial organisation. It not only made it easier for its members to adjust to new circumstances by finding them a job and a house and by giving them moral support in difficult situations. It also encouraged a turnover of workers in that it helped find jobs for its members and also had a certain say in the day-to-day work routine.

We now know a great deal about the part played by kinship networks in migratory processes, but less about family power in the unit of production as shown in the Amoskeag example. Within the factory, each shop was organised on a basis of kinship and ethnic group. The reconstruction of kinship networks by unit of production shows that in certain cases 90 per cent of the workers belonged to the same ethnic group. Thus the group was cohesive for two basic reasons, namely cultural affinity and kinship, and could in certain circumstances resist the wishes of the bosses by delaying the introduction of changes in the tempo of work and so on.

Hareven's study shows clearly how flexible the family was and that its power as an institution with regard to the unit of production remained considerable. It could soften harsh contacts with industrial society by providing a framework within which its members could adapt themselves to new demands. Clearly it is important to describe, as the author does, the exact extent of such power, which varied according to economic contexts. Amoskeag was obliged to tolerate family resistance to modernisation before the First World War, as there was competition from other firms and labour was scarce. After the war, however, the situation was reversed and the company had the upper hand and regularly sacked workers. Thus, Hareven notes, kinship in an industrial society is apparently not an archaic survival from a rural one but rather the development of new responses to needs created by new conditions. In the context of industrialisation, its networks operated in two areas – origin and arrival. In the former, their strength was linked to their stability and in the latter to their ability to reorganise in relation to other networks, such as those of neighbourhood.[8]

The part played by family nepotism has still to be described. We tend to see it as a feature of the dominant classes, but it also played a part in working-class life, especially when working conditions were particularly bad. In sectors thought to provide relatively favourable conditions of work and pay, new or vacant jobs were by custom kept for close relatives, as in the case of women working in the state tobacco monopoly in France 'who managed to impose the idea that members of their families had priority when new workers were being set on'.[9] Young and Wilmott also note in *Family and Kinship in East London* that such practices seem to be a kind of protection provided by the working-class family for its members. They quote a newspaper advertisement published by the National Union of Printing, Bookbinding and Paperworkers announcing the taking on of new workers:

The members' sons and brothers list is again being opened. . . . Members of the London Central Branch who have sons and brothers of twenty-one and over whose names they wish to place on the list, should make immediate application for a form.[10]

The same thing happened in the large banks and insurance companies. Husband and wife would obtain clerical posts and would be followed by their children. Junior posts of this kind were later to disappear under the impact of mechanisation and data processing in both factories and offices.

Industrial development. At the other end of the social scale, both kinship and kindred groups also kept their power, frequently presiding over the introduction of the capitalist system and, from the basis of their structures and their traditional patterns of behaviour, often contributing to its development. There were great industrial dynasties of steelmakers, bankers and perfume manufacturers.

In an article on the role of family structures in the growth of Roubaix in the nineteenth century in *Colloque de l'histoire de la famille* (October 1979), Pierre Deyon has shown the extent to which the persistence of traditional mentalities and inheritance patterns and of the structure of roles predominating in a largely peasant society was transposed when large concerns were created. Deyon stresses the frequency of endogamy, the functions of which were even more precise in an industrial than in a rural milieu. In the latter, they united kindred groups of the same social and symbolic capital. In the former (as the author emphasises) they generally brought together two complementary businesses, two sets of customers and two patrimonies, and the legal arrangements connected with them show just how interwoven were family marriage strategies and the economic plans of the great industrial dynasties. In addition, women took an active part in running the family business and, at the beginning of this century, often did the accounts and dealt with the correspondence. Their labour, and that of the older children, often helped cut training and supervision costs. Significantly, the name under which the business traded often included those of both husband and wife.

Furthermore – and this is very important – the capital of most businesses came exclusively from within the family, and industrialists, who had no faith in medium-term credit, believed in self-financing whenever possible, automatically reinvesting most of their profits in the firm. Many partnership agreements even made this obligatory. If we also bear in mind that help from the family was a major factor in setting up or saving many businesses, it is easy to see why the French textile industry was able to resist domination by capital from banking institutions until 1914. These family powers were later to work against those wielding them, by leading to a lack of the necessary flexibility.

The same trends were at work in seventeenth- and eighteenth-century New England, where kinship also played a major part in economic and social life. Peter Dobkin Hall has clearly illustrated the intimate link between business and kinship there:

Families supplied merchant firms with manpower and capital. Business relationships and capital combinations were cemented by marriages. And businesses provided basic career training and livelihoods for family members. In addition, because of the dependence of the state on the family for the implementation of social policy, the family continued to provide basic social services for the society as a whole.[11]

Social and kinship change

Powers and kinship

Another test of the ability of kinship and kindred groups to adapt to changes brought about by industrialisation is the continued existence of their social, political or professional powers. The fact that they did persist is due to a process of adaptation to new economic and social conditions. The families of southern France provide an example of this.[12]

The traditional dominance of leading families was challenged by social and economic developments and in particular by the fall in income from land, which had been the traditional basis of their power. Under the Third Republic, that power passed to new people, but the kinship networks offered a threefold resistance to political changes, and certain kindred groups managed to adapt to the new forms of economic power. In both the agricultural and industrial spheres, they appeared on the boards of banking, commercial and industrial establishments. Second, political power based on a traditionally faithful clientele often remained in the same hands. Third, the old networks were strenghtened by their links – which were very often the result of marriage – with the new man on the political scene.

A study of the heads of professional agricultural associations in the French department of Meurthe-et-Moselle shows the same persistence of the power of certain lines despite the restructuring of agriculture since the beginning of the twentieth century. By means of a diagram showing the relationships between leading figures, the author demonstrates that 'one or two important families have the great social privilege of a manifold accumulation of capital inherited by these leading figures'.

What clearly emerges here is the remarkable capacity for adaptation developed by families in a sector often thought to be more passive than the industrial one. In addition to their economic capital, the great peasant dynasties held a symbolic capital based on the accumulation and transmission of public duties. The whole department was encompassed by the network of their connections, and thus they managed to retain a determining role in the professional agricultural organisations. There was a circular reinforcement of their power:

They are elected because they are thought to have 'a hand in everything' and 'connections everywhere' and these members of great families owe their increased power to the influence that the other farmers rightly or wrongly attribute to them.[13]

Aristocratic kindred groups too continued to find a power base as a result of the great efforts they put into elaborating new marriage strategies. Like the *notables* in southern France they diversified their assets following the decline in income from land and thus renewed their social capital. Monique de Saint-Martin gives an example of this kind of renewal in the de Brissac family. The grandfather of the present duke, Pierre de Brissac, the twelfth of the line, married Jeanne Say, the daughter of Louis Say, the founder of a large sugar refinery. His maternal grandfather had married the only heiress of Madame Clicquot (the famous Veuve Clicquot of the great champagne firm). By becoming related by marriage to May Schneider, who was a member of the great iron and steel dynasty, Pierre de Brissac entered the world of business, industry and finance. The marriages of the children were characterised by a diversification of the positions they held, and this tended to increase as the generations went by. Belonging to the line meant that each member enjoyed varied and cumulative symbolic profits. Kinship networks were strengthened by those of friendship and business relationships were often added to these, ensuring that this particular 'large family' enjoyed both the profits related to a social capital and the means of reproducing them.[14]

LINES AND KINDRED GROUPS IN CONTEMPORARY SOCIETY

Recent studies showing the predominance of the nuclear domestic group illustrate the ideas that Parsons put forward. That particular family structure, however, is no longer seen as being perfectly adjusted to a modern economy, but rather as a shelter, a retreat from the external aggressions of society, a place in which all the emotion needed to counteract an inhuman society is turned towards a very small group of people. In distinction from the concept Parsons proposed, this view sees no functional structuring between society and family – only disharmony and even antagonism. It is to protect its members against the dehumanised life-style imposed by the means of transport, housing conditions and the relationships in the world of work that are part and parcel of modern society that the conjugal domestic group (called a 'nucleus' to stress its diminished importance) becomes a centre of affectivity and turns in on itself. This pessimistic thesis is advanced by Louis Roussel in *Le Mariage dans la société française:*

The family has become the privileged means of achieving psychological equilibrium for adults and the chief area in which everyone's psychological

80

history unfolds. . . . When couples shut themselves off from the world and seek a high level of emotional satisfaction, they are not only following the internal logic of the romantic model [that of freely chosen partners]: this behaviour is also linked to the individual's situation in contemporary industrial societies.[15]

Thus, as social space increases, there is a corresponding decrease in the family, whose functions are now reduced to bringing up children and providing emotional and sexual satisfaction for the husband and wife. Although this view offers some explanation for the high divorce rate, it is not entirely consistent. It is hard to see the functions of the family as being *reduced*. They have never been so obsessive, so important for the whole future of the individual and society. Roussel is bound by the logic of his research to contradict his own argument in part, since he admits that the area of emotional satisfaction is not limited to parents and their young children but includes the domestic groups of older generations beyond the conjugal cell.

The members of most families do not experience them as being 'nuclear' and know that they fit into a wider framework of near and distant relatives.

Relationships between parents and married children

It should be made clear here that we are not examining relationships within the family cell, which is the task of a psychosociological approach to parental and conjugal roles (Chapters 6 and 7), but rather relationships between parents and married children, which to some extent form the first degree of kinship relations.

Empirical studies to test Parsons's hypotheses have been carried out in America and subsequently in Belgium and France. Andrée Michel investigated 450 urban families in the Paris area and a further 100 in Bordeaux in connection with the help received by young couples with regard to housing, child care and, where necessary, financial aid. In particular, the author was trying to assess the role of social class. She herself observed that help was given mostly in the higher social classes, but this does not seem to have been borne out by later studies:

The individual's chance of moving up the professional ladder as a result of the isolation of the couple is still theoretical. In fact upwards movement here is more likely in the upper classes than amongst skilled employees or semi-skilled workers, and so is parental aid, most often of either a financial nature when the couple is setting up house or in the form of a service such as looking after children. The continued existence of a greater degree of parental help in these classes encourages the maintenance of status and consequently makes it easier for married children enjoying parental help to progress socially and professionally.[16]

Comparing families in Bordeaux and Paris, Michel notes that the former were much more 'traditional' in outlook than the latter. The reason could perhaps be that there are degrees of urbanisation, with Bordeaux still functioning as an older French town with district networks superimposed on kinship ones and Paris and its suburbs offering a new urban model. We will return to this difficult problem of cultural specificity later and attempt to decide whether the Parisian conurbation should perhaps be considered separately.

Louis Roussel, in *La Famille après le mariage des enfants,* put the same questions to young couples and to couples who were old enough to have been their parents. This was a national survey attempting to measure proximity of residence, frequency of contact, the level of the sevices rendered and the ways in which property was transmitted. His first conclusion, which went against all our stock ideas on the contemporary family, was the astonishing proximity of the parents' residence and that of their married children. Of the national sample, over 75 per cent of the latter lived less than twenty kilometres from their parents. This argues that industrial society does not necessarily entail a mobility that splits up families over wide distances. Although geographic proximity is not a determining factor in the frequency of children–parents contacts, it is clearly a contributory one. Once children are married, it is by choice that they wish to remain near their parents and the scenes of their childhood and adolescence and stay in the town or region whose way of life is well known to them and where they feel at home. The claims of ecology and movements linked to the quality of life merely accentuate the need to live and work in one's home region, near both parents and married children.

Catherine Gokalp's study of people at a point in family life when they had both living parents and married children shows how close together the various generations lived. Of all respondents, 63 per cent lived less than twenty kilometres from their parents (this confirmed Roussel's findings), 60 per cent lived less than twenty kilometres from their parents-in-law and 51 per cent less than twenty kilometres from their married children. The tendency was thus for people to live rather nearer to parents than to married children, but the difference is slight, since although the study showed that children gradually moved away from their parents, it also suggested

Table 3.1. *Real distance between subject and surviving family*

	N	Living together	Same commune	20 km	20–100 km	100–500 km	Over 500 km	Total (%)
Mother	869	16.7	25.0	21.4	13.2	15.3	8.4	100.0
Father	412	10.7	26.7	24.3	14.1	15.5	8.7	100.0
Mother-in-law	679	8.7	25.3	22.1	19.0	16.2	8.7	100.0
Father-in-law	372	7.2	23.7	23.7	20.7	15.3	9.4	100.0
Brothers & sisters	3,849	1.6	17.7	23.5	21.3	20.7	15.2	100.0
Brothers-in-law, sisters-in-law	3,124	0.7	17.0	23.0	22.9	21.8	14.6	100.0
Children (total)	4,459	43.1	13.9	12.9	12.0	12.2	5.9	100.0
Children married	2,034	3.0	23.9	24.3	20.8	18.7	9.3	100.0
of these, sons	962	4.2	24.1	23.3	19.9	19.4	9.1	100.0
of these, daughters	1,072	2.1	23.7	25.0	21.7	18.1	9.4	100.0
Mothers and children	1,815	5.2	20.2	18.5	15.9	40.2		100.0
Of these, married children	631	0.9	13.3	13.5	14.3	58.0		100.0
Of these, single children	1,184	7.5	23.8	21.1	16.8	30.8		100.0

Source: Catherine Gokalp, 'Le Réseau familial', *Population* 6(1978):1087.

that at a later stage the trend was to a certain extent reversed.[17]
Gokalp's survey also quantified the frequency of meeting between
parents and married children. When they lived in close proximity or
even shared a home, 90 per cent of those questioned said that they
saw their daughter at least once a week. For mother, son and
mother-in-law, the figures were 86 per cent, 83 per cent and 82 per
cent respectively. When they lived far apart (over 500 kilometres) it
was still common to see children several times a year, and 77 per
cent saw their daughter more than once and 67 per cent their son.
However, they saw their own parents about once a year, with 55 per
cent seeing their mother more than once and 42 per cent their
mother-in-law.[18]

From the detailed study of the transmission of property and of
occasions when meetings occurred or when services were performed
(e.g. giving financial help, looking after children either in an emergency or in a more regular way during long summer holidays and so
on) a coherent model emerges. Residential proximity meant frequent
contact provided the independence of the young couple was preserved. Both sides wished to preserve their freedom, and consequently contacts and help were a voluntary matter. There was a
desire for contact, but contacts were asymmetrical as a result of a
desire for autonomy. In the case of the transmission of property, for
example, the children made a point of stressing their wish to be
independent, for gifts and loans made by parents are not always
disinterested, and warm-hearted generosity may go hand in hand
with an ulterior possessive motive, as emotional needs are strong in
parents.

As a study by Françoise Cribier of a group of retired Parisians has
shown, contacts between married children and their parents become
more frequent when the latter have retired.[19] Although a minority of
men and only a third of women saw their role as grandparents as an
essential one, contacts were very frequent and close. The great majority of retired people were both pleased with what their children had
given them and experienced a sense of being useful, which gave a
point to their lives. At that age, parents, who throughout their lives
have given, take their turn at receiving, often in an indirect way.
Financial help from their children helps maintain the flat or the subur-
ban or country home that they will one day inherit. For retired
people, the importance of contacts with their children is not limited to
emotional or financial affairs, and it is often through them that they
keep up a network of friends. The content of relationships between
married children and their parents can thus be seen as undergoing
continuous modification throughout the cycle of family life.

Lines and kindred groups in contemporary society

A further aim of Roussel's survey was to define the continuity of culture from one generation to another. The general social mobility of young married couples in relation to that of their parents was observed in the hope of discovering whether the same models of the family, characterised by such variables as opinions about the allocation of male and female tasks, the wife's work outside the home and so on, were transmitted from father to son or whether the fathers adopted those of their sons. Three situations were noted. In the first a model of the family was characterised by a certain hierarchy of the spouses' and a sharp distinction between roles, a fairly strict upbringing and sexual reserve were transmitted. The second was typified by a certain convergence of opinions, arising in part from the transmission of particular ideas and in part from a more or less willing acceptance by the parents of positions they had not had in their younger days. In the third, there was a discernible distance, and perhaps even a contrast, between the two sets of ideas but no direct clash, as some subjects were systematically avoided to prevent conflict. Thus there was a cultural transmission between generations, but when values conflicted taboo subjects were not discussed, since the maintenance of relationships was even more highly esteemed than differences of opinion. Preserving these relationships was seen as more important than ideological reasons for a break.[20]

The aim of the in-depth investigation was to cast light on the findings of the national questionnaire. Forty very detailed interviews were devoted to examining the type, nature and frequency of contacts between parents and married children and views of marriage.[21] Given the major influence of social class on models of the family, the survey concentrated on the middle classes. These qualitative investigations confirmed Roussel's statistical findings and showed the high level of family ties and relationships between parents and married children. They also offered an explanation of the phenomenon. In a rapidly changing society, the family, since it is based on powerful unconscious forces, appears as the stable and permanent element and a 'refuge', particularly amongst the middle classes, who are the most sensitive to change. It is important to remember that in this context, the reference was to links between domestic groups covering two generations and not to 'family' in the sense of the couple.

Upward mobility and the achievement of a standard of living unknown to the earlier generation seem fragile things, to be protected by maintaining frequent contacts between the generations. This is something to be done at all costs, even if it means an ideological compromise when there is disagreement on political or family problems or on philosophies of life in general. Moreover, when the couple was in serious difficulties there was recourse to the parents.

These face-to-face interviews confirmed the importance of emotion:

All exchanges within the family and all the transactions carried out there are the vehicles of intense emotional relationships and are only fully meaningful if referred to them. . . . Emotional interdependence is one of the bases of family continuity.[22]

As was also shown by Roussel's national statistical survey, this affectivity is asymmetrical. If we follow the interviews through, we can see why. Parents – and this becomes more and more the case with the passage of time – are increasingly dependent on the affection of their children, and their many gifts, loans and services become the means by which they ensure it. This is clearly perceived by both sides, but must not be put into words. 'It must be as if the parents gave nothing and the children accepted nothing',[23] and the grandchildren are the means by which such transmissions occur. This lack of symmetry can also be interpreted in another way: Married children are in a dominant position for only one generation, and the imbalance in the situation is corrected when they will in their turn become the parents of married children. Alternatively, it would be possible to question the position of strength enjoyed by children who unconsciously trade their love and to see them, even when they are married, as being still emotionally dependent on their parents. There would then be a reciprocity of affection, even if the affection were shown in different ways. Noting that 'everything not connected with what is immediate and affective is seen to be of less value', Roussel concludes that

in its own way, the solidarity between the generations completes the conjugal cell. In a society in which relationships are increasingly functional, it is a part of that one area outside such a nexus: the family.[24]

Thus, the conjugal nucleus is seen as opening up only in order to absorb parents into that world of love and warmth that acts as a protection against society. Although the author tries to refute the possible charge, his view is very reminiscent of that of Parsons in that it stresses the high degree of isolation of a conjugal nucleus whose considerable emotional content is extended backwards to cover the previous generation. The isolation is thus no more than displaced and still emphasised.

It may perhaps seem false to make a sharp distinction between parents and married children on the one hand and other domestic groups composing kinship on the other. It is true that the clearly defined aim of Roussel's survey was to measure contacts between parents and married children, but it seems to include the whole field of kinship in these contacts. In addition, it is also very much characterised by the social category examined, since it is perhaps in the middle classes that families are most inward-looking.

If we take into account the goods and services exchanged within family networks, we can see the link between the domestic group, preceding generations and other members of the kinship group. Agnès Pitrou sees two types of aid in the flow within urban kinship groups, which she calls 'subsistence aid' and 'improvement aid'.[25] The former is aimed at maintaining a standard of living by helping in cases of unexpected difficulties and the latter at improving status.

These findings are important in two ways. First, they approach family relationships not from the point of view of the affectivity they contain but from that of the nature of their function in social strategies. Second, the relationships described go beyond the narrow framework of parents and married children and clearly show the importance of the role of the sibling group, that of the extended field of the family, backed up by the network of friendships.

Mother–daughter relationships

Demographic changes over the last hundred years have revolutionised women's lives much more than they have men's. With a longer life expectancy and fewer pregnancies (which are concentrated very early in an earlier marriage), a woman of around forty who has brought up her children now has on average another thirty-five years of life before her. These far-reaching changes and their effects on the position of women in society and the family will be examined later, but for the moment we will simply consider their effect on the frequency of family contacts and in particular on the mother–daughter relationship. Indeed, a leaning towards that particular relationship can be discerned in contemporary society, and as a result there is to some extent a move towards a certain matrilateral situation.

In the past, a trade, a status or the acquisition of technical skills was transmitted from father to son. By the nineteenth century, when both were hourly-paid workers in different factories, there was a break in transmission along the male line. Sometimes the mother emerged as the pivot of family life and her affective role increased as the father was more and more seen as a worker struggling with the harsh and painful conditions of proletarian life.

The affective relationship between mother and daughter, acting as a means of transmitting technical skills and values, is still present in the working class of the twentieth century. Michael Young and Peter Wilmott, studying Bethnal Green, a working-class area of London, have shown in *Family and Kinship in East London* that residence was most often 'matrilocal', as the majority of couples lived near the wife's parents. This, however, only partly explains the very high daily level of the exchange of contacts, visits, services and advice between mother and married daughter. When the latter married, her mother, whose own children were now grown, had more free time than her daughter, who was just entering the cycle of pregnancies, births and looking after young children. The mother's moral, emotional and material support was most needed at a time when she was most able to give it. A relatively clear distinction of roles and tasks between spouses encouraged the mother's day-by-day involvement in her daughter's household. In *Two Studies of Kinship in London*, Raymond Firth describes this type of family organisation as a 'matri-centered family'. It is typical of family organisation in Bethnal Green as described by Young and Wilmott:

But when she [a daughter] marries, and even more when she leaves work to have children, she returns to the woman's world, and to her mother. Marriage divides the sexes into their distinctive roles, and so strengthens the relationship between the daughter and the mother who has been through it all before. The old proverb applies:

> My son's a son till he gets him a wife,
> My daughter's a daughter all her life.[26]

But perhaps Bethnal Green is an unusual case. It may be a question of behaviour patterns characteristic of the working class as a whole, of a specific urban environment so closely knit as to be almost a village, or of one generation (the survey took place in 1955). However, this tendency for the wife's mother to become a focus does seem to have been confirmed by later studies carried out in Britain and involving different social environments. In 1961, Rosser and Harris conducted a survey in Swansea, an industrial Welsh city of over 167,000 inhabitants. They noted a whole pattern of visits very like that in Bethnal Green, particularly with regard to the different frequency for men and women. Over half the married women interviewed had seen their mother during the preceding week. In middle-class Woodford, the same mother–daughter link as in working-class areas was maintained. It is true that to the extent that the residential area was an indication of the daughters' upward mobility there had been changes in both the mother–daughter and the husband–wife relationships. The latter was stronger than in the working class and tasks and roles were less separate, and yet the mother–daughter relationship, much more than that between father and son, persisted. The mothers, however, did make much less display of their authority, particularly when they disagreed with their daughters about bringing up children, and were willing to accept the new cultural model of the upwardly mobile generation.[27]

In the United States, surveys have also shown that when families cohabit it is more often with the wife's parents than with the husband's and that aged parents more often ask for help from their daughters than from their sons or daughters-in-law.[28] Sylvia Yanagisako stresses the importance of the mother–daughter relationship in the American family and sees it as having a social and symbolic value beyond its functional aspect: 'Horizontal solidarity and female solidarity mediate between the mutual dependency of households and the ideological stance of nuclear family independence.'[29]

Thus, the mother–daughter relationship is not specifically a working-class phenomenon, even if the objective conditions for its pre-eminence are more fully present in the working class than in other social categories.

There is very little in the way of French data on this question. Roussel does not take it into account, but then his survey was concerned with 'children' and 'parents' and made no distinction by sex. On the other hand, Pitrou notes that in the middle classes aid from the wife's parents most frequently took the form of material services, whilst that from the husband's tended to be financial. Conversely, when it was a question of aid *to* parents, it was the wives who primarily provided visits, services, care and, where necessary, accommodation. Gokalp also established that there were more frequent contacts with married daughters.[30]

At the present time, a trend seems to be emerging in rural areas in France. The farmer's wife has a smaller role to play in agriculture as a result of technical developments and has consequently set up a new focus for her activities around her home, her children and the family with which she provides contact. The link with her mother is particularly close.

Genealogies and kinship networks in urban environments

As was the case with urban environments, the concept of lines and kindred groups is relevant to the analysis of kinship in urban environments. In that context, investigators must patiently construct the genealogy of the individual or domestic group they are studying, like anthropologists studying peasant or exotic societies. In order to do that, he must introduce himself into the human group he is investigating and become involved with it. But how can this be done in an urban environment outside the overbroad classifications into social category or profession? The earliest studies of kinship dealt with easily identifiable groups such as immigrants. Thus Firth, in *Two Studies of Kinship*, examined that phenomenon amongst working-class people in South London and an ethnic group of Italian origin scattered throughout the city. Firth was surprised at the extent of what he calls the 'kin universe':

The genealogies collected in the inquiry reveal that the total number of relatives reckoned in the kin universe of any household is usually more than one hundred. For the twelve households for whom data are most complete the kin universe varied between thirty-seven and 246, with an average figure of 146. Such figures were surprising to both investigators and informants, neither of whom expected them to be so high. . . .

[Another] point is the *inclusion of dead kin* among those cited. This has several functions. Memory of dead kin is part of the social personality of an informant; the dead serve as a focus for sentiment; they are links of justification for active social ties with other kin. All the genealogical material collected in the survey contained some references to dead kin. Of 1,150 kin cited in a set of nine genealogies from the families studied, just over 184, or approximately fifteen per cent, were dead kin. About two-thirds of these dead kin were consanguineal and one-third affinal kin.[31]

Remembering dead relatives is thus a selective process. It is agreeable to recall a link, even a distant one, with a given relative, because it is flattering to be able to display such a connection. That selectivity in both genealogy and the choice of relationships is moreover one of the characteristics of the European kinship system, and we will return to it later.

Although the sheer size of the kin universe is important, it is more a question of collateral extent than genealogical depth. Five or six generations at most are covered in all, usually two earlier ones and two subsequent ones starting from Ego, if Ego is in an average age-range. In every genealogy, there is a relative who can be seen as a pivot, a kind of junction point in the structure, either because he is important from the point of view of such matters or because of his knowledge of the ramifications of the family tree. Ego could appeal to this relative to help his failing memory just as he could refer to his wife's knowledge of relatives. Consequently, in these British surveys, genealogies are those of a family social group rather than of an individual.[32]

Every kindred group contains someone who is the family memory bank, and when anyone is asked to construct a family tree, he can turn to this individual. Maupassant depicts just such a family genealogist in his story *Pierre et Jean:*

Madame Roland had an excellent memory for kinship and began at once to trace all the relationships by marriage on her husband's side and her own, to go back through lines of descent and to follow the branches of cousins.[33]

An American study of Jewish families from Western Europe who had immigrated to the United States provided similar information.[34] There was the same feeling of satisfaction amongst those respondents who, once their genealogy had been established, could trace the wider network of kin both over generations and collaterally. The average number of relatives, living and dead, who could be recognised was 241 for ten families, which was higher than for the British families but is explicable by the specific cultural character of the group studied. The same characteristics of the networks were apparent here; there was great collateral width but little genealogical depth, and up to 20 per cent of dead relatives were included in the genealogy. The figures established by Elizabeth Bott in *Family and Social Network,* which were based on a study of the kinship networks of three middle-class English families, approach those provided by Firth. The Newbolts recognised 156 relatives, including 17 deceased ones, the Daniels 124 (34 deceased) and the Hartleys 60 (27 deceased).

We have scarcely any information of a similar kind for France, since the study undertaken by the Institut National d'Etudes Démographiques (INED) arbitrarily established a 'family group' made up of the parents of the couple, the couple themselves, their children and their spouses, the grandchildren, the brothers and sisters of the couple and their children, totalling on average twenty-three persons with little variation according to age.[35] For obvious reasons, we know nothing of the extent of kinship beyond these relatives.

The fact that relatives are known and can be named does not necessarily mean that contacts exist, and we must distinguish between knowledge of a kinship network and those interacting links for which it may provide a theatre. Bott distinguishes between 'effective' and 'non-effective' relatives. The former are those with whom there is a fair degree of intimacy, the latter those with whom there is no contact and about whom one merely knows a certain number of facts, such as their name or job or the number of children they have. Finally, there is the group of distant or 'unfamiliar' relatives about whom one simply knows that they exist.[36]

Firth distinguishes in the way his genealogies were recorded between 'recognised' and 'named' kin, the latter being a more restricted group than the former since it included only those relatives who could be addressed by name. There were often very large numerical differences between the two categories. The principle of selectivity seems characteristic of the kinship system in Western societies, operating both in the establishment and the content of social relationships, and functioning as a system of social landmarks. In our societies it is no longer the only one, but it does occupy a major role amongst all the other social identities that the individual is more or less free to choose. This act of social identification can fulfil a number of other real or latent functions, and even if its only place is in the world of the imagination it is worth close attention. Basing his remarks on British research, the anthropologist Christopher Turner describes the selectivity principle in these terms in *Family and Kinship in Modern Britain:*

The permissiveness allowed in establishing social relationships with kin, and the openness of a multi-lineal system means that an individual may choose whether or not to recognise more distant kin, and has a further choice concerning whether or not to establish social relationships on the basis of known kinship links. Generally speaking an individual actually recognises first and second degree relations, and maintains some form of social contact with first degree kin, and with second degree relatives in the direct line of descent. Knowledge of or contact with peripheral kin is extremely variable.[37]

Functions of kinship

There is too great a tendency to reduce kin relationships to affective, ritual or symbolic functions. The widest range of relatives is invited to those great rituals that mark the ending of one stage of life; in a French context these are baptism, first communion, marriage and – in particular – funerals. These family reunions are only points in a general process of identification with the family that has its own range of functions. Beyond contacts, visits, exchanges of services and family reunions, kinship creates a set of more or less constraining moral obligations and provides a frame of reference that has its own importance in relationship to others such as those set up by profession, place of residence or birth or the make of car driven. This competition with other subsystems is characteristic of the kinship system in urban societies. However, as the empirical studies undertaken in the 1960s by the American sociologists Marvin Sussman, Lee Burchinal and Eugene Litwak have shown, this has in no way weakened its functions.

Lines and kindred groups in contemporary society

Identification. The latent existence of kinship networks assumes great importance in a society that isolates the individual, and the idea of the family as a refuge re-emerges. It is no longer a question of immersion in the conjugal domestic group but rather of finding a place in the family network that will enable individuals to get their bearings in time and space and of establishing an identity and an origin by means of family history. Each individual, once he is enclosed in the sequence of generations, part of a collateral network and defined by the place of origin of the family, finds a proper niche. Networks give a feeling of stability and belonging, and function as a system of identification.

They do so all the more successfully when all the relatives live close together, but those who are distant in terms of kinship or location have a latent function, and networks can be suddenly reactivated if a crisis or a need arises. We are once again faced with the kindred group, a malleable network in terms of needs.

Kinship also serves as a kind of identity or 'identification' card when the individual is in contact with other people. Rosser and Harris quote the example of the man arriving at his aunt's house in Swansea. He did not know her, but did know that he had the right to knock at her door. As soon as the kin relationship was expressed, the woman was able to place the stranger:

'There was a knock on the door one Sunday evening,' said Mrs. Price of Cwmbwrla, 'and the chap standing there said "I'm Donald from Bolton. Hullo, Auntie Rhoda. Dad said to come and look you up. I've been sent down here for four months by McAlpine's. Can you put me up?" "Good God!" I said "come in, boy!" I hadn't seen him since he was about six, more than thirty years ago I suppose. My brother moved up to Lancashire in the Depression and made his home there – never came back this way. I could hardly understand Donald's accent with all that funny Lancashire twang. But of course he stayed with us, and went round to see all the family down here. He even turned up my cousins over in Llanelly and I haven't seen them for years. He just walked in the British Legion Club one Sunday and said to one of the older chaps "Are there any Loosemores here tonight? I'm Dick Loosemore's boy from Bolton." They turned out half a dozen relatives (that he'd never seen) for him in no time, and many of Dick's friends from the old days.'[38]

A whole variety of kinship functions emerges from this example. Materially, it produced a lodging and, less directly, it enabled the other members of the group, whether relatives or friends, to integrate the newcomer into the pre-existing network. Kin relationships thus offer a means of access to the community.

Acculturation. In an urban environment, kinship is particularly functional for immigrants and political, religious and other minority groups. It is a two-way process, at once a means of integration into the whole of society and something that slows assimilation and social mobility. For such groups, whose role has been particularly studied in the melting-pot of the United States, kinship is a network of support and a source of identification providing norms and values that ensure transition between original and host groups.

In this context, a study of a New York Jewish group showed that relatives lived close together, which meant frequent visits and a great number of telephone calls. A number of relatives had the same type of job, and there were even institutionalised kinship groups, a variety of what anthropologists call 'corporate groups'. Family circles or cousins' clubs were organised, each with its chairman, treasurer, secretary and so on. The apparent function of these associations was of a purely recreational nature, such as organising theatre trips and Hanukkah parties. Whereas associations like the Goldman Family Circle emphasised links between the various generations, the cousins' clubs encouraged horizontal links within a single generation. The function of these associations was acculturation.[39] Amongst Jewish relatives who had emigrated to Canada there are examples of kinship networks functioning like true lineages, with members working and living together and jointly owning property.[40]

It was with the aim of evaluating the specific nature of English kinship that Firth studied that of the 'Italianates' in London. These were either recent immigrants or the children of immigrants who had moved to England before the Second World War. Some of their kinship characteristics were similar to those noted amongst the working-class groups of 'South Borough' in London, for example their degree of knowledge of genealogical depth and the existence of a 'pivotal' relative who was the repository of family group memory. There were nevertheless a certain number of particular features characteristic of a fairly specific kinship bearing witness to the Italian influence and ensuring continuity. In the first place, although kinship in South Borough (and in urban societies in general) is characterised by selectivity, that is, by the choice of either having or not having contacts with a given distant relative, all kinship links amongst the Italianates were definite and entailed rights and duties. Mutual aid within the network was an obligation, and a certain kind of relationship, based on mutual trust, was expected. There were usually frequent contacts within the kinship group, despite the fact that it was scattered over several areas of London and despite the distance separating relatives who had emigrated and those who had stayed in Italy. In many cases, there were no social contacts outside the kinship framework. The domestic groups involved were rarely nuclear and would take in a distant relative. The scarcity of flats in London also served to mask the true extended nature of the groups, as nephews or cousins, even though they were part of them, had to be given accommodation where they worked in the restaurant or hotel belonging to the head of the family.

This kind of kinship-based structuring of relationships within an immigrant group slows considerably the process of assimilation into the dominant group. Thus, one can make a striking comparison between the London Italianates and Italian immigrants in the United States. The latter were not supported by their kinship network and became Americanised within a generation, whereas it took several generations for the former to become fully integrated into English society. Maintaining a kinship network providing the complete framework for social interaction means that certain distinguishing features of the original culture will persist. Giving personal names from the family stock, and giving them to first-born children in the traditional way (with the son taking his paternal grandfather's and the daughter her paternal grandmother's), marrying within the Italianate community, the high level of economic flow between the family at home and those who had emigrated to London, the retention of Catholic culture and morality, all helped to perpetuate the kinship organisation.[41] Social category, however, introduced differences into the slowing-down process, for even in a cultural milieu that at first glance seems very homogeneous, social stratification and family organisation were interdependent. Thus, those towards the top of the social scale such as doctors, lawyers, managing directors and the like were wealthier and could go back to Italy two or three times a year and thus keep up closer links with those at home. This occurred to such an extent that their life in England seemed to be merely an extension of their way of life in Italy, whereas the further one went down the social scale, the looser the ties with the family in Italy became, as visits were more difficult. This was particularly obvious in the case of the children of workers or servants.[42]

Even in the case of groups achieving a high degree of cultural integration, the social category variable seems to be the major one with regard to the recognition and implementation of relationships within the kinship group.

Kinship is not the only means of access to the community. The schoolroom, the army and the place of work are others. Increasingly nowadays there are other formal groupings that offer immigrants an opportunity to integrate. They have contacts through children in school, through playing tennis or bowls, through collecting stamps or butterflies or through fighting to preserve an old building or their local environment, and yet kinship remains a major way of making contact with others and creating social links.

Access to the labour market. Kinship often provides a way into the labour market, especially in the case of first employment in any field. The young person of an age to start work will have formed an image of the job or of factories likely to hire him from what his relatives or friends have been able to tell him. In the upper sections of the social scale, reference to a particular member of the kinship group serves as an identifier and may carry as much weight as a formal qualification when a selection is being made.

Certain ethnic groups with close-knit kinship patterns enjoy a real monopoly of some jobs as generations and kindred groups come and go. In the United States, for example, it has been observed that policemen were recruited essentially through the kindred group. In one town where most of the force were of Irish origin, 76.2 per cent of policemen had close relatives in the force and 29.2 per cent of their fathers were either still in it or had retired from it.[43] Similarly, in a large factory in Cleveland using semi-automated assembly methods, 13.5 per cent of workers hired for the summer of 1963 were the sons or relatives of middle or higher managers in the company.[44]

Danièle Auffray and colleagues have shown the part played by the family with regard to the labour market in a working-class area in the Mayenne region of France.[45] They observed the frequency of town–country contacts based on deep-freezers and gardens, allowing for the exchange of cuts from a pig killed at home and vegetables. They saw the family network as particularly important in connection with the small factories located in Laval and Mayenne, where kin contacts were in the first place a system of information about jobs, providing a certain picture of working conditions in the factories and encouraging a rapid turnover of labour. Since industry in Laval offers a tiny variety of jobs, the worker sought out the company offering the best wages. For 'shoe-string' concerns of this kind, turnover is an expensive business and they are obliged to come into line to some extent:

The labour market is not the vast, featureless area some neo-classical economists have described within which the worker is moved around like a pawn in accordance with the needs of employers. It is rather an essential stake in the social conflict in which are at play those family and territorial practices which give each region its own economic and social configuration.[46]

Nowadays we note the refusal of mobility. Industrial ideology presumed that workers would necessarily follow the demand for labour wherever capital set up factories, but families, once the great population movements of the Industrial Revolution were over, showed their wish to stay where they lived and organised their kinship and friendship networks. Not only do those unemployed who could find a job elsewhere refuse to move and uproot themselves, but young people too increasingly look for work in their home area. There is a spatially and temporally limited, but significant, example of a change in behaviour patterns in which the family played a major part.[47] In the southern part of the Cornouaille area of Brittany, which was over-populated after the Second World War, a generation of men broke with agriculture for good in the 1950s and 1960s and went to Nantes or Paris to find work in factories or in the national police force. Young people today take exactly the opposite attitude, and their behaviour shows their wish to remain in their own area. 'Building' is their aim, and they want to give a material expression to their desire to keep their roots. The building industry offers the chance of a local job, and young men have become skilled workers, heating engineers, bricklayers, roofers and the like. The lack of industrialisation is certainly a handicap at the regional level, but it also means a gradual adaptation to the modern world. By staying in their own area, they can enjoy a more genuine quality of life and remain in the cultural milieu within which they were brought up. Some are even willing to take a cut in wages or accept a lower grading than they are qualified for. If they live and work where their kinship and friendship networks are, they can soon make up the money they have lost by not moving to the towns, for those networks are multi-functional, and as well as providing psychological and emotional support, they also provide material exchanges, goods, services and advice, and an informal economy is gradually becoming apparent. One of its nodal points, in fact, is the family building of houses. The young men, who are mostly farmers' sons, inherit a piece of land. They then set up a construction team using the technical skills available in the kinship network, and this team, working in its spare time in the evenings and at weekends, builds the house from the cellar to the attic without calling on regularly paid skilled labour unless there is a skill the kinship group cannot provide. The networks also provide help with young children and food exchanges in the form of garden produce, and have important functions at the level of jobs and employment. Since they extend into both town and country, they provide high-grade information about the labour market. Everyone knows where everyone else is working, and the reputation of different companies is built on these informal contacts. As soon as a job becomes vacant or a new one is created, the kinship network, as was the case with Amoskeag, is responsible for filling it. The various layers of social positions also give those who hold power at the local level a whole range of high-quality information. The branch manager of the bank giving loans for house-building may also be the manager of the local sports team, and in the vast majority of cases he knows the applicant, his family circumstances and his creditworthiness personally. In cases in which, in an impersonal environment, lengthy inquiries would be needed to complete the file, the network of mutual acquaintances is enough. Kinship networks are mediate institutions between the individual and society. They help to reduce the traumas of economic and social changes and to let the individual find his place in a world which is overformalised, difficult to enter and opaque.

Kinship and the urban environment

Of course, the more stable the group, the longer established the residence, the lower the incidence of social and residential mobility and the greater the degree to which kinship links multiply and become superimposed to form a society of mutual acquaintanceship of the kind characteristic of village communities or old parts of towns. In Bethnal Green, that archetypal district studied by Michael Young and Peter Wilmott in *Family and Kinship in East London,* the movement to friendship was via kinship. The various neighbourhood and kinship networks were very much alive in this working-class district of London. At the time of the survey, all the inhabitants of a relatively restricted area were either related or knew each other through relatives or mutual friends, and the residential proximity of parents and married children (and also of other more distant relatives) was great. There was no need to travel far to work, and the social hierarchy was very limited since most of the men were manual workers and white-collar workers employed in the district did not live there. In short, kinship relations were the overriding factor in the local cluster of social relationships and the district functioned in the manner of a village. It seems unlikely that towns are still made up of juxtaposed villages, and the effects of urban renovation on kinship networks must be considered. Major rebuilding has seriously affected the urban web of old towns or led to the creation of new ones.

Young and Wilmott continued their analysis in *Family and Class in a London Suburb,* following up some of the Bethnal Green families who were rehoused in Greenleigh. This was something of a laboratory experiment, with most of the variables controlled, since comparisons between the two situations could be made. Forty-one of the worst-housed couples in Bethnal Green were moved into an estate of identical rows of houses round a shopping centre. Little information about contacts with the wider kinship group is available, as this was not part of the survey, but a certain number of changes with regard to close relatives were apparent. Contact with the mother became less frequent than in Bethnal Green, where it had been exceptionally high, since the distances involved were now greater, and the new isolation of the couple meant that the husband–wife relationship became closer and stronger and the distinction between their respective roles increasingly blurred. In an anonymous urban community of that type, status replaces the network of mutual acquaintance. The individual can no longer be identified as a member of his kinship group, no longer has a share in a long history that is part of a collective patrimony, no longer has qualities, defects and a personality that are part of the public domain, and is therefore identified by other people by means of external criteria, such as the way his children are dressed for school, the sort of car he drives and how he looks after his garden. Kinship and sociability networks thus function on the basis of different criteria and are not interchangeable.

Is it possible to maintain that the less favourable the urban environment is to human contacts, the less human beings interact in their daily lives and the more kinship narrows towards the domestic group? This seems to be what has in fact happened in the greater Paris area, where Agnès Pitrou has observed very different behaviour patterns from those in medium-sized towns of over 10,000 inhabitants, where contact with relatives is very much a vital phenomenon. In Paris and its surrounding area, the domestic groups she questioned had, on average, the least frequent contacts with relatives and a high proportion of them had none at all, particularly working-class families:

The tempo of life in Paris, transport and traffic problems, frequent moves to increasingly outlying suburbs paradoxically means that hyper-concentration makes visits and exchanges more difficult over a distance of ten kilometres than over one of fifty or a hundred in the provinces. Very large cities are a haven for many voluntarily or involuntarily rootless people with only the most tenuous links or none at all with their families.[48]

And yet another study by Béatrix Le Wita in *La mémoire familiale des Parisiens des classes moyennes*[49] shows that the domestic groups living in the thirteenth *arrondissement* of Paris have a high level of kinship contact. Most of them are provincial in origin and the telephone provides for those who wish to do so – the majority, in fact – an easy means to maintain this level. Relatives are visited on weekend outings, and holidays are spent in their original area in a family house that two or three times a year sees the renewal of contacts with the kindred group. In our age, residential distance no longer seems to be a cause of the loosening of kinship ties.

The importance of a kinship network cannot be measured solely in terms of its tangible functions, for it refers to a whole active imagination and its role is perhaps more important as a result of that latent function. It enables an individual who is unhappy in his job or the place he lives in to situate himself in space and time and to stand in a relationship to a family history which gives him an identity and an identification that his work and place of residence cannot provide. The imaginative landscape of the family also offers comfort and assurance. In a world in which there is a lot wrong with the family, yours is all right. The ability to produce a large number of collateral relatives, ancestors and descendants means that you yourself are socially normal in a world out of control.

Kinship and social class

The first studies stressing the importance of kin relationships and their role were concerned with working-class families. What is the situation in the middle and upper classes?

First, it should be noted that there is no universal agreement about the place of kin relationships in working-class families. Andrée Michel, in a study of the urban family and kinship in France published in *Families in East and West*, notes that:

The families of labourers and semi-skilled workers are the most nuclear and the most cut off from parental help, with only 16% asking parents for help in setting up a home, 24% requesting it at times of financial need and 17.9% seeking it in connection with looking after children.[50]

Pitrou believes, however, that in fact working-class social relationships are almost exclusively with the kindred group.[51]

In France, it is no longer workers, but the subproletariat, who have no family and are also the poorest off as far as kinship is concerned. In a comparison of French and foreign subproletarians, Colette Pétonnet notes in her *On est tous dans le brouillard* that the former, whether they come originally from the town or the country, have broken their links with their kin and often do not know where they come from, unlike Spaniards or Portuguese, who receive emotional, moral and material support from their compatriots. The French subproletarians, says the author, have no sense of a family past and feel this as a loss of identity. The lack of any family transmission means that there can be no memories attached to a particular place, no sense of roots, even imaginary ones, elsewhere.

The authors who studied Bethnal Green, along with other English anthropologists, have studied kinship in the working and middle classes, and these studies have provided a whole range of interesting data.[52] However, since no similar studies have been undertaken in France, it cannot be assumed that their conclusions can be transposed from one country to the other, where the same name for a social class includes situations that are sometimes different.

According to the hypothesis that we have already mentioned on several occasions, social mobility, which is frequently geographic mobility, often greatly distends kinship links between parents and married children, and to an even greater degree amongst kindred groups. It is true that in comparison with the interaction observed in working-class contexts there are fewer kin relationships in a middle-class one if these are measured in terms of the frequency of visits, as we have already noted. An upwardly mobile couple is ready to give up the advantages of residential proximity for those offered by a better job in a distant town or part of the country. As the couple becomes integrated into a neighbourhood composed of people with a roughly equivalent standard of living, they will acquire new cultural behaviour patterns, and sociability with friends will take the place of sociability with the family. This process has been shown quite clearly in Woodford, an English suburb with two social classes distinguished by their type of sociability. For working-class inhabitants, institutionalised sociability had little appeal, whereas those from the middle classes favoured meetings within the framework of the parish, the tennis or golf club, the choir, the drama society and so on.[53] Here, we are leaving the family sphere proper. The upwardly mobile middle classes acquire a whole leisure culture that is unknown to the working classes, and that perhaps replaces all forms of family sociability with those that grow up around the leisure society, or at least adds the latter to the former. There may be no direct competition, but the middle classes certainly acquire other centres of interest. Work and the family are no longer the only poles of attraction in social life.

Nevertheless, it is difficult to maintain a single view of kinship and sociability networks in that social category. We have already said that the English middle class is not strictly equivalent to its French counterpart. Its boundaries are vague, and when we speak of kin relationships between generations, we need to know whether we are dealing with patterns with a heightened social mobility (where, for example, the father is a workman and the son a manager) or whether there is still a relative stability between the generations. It is perhaps the very blurred outline of that class that means that apparent contradictions can be reconciled. We have seen the high degree of interaction within the kinship group in the English middle classes, which is still present even when face-to-face contact is often replaced by telephone calls or letters. All this therefore disproves the hypothesis of an inevitable break in relationships either because reciprocity is impossible or because the status of various relatives is different, or because their ideologies and norms are too divergent, particularly with regard to bringing up children. All the studies also stress the existence of frequent contacts between parents and married children, particularly in a middle-class context where people have to preserve a fragile status and invest considerable emotional energy in close family relationships, even when this entails avoiding subjects likely to provoke conflict.

We really do not know any more about the rest of the kinship network. Is it at this level that the family breaks up when conflicts related to status, ideology and culture become too great or when such relationships no longer have an emotional content? Are relationships with uncles, aunts and cousins, met at holiday times and with whom one shares an identification, kept up? There are no studies to provide answers to such questions.

There seems to be more general agreement with regard to the upper classes, despite the absence of in-depth studies and the fact that what has been said comes from subjective presuppositions. In such a context, kinship relations are no longer necessary, to the extent that services provided in other social classes by kinship (such as a nanny or a woman to look after the children) can be purchased elsewhere. As in a middle-class context, there is also a considerable social interaction outside the kinship group here, by virtue of membership of clubs and associations and/or by the extension of friendship networks. On the other hand, it is in upper-class contexts that there is the greatest amount of family financial help in the form of goods and services, particularly when married children are setting up house. The young couple's independence is preserved, but they are given the means to reproduce their parents' social level immediately. Here, kinship provides the moral and material help to maintain it. If the married children have to undergo the temporary setbacks associated with embarking on a career, the kinship network functions fully, with recommendations and the use of its name as a social reference to ease entry into the professional milieu.

A number of studies see social class as one of the major variables concerned with the existence of kin relationships, but there are not enough of them to extend the correlations. It is nevertheless no longer possible to claim that industrialisation has cut off the domestic group from its kinship network.

KINSHIP GROUP VERSUS NUCLEAR FAMILY: AN IDEOLOGICAL POSITION

If relationships with the kinship group are such an abiding phenomenon, why has their existence been so often hidden and indeed denied over the last twenty years or so?

State action has been a factor here for the last century. It is impossible to tax kindred groups and close relatives or to produce figures for scattered kinship networks, and the state has had to single out individual domestic groups within their kinship networks for its purposes of possession and manipulation.

The ideological significance of the nuclear family must also be recognised. In his *World Revolution and Family Patterns*, William Goode has shown the importance of the gap between representations and practices with regard to the phenomena connected with the family and has stressed the independence of ideological variables. The ideology of the nuclear family proclaims the right of the individual to choose a marriage partner, a place of residence and the group of relatives he or she wants to see. Goode maintains that it contains an ideal of democracy and freedom and insists on the unique nature of every individual even in those societies in which kinship systems are the most constricting.

Consequently, it is not surprising that an image and an ideology of the nuclear family are transmitted by the press and television. These are not, however, adopted by domestic groups themselves, since the latter recognise their relationships with their kin.

SUGGESTED READING

Auffray, Danièle, Thierry Baudoin, Michèle Collin and Alain Guillerm. *Feux et lieux, histoire d'une famille et d'un pays face à la société industrielle*. Paris: Galilée, 1980.

Bott, Elizabeth. *Family and Social Network*. 2d ed. London: Tavistock, 1971.

Chalvon-Demersay, Sabine. 'Aimée ou haie: la famille'. *La Sagesse et le désordre*. Ed. Henri Mendras. Paris: Gallimard, 1980.

Kin relationships in urban society

De La Tour, Charles-Henri. 'Le Système de parenté dans les grands ensembles de Montbeliard'. *Bulletin de psychologie* 1978: 335.

Farbes, Bernard. *Kinship and Class*. New York: Basic Books, 1971.

Firth, Raymond, ed. *Two Studies of Kinship in London*. London: Athlone Press, 1956.

Firth, Raymond, Jane Hubert and Anthony Forge. *Families and their Relatives. Kinship in a Middle-Class Sector of London, An Anthropological Study*. London: Routledge & Kegan Paul, 1969.

Hareven, Tamara K., ed. *Family and Kin in Urban Communities, 1700–1930*. New York, London: New Viewpoints, 1977.

Hareven, Tamara K. 'The Dynamics of Kin in an Industrial Community'. In *Turning Points* 84(1978): 151–82. Supplement of *American Journal of Sociology*. Ed. John Demos and Sarane Spence Boocock.
Family Time and Industrial Time. Cambridge: Cambridge University Press, 1982.

Harris, C. C. *Readings in Urban Kinship*. Oxford: Pergamon Press, 1970.

Litwak, Eugene. 'Extended Kin Relations in an Industrial Democratic Society'. In *Social Structure and the Family*. Ed. Ethel Shanas and Gordon F. Streib. Englewood Cliffs, N.J.: Prentice-Hall, 1965.

Michel, Andrée. *La Sociologie de la famille*. Paris: Mouton, 1970. (Covers the main articles and books up to the date of publication.)

Mogey, John. *Family and Neighbourhood*. Oxford: Oxford University Press, 1956.

Pitrou, Agnès. *Vivre sans famille*. Toulouse: Privat, 1978.

Rosser, C. C., and C. Harris. *The Family and Social Change*. London: Routledge & Kegan Paul, 1968.

Roussel, Louis. *La Famille après le mariage des enfants*. Travaux et documents, Cahier. no 78. Paris: PUF, 1976.

Smelser, Neil. *Social Change in the Industrial Revolution*. Chicago: University of Chicago Press, 1959.

Sussman, Marvin B., and Lee Burchinal. 'Kin Family Network: Unheralded Structure in Current Conceptualisation of Family Functioning'. *Marriage and Family Living* 24(1962): 231–40.
'Parental Aid to Married Children: Implications for Family Functioning'. *Marriage and Family Living* 24(1962): 320–32.

Turner, Christopher. *Family and Kinship in Modern Britain*. London: Routledge & Kegan Paul, 1969.

Young, Michael, and Peter Wilmott. *Family and Kinship in East London*. London: Routledge & Kegan Paul, 1957. The Penguin edition (rev. 1962) is referred to here.
Family and Class in a London Suburb. London: Routledge & Kegan Paul, 1968.

PART TWO

The making of the domestic group

Chapter 4

vvvvvvvvvvvvvvvvvvvvvvvvvvvvvvvvvvvvvvvvvvvvvvvvvvvvvvvvvvvvvvvvvvvvvvvvvvv

The historical sociology of marriage

The institution of marriage, on which the family is based, is becoming better understood as a result of recent historical, demographic and anthropological research. To some extent, the methods and approaches to problems used by these disciplines have converged, providing fresh data in this area. Over a time-span stretching from the sixteenth century to our own age, we are in a position to reply to a certain number of questions capable of casting light on the meaning of the family as an institution. These questions are related to the choice of marriage partners, the age at which marriage takes place and its functions.

By studying the way in which the conjugal couple is made up, we can also understand changes that have occurred in the family and that are linked to modifications arising from industrialisation and urbanisation. Such relationships, however, as we have already seen with kinship, are never simple or linear. If we are to perceive certain mechanisms of change, we must study times, places and social milieux in detail.

Right from the start, we must reject the general misconception that nowadays we marry for love, whereas in the past people married for pecuniary or other advantages, and that now we choose a spouse ourselves, whereas in the past marriages were arranged by parents. Stereotypes of this kind are linked with the supposed development of the domestic group. If marriages were arranged, people could live in fairly large domestic groups because their emotions were not tied up in them; today, our life would be much more centred on the couple, as the couple could be based only on love, and hence marriage can have no other aim than the emotional and sexual satisfaction of the couple.

The historical sociology of marriage

FROM ALLIANCE TO MARRIAGE

In a society based on Christian belief and morality, marriage is authorised by laws governing sexuality. Within a legal and ecclesiastical framework, the institution is embedded in very varied social, economic and cultural contexts.

The religious framework

In so far as law is a constraining framework, it establishes the norm in matters relating to marriage, but because it declares which practices are unlawful, it also shows up deviant or minority behaviour. The canon law drawn up in the twelfth century defined marriage as an indissoluble sacrament of which the matter consists of the mutual consent of husband and wife. The doctrine meant that child marriages were possible, hence the image of young Romeo and Juliet legally and properly wedded in the presence of a monk who hears their vows. Such marriages, where parental consent was not required, were potential causes of social disorder. Perhaps princes might marry shepherdesses.

Certain economic and social phenomena led parents to reassert their authority over their children in the choice of a spouse so as not to endanger the social order. The nobles, whose influence on ecclesiastical and secular power was greatest, brought pressure to bear to obtain new laws strengthening paternal authority and changed marriage from the union of two individuals into an alliance of two kindred groups and two patrimonies. The son of a Burgundian parliamentarian, inquiring about the qualities of the young woman he was to marry, was promptly told to mind his own business.[1]

The documents of the Council of Trent and the French royal ordinances of the late sixteenth and early seventeenth centuries established the official doctrine of marriage that was to remain in force until the nineteenth century, as amended by the Revolution and the Civil Code.

With regard to marriage, men were deemed to have reached their majority at the age of thirty and women at twenty-five. Before that, they had to have their parents' consent; once of age, they merely had to ask their opinion. Reading the banns three times meant that a certain interval had to elapse between requesting the nuptial blessing and the actual ceremony. This was needed to seek out any possible obstacles and publicise the action that committed the two individuals, their parents and the whole social group. The banns were read from the church pulpit on Sundays and made the couple's intentions official in the eyes of the community. The church would release the man and woman from them only to protect the honour of the families concerned, and detailed studies have shown that often this was when the woman had conceived before marriage, that is when a child had been born within three months of it.[2]

Until the Council of Trent, the priest was simply a witness to the couple's commitment to each other. Thereafter, however, his part in the sacramental act was greater, and it became his task to join them in marriage. There was a further reform that stressed the unique function of the marriage ceremony, for the clergy removed the confusion between marriage and betrothal by diminishing the importance of the latter. In the fifteenth and sixteenth centuries, the *verba de futuro*, the 'words about the future', seemed for many couples, at least amongst the people, to mark the beginning of cohabitation. In an attempt to give a moral nature to conjugal life, the church tried to bring the betrothal and marriage ceremonies closer together, and to avoid any ambiguity the former was celebrated the day before the marriage or on the wedding day itself.

During the seventeenth and eighteenth centuries the nature of marriage changed. It became less of a sacrament and more of a contract. This was partly due to the influence of the Reformation, which rejected its sacramental nature and, in the eighteenth century, to that of the 'natural law' school of jurists. According to André Armengaud, these thinkers saw it as a datum of natural law and hence anterior to the institution of any sacrament by religion. This idea was taken up by the philosophers, and Voltaire explained in his dictionary that marriage was a legal contract between human beings that the Roman Catholic church had made into a sacrament. But sacraments and contracts are very different things, the former being a focus of civil effects, the latter one of the graces bestowed by the church.[3] These two aspects were completely separated at the time of the Revolution, which marked the final point of the two tendencies by insisting on a civil ceremony to validate the religious one.

In this religious and secular framework, a practice with a certain number of characteristic features established itself between the seventeenth and nineteenth centuries. The age at which marriages were contracted, the conditions governing the choice of a partner and the very content of the institution varied considerably from one social category to another, and in all the different types of marriages distinct models entailing differing futures can be seen.

The historical sociology of marriage

The demography of marriage

The marriage rate. When demographers calculate the marriage rate – the relationship between the number of marriages and the population as a whole – they are asking whether in the past there were more marriages than there are today and at what times of the year people married. Such calculations are clearly not easy for periods when there existed none of the statistical apparatus we have today.

It is possible to study the number of marriages only if the territorial unit under observation had an uninterrupted series of marriage records extending over a long period of time. From the sixteenth century onwards, king and church both tried to compel the priests – those administrators of the sacraments that mark out the stages of a lifetime, birth, marriage and death, and their corresponding ceremonies, baptism, matrimony and burial – to keep appropriate registers. In France, the Ordinance of Blois, signed by Henri III in May 1579, imposed that obligation on them. Given the inevitable regional and individual variations, such registers were more or less well kept. Many of them, however, suffered as a result of later historical vicissitudes such as the Revolution and bombing. There are more or less continuous data, depending on the region, for the oldest periods, but from the second half of the eighteenth century their regularity and quality are generally more satisfactory and it is possible to calculate the marriages celebrated in each parish.

The second element of the relationship, that is the population figures, is harder to establish. Regular censuses did not become compulsory until 1836, and for the seventeenth century we have only the partial enumerations required for specific purposes such as taxation and conscription. For other periods, there is mention in learned works of the number of 'hearths'. This may call to mind the concept of the domestic group, that is, the unit of residence and production, but it gives no indication of what the multiplier should be in order to arrive at the number of individuals, for we have no way of knowing how many people each household contained. This means that the demographers can establish upper and lower limits for the earlier periods and that there can be no question of *national* figures. We must be content with limited results covering a single parish or a microregion.

Despite these restrictions, it is possible to trace developments. In the first place, the marriage rate is sensitive to demographic factors. It is well established that under the *ancien régime*, at times when the death rate was high during epidemics, the marriage curve tended to drop towards zero. Economic crises also tend to reduce it. It has even been possible to relate the graph of the marriage rate to that of the price of grain. Thus, Pierre Goubert describes how in the area around Beauvais one can see:

a fall in the number of marriages at times of crisis, with the curve reaching its lowest point when, or just before, that for deaths reaches its highest. . . . The population rushed into marriage as soon as there were fewer burials, the epidemic began to die out and the high price of grain to come down.[4]

Certain kinds of political events such as wars and revolutions are also detrimental to the marriage rate, as we have seen in our own century at times of massive conscription for war. On the other hand, some kinds of legislation do encourage a high rate. An example of this is the lowering of the age of consent to twenty-one by the Constituent Assembly. This measure helped to release onto the marriage market a large number of young people who would otherwise have had to wait until they reached the fateful age and produced a significant, though temporary, increase in the rate.

It might be surprising to learn that over the long period of time from 1740 to our own day the absolute number of marriages has continued to increase slightly, except in certain wartime periods, whereas the crude marriage rate (i.e. the number of newly-weds per thousand inhabitants) has remained more or less stationary (Fig. 4.1). It is only in very recent years that there has been a fall in the rate. From 1775 to 1900, the average rate was sixteen per thousand, with moderate reductions to fifteen per thousand during the First Empire and in more recent years since 1932, when it fell further to fourteen per thousand apart from disturbances brought about by the wars associated with the Revolution and the Empire and those of 1870–1, 1914–18 and 1939–45, when many marriages were postponed and later swelled the figures for the years immediately after the end of hostilities.[5]

These crude rates are obviously very rough and ready, but we need them if we are to place the development of mentalities and attitudes in context. It is perhaps striking that the marriage rate in France has remained so stable for almost three centuries.

On the other hand, the time of year when marriages took place changed a great deal. The seasonal patterns of former times were characterised by the alternation of intense activity and slack periods during major agricultural work or at times when the church forbade marriage, such as Advent (the four-week liturgical cycle before Christmas) or Lent. In most monograph studies of parishes, the curves for each month took on a characteristic shape during the seventeenth and eighteenth centuries. At that time, most marriages

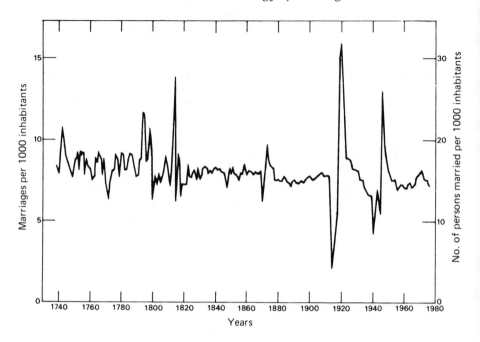

Fig. 4.1. Crude marriage rate in France since 1740.

were celebrated in February and November. July and August were the slack months, as farm-work kept all the labour force busy and left little time for the pleasures associated with marriage. Later in the nineteenth century, there was a reluctance to marry in May, the month of the Virgin Mary.[6]

Certain days of the week were also preferred to others. Friday was excluded, being unlucky as it was the day of Christ's death and a day of fasting and abstinence on which there could be no marriage feast. So was Thursday, which popular belief also held to be unlucky. Tuesday was a popular choice, as it left two days for the preparations and another two before Friday, the holy day during which there could be no feasting. Sunday was excluded, as the nuptial mass might have interfered with the main Sunday mass. Local circumstances also influenced the choice of day. In seventeenth-century Fontainebleau, for example, where there were markets on Mondays, Wednesdays and Fridays, 56 per cent of weddings were held on Tuesdays.[7] Without being too hard and fast, we can relate Tuesday to the day preferred in country parishes in the

Gers area: cut the rushes on Sunday, prepare the feast on Monday, wedding day on Tuesday.[8]

Nowadays, weddings take place throughout the year, with the summer months being the favourite time, and almost 80 per cent of couples marry on Saturday to benefit from the weekend break.

Single persons. Single persons are bachelors or spinsters, and this enables us to measure the numbers of those marrying in terms of those remaining single, especially for periods when it is difficult to establish the nuptiality rate. It is easy to do so, since all one needs to do is to take from the censuses the number of bachelors and spinsters aged fifty, as above that age they had virtually no chance of marrying. It is also a fairly reliable measure, yielding data enabling comparisons between men and women, and so confirming results obtained from calculating the marriage rate, which indicate that permanent bachelorhood or spinsterhood was rare. In the eighteenth century, between 10 and 15 per cent of women never married, and the figure was even lower for men, as there were fewer of them as a result of higher mortality and emigration rates. The proportion of people who never married increased during the century. In the generation born around 1765, it was between 6 and 7 per cent for women and rose to 12 per cent for women born ten years later and reached a maximum of 14 per cent for those born around 1790. Thereafter, there was a long decline in numbers, slower than the rise in the eighteenth century, which brought back the level of those born around 1850 to that of those born around 1760. The rapid increase for those born between 1760 and 1790 was due to the gaps in the male population caused by the revolutionary and imperial wars.[9]

For men, the highest frequency of those never marrying was later than for women. It was around 10.5 per cent and covered those born between 1805 and 1844. This increase can be explained by the fact that the population in an agrarian economy with no new land to take into cultivation was increasing. The result was that both marriage and birth rates were restricted.[10]

The rates fell slowly during the nineteenth and twentieth centuries, but developments were complex (see Table 4.1).

Between 1821 and 1880, if the excess mortality rate for single people, which was higher for men than for women, is taken into account, the percentages of unmarried persons was roughly the same for both sexes. From 1881 to 1905, the proportion of unmarried women increased significantly as a result of the high rate of male mortality due to wars. In the twentieth century, male emigration has

Table 4.1. *Proportion of unmarried persons aged fifty grouped by year of birth*

Year of birth	Men(%)	Women(%)	Year of birth	Men(%)	Women(%)	Year of birth	Men(%)	Women(%)
1821–1825	11.4	11.8	1861–1865	(10.8)	(11.2)	1901–1905	9.7	19.6
1826–1830	11.8	(11.8)	1866–1870	(10.8)	(11.4)	1906–1910	10.2	9.5
1831–1835	12.7	13.3	1871–1875	9.9	(11.3)	1911–1915	9.6	8.5
1836–1840	13.3	13.6	1876–1880	9.8	(10.5)	1916–1920	9.5	8.4
1841–1845	12.3	13.0	1881–1885	9.0	10.9	1921–1925	10.5	8.1
1846–1850	11.5	12.2	1886–1890	8.2	11.6	1926–1930	(10.6)	(7.5)
1851–1855	10.4	11.2	1891–1895	8.6	12.5	1931–1935	(10.7)	(7.4)
1856–1860	10.7	11.3	1896–1900	9.1	11.9	1936–1940	(8.2)	(7.2)

Note: The numbers in brackets are estimates, as the basic data do not distinguish between the two age-groups (forty-five to forty-nine and fifty to fifty-four) round the fiftieth birthday. For the years after 1926, the figures are estimates based on extrapolations.
Source: 'Situation démographique de la France', *Population* (1978): 307.

led to a higher number of bachelors. In the case of those born between 1921 and 1925 and 1926 and 1930, the continued fall in the
birth rate meant that there were always fewer women than men if
an average age difference of three years between husband and wife
at the time of marriage is taken into account.[11]

The need to marry to acquire adult social status explains the small
proportion of unmarried people in earlier times. When the domestic
group, the farm or the artisan's shop were essentially synonymous
and the organisation of work was based on the complementary nature of male and female activities, marriage gave the individual a
place in society. The bachelor was a marginal figure, a servant on his
brother's farm or perhaps an emigrant. The celibate life was not
'chosen', unless it was for military or religious reasons, and celibacy
was often a last resort.

Although we have few data for the towns, the proportion of single
persons in them was probably greater than in the country, at least in
the large towns undergoing urbanisation and attracting workers
who would have been unemployed and without status in the country. From the census taken in Lyon in Year IV (1795) we can see that
of women aged fifty and over almost 40 per cent were spinsters. The
percentage was particularly high in the silk mills, where over 25 per
cent of the women over thirty were unmarried.[12]

In certain urban areas of imperial Germany, the proportion of
bachelors and spinsters and the average age of marriage were typically higher than in country areas.[13] Louis Roussel, in his study *Le
Mariage*, observes the same phenomenon in France between 1853
and 1900. Marriage took place at the lowest age in rural areas, and
the Seine department had the highest average age of marriage.[14]

The reflections of those writing about Germany clearly present the
complex problem of the relationship between industrialisation, urbanisation and new marriage patterns. If the comparison is refined
by taking the size of the town into account, it becomes apparent that
people married later and that there were more unmarried persons in
major cities than in smaller towns and that sex ratios were also
different in administrative centres and working-class towns. Women
were mobile over only short distances and they were usually employed as servants, the normal situation for spinsters. These females
had left country areas because they could find neither work nor a
home there, and their employment conditions in towns forced them
to remain unmarried.

This offers an explanation of the paradoxical relationship between
urbanisation and an increase in the number of single persons, who
sometimes were mostly male and sometimes mostly female. Here,

there was a major difference between male and female chances of marriage within the context of massive industrialisation and the high degree of proletarianisation it entailed. A man had access to two marriage markets, that in his place of origin and that in the town to which he had migrated, whereas a woman had to marry where she was, since migration had completely deprived her of a possible home in her own district or, more exactly, it was because she had not been able to marry and set up home that she had joined the swelling ranks of those migrating to the towns.

The age of marriage. A number of familial behaviour patterns depend on the age at which young people usually marry, which in its turn depends on social, economic and cultural conditions. The age of marriage is thus a pivotal point in the development of the family, and diligent searching in parish and later secular registers and the introduction of the *fiche de famille* have made it possible to correct the often approximate information provided by marriage certificates.

Contrary to what is commonly believed nowadays, people did not marry younger in past times. Indeed, seventeenth- and eighteenth-century Europe probably offers a unique model in the range of cultures, one characterised by marriage at a late age, which was linked to the need for an independent establishment. If he wished to marry, a man had to have finished his apprenticeship and found a position or to have his farm and his own share of the family inheritance. In Eastern and exotic societies, however, the young couple, as soon as they married, became an integral part of wider kinship groups in which property was not divided.[15] A number of factors combined to produce a situation in which late marriages were the norm.

As François Lebrun has noted in *La Vie conjugale sous l'Ancien Régime,* with the exception of aristocratic families (whose sons were on average twenty-one when they married and whose daughters were eighteen), the average age amongst the lower classes in both town and country was twenty-seven to twenty-eight for males and twenty-five to twenty-six for females, apart from certain regions such as the country to the south of Limoges or in the Midi (where there was a kind of tacit community that distinguished between marriage and setting up house). Not only did men and women marry late, but the age at which they married rose during the first fifty years of the eighteenth century (Table 4.2).

Marrying at such a late age raises a problem. It perhaps imposed a period of sexual abstinence on young people, in so far as the church condemned sex outside marriage. For some ten years between puberty and marriage, young people had to remain chaste. Could they

Table 4.2. *Average age at time of first marriage in some French towns and villages in the seventeenth and eighteenth centuries*

	Year	M	F	Year	M	F
Meulan	1660–1739	26.5	25.1	1740–1789	27.6	26.2
Saint-Malo	1650–1750	29.7	27.2			
Reims	1668–1724	27.7	25.2	1725–1791	28.1	26.2
Caen (centre)	1740–1749	30.6	28	1780–1789	31.1	28.1
Lyon	1700–1750	29	27.5			
Villages						
Crulai	1674–1742	27.5	25.1	1770–1789	27.2	26.8
Vraiville	1706–1752	25.4	24.2	1753–1802	26.9	26.3
Thezels	1700–1766	26.8	23.8	1767–1792	27.1	26.3
Azereix				1732–1792	30	26

Source: F. Lebrun, *La Vie conjugale sous l'Ancien Régime*, p. 32.

and did they? Historians, referring in particular to the increase in illegitimate births and premarital pregnancies, a sign that the young were breaking ecclesiastical taboos, have read the situation in several different ways.

The very noticeable consequence of these delayed marriages was a shortening of the child-bearing period in women. Instead of having children from the age of twenty and up to about forty-five, they did not start to do so until they were twenty-five or twenty-six, thus reducing the possible number of children by at least three, for as we now know, the typical fertility pattern in earlier times was a child every eighteen months or two years rather than every year (see Chapter 6). At a time when birth control was not part of moral thought and practice, late marriages were, in the well-known words of Pierre Chaunu, 'the real contraceptive weapon of classical Europe', the conscious or unconscious response to population increases, stable resources and less frequent and less deadly famines.

Changes in the times of marriage are of interest to demographers and historians, who study their fluctuations in detail and relate them to economic and social changes. They fell considerably during the nineteenth century, at a time when deliberate birth control was coming into use in France, and demographers have thought that the fall might have been the cause of an increase in population. It is a complex question, since many factors, such as the wide range of social categories, differential urban–rural phenomena and the falling death rate, have to be taken into account. As far as we can say in the present

Table 4.3. *Average age at time of first marriage (by year of birth, in years and tenths of years)*

Years of birth	M	F	Years of birth	M	F	Years of birth	M	F
1821–1825	28.7	26.1	1861–1865	27.8	24.4	1901–1905	26.2	24.1
1826–1830	28.4	25.8	1866–1870	27.8	24.3	1906–1910	26.3	23.2
1831–1835	27.9	25.0	1871–1875	28.0	24.3	1911–1915	27.0	23.3
1836–1840	27.7	24.8	1876–1880	27.7	24.2	1916–1920	(27.6)	23.7
1841–1845	27.4	24.5	1881–1885	27.5	23.6	1921–1925	26.0	23.8
1846–1850	27.7	24.4	1886–1890	28.0	23.7	1926–1930	25.9	23.3
1851–1855	28.0	24.6	1891–1895	27.2	24.1	1931–1935	26.0	23.3
1856–1860	28.0	24.6	1896–1900	26.2	24.1	1936–1940	25.8	23.2
						1941–1945	25.2	22.8

Note: The figures in brackets for men 1916–1920 are approximate, as the basic data are uncertain.
Source: 'Situation démographique de la France', *Population* (1978): 309.

state of research, population increases in the nineteenth century seem to be much more the result of a fall in the death rate (particularly in infant mortality) than of a fall in the time of marriage.

A national survey carried out by the Institut National d'Etudes Démographique (INED) shows that from the first groups studied (those born between 1821 and 1825) to the last (1941–45), there was a slow and regular fall in the average age, from 28.7 to 25.2 for men and from 26.1 to 22.8 for women (Table 4.3).[16]

This fall reveals a certain number of changing ideas about marriage and the choice of a partner. In the case of those engaged in agriculture, it no doubt reflects the fact that it was easier to gain access to land, for fewer children and migration to the towns meant that problems of succession were less acute, since an increase in agricultural incomes meant that a certain amount could be put aside for parents to enable them to hand over the farm to their children. In that social category, the model of marriage remained unchanged. With agricultural or industrial wage-earners, however, the fall in the age of marriage may well indicate a new independence from parents, since they were apt to make their own arrangements for setting up house, which their pay enabled them to do at an early age. They had no need to 'kill the father' and take his place. On the other hand, although this fall in the marriage age in the nineteenth century was an expression of new ways of thinking, it did not mean that marriage and setting up house or marriage and entry into adult life were seen as separate things. That is a characteristic phenomenon of our own age.

The homogamy rule

In the past as now, people tended to marry their social or professional peers. A suitable match and comparable situations were desirable. One of the functions of marriage seen as an alliance between two lines was the transmission of patrimonies. The best way to protect this was to make sure that one's spouse was from a similar social background. This is confirmed by all historical, demographic and ethnographic research involving written sources such as marriage certificates, by proverbs and the like collected by folklore specialists and by field-work.

The homogamy rule was observed in all social categories. This is what happened at the top of the social scale:

Between 1665 and 1789, of the thirty-three marriages entered into by the *intendants* of Tours and Orléans, seventeen were with the daughter of an *intendant* or member of a sovereign court and eight with the daughters of men holding office. The same attitude can be observed amongst the magistrates of the parliaments of Paris, Rennes and Besançon: In the eighteenth century more than two thirds of the Besançon parliamentarians took a wife from a judge's family and half of them chose a wife at their own level, that is from the family of a magistrate of the sovereign court (parliament or revenues court).[17]

In order to find a husband or wife of the same rank for their children, men of social position such as notaries, *lieutenants* and lawyers had to search far and wide. As Alain Collomp notes:

Matrimonial alliances in the most eccentric circle (with its centre in the commune being studied) almost always involved the bourgeoisie, the three or four richest and most honoured families in Saint-André who married into the leading families of all the farthest communes. . . . Bernardin Simon, *lieutenant* and judge, living in Saint-André and of the bourgeoisie, had from his marriage with Anne Trabaud in 1677, the daughter of an advocate of St Vallier (above Grasse and 75 kilometres from Saint-André) three sons and four daughters who lived to adult age. One of the three sons was a priest in Paris, the other two married women from a distance away, Jean-Baptiste marrying an heiress from Puget-Théniers in Savoie and taking up residence with his wife's family, and the other remaining as a notary in Saint-André and marrying the daughter of a notary from Riez.[18]

For peasants, however, homogamy meant endogamy, that is, marrying locally, at least within the nearest villages. Marriages of this kind meant that people knew the families with whom marriage was planned and could keep a watchful eye on the arrangements concerning the patrimony, which was often in the form of land. Given the state of communications, it is understandable that the area of choice was limited to inhabitants of the same village or of those in the immediate vicinity. Every monograph study bears witness to the high degree of endogamy in the rural society of the seventeenth and eighteenth centuries. Frequently, endogamous marriages accounted for almost 80 per cent of the total, with the rest being between people from neighbouring villages. The figures for a small community in the Eure department, Vraiville, showing the marriage rate from 1706 to 1962, are given in Table 4.4.

Lebrun notes that the situation was not quite the same in towns:

Things were rather different in towns, and this illustrates the relatively greater mobility there. In Meulan, between 1690 and 1798, 50% of spouses were born in the town and 20% in the parishes within a radius of 10 km, or only 70% of the total number. In Angers, of the 1255 marriages celebrated in the sixteen parishes of the town between 1741 and 1745, 855 were between men and women from Angers. In the 400 other cases, i.e. in almost one marriage in three, at least one of the spouses (and indeed both in 36 cases) was not from the town. This mobility was more evident in the case of men than of women: almost 25% of the men, but only 10% of the women marrying in the town came from outside it, usually from nearby parishes but exceptionally from parishes outside the province of Anjou. In Lyon, the breakdown of spouses by geographic origin at the beginning and end of the eighteenth century is given in the table below:

Region of origin	1728–1730		1786–1788	
	M	F	M	F
Lyon and suburbs	52%	61%	42%	47%
Lyonnais, Dauphiné, Bugey	28%	28%	30%	39%
Total	80%	89%	72%	86%

The proportion of married people in Lyon coming from the town and its suburbs was slightly above average at the beginning of the century but below it at the end. It is true to say that beyond the urban area, marriage partners were increasingly chosen from the immediate hinterland, the Lyonnais, the Dauphiné and Bugey. A final example: In Saint-Malo, a large port with foreign connections, one husband in two (56%) and almost one wife in four (24%) marrying between 1700 and 1750 came not only from outside the town but from outside the diocese too.[19]

Table 4.4. *Domicile of spouses at time of marriage (in %)*

	No. of marriages	Vraiville	N^a	S	Louviers	Elbeuf	Le Neubourg	Eure	Seine Maritime	Paris	Other
Men											
1706–1752	162	62.2	17.2	7	1.2	0.6	–	11.2	0.6	–	–
1753–1802	204	63.4	12.9	8.4	1	0.5	–	12.3	0.5	–	0.5
1803–1852	197	67.1	12.7	3	–	2	–	12.2	0.5	–	2.5
1853–1902	184	41.9	24.4	9.2	3.8	6	–	12	1.1	0.5	1.1
1903–1962	173	45.1	17.3	5.2	1.2	5.2	–	16.8	2.3	2.3	4.6
Women											
1706–1752	162	88.8	5	2.5	0.6	–	–	2.5	0.6	–	–
1753–1802	204	86.7	1.5	1.5	2	0.9	0.5	6.9	–	–	–
1803–1852	197	94.5	1	0.5	0.5	0.5	–	3	–	–	–
1853–1902	184	89.2	3.3	1.6	–	1.6	–	2.2	1.1	0.5	0.5
1903–1962	173	83.1	3.5	1.2	1.2	1.2	–	6.9	0.6	0.6	1.7

[a]N = 7 nearest villages north of Vraiville (maximum distance 10 km)
S = 7 nearest villages south of Vraiville (maximum distance 6.5 km).

Source: Martine Segalen, *Nuptialité et alliance. Le choix du conjoint dans une commune de l'Eure* (Paris: Maisonneuve et Larose, 1972), p. 90.

To describe populations marrying within limited geographic areas, demographers use the term 'isolates', specific zones within which spouses are chosen. The human groups in certain exotic societies, observed as a whole, are isolates because they are finite populations, but that is never the case with European populations, which always have a certain degree of mobility and contain no totally introverted human groups. But endogamous marriages, where there is a stable population, lead to marriages between relatives, and the search for a suitable partner strengthened this trend. There would have been many marriages between blood relatives if the Church had not had laws governing such unions.

Because incest is forbidden, the church does not allow marriage between excessively close relatives. We will not go into details of such laws since the Middle Ages, but it must be appreciated that it was forbidden to marry blood relatives within the fourth degree, that is up to and including the children of first cousins.[20] The doctrine of impediments was linked to the Catholic idea of marriage, and if the church forbade incest, it was, in the words of Jean-Louis Flandrin in his *Amours paysannes*, 'to strengthen cohesion by multiplying kinship links amongst Christians'.[21] The same was true for remarriage, which in principle was forbidden within the second degree of kindred of the deceased spouse.

But applying these rules rigidly and forbidding such unions would have severely depressed the marriage rate in rural communities where layers of family and social networks created the conditions for marriages between relatives, and the church was forced to grant dispensations for them. Marriages between blood relatives played scarcely any part in the genetic heritage of the population, however, and were soon absorbed into the complex kinship networks that grew up over the generations. Even human groups conscious of a cultural originality they wish to preserve by means of marriage between blood relatives need only a few partners from outside the group to renew their genetic patrimony completely. With Albert Jacquard, the author studied a very endogamous Protestant community in the *bocage* area of Normandy. Of 154 Protestant marriages celebrated between 1860 and 1868, 7.1 per cent were between blood relatives. Using genealogies, it was possible to determine for every individual alive at a particular time the share of his genetic patrimony coming from each of the 'founding fathers' (defined as an ancestor beyond whom ancestry was unknown) who together made up the multiple source of the genes in the community. The two major 'founding fathers', whose descendants make up over half of the present-day population, contributed only 4.1 per cent each to the stock of genes. The annual arrival of spouses from outside the group was sufficient to maintain considerable genetic diversity. Despite its affirmed awareness of its own cultural identity, which was closely linked to its ancestors, the group had no specific genetic characteristics.[22]

Marriage strategies

Even if marriages between blood relatives have no consequence genetically, they clearly show the role of kinship in marriage. One cannot marry *close* blood relatives, but beyond that there is theoretically a free choice. And yet marriages between blood relatives and homogamous and endogamous marriages presuppose unspoken rules and indicate family marriage policies.

This takes us back to anthropological theories of kinship and marriage. Between our own systems and those operating in exotic societies there is a difference of degree, but not of kind.

In past societies, whether peasant, aristocratic or bourgeois, husbands and wives depended on the patrimony of their parents when they wanted to set up their own establishment and move into active life, and marriages were governed by patrimonial strategy. In 'Célibat et condition paysanne', Pierre Bourdieu writes:

> Before 1914, marriage was governed by very strict rules. As it entailed the whole future of the family farm and was an occasion of the most important kind of economic transaction and as it also helped to reaffirm the social hierarchy and the family's place within it, it was the concern of the whole group rather than of the individual. The family married and the individual married with it. . . . The first function of marriage was to ensure the continuity of the lineage without compromising the integrity of the patrimony.[23]

The area Bourdieu studied was Béarn, where the stem family is dominant. The custom there was that the eldest son received the house and lands attached to it without division as symbols of family continuity, whereas the other children received only cash dowries. The strategy was to marry the eldest son to the youngest daughter of a house, of equivalent status if possible, which would then pay the head of the family, the future bridegroom's father, a cash dowry. As for the younger sons, they either married a younger daughter, in which case their economic situation was poor, as the girl would receive only a small dowry, or they left home, or kept their bachelor status in their eldest brother's house, giving up all claims to an inheritance and putting the ideology of the unbroken patrimony above their own position. In such circumstances, it is easy to understand the importance of making the proper choice of a new wife or husband, which both families would have to evaluate in terms of the two patrimonies and the honorific capital associated with each of them.

It can be seen that matrimonial strategy was one of the modes of the wider 'strategy of biological, cultural and social reproduction that the whole group set in motion to transmit, maintained or increased, the powers and privileges it had inherited to the next generation'.[24]

All peasant marriage strategies are endogamous, but some are more endogamous than others. One or two lines, frequently the richest (or the least badly off), systematically arranged marriages with related lines, whilst others would marry non-relatives, but within a closed geographic area. After a few generations, it can be observed that with the former there were certain regular patterns, certain preferential marriage systems that, although they were not as rigorous as those operating in exotic societies, came quite close to them. In the parish of Ribennes in Haut-Gévaudan, which had 550 inhabitants, Pierre Lamaison has been able to show 'patrimonial cycles'. The upkeep and transmission of the *ostal* provided the underlying logic of marriages, and to keep a balance between all the families, the rule was that the heir to an *ostal* should marry an endowed daughter from another *ostal,* the *cadette.* The nucleus of each line was thus constituted by the succession of heirs to the patrimony held by the oldest couple of ancestors, and the permanence of the line lay in the property transmitted and the place to which it was attached. The corollary of the exogamy practised by the lines was a renewal of marriage alliances between two of them. Thus it is that Lamaison was able to bring out strategies with cycles by concentrating not on every line but on those he calls patrimonial. These cycles usually unfolded over several generations and involved both main and subsidiary heirs, and they covered the families of the canton.[25] Lamaison distinguishes cycles that were restricted or generalised exchanges.

A restricted exchange involved two groups of siblings, an heir and his sister, who had a dowry. The former would marry a younger daughter with a dowry and the latter one of her brothers who was an heir. As both dowries were of equal value, no money would really change hands. Generalised exchanges involved several families; the dowry would circulate and, at the end of the cycle, finally return whence it came.

Figure 4.2 presents an example of generalised exchange taking place amongst seven *ostals* and extending over several generations.

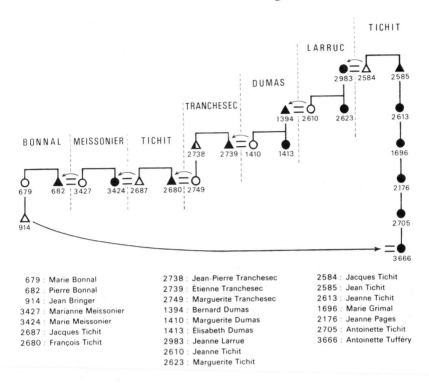

679 : Marie Bonnal
682 : Pierre Bonnal
914 : Jean Bringer
3427 : Marianne Meissonier
3424 : Marie Meissonier
2687 : Jacques Tichit
2680 : François Tichit

2738 : Jean-Pierre Tranchesec
2739 : Étienne Tranchesec
2749 : Marguerite Tranchesec
1394 : Bernard Dumas
1410 : Marguerite Dumas
1413 : Élisabeth Dumas
2983 : Jeanne Larrue
2610 : Jeanne Tichit
2623 : Marguerite Tichit

2584 : Jacques Tichit
2585 : Jean Tichit
2613 : Jeanne Tichit
1696 : Marie Grimal
2176 : Jeanne Pages
2705 : Antoinette Tichit
3666 : Antoinette Tufféry

Fig. 4.2. Example of generalized exchange amongst seven *ostals* over several generations. The numbers are those of the proposers, the allocation of numbers having been effected after a twofold classification (with a computerised preliminary sort) alphabetically and, for each patronymic, by order of the seniority of the marriage. Heirs are shown in black. (From Pierre Lamaison, 'Les stratégies matrimoniales dans un système complexe de parenté: Ribennes en Gévaudan 1650–1830', *Annales Economies, Sociétés, Civilisations* 4[1979]: 735.)

It can be seen how the cycles linked together, intersected and became superimposed over the generations.

These marriage strategies show the decisive importance of the patrimony; and both were indissolubly linked by the system of devolving property. The examples we have studied so far have been taken from societies in which the stem family was predominant.

Can we also speak of strategies when referring to societies in which the inheritance system was an egalitarian one and the patrimony was shared amongst all the heirs; in which the peasants had rented farms or were share-croppers with little property to pass on,

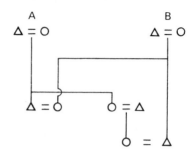

Fig. 4.3. Matrimonial relinking between A and B.

in which there was high mobility and domestic groups were much more independent of their lines?

A number of studies show that even when no land was involved it is still possible to detect family marriage policies, because in the seventeenth and eighteenth centuries peasants did own *some* property – agricultural implements, livestock, the lease to their farm, for example. The capital they owned in the form of family prestige, an ancient name and fame, was just as important, and perhaps even more so, in a poor society. In an economic system where it was impossible to amass wealth, the ultimate aim of marriage strategies was to maintain the position of the family, and sons and daughters adapted themselves to it all the more willingly as there was no social status outside the family.

One indication of marriage strategies in egalitarian societies was the large number of cases in which a widower married his dead wife's sister, that is, in which there were second marriages between sibling groups. What Françoise Zonabend and Tina Jolas have called *renchaînement d'alliance* (matrimonial relinking) has been observed in a number of peasant societies. It strengthened links between kinship groups and created alliances between neighbouring villages as well as introduced a certain degree of exogamy (Fig. 4.3).

In *Nuptialité et alliance,* by studying in detail marriages between sibling groups in Vraiville in the Eure department (Normandy), the author was able to establish that between 1730 and 1950, of 828 marriages, almost 40 created links within neighbouring communes, often over several generations, through two brothers marrying two sisters or two cousins or by a brother and sister marrying a sister and brother. We also noted that in the south of the Bigouden region ecclesiastical dispensations were given for marriages between blood relatives who never lived in the same commune.[26] A similar phe-

126

nomenon has been noted in the Pays de Sault area where, 'the number of marriages involving blood relatives from different villages was higher than had been expected when working on the hypothesis that choice operated independently of the kinship criterion.'[27] It is not hard to see what is happening in such cases: The knowledge necessary to an understanding of the groups allied by marriage is acquired when the second marriage takes place. The first had brought strangers together, the second brings together families already allied.

Such strategies were also practised in the upper levels of society, in American societies in the early stages of capitalism, for example. Peter Dobkin Hall notes two types of matrimonial strategy amongst Massachusetts merchants in the eighteenth century. Marriage between first cousins kept inheritances in a small number of hands, as was the case in peasant societies, and marriages between sibling groups also helped to consolidate capital.[28]

Another way of detecting the presence of matrimonial strategies is by analysing rituals, for example the use of a go-between in certain societies. His task was twofold: to give one family group a better understanding of the social and symbolic possessions of the other and to negotiate contributions on behalf of both families. If nothing came of the negotiations, neither family would feel insulted, since there had been no official commitment. His role was to cope with the possible breakdown of negotiations and to guarantee the continuity of social relationships.

Other rituals associated with marriage symbolise and make explicit the role of kinship in the making of marriages, and also help to produce matrimonial relinking. A wealth of articles and books on this question has been brought together by Arnold Van Gennep in his *Manuel du folklore français contemporain*.

Rituals of this kind are a symbolic discourse, and what is said and done in varying ways expresses the importance of marriage for the community in the same way that bridal processions do. Rituals are a language that in a traditional rural milieu blesses marriage as an alliance between two kinship groups and provides great publicity for an event involving the whole of society. Processions in which the young people of both families are matched in the conscious or unconscious hope of further links of the same kind, wedding feasts joining both families and turning strangers into in-laws, the coming and going between the two houses are all rituals symbolising the alliance taking shape and the bride's move from her father's house to her husband's.[29]

One might wonder what room was left, in such a context of strate-

gies and transactions, for the young people's personal preferences
and how important love and mutual attraction could be.

Love in peasant societies

Nowadays we unreflectingly think that people marry for love and
that they married for material advantage in the past; we suppose
that love and concern with an inheritance are irreconcilable. From
there we go on assume that we now have something called a
'modern' family and take it as an article of faith that our present-
day institution is a more highly developed form, based on love and
the freedom of the partners, and obviously the 'best' of possible
families.

There is no more problematic area than that of the history of
sensibility. We can draw up and study graphs showing the marriage
rate, analyse the intervals between births or the geographic catch-
ment area for marriage partners, but once we are dealing with the
personal sphere of emotions and sexual relationships it is hard to
find documentary evidence and even harder to interpret it. The
vagueness of our vocabulary is just as much a hindrance. Do we all
mean the same thing by love? The analyses we read are often highly
subjective, the work of authors who interpret the available data in
the light of their own philosophical, political or religious ideas, and
men and women interpret the same facts in different ways. With
regard to love and sexuality in past times, for which we will never
have the equivalents of the Kinsey or Simon reports (though they
too raise problems, of course), we can only suggest hypotheses. We
will summarise them here, suggesting that that will always be the
most we can do in this area.

Did young people who had to wait many years to have legitimate
sexual relations transgress religious and social prohibitions? What is
even more important, did they experience emotional and sexual impulses? Were they capable of loving? The fact that illegitimate births,
a sign of extramarital sexuality, and pregnancies before marriage, a
sign of premarital sexuality, were very few in number between the
middle of the eighteenth and the middle of the nineteenth centuries
and, it seems, lower than in earlier periods, perhaps indicates that
the church was successful in imposing a sexual morality. In a mental
world totally different from ours, young people perhaps had internalised prohibitions and the model of marriage created by their parents and remained sexually inexperienced before marriage, for in a
society ignorant of contraception, the low illegitimate birth rate and
the few pregnancies before marriage suggest that prohibited sexual

relations were almost non-existent. This is the hypothesis adopted by the American historian Edward Shorter in his *The Making of the Modern Family*. He accepts that peasants were chaste, but attributes their chastity to doltishness and insensitivity rather than to a sublimation of prohibitions, seeing them as stupid brutes easily manipulated by their parents. On the other hand, Flandrin expresses in *Amours paysannes* the view that partners could be relatively freely chosen within the framework of prohibitions accepted by the people seeking to marry and that consequently love matches were much more frequent than we think. Jean-Marie Gouesse also thinks that in seventeenth- and eighteenth-century Normandy it seems not to have been parents who imposed marriages. He goes on to add, however, that 'that freedom could only be exercised within narrow limits fixed by economic, social and in particular demographic factors'.[30] In addition, the rituals of seeing each other, which peasants called 'making love', allowed of amorous relationships stopping short of the sexual act. Two traditions of peasant love-making have been very popular with historians. These are *maraichinage* and *kiltgang*. The first was specific to the Vendée marshes. It was a collective ritual and allowed young people to 'go marshing' under an umbrella or in a room in an inn. The second took place in the young woman's bedroom with her parents' permission. Both allowed the declaration of feelings and, with certain conditions, sexual contact between unmarried young people. Flandrin believes that in one form or another *maraichinage* was widespread in France[31] and suggests that premarital chastity cannot be measured simply in terms of low illegitimacy figures. Love amongst the peasants existed in its way and young people were free to marry. This suggestion, however, seems perhaps rather simplistic.

There are many indications that love was not an unknown phenomenon in rural society, and proverbs, gifts and rituals all suggest that it existed and was recognised. Proverbs concerned with love are very widespread: 'Love and a cough cannot be hidden' (Catalonia, the Limousin and the Val d'Aoste); 'Those not in love are very ill' (Provence); 'Love is like death; if it doesn't come in by the back door, it will come in by the back window' (Normandy). And when it has negative connotations it is associated with marriage: 'Marry for love and you will have good nights and bad days' (Languedoc, etc.). Love might be feared and shunned in marriage, but it was recognised as indispensable in the mechanics of the making of the couple. Love as it was recognised in past times in rural society was something different from the eroticised and exhibitionist form of it that we have today.

In peasant societies, love was highly codified and the interchange of presents, gestures and speech between lovers followed strict stereotypes. That does not, of course, mean that feelings were insincere, for such structuring was rather a result of the phenomenon of social reproduction observable here as in other areas such as those of costume, furniture and the transmission of tales and legends during long evenings spent together. Each region had its own love-gift. Sometimes these were rings of no great value, which the young woman kept if the relationship lapsed or, as in the Bethmale Valley, nailed clogs with the length of the point indicating the intensity of the lover's feelings. As Arnold Van Gennep observes, each action had its precise meaning: 'Lovers jostled each other, threw small pebbles at each other, prodded each other or gave each other taps on the shoulder or knee or squeezed each other's fingers until they were completely out of joint.'[32]

And yet the part played by love in the choice of a marriage partner perhaps varied significantly from one region to another, depending on the degree of social and economic differentiation within the human group. One can put forward the hypothesis that the more egalitarian the group, the greater the degree of choice. Breton society in the south of Cornouaille, for example, was very hierarchical, with strict separation of the sexes, a system of limited contact and an active role for the go-between. In Maurienne, where the social structure was much more egalitarian (chiefly as a result of sharing large commons, which tended to blur social distinctions), young people were allowed to 'bundle', that is to engage in premarital sexual activity of the *kiltgang* type. Breton society could not risk a daughter becoming pregnant by a day-labourer and contracting a hypogamous marriage, which would endanger all the subtle play of exchange involving women and land. Things were different in Savoie, where all families were at much the same level and the system could cope with choices left to personal inclination. Freedom certainly was not complete, and relationships of the kinds described were tolerated only *before* marriage. Young women were allowed only one choice, or at most two, for after that their reputation would be lost, and the fact that they had allowed a particular man into their bed made sure that a marriage would soon take place.

Pierre Caspar has made a study of pregnancy before marriage in the principality of Neuchâtel between 1678 and 1820.[33] In that region, *kiltgang*, a nocturnal meeting of the sexes conducted with parental approval, resulted in many such pregnances (31.3 per cent at the end of the seventeenth century) but very few illegitimate births.

Caspar notes that they increased in number during the course of the eighteenth century, but only in certain social categories, with the number falling the further up the social scale one goes. Sexual relationships amongst young unmarried people were limited only in those social classes obliged to defend their patrimony by means of a marriage policy based on social homogamy, which an unforeseen pregnancy could endanger. The rising number of pregnancies before marriage was basically a working-class phenomenon, a feature of the lives of agricultural labourers whose only asset was not a family patrimony but the labour force of a group of young people.

From around 1750, France experienced an increase in the number of both illegitimate births and pregnancies before marriage. This could have been due to a fall in the age of marriage, with a larger number of women conceiving earlier, even though unable to marry, or to a higher female fertility rate as a consequence of a better diet or an improvement in child care and stronger children at birth, and so on. No single factor is enough to explain such a major phenomenon affecting chiefly urban (though preceded, it seems, by country) areas.

The distinction between premarital pregnancies and illegitimate births is an important one. One can see the former as a way of forcing a family's hand and making them consent to a marriage. It is also possible to assume – and this is perhaps more probable – that once the family and the young couple had agreed, the latter saw themselves as virtually married and anticipated their conjugal rights; in short, the church's attempt to clarify the situation of young betrothed couples and to abolish trial marriages without cohabitation had failed by the second half of the eighteenth century.

With regard to the increase in illegitimate births, interpretations vary even more. Flandrin declares in *Amours paysannes* that the sexual repression that had become ever stronger up to the beginning of the twentieth century had the opposite effect to the one anticipated, and that young men, no longer having the right to woo young women in a sexually satisfying way that stopped short of making them pregnant, had become accustomed to have more sexual relationships outside marriage. He also suggests that in rural areas where demographic pressures made it hard to set up house, not as many illegitimate births could be transformed into 'pregnancies before marriage'. This would mean that, paradoxically, sexual freedom had been a result of the church's repressive attitude. Illegitimate births, however, are scarcely an indication of sexual liberation of the type the modern family is experiencing. They are rather the sign of cultural, economic and social changes.

The historical sociology of marriage

TOWARDS CONTEMPORARY MARRIAGE

Artisans in protoindustrial society

A distinction between the rural and the urban world has to be made as soon as one reaches the end of the eighteenth and the beginning of the nineteenth centuries. Until then, in France at least (urbanisation and industrialisation had taken place much earlier in England) towns functioned more or less like villages, with quarters centred round parishes being akin to small village communities and little market towns showing matrimonial models very like those of the countryside. We have an example of this in the detailed study of marriage in Fontainebleau referred to earlier. As industry grew and the concentration into towns became more marked, the split between town and country deepened like that of the difference in matrimonial behaviour patterns reflecting the difference between social classes.

In the nineteenth century, the social make-up of villages became more homogeneous as depopulation removed the most marginal of their inhabitants, in particular day-labourers and artisans whose trade could not compete with industrial production. For the peasants remaining in the village, marriage was more than ever a strategy for obtaining land. Maintaining or increasing one's property, the farm, and keeping one's place in the community were prime objectives. Marriage was still controlled by kinship and class endogamy still the rule. Modern developments in agriculture have not made such models out of date. As long as the family farm remained the framework of production, marriage strategies still had a certain traditional look about them. They were to disappear, relatively speaking, as agricultural production became increasingly part and parcel of the capitalist system in which the ability to obtain credit becomes more important than what husband and wife bring to their marriage in the way of personal wealth.

For village artisans, marriage was no longer the setting up of a home organised by parents who had the means – land and dowries – to do so. Their only capital was their labour, which meant that as far as setting up house was concerned they could show their independence of the family group. This did not mean, however, that they had any greater freedom in their choice of spouse. In a rural milieu, artisanal labour was organised on the basis of the close complementarity of the labour of the artisan and his wife. Amongst weavers in rural Normandy, each couple had two looms. The husband wove the heavy woollen cloth and his wife the lighter cotton materials.

There too a high degree of endogamy was vital and determined how the couple was made up. These 'protoindustrial' families had a high fertility rate (as did peasant families) because they needed as large a labour force as possible since their production was subject to the varying demands of the capitalist market. Births were frequent and the children started work in the family shop at a very early age. In their fertility, their way of thinking and their part in the village community, such families belonged to the system of former times, but in other ways they were a new form of the couple providing a new model of marriage. One of the features supporting this view was that the way the household was made up was no longer determined by property relationships of the patriarchal type and had moved outside the control of parents, even if their material foundations were still essential. They represented a step in the direction of a union of the 'association of individuals' type.

The protoindustrial family thus heralded the working-class family. The status of wage-earner meant that young people could soon save up enough to get married and did not need to wait for a parental dowry. They married younger and in a more independent way. The appearance of this new kind of marriage coincided with a leap in the number of premarital pregnancies. Caspar, noting the increase in the number of pregnancies between the fourth and six months of marriage in a village in the principality of Neuchâtel in French-speaking Switzerland, links the phenomenon to an increase in population and the introduction of the printed-cloth industry, which created a large wage-earning class. Factory workers were indeed the first to be affected by 'shotgun' marriages indicating premarital sexual relationships:

For them, marriage was less and less a business transaction and more and more a union in which instinct and feeling played a part right from the beginning. Economic calculation did not necessarily disappear from it, but it was based on new factors, of which the chief one was the taking into account of the spouse's labour.[34]

The differences between social categories were subtle and the recent growth of studies on societies undergoing industrialisation show the links between certain older models of marriage and the emergence of new ones. Workmen in Lyon from 1848 to 1914, for example, observed the same marriage patterns as the rural protoindustrial artisans we have been examining. They had a high rate of endogamy and strong social continuity, with between 50 and 60 per cent being the sons of workers. Their endogamy was scarcely affected by migration, since the latter was always within the same trade. Lyon silk workers, clothing workers from Vienne and ribbon-makers from Saint-Etienne were the sons of spinners or weavers who mostly married the daughters of textile workers:

The organisation of work in small family units in premises that were also houses in which master and men lived side by side and related jobs called for a large female work force and encouraged marriage within rather than outside the trade. . . . The workshop was such a melting pot that it was commoner than not to find families entirely composed of textile workers.[35]

Amongst these workers, marriage continued to reproduce social structures but made way for a new system of male and female tasks and roles. The structures, however, were fragile. If there was an economic crisis and all a father could leave his son was his skills, the latter would abandon his trade and his family milieu and become a part of the general flotsam of rural poor, small farmers without an inheritance and artisans displaced by the new machinery, all caught up by the tide of industrialisation and urbanisation.

What were the marriage patterns of these new migrant workers? What was marriage for them? Did they marry more frequently or less frequently than in the country? When they were older or younger? Here we will deal only with the factors related to the making of the couple, examining later the question of roles and organisation within the working-class conjugal family. It is, of course, rather arbitrary to separate the two, since it is clear that both parts of the process influenced each other.

Common-law associations and working-class marriages

Studying unmarried cohabitation as a different model of marriage from the 'traditional' one and the definition of the couple implied by it would mean that we would first need a demographic framework, and amongst specialists there is by no means any general agreement as to what that would be. It is possible to talk about common-law associations only after having marshalled such demographic data as the major imbalance in male–female ratios following massive migration or a change in an indicator such as the age of marriage, which means that there are more 'marriageable' people available. Until recent years, it was supposed that a fall in the age of marriage was due to better job opportunities (and hence the possibility of setting up house at an early age), a hypothesis that made it possible to link increases in population and industrialisation.[36] This hypothesis is now in question, for relationships between demographic, social and cultural factors are complex. By paying particular attention to changes in mentality, which have moved from the concept of marriage as a process of 'settling' to one of 'feeling', we can more easily fit into this process the great increase in illegitimate births whose burden fell solely on unmarried women in very difficult urban circumstances.

It is here that what could be called the paradox of pregnancies before marriage and illegitimacy comes into play. As we noted in connection with Neuchâtel, an increase in the latter, subsequently 'regularised' by marriage, was a reflection of the appearance of a new sexual order and a new view of marriage as being both based on the ability of the partners to work, irrespective of what the parents of either owned, and freed to some extent from the constraints imposed by village life. But *illegitimacy* is not a sign of a new sexual morality or of the immorality of the popular classes. It is a sign that a traditional marriage policy has broken down. Recent studies have shown that these illegitimate births would have been legitimised if the women had been able to marry as they wished. Illegitimacy is not the rejection of marriage, but rather its failure to take place.[37]

A detailed study of common-law associations in Paris shows the meaning of such failures.[38] Such associations were something second-best, entered into in the hope of marriage. It is true that a greater degree of independence for women encouraged these associations as much as it encouraged marriage, but the latter remained the model.

The conditions the female urban industrial worker had to endure meant that she had to seek some association with a man. Young women with no qualifications worked in the textile trade, where the workshop was the unit of organisation. Working conditions were dreadful. Wages were not high enough for day-to-day subsistence, there was seasonal unemployment, and at busy periods the working day was between eighteen and twenty hours, quite incompatible with family life. Thus, according to one late nineteenth-century observer, 'The working woman's downfall is the working-man.' She was forced into love affairs. Until the first child came, both were working and life was bearable. When it came, he beat her. When the second came, he left her,[39] and socially she was led towards prostitution.[40] Thus, economic conditions made working women very vulnerable, and they were the chief victims of common-law associations.

Michel Frey, however, has noted that even in the middle of the nineteenth century, although the working class had the highest proportion of such associations, it also had the highest proportion of married people, with maps of Paris showing marriage rates and working-class settlement matching each other quite exactly. The wage system encouraged working-class marriages and hence industrial development; the slowing down of population movements gradually stabilised the working class and integrated it into society as a whole in towns, and the major process involved was the integration of the family. Observing changes in the demand for prostitutes, Alain Corbin notes that in the second decade of the Second Empire, the new urban proletariat became integrated and that 'the sexual imbalance fell, the conjugal family model and that of middle-class intensity were gradually assimilated by the urban proletariat'.[41] A freer marriage, in which feeling played a larger part and two capacities for work and two wages were pooled, was the new modern model arising from the working class, with the norm still dictated by a bourgeois model. The latter was to take several decades to lose if not its strategies of homogamy at least its near synonymity with a pattern of setting up house. The working class, by establishing its place and becoming more bourgeois, reproduced the model of middle-class family closeness visible in its new child-centred nature. Rather than seeing imitation, we should see in it a coming-together of images of the family that still, however, are noticeably different, particularly with regard to the roles carried out within it.

Bourgeois marriage

Bourgeois and petty-bourgeois marriages were still the object of classical strategies at the end of the nineteenth century and the beginning of the twentieth, and this explains why there were more common-law unions in these classes than we might expect. This is what Frey has to say on the subject:

There were proportionally fewer bourgeois marriages than working-class ones, as the middle classes married for acquisitive purposes, that is, to maintain and transmit a patrimony. These functions determined the nature of the matrimonial strategy of owners of property, which reduced chances of marriage. The opposite was the case with economically independent wage-earners whose matrimonial strategy was carefree and who married much more readily.[42]

The model of bourgeois marriage continued to be, in the full sense of the word, an alliance between two family groups. It was not in country areas, where the future partners would know each other directly or as a result of the interplay of kindred groups, but in bourgeois marriages in towns, that the young people were most likely never to have met; it was in marriages of the latter kind that financial arrangements were most openly of prime importance, quite apart from any personal consideration. In the nineteenth century, in a society characterised by social mobility, marriage had a crucial role to play in a career, and it was in bourgeois circles that a misalliance was most feared. The lower middle classes for the most part saw marriage as an establishment, for these social categories were both the most fragile and the most desirous of protecting their precarious status.

SUGGESTED READING

Armengaud, André. *La Famille et l'enfant en France et en Angleterre du XVIe au XVIIIe siècle*. Paris: Société d'Edition d'Enseignement Supérieur, 1975.

Duby, Georges. *Le Chevalier, la femme et le prêtre. Le Mariage dans la France féodale*. Paris: Hachette, 1981.

Dupâquier, Jacques. *Marriage and Remarriage in Populations of the Past*. E. Helin, P. Laslett, M. Livi-Bacci and S. Sogner, eds. London: Academic Press, 1981.

Flandrin, Jean-Louis. *Les Amours paysannes*. Paris: Gallimard-Julliard, 1975. *Families in Former Times*. Cambridge: Cambridge University Press, 1979. *Le Sexe et l'Occident*. Paris: Le Seuil, 1981.

Gillis, John R. *For Better, for Worse. British Marriages, 1600 to the Present*. New York: Oxford University Press, 1985.

Goody, Jack. *The Development of Family and Marriage in Europe*. Cambridge: Cambridge University Press, 1983.

Lebrun, François. *La Vie conjugale sous l'Ancien Régime*. Paris: Colin, 1975.

Outwaithe, R. B., ed. *Marriage and Society*. London: Europa, 1981.

Shorter, Edward. *The Making of The Modern Family*. New York: Basic Books, 1975.

Traer, James F. *Marriage and the Family in Eighteenth-Century France*. Ithaca, N.Y.: Cornell University Press, 1980.

Marriage in rural milieux

Augustins, Georges. 'Reproduction sociale et changement social'. *Revue française de sociologie*. 18 (1977): 465–83.

Bourdieu, Pierre. 'Célibat et condition paysanne'. *Etudes rurales* 5–6 (1962): 33–135.

'Les Stratégies matrimoniales dans le système de reproduction'. *Annales Economies, Sociétés, Civilisations* 4–5 (1972): 1105–27.

Claverie, Elizabeth, and Pierre Lamaison. *L'impossible mariage. Violence et parenté en Gevaudan, 17e, 18e, 19e s*. Paris: Hachette, 1982.

Collomp, Alain. 'Alliance et filiation en Haute Provence au XVIIIe siècle'. *Annales Economies, Sociétés, Civilisations* 3 (1977): 445–77.

The historical sociology of marriage

Segalen, Martine. *Nuptialité et alliance, le choix du conjoint dans une commune de l'Eure*. Paris: Maisonneuve et Larose, 1972.

Quinze générations de bas Bretons. Parenté et société dans le pays bigouden sud, 1720–1980. Paris: PUF, 1985.

Marriage rituals

Burguière, André. 'Le rituel du mariage en France. Pratiques ecclesiastiques et pratiques populaires (XVI–XVIIIᵉ s.)'. *Annales Economies, Sociétés, Civilisations* 3(1978): 637–49

Segalen, Martine. *Amours et mariages de l'ancienne France*. Paris: Berger-Levrault, 1981.

Van Gennep, Arnold, *Manuel du folklore français contemporain*. Vol. I, 1 and 2. Paris: Picard, 1943–6.

The Rites of Passage. First published in 1909. Chicago: University of Chicago Press, 1960.

Chapter 5

vwwwwwwwwwwwwwwwwwwwwwwwwwwwwwwwwwwwwwwwwwwwwwwwwwwwwwwwwwwwwwwwwwwwwwwwwwwwwwwwv

Marriage and divorce in contemporary society

MARRIAGES

Let us take another look at the marriage rate (see Chapter 4, 'The marriage rate'). It would seem that it is now lower in relation to the total population than it was in 1840. But, as Louis Roussel observes in his *Le Mariage dans la société française contemporaine:*

This index, highly sensitive to age structure and the apparent fall in the rate as compared with 1840, simply means that in the population of France the proportion of those 'too young to marry' and 'old and already married' has increased considerably.[1]

For the contemporary period, demographers use a more sophisticated method that relates the number of marriages to the total number of those of marriageable age rather than to the total population. Contrary to what the crude rates would suggest, there has been until very recent years an increase in the marriage rate in our own age, and the same phenomenon has been observed in every European country.

The trend has recently been reversed, however. Up to and including 1972, the rate increased, peaking at 416,500 for France and then falling to 355,000 (13,000 fewer than in 1977) in 1978, 340,000 in 1979 and 335,000 in 1980. As the population has increased, the rate is the lowest since the end of the Second World War, or 6.2 marriages per thousand inhabitants.[2] The downward trend is still too recent for us to be able to say whether it is temporary (an economic crisis causing people to defer marriage) or due to a changing attitude towards marriage on the part of young people. It is common to the whole of Europe, with France, England and Belgium experiencing a moderate fall and Germany and the Netherlands a much more severe one, such has already occurred in Sweden.

139

Table 5.1. *Average age at time of marriage in France since 1931 (corrected by age breakdown of the population in years and hundredths of years)*

Year	M	F	Gap	Year	M	F	Gap
1931	26.67	23.70	2.97	1957	26.40	23.54	2.86
1932	26.63	23.56	3.07	1958	26.32	23.45	2.87
1933	26.52	23.47	3.05	1959	26.15	23.36	2.79
1934	26.52	23.37	3.15				
1935	26.47	23.38	3.09	1960	26.05	23.27	?.78
1936	26.62	23.35	3.27	1961	26.01	23.27	2.74
1937	26.80	23.43	3.37	1962	25.82	23.17	2.65
1938	26.91	23.59	5.32	1963	25.42	22.99	2.43
				1964	25.30	22.96	2.34
1946	27.67	24.45	3.22	1965	25.22	22.95	2.27
1947	27.55	24.23	3.32	1966	25.24	22.97	2.27
1948	27.29	24.03	3.26	1967	25.20	23.01	2.19
1949	26.83	23.75	3.08	1968	25.14	22.93	2.21
1950	26.58	23.59	2.99	1969	25.12	22.93	2.19
1951	26.51	23.52	2.99	1970	25.07	22.89	2.18
1952	26.48	23.50	2.98	1971	25.02	22.85	2.17
1953	26.40	23.47	2.93	1972	24.94	22.75	2.19
1954	26.35	23.46	2.89	1973	24.94	22.70	2.24
1955	26.34	23.46	2.88	1974	24.97	22.77	2.20
1956	26.48	23.62	2.86	1975	25.03	22.91	2.12

Source: 'Septième Rapport sur la situation démographique de la France', *Population*, 1978, p. 320.

The age at which people have married has fallen continuously since the beginning of the nineteenth century. If we examine it year by year from 1931 to 1975, we can see, within the general downward trend, a slight increase between 1931 and 1938, then a temporary one between 1946 and 1948, due to the backlog of marriages postponed during the war, then a marked decline until 1973 and finally, over the last few years, a slight upturn, which could be either a cause or an effect of the fall in the marriage rate (Table 5.1).

The data in Table 5.1 pertain to the whole of France, with no distinctions as to social class or profession. It is known, however, that the marriage rate and the age of marriage are not the same for workers and the higher managerial grades, that marriage takes place later when long periods of study are involved, that the number of unmarried females is linked to educational level, professional qualifications and so on, and the national statistics have to be read in conjunction with the findings of detailed studies carried out by the INED. The latter, unfortunately, are based on out-of-date material –

a scrutiny of the 1962 census and a survey of 240,000 people establishing the age of marriage in terms of socio-cultural milieu and the frequency of marriage.[3] The chief facts to emerge were as follows:

1. There were major differences in the age of marriage connected with social and professional circumstances. Farmers married late and infrequently, whereas women connected with agriculture married at the same ages as those who were not. There was an imbalance in age between the numbers of the marriageable due to the movement towards the towns, which chiefly affected women, and the greatest difference in age between spouses was found in this group.

Amongst industrial workers, the best qualified men married earliest, which suggests that, as in the nineteenth century, it was insufficient economic resources and in particular the problem of housing that prevented marriage. Members of the liberal professions married latest in life.

2. Educational levels directly influenced the age of marriage, particularly in the case of women, and to a large extent this variable cut through that of social and professional category. On average, women without a diploma or who had only a basic education married much younger and married younger men. The better qualified a woman, the later she married, and the age gap between man and wife narrowed correspondingly.

This survey, which was carried out in 1962 and analysed in 1971, included couples marrying between 1919 and 1951. Since then, analysis of the 1968 census has produced more sophisticated findings, and it has been possible to do some work on the proportion of unmarried people by age group. In Roussel's view,

the frequency of marriage is a direct function of the level of professional qualifications in the case of men, and for women the relationship is the inverse. For them, the higher their social and professional category, the lower their final marriage rate.[4]

The proportion of unmarried women aged between forty and fifty is still very high, particularly among highly qualified persons in relatively easy material circumstances and of an above-average level of general culture.

Thus, in a group that although clearly a minority is socially important, the high level of permanent spinsterhood indicates that marriage is not universally a prime goal. This model is a significant one because upward social movement towards high qualifications is always dependent on lengthy studies of the kind that more and more young women are undertaking.

Table 5.2. *Indices of earliness and frequency of marriage by size of communes in 1968*

	Earliness		Frequency (incidence of persons never marrying)	
	M	F	M	F
Rural communes	44.7	53.1	16.1	7.9
under 20,000 inhabitants	57.3	58.9	9.4	8.9
Urban communes				
20,000 to 100,000 inhabitants	61.7	58.2	7.2	8.0
over 100,000 inhabitants	54.7	50.4	7.3	8.8
Paris urban area	49.0	48.0	8.9	11.0
All France	53.1	52.9	10.5	8.8

Source: Louis Roussel, *Le Mariage dans la société française contemporaine,* p. 102.

If we examine marriage in France on a regional basis, we see that there are now more and earlier marriages in towns than in the country (Table 5.2). The lowest ages of marriage are found in towns of under 10,000 inhabitants. There too, we note with Roussel that 'country areas discourage marriage for men, and Paris marriage for women'.[5]

A comparison of the data for 1911 and those for 1968 shows a change in the French geography of the marriage rate.

The areas with the most and the earliest marriages are no longer in the south-west, but in the north and the Paris basin apart from Paris itself. The latter is characterised by very late marriages and a low rate of marriage for men, and by fairly late marriages and a very low marriage rate for women. The low percentages of unmarried Parisians however are probably due to the difficulty of remaining in Paris after marriage than to a low propensity for marriage amongst Parisians.[6]

These variations within France show the significance of cultural and social phenomena amongst the factors determining the marriage rate (and the fertility rate). They assume even greater importance when examined in relation to populations of different ethnic origins in the same area. In the United States, for example, Irish immigrants married later than French Canadians or native Americans. The latter married earlier and entered their fertile period earlier than the Irish, who married later but had more children over a longer period.[7]

The characteristics of the marriage rate in our own times are thus beginning to take shape. These and the sparser data from past times illuminate each other. There is nothing definitive about them, and they are no more than signs, for populations have moved temporally, geographically and socially. A single phenomenon can also have more than a single meaning. Rural celibacy, for example, is no longer the way in which a society using marriage as the means of family and social reproduction regulates itself. It is now an indicator of the malfunction of agricultural society, stemming from the movement of women away from the countryside, which itself is linked to a whole range of disruptive economic, technical and cultural changes.

In French society, until around 1972, the pattern was that of early marriages and a high marriage rate. As a result of longer life expectancy, spouses can now expect to live their lives together for fifty years or so. The frequency of widowhood and remarriage has decreased, but marriages are now increasingly ended by divorce. A longer life span means that the generations now overlap rather than succeed each other, and people marry younger because it is no longer necessary to wait for their fathers to die. All this means that marriage looks less and less like a settling down and is no longer a break, a rite of passage to adult life, particularly when young people live together before marriage.

Early marriage, which has become so widespread that a mere 5 per cent of women born around 1940 will be spinsters all their lives, was a feature of the 'golden age' of marriage. In the 1960s there was already evidence of unstable marriages and an increase in the number of divorces, with the number of broken marriages rising from 6 to 10 per cent. Since 1972, the figures have gone in opposite directions, with the number of marriages per year falling and that of divorces shooting up.

CHOOSING A PARTNER: WHO MARRIES WHOM?

Theoretically, any male and female can marry each other. The choice of partner, however, is not a totally free one. Social milieux still reproduce themselves from within. The findings of many American surveys and of a major French national one bear each other out. Despite the mobility characteristic of industrialisation, people still marry partners from the same natal area for the most part. Even in a large city like Seattle, most men lived less than three miles (4.5 km) from their intended wives when they took out their marriage licence.[8]

Alain Girard's French national survey, *Le Choix du conjoint* (1959), produced the same conclusions (see Table 5.3):

Table 5.3. *Residence and place of birth of spouses*

	Residence of both spouses at time of marriage		Place of birth of both spouses	
	%	% Cumulative	%	% Cumulative
Same commune	57.4	57.4	21.6	21.6
Same canton	11.5	68.9	10.6	32.2
Same district	12.1	81.0	19.8	52.0
Same department	6.9	87.9	11.3	63.3
Same region	3.3	91.2	8.9	72.2
Others	8.8	100.0	27.8	100.0

Source: A. Girard, *Le Choix du conjoint,* p. 189.

Most marriages (seven out of ten) are contracted by people having the same origins. In two families out of ten, husband and wife were born in the same commune, three out of ten in the same canton and over five out of ten in the same district.[9]

One might think that this geographic homogamy has decreased somewhat since 1970, and this has indeed happened to a small extent. Examining place of birth in 1977, one notices a shift between the parental couple and that consisting of children. Of the former, 26 per cent stated that they had been born in the same commune and 71 per cent in the same department, whereas the figures for the latter were 18 per cent and 55 per cent respectively. The Nord/Pas-de-Calais and the Midi-Pyrénées areas were those in which both spouses most frequently came from the same region, and it was in the Paris area that there were the most 'mixed' couples, as Catherine Gokalp notes in 'Le Réseau familial'.[10] However, the fact remains that today half of all married couples still come from the same department, and it seems that given the recent resurgence of regionalist feeling and the wish to live and work in one's home area, homogamy will remain a feature of the way couples are made up in years to come.

Geographic homogamy decreases as social status increases, and the social homogamy that was a feature of marriages in past times is still found in those of our own. Post-war American commentators have stressed that there are many correlations, with choice being most likely to bring together spouses of the same race, ethnic group and

Table 5.4. *Social and professional category of wife's father related to that of husband's father* (in %)

| Wife's father | Husband's father | Marriages celebrated | | | | | | | | | |
| | | Farmers | | Employers, managers | | Artisans, small traders | | Middle managers, clerical | | Ind./Agri. workers | |
		Pre-1960	Post-1960	Pre-1960	Post-1960	Pre-1960	Post-1960	Pre-1960	Post-1960	Pre-1960	Post-1960
Farmers		67	65	3	6	19	16	10	10	16	12
Employers, managers		2	2	41	50	3	10	6	3	1	1
Artisans, small traders		9	7	22	8	30	28	19	15	9	12
Middle managers, clerical		6	7	21	19	16	13	32	35	14	18
Ind./Agri. workers		14	17	6	13	27	29	29	30	36	54
No profession		2	2	7	4	5	4	4	5	3	3

Source: A. Girard, *Le Choix du conjoint,* 2d ed., 1974, p. 26.

social class and sharing the same values.[11] Girard's major survey provides an accurate assessment of such phenomena in French society:

Social homogamy was twice as frequent than when marriages were contracted independently of the social origins of the partners. . . . Homogamy varies considerably from one milieu to another . . . being dominant amongst agriculture and industrial workers. In tertiary sectors, however, there was a much greater variety in the social origins of spouses, with social mixing occurring particularly in the lower middle-class groups.[12]

Given comparable social origins, it is not surprising to find that most spouses had an identical level of education (66 per cent). Religious homogamy was even more a major feature: In 92 per cent of cases, both spouses either had the same religion or none at all. For marriages contracted between 1960 and 1969, there was no decline in the frequency of social and professional homogamy. In the preface to the second edition of his *Choix du conjoint,* Girard observes that it even seems to have become more marked in the highest group for marriages contracted after 1960 (Table 5.4). These findings have been confirmed in Gokalp's recent (1977) survey.

In every social milieu there are places, institutions and practices whose function it is to enable young people to meet, get to know each other and choose partners.

Analysing the fundamental part played by dances in the making of marriages, Girard has pointed out that this term covers country

Table 5.5. *Place where meeting occurred* (in %)

Dance	17
By chance	15
Place of work or study	13
Family or childhood contacts	11
Neighbourhood contacts	11
Introduction	11
Place of entertainment	10
Club, interest group meetings	6
Family occasion	6
Others	0

Source: A. Girard, *Le Choix du conjoint*, 1st ed., p. 192.

dances attended by farmers and agricultural workers, balls held by the Grandes Ecoles, parties and middle-class gatherings and so forth. Each social category has its own type of dance, and when respondents said that they had met 'by chance', the fact most often seems to have been that they met as a result of a social process providing individuals from the same milieu with opportunities for meeting (Table 5.5). The agreement between the facts and Girard's opinion survey points to a general acceptance of a collective norm. Thus, Girard writes:

Despite the fact that liberal ideas are at work in the collective unconscious, there is still a very deep feeling supporting and sanctioning things as they are. The structures and forms of social life throw individuals from the same milieu together. Ultimately chances are greater amongst people of the same milieu, and it is there that it is fitting to choose one's spouse. The range of options gradually narrows if one has to meet a match in one's own circle.[13]

Paternal consent is no longer necessary for marriage to ensure social reproduction, but other strategies, less visible than those in the past, continue to operate.

A study of the population of Nantes shows a correlation between the woman's educational level and that of her husband, with a 'good' one leading to a 'good' marriage.[14] The findings of the Nantes study confirm both those for France as a whole and those of the American surveys. François de Singly notes the clear influence of educational levels on matrimonial mobility:

In the case of every social group, women who are upwardly mobile as a result of marriage have a better educational level than those who are immobile or downwardly mobile, and this is true of both working-class and middle-class women.[15]

Strategies of this kind for achieving upwards social mobility might appear to contradict homogamous practices, but in fact homogamy is a consequence of strategies aimed at either maintaining the social *status quo* or achieving some degree of social improvement. They are the permanent pole of tension running through marriage at all times.

Matrimonial society thus entails material, social, cultural and symbolic capital, and, as Alain Desrosières writes, 'There is no liking for each other unless likes and dislikes are shared, and social homogamy is high particularly in the dominant and the lower, but less so in the middle, classes.'[16] In the former groups, it is the result of selection mechanisms and the ability to control the future, and in the latter it reflects exclusion mechanisms, two different kinds of logic in choosing a spouse that both, however, lead to the same behaviour.

If homogamy is still so strong, how can it be compatible with the proclaimed freedom of the individual? What room is there in it for feelings? How does love fit into these strategies?

LOVE, A SOCIAL FORCE OF REPRODUCTION

French marriage sociologists do not very often mention love. In *Le Choix du conjoint*, Girard does so only once, in a single decorously phrased question: 'Do you personally think that in connection with marriage personal attraction or social position should be the main consideration?'[17] Nevertheless, a sociologist does encounter that fundamental affective factor of the formation of couples that permeates our present-day ways of thinking and feeling and for which the mass media – literature, the cinema and television – are a vehicle. People marry for love; just as they meet by chance, they marry because they love each other, and they stay married because marriage is the finest expression of love. And in neither traditional nor modern society should that affective dimension be seen simply as a sexual one, as it contains a mixture of both tenderness and sexual drives.

American sociologists, under the pressure of the ideology of love characteristic of North American society, have been interested in its 'theoretical importance', and this is particularly the case with William Goode.[18] Recognising its structural importance, which can be seen as either beneficial or harmful in connection with the institution of marriage, Goode first of all declares that it is an emotional potentiality observed in all societies. What differs is the way in which it is fitted into the social structure. In some societies, it is a tragic aberration. In ours, to admit that one had married without love would be shameful. North American and Northern European societies have to endure the dictates of love, which are far more constraining than those of any seventeenth-century father.

Every society uses means to control love (from child marriages to the separation of adolescents, from imposing prescribed spouses to devaluing feelings) and to avoid its harmful effects. In the United States, and to a lesser degree in Europe, the choice of spouse is ostensibly free. It is associated with the functioning of an age-group system in which love plays a large part. Children are socialised into falling in love as soon as they reach puberty. Until quite recently, this age-group – teenagers – seemed such a specifically American phenomenon that French had no linguistic equivalent for it. Its behaviour was orientated towards the appearance of those feelings of love associated with the formation of couples. In the dating process, young people go out in pairs as soon as they are teenagers, prefiguring married couples and not the gang. From that point, notes Goode in *The Family*, it is considered quite natural that they should all decide to marry as a result of a romantic attachment that will crystallise around one person within their age-group. In order to maintain their control over their children's choices, parents have to submit to those of the group, moving to 'good' districts, sending their children to 'good' schools, giving parties and saying who can come and who cannot. Thus, 'Since youngsters fall in love with those with whom they associate, control over informal relationships also controls substantially the focus of affection.'[19]

Goode stresses the threefold link between love and Western kinship structures. First, the couple, being relatively independent of its kinship network, can concentrate on itself the affective relationships it has no need to share with relatives. In a society in which the couple is only one strand in a close-knit network, affectivity can be shared amongst several relatives (e.g. in contacts with kin groups or privileged relatives such as an uncle), but love can flourish in the couple only when the latter is relatively independent of the kinship network. It makes the marriage very inward looking and is too disruptive of wider family solidarity to be tolerated in traditional society. Second, the parent–child tie is a very strong one, and falling in love gives children an emotional independence that turns them into adults who can break with the parents. Third, in a social pattern giving a great deal of freedom to adolescents, love can be seen as something that increases that freedom.[20]

COHABITATION AND THE YOUNGER GENERATION

In the last twenty years, the normative attitude of our society towards sexual relations before marriage has changed completely. In

Table 5.6. *Does the fact that young women today have greater sexual freedom seem to you unimportant, regrettable or satisfactory?* (in %)

	Married men					Married women				
	Pre-1951	1951–1960	1961–1964	Post-1965	All	Pre-1951	1951–1960	1961–1964	Post-1965	All
Unimportant	16	17	22	22	18	14	19	20	21	18
Regrettable	56	52	46	34	44	62	54	47	33	46
Satisfactory	21	23	27	37	25	18	21	28	37	24
Don't know	7	8	5	7	13	6	6	5	9	12

Source: Louis Roussel, *Le Mariage dans la société française contemporaine*, p. 234.

1958, in Girard's survey, young women were still expected to be virgins, even if practices differed from the expressed norm. Nowadays, all categories accept that young people live together.

What is striking is the speed with which norms and practices with regard to the sexuality of young women have changed. This is evident in Table 5.6, which gives the replies to a question regarding sexual freedom.

Today, even if they disapprove of it, the older generations accept the fact of premarital sexuality leading to marriage. As Roussel writes:

In the past, trial marriages were scandalous. Nowadays, in certain milieux, they are one possible model of betrothal . . . and 15% of recent marriages were preceded by a long period of cohabitation by the spouses.[21]

Perhaps such new and strikingly prevalent behaviour patterns – so widespread as to carry the penalty of being the subject of sociological studies – are taking shape within the institution of marriage or are an advance indicator of new models. Are young people engaging in trial marriages or inventing a new life-style when, between the ages of eighteen and twenty-five, they decide to live together outside marriage? Is it a sign that they want nothing to do with marriage, which will become increasingly clear in future years? A negative answer might be appropriate if we note that in most cases although 'juvenile cohabitation' is increasing, it ends in marriage, and that it is also sterile.

The practice has grown rapidly over recent years. For all couples stating that they had lived together before marriage, the figures were 24 per cent for marriages between 1970 and 1971, 26 per cent for those between 1972 and 1973 and 44 per cent for 1976–7. If we examine the proportion of those cohabiting in relation to a given age-group in a population, the figures seem much lower, amounting to 9.7 per cent for the eighteen to twenty-nine age-cohort.[22] Cohabitation and procreation are kept quite separate, with almost no births for cohabiting couples. Such cohabitation, which is accepted by parents, who see in the boy- or girl-friend their future son- or daughter-in-law, usually ends in marriage, and is thus to some extent 'salvaged' by the system. The parents may not interfere directly when the two young people move in together, but later they tend to press more or less directly for the situation to be 'legalised'. They are also ready to make any social sacrifice, being particularly willing to give up all the wedding festivities if that is the price to be paid for a marriage. Cohabitation is most frequently institutionalised when the young woman becomes pregnant, and indeed the very fact that she is pregnant may be the result of an unconscious decision to end a situation still experienced as temporary or marginal. This could explain the increase in premarital pregnancies (from 15 to 30 per cent over twenty years, observes Roussel).

Young people living together in unofficial unions meet in the same ways as those that fifteen years ago led to marriage, with selection being made on the basis of social possessions, type of studies and preferred leisure activities. 'The circumstances in which the first sexual partner was met,' notes Girard, basing his observations on French and Belgian surveys, 'were in all ways similar to those in which a spouse is chosen.'[23] Since the first sexual partner was in fact often the future spouse, it can be seen that 'liberal morals' ensure social reproduction just as much as older ones. Cohabitation of this kind goes back to some extent to the venerable 'trial betrothal' of the Middle Ages, which was acceptable to parents and society, but condemned by the church after the sixteenth century.

Are we coming closer to the 'Scandinavian' model? In Denmark and Sweden and to a lesser extent in Norway, Roussel declares that

the conjunction of a high standard of living, a Protestant culture and a practice based on a combination of freedom and solidarity has created the conditions for a kind of bold social experimentation.[24]

In these countries, there has been a fall in the marriage and fertility rates and a rise in the number of divorces and illegitimate births over the last fifteen years. Cohabitation outside marriage is increasing, and not only amongst young couples. This means that the boundary between the legitimate and the illegitimate is becoming blurred: In Sweden, 40 per cent of children born are conceived outside marriage, and unmarried mothers announce the birth of their children in the newspapers. Certain studies have shown that sexuality is linked to neither marriage nor love. Such developments mean that the very principle of marriage is in question.[25]

An examination of cohabitation in France shows how far that country is from the Scandinavian model. In the former country, the period of cohabitation is typically sterile and does not change the post-marital behaviour of couples, and legal marriage still cannot be dissociated from the formation of families.[26]

DIVORCE

Like marriage, divorce has also changed. Until recently, it was a sign of family instability and social and individual crisis, and represented the punishment of a fault against the partner, the couple, the children, the family and society. Nowadays, it is commonplace. A certain amount of historical background and some contemporary sociology will provide a clearer understanding of its place in the architecture of the institution of marriage. Jacques Commaille's detailed study will be of help here.

Divorce does not create a really new situation. We have already mentioned the considerable lack of stability in many domestic groups in former times as a result of a high mortality. Conditions in the past and those obtaining today differ in that the former were endured whereas the latter are the result of choice. The consequences are more or less the same: remarriage and children by several spouses, whose psychological welfare, to say nothing of their material interests, is hard to provide for. Our present-day demography, however, has upset the whole context of divorce, and our current life expectancy means that couples can look forward to fifty years together.

When, at the time of the French Revolution, marriage ceased to be an indissoluble sacrament and became a contract entered into before the civil authority, the way to divorce was opened, since any contract between two parties can be broken if they both agree. The law of 1792 introduced very liberal provision for divorce by stipulating three situations in which marriage could be ended. These were first, by mutual consent, with the spouses free to end their marriage if both agreed to do so; second, by the freedom of either spouse to preserve his or her freedom in relation to the other for reasons of psychological incompatibility; third, by the fact that divorce proceedings could be based on one of a given number of legal grounds, namely madness, the condemnation of one of the spouses to corporal punishment or punishment involving exile or the loss of civil rights, crimes, physical injury or serious moral injury to the other spouse, serious moral turpitude, and desertion for at least two years.

This list of grounds indicates the liberal spirit of the law, which facilitated divorce to such an extent that the rate soared in 1793. Napoleon restored a stricter ethos and made divorce a punishment for failure to maintain family and social order. Indeed, the law of 1804, which replaced that of 1792, practically made the only grounds for divorce the serious fault of one of the spouses (adultery, physical or serious moral injury and so on). It was rescinded in 1816, and only separation was admitted, as had been the case under the *ancien régime*. The Naquet law of 1884 reintroduced divorce for much the same grounds as those the 1804 law had recognised, and here too it was seen as a punishment of one of the spouses for infidelity or, more generally, for failing to honour the moral commitment accepted on marriage.

After 1884, divorce could be granted only if it was proved that one of the spouses had committed a grave fault of the kind accepted as an immediate reason for divorce (adultery, condemnation to punishment involving corporal punishment, exile or loss of civil rights) or one over which the judge had discretionary power (immorality, physical injury or serious moral injury). The Naquet law continued to regulate divorce until the law of 11 July 1975 came into force. This law incorporated a radically different view of divorce and, in certain conditions, authorised the ending of a marriage without the need for establishing guilty conduct on either side. It provided for divorce by mutual consent, either at the request of both spouses or an uncontested request from one of them, on the grounds of the breakdown of the marriage or for guilty conduct (see Table 5.7). The law had changed, but was increasingly out of step with real life. The legal machinery was a strait-jacket on the way in which ideas and behaviour were naturally developing.

There had been a gradual increase in the number of divorces since 1966 and this speeded up when the 1975 law came into force, making divorce easier and in general procedurally simpler.[27] Over recent years, younger couples have divorced more frequently than in the past, and older ones have also made use of the new legal provisions. This combination of circumstances has meant a rapid rise in the divorce rate (see Fig. 5.1). Commaille has pointed out that for couples marrying in 1900, one marriage in twenty ended in divorce, whereas for those marrying recently the proportion has risen to one in six. In the United States, there were forty-eight divorces per one hundred marriages in 1977.

Table 5.7. *Number of divorces, separations and marriages since 1884*

Year	Divorces	Separations	Marriages
1884	1,657	2,821	289,555
1885	4,123	2,122	283,170
1895	7,700	1,823	282,945
1905	10,860	2,238	316,200
1913[a]	16,335	2,466	
1913[b]	13,457	2,046	298,866
1914	10,154	1,696	168,923
1915	1,952	405	75,242
1925	22,176	3,354	352,830
1935	23,988	3,530	284,895
1945	37,718	4,806	393,000
1946	64,064	5,237	517,000
1955	31,268	4,097	312,703
1960	30,182	4,060	319,944
1965	34,877	4,771	346,308
1970	40,004	4,355	393,700
1971	46,788	4,238	406,700
1972	48,954	4,368	416,300
1973	50,267	4,078	400,700
1974	58,459	4,438	394,800
1975	61,496	4,625	390,000
1976	63,483	3,445	374,003
1977	77,709	3,504	367,000
1978	82,256	3,436	355,000
1979	88,831	3,831	340,000

[a] Statistics covering 87 departments.
[b] Statistics covering 77 departments.
Source: Jacques Commaille, 'Le Divorce en France', p. 41.

Divorce has changed in another way, namely chronologically, with marriages being dissolved at an increasingly early stage.

The demographic behaviour of divorced people is similar to that of those who stay married. The rate of premarital pregnancies is higher for the former, but they tend to marry at more or less the same age as the latter and to have a comparable number of children. The characteristic that really distinguishes divorced people is of a social and professional nature. If we compare divorce rates on this basis, we can see that clerical workers, followed by middle managers, are the groups divorcing most frequently (see Table 5.8).

The figures can be refined if we take into account, as Desrosières does, the cultural capital variable.[28] In the lower social groups, marriage is a means of legalising the *status quo* and getting rid of the

Fig. 5.1. Divorce rate in France since 1955. The index relates the number of divorces in a given year to the initial number of marriages in a year from which divorces resulted. This gives rates that when combined give the total of divorces 'reduced' for a given year. (From Institut National d'Etudes Démographiques.)

drawbacks of cohabitation, and divorce is rare because of the expense and slowness of legal proceedings. In the salaried middle classes, people marry because they have a certain cultural capital to transmit. Since, however, it is more often a cultural and social rather than an economic one, it does not rule out divorce, which is more frequent among these groups because it is financially and culturally more accessible. In the non-salaried middle classes and amongst farmers, it is less frequent because it is less compatible with the management and transmission of economic capital. It is also infrequent amongst the dominant classes because it represents a serious

Table 5.8. *Comparative socio-professional distribution of spouses instituting divorce proceedings with that of married people as a whole* (in %)

	Husband		Wife	
	Divorcing	Married	Divorcing	Married
Self-employed farmers	1.6	9.4	0.5	6.1
Agricultural workers	1.3	2.3	0.2	0.2
Industrial/commercial employers	8.9	9.4	3.7	4.3
Liberal professions	8.5	6.1	2.2	0.9
Middle managers	13.5	8.1	7.9	3.9
Clerical	14.9	7.2	29.0	8.3
Industrial workers	39.5	35.0	12.4	7.1
Services	2.8	1.4	11.9	3.3
Others	3.3	2.3	0.4	0.1
No profession	5.7	18.8	31.8	65.8

Source: J. Commaille and A. Boigeol, 'Divorce en France, année 1970', *La Documentation française*, 1973, p. 75.

obstacle to the reproduction of a much greater social, cultural or economic capital (Table 5.9).

As Commaille points out, a clear correlation can also be seen between the divorce rate and the woman's professional activity:

The proportion of divorced women with a profession is twice as high as that for married women as a whole. The divorce rate for couples by the husband's socio-professional group, of whatever nature it may be, is always considerably higher for couples in which the wife has a profession than for those in which she has none. On average, it is four times as high.[29]

The increasing number of middle-class women working (from a class in which they traditionally had 'no paid employment') is a major and recent phenomenon and has entailed significant changes in conjugal and parental roles. Women have become more independent at all levels, particularly economically, and the consequence of this is a relative independence if divorce takes place. It follows that more women seek divorce. This is more often the case when they have salaried employment than when they have none, and the higher the social status of the woman, the more likely she is to be the one instituting proceedings. The per centage of women doing so rose from 54.7 in 1965 to 66 in 1975.

We have described the new type of divorce that very often occurs early in marriage, but the more 'classical' kind, still taking place after

Table 5.9. *Divorce rate based on socio-economic group of spouses*

Husband Wife	Farmer	Ind./agri. worker	Clerical	Middle manager	Higher man + lib. prof.	Employer	All
Farmer	0.4	1.7					0.5
Ind./agri. worker	8.3	9.1	13.4	12.4	12.2	13.0	9.6
Clerical	20.6	16.6	21.0	19.1	20.1	21.8	18.9
Middle manager	5.5	9.9	15.0	9.8	12.9	11.9	11.0
Higher manager and liberal prof.		10.2	14.8	14.2	12.5	9.2	12.5
Employer		9.3	10.9	10.1	10.9	2.8	4.7
No profession	0.9	2.9	5.1	3.8	3.9	3.3	2.6
All	0.9	6.2	11.0	8.7	7.2	5.0	5.4

Note: The rates have been calculated by relating the number of divorces sought in 1970 to couples figuring in the 1968 census. To simplify the table only the main socio-professional groups have been used. The remainder are included under the heading 'All'.
Source: Alain Desrosières, 'Marché matrimonial et structure des classes sociales', *Actes de la Recherche en Sciences Sociales* 20–1(1978): 105.

fifteen or twenty years of marriage, should not be forgotten. In this older type, a wife with no paid employment generally pays the costs and is left with very little material or psychological support. In the newer type, the separation is usually by mutual consent, with the wife taking the initiative, which means that the divorce will be one in which both parties will be equally to blame and that she will lose her husband's financial support. In principle, her earnings will mean that she can do without it.

Thus, there are new attitudes towards divorce, just as there are new models of marriage. If we bring these together, we can see that divorce is no longer an aberration, but has become part of the new rationale of marriage.

Is it not in some way implicitly present right from the establishment of the couple? Nowadays, partners in marriage principally seek happiness and their emotions are inordinately invested in the idea of the couple. According to Roussel and Commaille, this attitude is extended over a greater period of time by the limitation of fertility. They have let their hearts lead them in their choice of spouse, and they freely share each other's lives with no legal blessing. When the latter comes, it is a commitment that is perhaps seen as only temporary. The matrimonial tie is all the more constraining because the association has been entered into freely. What can break it? The fact that the couple cannot keep their promises and in particular cannot meet the wife's expectations of the marriage. She has a job and expects to find personal fulfilment in other kinds of work than the purely domestic. After a year or two, she begins to see how relatively rigid male and female roles are and feels justified in expressing her disappointment in concrete ways. If that is so, why keep up the pretence of love and personal fulfilment if marriage hinders rather than helps this? Once there is disagreement, the husband accepts divorce. The concept of marriage as a free choice has a corollary in the notion of the least traumatic break possible for spouses and children.

Divorce is not a rejection of marriage as such, since it often leads to a new marriage. There has been an increase in France in the remarriage of divorced persons, with 34,476 men and 31,080 women remarrying in 1978, amounting to 9.7 per cent and 8.8 per cent of all marriages. Between 1955 and 1975, the proportion was around 6 per cent.[30] Divorce is now common, accepted and normal, and increasingly seen as a release from family tensions. To push the paradox a little further, one could say that it is a sign of the health of the institution of the family.

SUGGESTED READING

Marriage

De Singly, François. 'Le Mariage informel'. *Recherches sociologiques* 12 (1981): 61–90.

Girard, Alain. *Le Choix du conjoint*. 2d ed. INED, Travaux et documents, cahier no. 70. Paris: PUF, 1974.

Roussel, Louis, *La Mariage dans la société française contemporaine*. INED, Travaux et documents, cahier no. 73. Paris: PUF, 1975.

Roussel, Louis, and Odile Bourguignon. *Générations nouvelles et mariage traditionnel, enquête auprès de jeunes de 18–30 ans*. INED, Travaux et documents, cahier no. 86. Paris: PUF, 1979.

Divorce

Commaille, Jacques. 'Le Divorce en France. De la réforme de 1975 à la sociologie du divorce'. *Notes et études documentaires*, 29 September 1978, no. 4478, La Documentation française, new ed. 1980. Includes a detailed bibliography on divorce.

Goode, William. *Women in Divorce*. New York: Free Press, 1965.

Mixed marriages

Barbara, Augustin. *Mariages sans frontières*. Paris: Le Centurion, 1985.

Bensimon, Doris, and Françoise Lautman. *Un mariage, deux traditions: chrétiens et juifs*. Editions de l'Université de Bruxelles, 1977.

Ethnies, 4, numéro special. 'Mariages mixtes'. Paris: Mouton, 1974.

Chapter 6

The child and the family

This chapter is about the link between the number of children and family attitudes and, more generally, relationships between parents and children. 'Family' is used here in its most restricted sense, that of the conjugal cell made up by marriage or its extension and/or the children produced by it. It will nevertheless be impossible to keep discussion within those strict bounds, for models of procreation and upbringing, although they both, especially the former, seem to stem from the most intimate and personal aspects of our lives, also have links with social relationships at the level of the family and of professional life. Chapter 10, on relationships between the family and society, is concerned with questions of this kind, but we will also discuss them briefly here.

Our interest in that third being to whom two others give life will not simply be an interest in the new-born child closely dependent on others for all needs. We will also sketch in a history of adolescence and try to show what changes there have also been in relationships between parents and their older children. The dynamic aspect is important and will be the major one here.

Although psychoanalysis is of considerable importance in this area, we will not make much reference to that aspect of parent–child relationships, as it lies on the boundaries of our own field of scientific investigation. Several ways of filling the resulting gap are indicated in the Suggested Reading section at the end of this chapter.

We will also use the past as a point of reference in our efforts to understand parental relationships in our own age. Along with research on domestic groups, the study of the child in the family has been one of the most successful investigations in historical demography, which over the last twenty years has amassed a body of relevant data and raised some fascinating questions. These have been much discussed amongst historians and anthropologists in ways that highlight the complexity of the whole question.

After an examination of the child in the family under the *ancien régime* (and here politics and demography come together crudely), we will study the two contraceptive revolutions. What attitudes towards children illuminate and explain these upheavals? What were their consequences for parental relationships?

TOWARDS A NORM OF TWO CHILDREN

The demographic framework

The historical demography of France, which is quite distinct from that of other European countries, was characterised by an early fall in the birth rate. This occurred at a different pace and to a different degree in differing social milieux, but it was becoming apparent by the end of the eighteenth century. A number of studies have established that it had already occurred before the Revolution, with the demographic change just preceding that great political and social upheaval.

The birth rate – the annual number of births per 1,000 inhabitants[1] – has fallen consistently since 1800, except amongst those born around 1930. It was around 40 per thousand during the period from 1750 to 1754, 37 per thousand from 1795 to 1799 and 32 per thousand from 1800 to 1804. It fell to its lowest point (13.1 per thousand) in 1941 and then reached a new and totally unexpected peak of 20.3 per thousand between 1946 and 1953. In the United States, it fell from 24.5 to 14.7 per thousand between 1951 and 1976.

Demographers prefer to use a rather more sophisticated measurement, the fertility rate, which gives the average number of live births per woman. In France this fell from 3.4 for children born in 1825 to 2 for those born before 1900. For those born in 1950, the final number of offspring was 3.28 (England and Wales and Sweden had a fertility rate of 4.28 in that year).[2] After 1945, it was between 2.65 and 3 in France, reaching 2.9 in 1964 and then gradually falling to around 1.85, stabilising around this figure since 1976, with a slight rise to 1.95 in 1980 (see Figs. 6.1 and 6.2).

It is often said that before modern methods of contraception were introduced couples frequently had up to twenty children. This was certainly not so, for two reasons. On the one hand, a whole range of factors limited the number of births, and on the other, the death rate considerably reduced the number of children surviving their parents and producing children themselves.

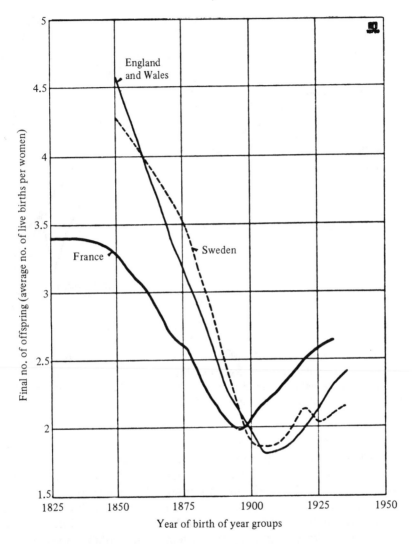

Fig. 6.1. Final number of offspring, 1825–1950. (From Roland Pressat, 'La Population française: mortalité, natalité, immigration, vieillissement', *Colloque national sur la démographie française*, June 1980, Institut National d'Etudes Démographiques, pp. 7–11.)

The age at which people married, as we have already noted, acted as a powerful brake on the number of births. We know that in the past this was on average twenty-six for women, higher than in the twentieth century. Religious practices imposed continence during

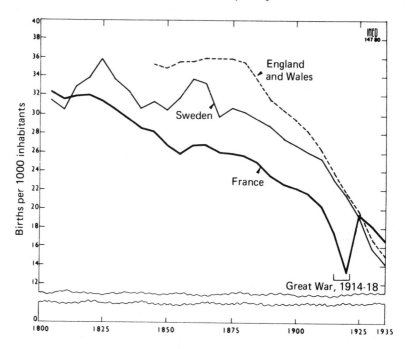

Fig. 6.2. Birth rate: England and Wales, Sweden, and France. (From Roland Pressat, 'La Population française: mortalité, natalité, immigration, vieillissement', *Colloque national sur la démographie française*, June 1980, Institut National d'Etudes Démographiques, pp. 7–11.)

certain periods of the church year, and cultural practices of extended breast-feeding generally meant a temporary suspension of fertility. Economic conditions of both a temporary and a structural nature had an effect on diet and caused periods of amenorrhoea or miscarriages. For all these reasons, women did not have a child a year for twenty-five years of married life, but twelve or fifteen children altogether at the very most. In fact, if female and infant mortality are taken into account, they had far fewer. Only one woman in two of those born in 1750 reached the age of fifteen and only one in three her fiftieth birthday (Table 6.1). The risks attached to pregnancy and childbirth were considerable. As we have seen, marriages were often ended by the death of one partner, and frequently remarriages only partly made up for the 'missing' children who would have been born if the marriage had not come to an end.[3]

Women born in 1750 had on average only five or six children per marriage. An additional cause to those already given was the high

Table 6.1. *Mortality, marriage, and legitimate fertility of women born in 1750 and 1950*

	Born 1750	Born 1950	
		Maximum fertility	Probable history[b]
Girls surviving			
to age 15	48%	94%	94%
to age 50	30%	90%	90%
Average age at puberty	16 yrs.	13 yrs.	13 yrs.
Average age at 1st marriage	26 yrs.	23 yrs.	23 yrs.
Percentage of spinsters at age 50	11%	8%	8%
Average age at 1st birth	27 yrs.	24 yrs.	25 yrs.
Average age at 2nd birth	37 yrs.	38 yrs.	30 yrs.
Average no. of children, per woman			
married at age 20, still married at 50	8.7	12.3	2.8
per married woman	5.3	10.1	2.2
per woman aged 15	4.2	9.3	2.0
in the group	2.0	8.7	1.9

[a] Theoretical fertility, assuming no birth control (contraception or abortion).
[b] Estimate, taking no account of illegitimate births (+0.15 children per family) or divorce (difficult to calculate its effects on the family).
Source: Henri Léridon, 'La maîtrise de la fécondité: ses motifs et ses moyens', *Colloque national sur la démographique française*, Paris, June 1980, p. 51.

number of unmarried women. As a result of mortality, the net number of children was four, of whom only two reached child-bearing age. Table 6.1 summarises the demographic situation under the *ancien régime*: no contraception and a high death rate, which explains why, despite a high birth rate, population growth was slow.

The comparison with the present situation is particularly illuminating. If we imagine an absence of birth control, the fall in the death rate in the twentieth century would mean that our society would have the kind of high number of births we have mentioned, namely 12.3 children for every woman marrying at age twenty (which in fact contraception has reduced to 1.8).

Thus, the demographic context of the family of past times is clear. Families were prolific and did not attempt to control their fertility. There were births and the deaths of adults and children. Children were socialized as a group within the household and the village community. The relationships governing parent–child contacts were linked, like those governing the contacts between the couple and the kinship group, with the wider social group.

The two contraceptive revolutions

We must distinguish between natural contraception and the recent development of chemical contraception. The two are very different by nature, in their effects on family relationships and in the attitudes towards children they imply, even if their aim seems identical.

Natural contraception and the new place of the child. Philippe Ariès has described the characteristics of the revolution that went beyond the sex act and brought about a major change in attitudes towards bodies, life and death. His views, which are well known, can be summarised as follows.

Natural contraception as practised in France from the end of the eighteenth century was a masculine form of birth control, an ascetic one, as Ariès says, in that the man controlled his sexual impulses and withdrew at the height of his pleasure.

Until then, people had not even imagined the possibility of influencing the sexual act, which was an act of nature, and it was this change in attitude towards their bodies that constituted a revolution in mentalities. Ariès stresses that 'contraceptive practices were unthinkable in older societies because they were outside their mental universe'. Their attitudes towards sexuality were also supported by church teaching, which saw chastity as the optimal state. Marriage was a lesser evil, but every sexual act had to be open to the transmission of life, and deliberately sterile sexuality was condemned.

At the end of the eighteenth century, however, in Catholic France, the practice of *coitus interruptus* affected various social levels of the bourgeoisie and the peasant classes. The technique was, of course, already known in certain circles, such as those of prostitution and the *salons* of society, but what was new was the rapidity with which the 'deadly secrets' spread. Fertility was rapidly affected and statistically the effectiveness of the method was considerable, since it reduced the number of births. At the level of individual couples, however, the picture is less certain. Even if they had 'been careful', that is, separated pleasure and the risk of conception, more children were born than were wanted, and it is this lower safety margin that distinguishes older from more modern methods of contraception.

Ariès's views have been criticised by historians such as Jean-Louis Flandrin and Edward Shorter, particularly with regard to the delicate question of the move from a non-contraceptive to a contracep-

164

tive society. André Burguière stresses that the spread of contraception corresponded to a change in attitudes to life:

It was an affective change leading to a desire to ensure the future of their children by means of education and a higher standard of living rather than simply bringing them into the world. It also led to an increase in the value given to the couple and the 'civilising' of conjugal relations. . . . The apparently paradoxical idea that birth control can be encouraged by an increasing attention to children is supported with regard to eighteenth-century France by many literary and iconographical studies. Dr J. Sutter summarises Ariès by saying that it was when the French began to be interested in children that they started not to have so many. We should add that it follows the logic of the demographic situation. The drop in infant mortality has led to birth control to stop families getting too big and also to increased material and affective investment in children whose birth and survival are no longer completely random.[4]

These new children fit into a strategy of upward social mobility or a patrimonial one. Their upbringing is ever more constrictingly sheltered. The world of school cuts them off from the adult world and they no longer learn by watching their elders or by being directly taught by them. There is also a great deal of emotional and medical investment in them.

The second contraceptive revolution. For over ten years, modern contraceptive techniques have increasingly become an integral part of our customs and morality. In many ways, they are very unlike classical ones. Those opposed to them describe them in passionate, ideological terms, using such phrases as 'non-parental pleasure' and 'children when convenient'.

The drop in fertility has alarmed the leaders of various governments in the West. One useful result of this has been a number of detailed studies of the phenomenon of the use of new contraceptive techniques and their effect on fertility. They help us understand new parental attitudes to society, the family and children.

It has been established that the rapid decline in fertility came before the almost universal use of modern contraceptive techniques. There was a sharp fall in fertility in 1964–5 whereas, as has been said, the almost universal use of the pill and the coil did not really begin until the early 1970s. This trend is all the more noteworthy in that it affected the other European countries in much the same way. Gérard Calot offers this explanation:

Reduced fertility was something desired and not something simply accepted, and it came before new contraceptives and legalised abortion. Consequently, it is not simply a result of more permissive legal or technical procedures, but comes from a deliberate wish on the part of couples and families.[5]

A detailed demographic analysis of the phenomenon will show just how old it is:

The downward trend in fertility from 1930 onwards is extremely marked, and there has been no sign of a slackening of the fall over the subsequent twenty years. In 1950, the 1896 figure, the lowest ever recorded in France, was reached again.[6]

What is striking is the way in which the French figures match those for every European country, some of which have very different legislation on the pill and abortion. Whether they are traditionally highly fertile, like the Netherlands, or relatively infertile, like Sweden, they all experienced the same sharp fall around 1964–5. France fell between an upper and lower limit of 1.9 and 1.4 children per woman (Fig. 6.3). This collapse was thus part of a long-term movement in that country, occurred in a similar way in other Western nations and seems to have come about before modern contraceptive techniques came into general use. Why then are the latter so important?

There have been other ways besides those provided by medical research for Northern European and North American couples to achieve their wish of having fewer children. The reduction in fertility certainly began without them, but it was consolidated with their help. The major fact has been that pleasure and reproduction are now seen as separate matters, and yet to see a contrast between older forms of contraception as a reflection of an ascetic society and modern ones as the symbol of one based on hedonism and personal pleasure is moralistic and simplistic. The *real* difference between them is that modern contraception is a female matter. For the first time, the responsibility for creating life is given to those who bring it forth.

Nowadays, expressing everything in statistical terms seems so pervasive that there is nothing at all surprising about a survey of contraceptive techniques used, and yet this in itself is a sign of just how much our behaviour has changed. Twenty-five years ago, a survey of this kind, touching on the most personal aspects of a couple's life, would scarcely have been possible. Both the findings and the fact that the survey took place reveal the relative disappearance of the taboo on discussing sexual matters and the deprivatisation of the sexual life of human couples.

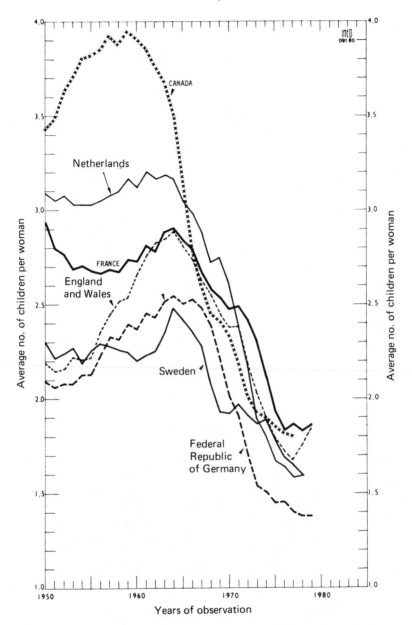

Fig. 6.3. Multifactorial indicator of fertility in various Western countries since 1950. (From Gerard Calot, 'La Baisse de la fécondité depuis 15 ans', *Colloque national sur la démographie française*, June 1980, Institut National d'Etudes Démographiques, p. 36.)

Table 6.2. *Contraceptive method used by age* (all women between 20 and 44 years of age at 1 January 1978; in %)

	20–24	25–29	30–34	35–39	40–44	All ages
Pill	38.3	35.2	30.4	20.5	9.8	27.9
Coil	2.0	10.9	13.4	11.5	6.4	8.8
Withdrawal	11.6	13.7	18.8	22.3	28.0	18.3
Sheath	3.5	4.6	5.9	6.2	6.3	5.2
Periodical continence	3.5	4.4	4.3	7.3	9.7	5.6
Others and unknown[a]	0.3	2.5	1.6	2.9	4.0	2.2
Total	59.2	71.3	74.4	70.6	64.1	68.1
None	40.8	28.7	25.6	29.4	35.9	31.9
Sterilisation (contraceptive)	0.5	1.0	4.6	9.4	6.9	4.1
Sterilisation (non-contraceptive)	0.1	0.3	1.5	6.4	9.9	3.2
Sterile	0.3	0.1	1.6	1.2	4.5	1.4
Pregnant	9.6	6.0	4.5	1.0	0.4	4.6
Alone (no regular partner)	18.0	9.7	4.1	4.1	6.3	8.7
Others						
wanting another child	9.9	8.7	7.3	2.6	0.6	6.2
not wanting another child	2.4	3.0	1.9	4.7	7.4	3.7
Total number of women in the population	2073	2128	1755	1400	1543	8899

[a] Diaphragm, jellies and spermicidal pessaries: 0.8% of the 20–44 group; washing, douche: 0.9%

Source: Henri Léridon, 'La Maîtrise de la fécondité: ses motifs et ses moyens', p. 54.

Table 6.2 shows clearly the importance of the use of the pill (almost 30 per cent of the women surveyed). It should be noted that all kinds of women were questioned – sterile or sterilised, pregnant, those living alone, and so on. The pill was the leading contraceptive method, and if these findings are compared with those of a survey conducted in 1971, it is clear how pre-eminent it now is, since the figures are 10.5 per cent and 31 per cent respectively.[7] As we examine the make-up of the family, it emerges that even couples still wanting a child use the pill, and it is increasingly used as the desired number of children seems to be reached. From the survey we can also see that 96 per cent of women not wanting more children used some form of contraception.

The pill and the coil were also used from the beginning of the reproductive period by unmarried couples living together (61 per cent) as a typical 'waiting' contraceptive. It was not a case of not wanting children, but rather of not wanting them at once.[8] This explains why the number of illegitimate births remained stationary at a time when young people between ages twenty and twenty-five were increasingly cohabiting.

The analysis of the use of modern contraceptive methods can be extended to cover socio-professional categories (Table 6.3).[9]

The most striking conclusion to be drawn from Table 6.3 is the relative balance between the various categories chosen for the survey. Whatever the place of residence, the level of education, the socio-professional category or the importance given to religion, the per centages were much the same. Whether the women in question had a job or not, their behaviour was also more or less identical, and this is important in view of the frequent association of women with jobs and a reduced fertility.

We must also include abortion amongst the methods of birth control used. Demographers estimate that the real number of terminations of pregnancy in France is around 250,000 a year, or one abortion for every three births. The figure has been calculated at 0.3–0.4 per birth, and abortion is used chiefly as a safety net if contraception fails. Most abortions are carried out on married women.[10]

Modern methods of contraception would thus appear very effective on the whole. Procreation is now a deliberate choice and no longer the result of a failure of birth control in one form or another or of the unthinking acceptance of a birth, as was the case with classical techniques. Pierre Chaunu, a historian deeply committed to a rising birth rate, remarks that

with natural forms of contraception, procreation is not separated from the natural state. It remains deep in the recesses of the mind. . . . Nowadays, it is not enough not to want; there must be a clear wish.

For couples today, the natural state is that of non-conception, and instead of being suffered and accepted, conception has to be decided on. Consequently, Chaunu goes on, 'It becomes necessary to find "reasons" for having a child instead of merely having reasons for not having too many' (see Table 6.4).[11]

Nevertheless, modern contraceptive methods, although they both reflect attitudes to life and the body based on freedom and a liberalisation of mentalities and change the relationships between the sexes, do not mean a rejection of children. Demographers have established that the reduction in fertility cannot be attributed to selfishness and a desire for self-sufficiency on the part of couples since 'almost all those couples capable of having a child have at least one',[12] with the fall in fertility occurring at and after the third child. With techniques that are almost 100 per cent safe, couples chose to have two children, usually fairly close together. The real change has

Table 6.3. *Use of modern contraceptive methods by various socio-economic characteristics* (women aged between 20 and 44; in %)

	Using pill or coil
All women	36
Matrimonial situation	
Married, husband present	36
Unmarried, cohabiting	61
Unmarried, partner not cohabiting	61
Unmarried, no partner	15
Place of residence	
Rural commune in an entirely rural canton	27
Rural commune in a partly urban canton	34
Town of 5,000–20,000 inhabitants	31
Town of 20,000–100,000 inhabitants	38
Town of over 100,000 inhabitants (excluding Greater Paris)	39
Greater Paris	47
Nationality	
French	37
Other	34
Educational level	
Primary	29
CEP (primary studies certificate)	31
CAP (vocational certificate)	39
BEPC (school certificate at age 15)	40
Baccalaureate	44
Higher	44
Professional activity	
Working	37
Not working at present	36
Never worked	34
Socio-professional category of spouse[a]	
Agriculture (self-employed or salaried)	23
Labourer, unskilled worker	31
Skilled worker	37
Clerical	33
Artisan, trader	38
Middle management, supervisory	38
Higher management, liberal professions	43
Importance of religion[b]	
Very important	27
Fairly important	34
Unimportant	43

[a] Or of the wife, if she has no spouse.

[b] The question was, 'What importance do you attach to religion in your everyday life? Would you say that it is very important, fairly important or unimportant?'

Source: *Population et sociétés*, January 1978, no. 128.

Table 6.4. *Contraceptive methods used, 1971 and 1978 and at different stages of family composition* (1978)

Method used	1971 All	1978 All	Childless women wanting a child	Women with one child wanting more	Women with 2 children not wanting more
				1978	
Pill	10.5	31	22	29	34
Coil	1.5	12	1	8	16
Other methods	58	44	19	36	46
None	30	13	58	27	4

Source: Henri Léridon, 'La Maîtrise de la fécondité, ses motifs et ses moyens', p. 51.

been the disappearance of families with more than three children. In France, the proportion of childless couples is still small and the number with one or two children is increasing. Here, as in the other countries of Western Europe and North America, there is clearly a deliberate intention to have no more than two children, and one can see the emergence of a new model of the family.

An opinion poll has shown the obvious change over the last ten years in the general notion of the ideal size of the family. Alain Girard and Louis Roussel have noted that in the 1960s, estimates of the real (i.e., final) number of children of couples was around three, and that this number then fell slightly from 1959 to 1967. Since 1970, large families of four children or more have almost disappeared, being basically replaced by families with two. In 1959, 34 per cent of those interviewed thought that French families would have an average of four or more children; in 1978, it had fallen to 2 per cent. In the opinion of the present-day public, families rarely go beyond two children, as Table 6.5 shows.[13] Demographic studies have the merit of refuting the ideological views of those favouring a high birth rate and opposed to abortion. Contrary to what they maintain, it is not the 'radical category of non-parenthood' that has caused the fall in the number of births as a result of an 'abortion for personal convenience'.[14] We are not witnessing the birth of a new hedonistic society based on pleasure and selfishness. The fall in the birth rate reflects complex phenomena in which social, religious and cultural factors all interlock. All those limiting their families to two children were

171

Table 6.5. *How many children do you think a French family nowadays has or will have?* (in %)

	1959	1965	1966	1967	1978
One	1	1	–	2	14[a]
Two	20	24	23	31	66
Three	45	44	51	48	18[b]
Four	25	23	22	14	2[c]
Five	7	6	3	4	–
Six or more	2	2	1	1	–
Mean	3.24	3.14	3.09	2.89	2.09

[a] Including 6% of answers in the form, 'One or two children'.
[b] Including 4% of answers in the form, 'Two or three children'.
[c] Four or more children.
Source: A. Girard and L. Roussel, 'Fécondité et conjoncture. Une enquête d'opinion sur la conjoncture démographique', *Population* 3(1979): 572.

born after the war in a climate of economic expansion but without any collective movement to mobilise energies. Traditional religion has lost many of its adherents and those belonging to new ones are relatively marginal groups. Young people have lost faith in themselves and in the world, so why should they have a lot of children?

The growth of the number of working women in age groups in which women had never previously worked is closely linked to these other factors. As Jean-Claude Chesnais says:

The world of woman is gradually ceasing to be coterminous with the domestic sphere. The relationship between women working and fertility may be ambivalent, but it is clear that on the one hand, a second salary raises the aspirations of couples and hence increases the cost of having children (loss of salary as a consequence of having to give up work) and on the other, reconciling a job and motherhood becomes more difficult as the number of dependent children increases.[15]

A phenomenon as complex as a fall in births is thus not the result of a single cause, but of several converging ones, and effective contraception and an economic crisis combine to produce the same result. However, whereas the economic crisis is a long-term phenomenon and unemployment is still increasing, the reduction in fertility now seems to have become stable. In matters connected with the number of births, there is no mechanistic link between cause and effect.

THE DIVERSE AND CHANGING NATURE OF PARENTAL RELATIONSHIPS

Any biological event is dealt with differently in different societies. The way children are brought up and the relationships between them and their parents, which seem 'natural', are in fact shaped by various cultural modes. The first menstruation of young girls, for example, as Margaret Mead has noted,[16] is socialized in very different ways. Amongst certain North California Indians, young girls reaching puberty were thought to bring great dangers to the tribe and were urged to move about as little as possible to prevent damage to crops, and in the tribes of British Columbia girls at that stage in their lives had to carry out certain magical actions that would shape their whole future as women. In the Gilbert Islands in the western Pacific, however, such girls were not seen as dangerous but rather as being in danger themselves and were consequently protected. Contrasting adolescence in Samoa and Manus, Mead pointed out that in the former there was no conflict: Menstruation was not surrounded by ritual and puberty was simply a time of peaceful maturation. In the latter, adolescence was a time of fundamentally cultural anxiety and involved ritual, taboos and conflict situations. Western society is still influenced by Victorian taboos relating to menstruation and puberty. Thus, the period of stress that accompanies adolescence in our culture is linked to prohibitions concerning the acquisition of physical and sexual knowledge, which are cultural attitudes and not part of any 'human nature'.

Seeing the spatial and temporal relativity of our own culture also enables us to observe the different influences of parents and peer group in the socialisation process. According to Mead, one can distinguish the 'post-figurative' culture, in which children are chiefly taught by their parents and which is authorised by the past; the 'co-figurative' one, in which both children and adults learn from their peers and have a culture based on the peer group; and the 'pre-figurative' one, in which adults also learn from their children.[17]

In a post-figurative culture, the past of adults is the future of each generation, since the older generation cannot conceive of change and transmit to their descendants a sense of immutable continuity. Grandparents with their grandchildren in their arms cannot envisage for them a future different from their own past. Very slowly changing peasant societies are of this type. In co-figurative cultures, older generations remain dominant by determining the style and the limits within which co-figuration can be expressed in the behaviour of the young. In such societies, new models proposed by the latter still need the acceptance of their elders. A number of factors can bring about development from a pre- to a co-figurative culture, and the children of families moving from the country to the town and children in Israeli *kibbutzim* move from one to the other. When there is co-figuration, the experience of the younger generation is radically different from that of its parents and grandparents. Mead's third model, the pre-figurative one, with its suggestion of children and not parents or grandparents representing the future and teaching their elders, is probably the most debatable one, and the generation gap she notes should probably be stored away with all the other lumber of myths about the family.

Parent–child relationships in pre-industrial societies

Here, it is difficult to propose clear-cut chronological periods. Attitudes and behaviour patterns proper to one age reappear a generation or two later and, conversely, pockets of modernity can sometimes be observed in a group characterised by occupation, level of education, religion and so on. An intellectual need to divide things into distinct chronological stages does not imply that reality is separable in such ways, for family behaviour patterns change only slowly.

In this connection we should distinguish, as we will later with regard to the contemporary period, the phases of the child's growth and development from baby to child and from child to adolescent. A number of books on the young child (see Suggested Reading section) have recently been published. The false problem of maternal indifference to the infant in past times can be disposed of at once.[18] No woman and no couple can undergo the shock of repeated births and rapid deaths – whether in a matter of hours, days or months – without trauma. A whole range of popular prophylactics and remedies surrounded the most dangerous moments of the infant's life. Even if their curative power was limited, such practices bear witness to the loving anxiety of women who were powerless in the face of catastrophe. Psychoanalysis, rediscovering the major importance of the earliest years of life, gives us reason to believe that children in these non-contraceptive societies were brought up in an environment pulsating with interactions. The techniques of traditional ways of bringing up infants respected their natural rhythms, and they were fed, changed and put into the cradle on demand. It was the nineteenth century with its doctors and their rigid timetables that was to make changes.

Those children fortunate enough to survive were brought up, fed and socialised at one and the same time in the parental and grand-parental domestic groups, even when there was no cohabitation. There was often some harshness in relationships with parents, with a compensatory ease and complicity in those with grandparents. This latter relationship showed the real position of children with regard to adults, for in a society with no system of social security or provision for old age, having children brought precisely those bene-fits now provided by social security. The often special relationship between grandchildren and grandparents was a symbol of intergen-erational solidarity and ensured the transmission of values. Educa-tion was also part of the duties of bigger brothers and sisters, who were often much older than their smaller siblings, and of servants and farm-hands. Children were a collective responsibility, and this too provided a means of social transmission.

One of Ariès's most provocative ideas, that of the 'rediscovery of the feeling for childhood', is criticized today. He has been accused of ignoring infancy, and it has now been established that in pre-contra-ceptive and even later societies, infants were loved and surrounded by precautions that medically speaking were perhaps excessive or inept and that those around them were not indifferent as to whether they died or survived. Ariès also suggests that affective relationships were not frequent and that socialisation was largely out of the family's hands:

Feeling between spouses, parents and children was not necessary either to the existence or the equilibrium of the family, and was at best a bonus. Affective exchanges and social communications were therefore ensured out-side the family by a very close and warm milieu of neighbours, friends, masters and servants, children and old people in which inclination had a fairly free play. French historians now call this propensity in traditional communities towards visits, get-togethers and festivities 'sociability'.[19]

In his view, children were socialised less within the family than by a scattered but culturally homogeneous milieu that reproduced the norms, practices and values of the older generation. This both mini-mises the role of the family and leaves that of society too vague. As children grew up, became continent and learned to speak and move about, their world gradually extended outside the family household as far as village society, but not as far as society as a whole.

The chief influence was that of the peer group. Maurice Crubel-lier, working from literary or ethnographic references,[20] describes this group of young people, which was based on sexual segregation, territorial rivalry, solidarity, initiation rites and a special vocabulary. This mode of socialising children persisted for a long time over an enormous sector of French society, and it can be seen that even in the past the family never had the monopoly of educating and social-ising children, but shared these functions with other more or less institutionalised groups. What Ariès calls the 'discovery' and Cru-bellier the 'colonisation' of childhood took place to the detriment of the freedom that young children shared with their comrades. Child-hood, from six or seven to thirteen or fourteen, has always been a special period, outside traditional society and seen as such. Its dis-covery came about through the break-up of the age-group and the suppression of its freedom, but only in the case of the nineteenth-century bourgeoisie, as education increasingly encroached on it spa-tially and temporally.

Adolescence is perhaps a modern invention. Ariès maintains that this is the case, although several historians reject the idea, taking the view that every society recognises in one way or another the period from the beginning of puberty to the full exercise of adult roles. Natalie Z. Davis, studying popular cultures in the sixteenth century, writes that

although villagers have no theories about the psychological development of the young adolescent and rural society does very little to encourage the search for other forms of identity, youth organisations, in their own way, do stress that marginal period and channel the first sexual impulses.[21]

And traditional society did in fact recognise and institutionalise 'youth', a time of life generally reached after first communion, by giving it specific tasks within the community, particularly those of safeguarding the social order, watching over the private lives of couples and organising festivities.

Within the family group, education became increasingly a matter of learning a trade. As far as their strength and skill allowed, chil-dren were closely linked to the running of the family concern, look-ing after the cows or the geese, winding the spools in the weaver's shop and later participating more fully in agricultural or craft work. Adolescents started their trade training within their domestic group. In Anglo-Saxon societies too, training started early, but it was cus-tomary to place children with artisans or as servants in other fami-lies. They were socialised outside the family group, perhaps with the intention of hardening them more.

For young people in traditional societies, there was no salvation outside the family, from which everything – possessions, knowl-edge, and patrimony – came. Youth lasted for varying periods and ended at marriage. Youth and the single state were synonymous, and marriage, which imposed economic responsibilities and gave the right to licit sexuality, meant the end of youth.

But in so far as the psychological needs associated with that period of affective and sexual maturation were not explicitly recognised, as the rites of passage socialised personal tensions and made it possible to go beyond them and necessity knows no law, youth was not adolescence in our sense of the word.

Parent–child relationships in the nineteenth century

The bourgeois family. As Ariès has shown, the development of a feeling for childhood has been marked by a new awareness of the existence of the personality of the child and a lengthening of the period of childhood. As the couple withdraws from public functions and becomes more private, children, now fewer in number, are more esteemed. Marriage, as we have seen, is an institution in which interest is a predominant factor. Extending this has meant a smaller number of better-educated, better-cared-for children who will be entrusted with the task of reproducing the family model or successfully achieving its upward social movement. There is a growing feeling in both the family and society that the child is a kind of capital and that the birth of a lot of children who never reach maturity is wasteful in human, social and economic terms. Fewer but healthier and better-educated children are a sign of the interdependence of strategies of biological reproduction, education and social reproduction.

As a result of this, medicine and education assumed increasing importance. The educative function expanded, and specialisation in child health and, at the beginning of the twentieth century in psychology, led to the accumulation of a body of knowledge. It may be that social institutions to some extent removed the family's traditional functions. All of them have the same aims and help achieve a common goal accepted by parents, teachers and doctors. The new mode of education did not encroach on the territory of the family, but developed to the detriment of the peer group socialising children through contact with other children, whose cutting remarks and violence had to be endured, or by contact with other adults as a result of the learning process.

Bourgeois childhood and adolescence were marked by medical and educational provision and also by enclosure. In England, the boarding-school system spread, whereas in France day-schools were preferred. In both cases, however, children now lived in an enclosed space. Crubellier has stressed the break in bourgeois childhood, an age when the child was to be isolated, controlled and sown with the right ideas (p. 70).

During this process, a marked differentiation of parental roles was taking place. The father was the head of the domestic group and was responsible for the education of his children and its general shape, but everyday relationships were the mother's domain, and women with no outside work could actualise their potentialities in the maternal role. As Yvonne Knibiehler and Catherine Fouquet note in *L'Histoire des mères du Moyen Age à nos jours*, the new framework of liberal society had a place for female initiative. Middle-class mothers, of course, had a great deal of help in their task and enjoyed the services of governesses and nurses. At both the material and the affective level, the first months of the child's life were the responsibility of the latter. Fanny Faÿ-Sallois, in her *Les Nourrices à Paris au XIXe siècle*, estimates that during the Second Empire half the babies in Paris were breast-fed in their bourgeois homes by live-in wet nurses (p. 57). She explains the development of this practice thus:

Relieved of the burden of breast-feeding, the mother who had been replaced could now serenely enjoy the pleasure of family life without having to give up her social obligations or her wifely duties. Everything that the mother acquired, the wet-nurse lost. The latter's breasts hung wondrously heavy in her low-cut dress, and the costume she was obliged to wear both emphasised the wealth of her employer and hid a function often seen, in the imagination of the time, as 'bestial and repugnant'.[22]

Children, with their importance within the family, were brought up strictly and, by governesses or tutors, without affection. Education was based on authority and control.

The separation of children from the adult world and the development of education over an ever-increasing length of time led to the emergence of a new age in the bourgeois world, that of adolescence. Medical science also began to be aware of its specific nature and needs, which were quite distinct from those of the childhood left behind and the adult life still to come.

It was an age, created by a society believing in education, that the bourgeois family distrusted. Adolescents were still kept in their place. Girls were to remain cloistered within their homes for a long time, and boys enjoyed only a comparative freedom. The type of education received was hardly conducive to the development of the personality. Outings were also rigidly supervised and adolescents were expected to remain within the family circle. Towards the end of the century, sports clubs on the English model began to grow up.

They had an integrative function, but not at the professional level, and were self-contained in a way that permitted indirect family control. They also acted as a channel for sexual drives, but did not have the institutional weight of the youth groups of former times.

The peasant family. The peasant family had some of the characteristics of the bourgeois family, but also some of those of lower-class ones. The type of upbringing found in older societies continued unchanged, but was now in competition with that provided by the growth of formal education, which encroached on the territory of the family in as much as it deprived the domestic group of part of its labour force. It also proposed a model and provided an education conflicting with the aims of family succession. Some families, however, encouraged academic success as a way of escaping from poverty. In the nineteenth century education was the instrument by which the dominant culture controlled dominated ones and forced children to give up their native language and culture if they were to rise in the social hierarchy. It was an ally of families only when they sought a non-agricultural career for their children. Doctors critically examined family practices too, seeking to replace with their own scientific knowledge and methods, popular cures that had been handed down from mother to daughter from time immemorial and that were an intimate part of family wisdom. They did not succeed as well as schoolmasters had done, to judge by the number of such practices surviving to our own times.

The nineteenth-century child from a peasant home was the point where two cultures met and the object of both of them. Adolescence and its specific problems were barely in evidence. Either the young man remained within the traditional system, working on the family farm until he married, or he left to work in the towns and gradually became part of the working-class world.

The working-class family. In the new urban areas created by industrialisation in nineteenth-century France, the working-class family seems, during a short period, to have had no culture of its own. Its attitude to children oscillated amongst several models, and unlike the bourgeois or peasant family, it was defined by a series of negative characteristics.

It was affected by the unreliability of work and housing and had no strategy. The future was difficult to picture. What pattern of events to come could be imagined for it and its offspring when it had no patrimony and was living from hand to mouth on one or more wages? What means of envisaging a future could it have in its state of deprivation?

It took no thought for the morrow, hence its abundant fertility. The sign that the working-class family was moving towards bourgeois status was to be the sudden appearance of birth control. Instead of wondering why he should have children, the working-class man wondered why he should not. In her studies of today's subproletariat, Colette Pétonnet analyses the reasons for the high number of births currently characteristic of the most deprived families and constituting a kind of family counter-culture. When there is no hope, when the depths of poverty have been reached, 'their pregnancies are all that women can give to men who have no other way of proving their virility. . . . It is not so much a question of the child as of its conception' (p. 92).

As was also the case in peasant society, a large number of children meant the chance, once they no longer needed constant care and attention, of extra income to eke out the wages of the father or of both parents, and in a society with no provision for social security children offered a possible source of support when their parents were old.

Malthusian views and practices occur only when there is the chance of a family strategy and the hope of improving the social position. In that sense, one can say that it is not the nuclear family that encourages social mobility but a premeditated desire within the couple that prepares the way for it. This has been shown by Ariès in connection with the population of Paris:

In the space of a single generation, a prolific proletariat adopted a radically contraceptive mentality, . . . passing in one generation from a sexuality entailing an almost physiological fertility to a voluntary sterility with no counterbalance.[23]

In this working-class milieu, parental relationships were necessarily shaped by the factor of domination. Doctors, and the educational system trying to enclose children, were involved. There was an attempt to keep mothers out of factories and to encourage them to stay at home and look after their children, and one can see extraneous strategies being imposed on the working class that in wider terms were part of the aims of the dominant bourgeoisie.

Adolescence as a phenomenon was a late arrival in the working-class family. Crubellier reminds us that young workers were never called adolescents and that the term was reserved for the young of the middle classes. Without education or the sociability characteristic of traditional rural life, the young worker could only strengthen the image nineteenth-century philanthropists had of the working-class family. His behaviour was only what could be expected when such families were disorganised and incompetent, particularly with regard to their young people, who drank, fought and became delinquent. Organisations involved in social improvement were to try to 'normalise' them and turn them into adolescents who would be rebels only within their own families, but this was an aim that was to be constantly questioned and one that the consumer society has made even more difficult to achieve.

THE FAMILY LIFE CYCLE

Talcott Parsons's ideas (see Chapter 3, 'Social and kinship change') now have very little influence. His view of the rigid distinction between paternal and maternal roles as producing a stabilising framework for the child's personality has remained largely theoretical and unconnected to real family behaviour. The notion of a cycle of family life introduces a chronological dimension and is therefore nearer to actual practices.

The cycle of family life can be established on the threefold basis of the number of positions within the domestic group (father-mother-young child, number of children, etc.), respective age distribution and changes in roles (particularly in the father's from when he is working until he retires). The following is the framework of the cycle of family life proposed here, characterised by its various roles[24]:

1. The young married couple with no children.
2. Young parents, with children up to three years of age.
3. Domestic group with children of pre-school age (from three to six years of age with younger brothers and sisters).
4. Domestic group with children of school age (eldest child between six and twelve years of age, with younger brothers or sisters).
5. Domestic group with adolescent children (with the eldest between twelve and twenty years of age).
6. Domestic group with one young adult (from the eldest child reaching twenty years of age until the first child leaves home and marries).
7. Domestic group helping its children settle in life until the last has achieved this.
8. 'Post-parental' domestic group, a period lasting from the time the youngest child leaves home until the father retires.
9. Ageing domestic group after father's retirement.

This analytic framework indicates transition from one phase to another, which are critical points in the cycle. The parental roles it implies necessitate adapting from one period to another and read-justing aims and means in accordance with the age of the children and the stage in question.

This system has been used by researchers to classify family samples. For example, in a given population, the duration of marriages, the size of the domestic group or the age of husbands at given stages of the cycle have been established. With regard to the education of children, researchers working in the field of social change cut across the stages with variables such as the size of residence, the type of domestic group, the level of income and the size of the kinship and friendship networks.

This representation of the cycle of family life has received a great deal of criticism. It is very much influenced by its time and environment, and focusses on American middle-class families. Consequently, it is difficult to apply it to other times and places. Jean Cuisenier has criticised it from two points of view. In the first place, it totally disregards all types of family organisation with no legal sanction. Nowadays, for example, the cycle starts more and more frequently before marriage, with young people living together. There are family communities. What type of cycle are divorced people in, unmarried mothers, divorced women and so on? Second, it seems less valid if one takes into account changes in family models, such as the disappearance of the authoritarian father over the last few years. Experience is no longer handed down from one generation to another, and parents can no longer propose the models of their own upbringing to their children. All this means that it is not so much the way in which different phases are linked that is critical but rather the totality of the phases themselves.

Cuisenier also maintains that the cycle is at most a descriptive representation and that its analytic value is more doubtful, as there is no consensus on the criteria for establishing the phases. Such differences are fundamental, since they represent more or less diametrically opposed views of the family, depending on whether it is seen as all the pairs of related individuals making it up (husband–wife, father–daughter and so on) or in terms of its functions. If the latter is the case, comparisons are difficult as the family as an institution does not occupy an identical place in every society.[25]

Although it is peripheral to our study, the influence of psychology and psychoanalysis must also be stressed. From D. W. Winnicott to Françoise Dolto, doctors and researchers have shown the great importance of the first days and months of the infant's life and their influence on the subsequent development of the personality of the young child. They have also put great stress on the fundamental relationship between the mother and the child until it is weaned and on the role of infantile sexuality. Psychological theories have been very important in medical circles, but the often inept way in which they have been popularised by the mass media has meant an inadvertently ideological approach. There is no scientific proof that absolute paternal authority is good or that the mother–child relationship should exclude all others. A certain humility is called for here. Grandiose theories would be out of place, and those that, in the name of science, seek to impose behaviour aimed at solving problems that have nothing to do with the well-being of the child should be mistrusted. If we were to stress the primacy and the exclusive nature of the mother–child relationship, could we not reduce the problems associated with the economic crisis, unemployment and so on by suggesting that women should stay at home?

NEW KINDS OF PARENTS AND CHILDREN?

The period of natural control of fertility was perhaps the corollary of a new interest in the child, but that did not necessarily mean that life was easy or childhood a happy time. We have seen that in the bourgeois family children were subject to strong parental or, more frequently, paternal authority. This was often typified in that characteristically middle-class saying that children do not speak at table (always assuming that they are allowed to eat with their parents). Methods became more flexible when paediatrics and infantile psychiatry began to maintain that too close a dependence was not beneficial to the formation of character and to discover the need for some autonomy for the child.

In the 1950s, we exchanged a relatively repressive model of upbringing for a more permissive one, but cultural differences between one class and another and one country and another are still very noticeable. The United States represents one of the extreme forms of the new permissive model, in which parent–child relationships are part of a context in which children are the first concern. Family values revolve around them, their development and their education, and everything is organised in terms of their needs. In this model, the place of the mother is both disproportionately great and yet quite secondary. She does not work, and caring for the younger children and educating the older ones fall into her province. She has some very responsible functions, but at the same time her power is limited by that of experts such as doctors, teachers, psychologists and so on. It is true that the degree of control varies amongst social categories, and that more generally where family difficulties are concerned, but it is always there and perhaps all the more so for being internalised.

The few surveys we can consult show that models connected with the way a child is brought up are now closely linked to social category. That on *Liberté 81* (22 February 1981), conducted by *Le Monde*, contained a question giving four definitions of 'the most important thing that young children should be taught'. The replies were broken down according to profession, political allegiance, age, sex and religious practice. The first reply ('We must respect existing rules') was preferred by those engaged in agriculture, industrialists and higher managers, members of the far right and right-wing political parties, those under twenty years of age, those over forty-five and practising Catholics. The second ('You have to work hard and get a position or job') was chosen by industrialists, higher managers and engineers, Communists, members of right-wing political parties, men and those over forty. The third ('You have to make your own way') attracted middle managers, students, the unemployed, ecologists, those on the left and the extreme left, women, those under forty and those with no religious beliefs. The fourth ('Do what you feel like doing') was preferred by workers, primary-school teachers, technicians, those on the extreme left and left, ecologists, those under thirty-five and those with no religious beliefs.

Four very different concepts of upbringing related to political opinions and professional milieu, are thus apparent, and this is confirmed if one compares the findings here with those of a national sample of parents.

Table 6.6 gives comparative per centages of responses to the same questions in *Liberté 81* and in surveys conducted in France in 1975 and 1980.

The 'population' surveyed in the *Liberté 81* study was of a very particular kind, being largely composed of intellectuals and teachers, mainly left wing and chiefly male. The replies to the questions on the degree of freedom enjoyed by young people were markedly more liberal than in the national sample. It therefore seems that opinions are determined by a range of socio-professional variables as well as age.

We will now return to the analytic framework of the cycle of family life and follow parents and their offspring from birth until they leave home. Our procedure will be to raise one or two problems specific to each phase of the cycle rather than to present an exhaustive study.

Table 6.6. *Some people say that young people have too much freedom nowadays. Do you think that this is?* (in %)

	Liberté 81	National sample (COFREMCA June 80)
Completely true	5.6	36.3
True to some extent	28.4	30.2
False to some extent	27.9	17.4
Completely false	36.3	14.6

Some children do not tell their parents everything.
Would you find that normal or not? (in %)

	Liberté 81	National sample of parents (IFOP Nov. 75)
Normal at any age	49	17
Normal over 12	12.6	6
Normal after 15 or 16	27.4	27
Never normal at any age	8.6	47

Source: Le Monde, 22 Feb. 1981.

The young child

After birth, mother and child establish an intense emotional bond capable of generating conflict. The child has to acquire the basic elements of psychomotor development and to move beyond the relationship with the mother. She too must be able to pursue her personal development in terms of current norms. It is very difficult to judge the impact of psychoanalytic research on behaviour, since on the whole it reaches the public at large only through the media, via radio and television programmes and the major newspapers, as well as through the medium of practitioners or paediatricians or those in charge of kindergartens or paediatric departments in hospitals. Nor are specialists always in agreement. Some think that mothers need only be left to follow their instincts and their own common sense; others see them as incompetents to be fitted into a highly professionalized medical structure.

We will not examine such problems in detail and intend only to examine early childhood in relation to conjugal, family and social institutions. The first question to arise, given the increasing number of working women, is that of the way in which very small children should be looked after.

The possibility of a real choice – to work or not, to look after one's child oneself or to find an alternative – has to be examined at the very start. Surveys carried out by the Institut National d'Etudes Démographiques (INED) have shown that 74 per cent of men and women, whether working or not, think that up to the age of two or three a child should be looked after by its own mother, and 95 per cent accept the idea of two months' unpaid leave for a mother working before giving birth. At the same time, nine out of ten women want to be able to work part time, and three out of four would like to start work again, mostly for financial reasons.[26]

Anne-Marie Coutrot examines the bases of these mutually contradictory declarations and the social constraints on the family that mean that women only have the illusion of choice.[27] The only ones to be free of it are women who can afford to have their children looked after in satisfactory conditions, but even they are subject to the pressures of a 'maternally orientated' society in which the 'excessive value placed on motherhood becomes the most powerful tool for the exploitation of women', and their whole environment can exert hidden and guilt-producing pressures on them. Difficulties are compounded in the case of other women who want to work when they have young children, and working hours, transport and badly organised social amenities are all problems. There is a widespread image of the 'feckless mother' who 'lets her children fend for themselves' and is seen as blameworthy by those around her and by the institution looking after her children.

It seems harder today to have a child looked after than it was to keep it alive in times gone by. A 1976 survey conducted in France looked at the provision for caring for the 800,000 children under three with two parents working. The survey revealed 50,759 children in official kindergartens, 25,910 in family kindergartens taking children from six weeks to three years of age and 66,949 recognised nurses. In effect, 143,618 children were in institutions organised and supervised by public authorities, 70,000 were looked after at home by persons paid for the work, and 85,000 were looked after by a grandmother. The other 500,000 were looked after by 'unofficial' nurses, by a neighbour, or in some other makeshift way.[28]

To these figures can be added those for children old enough to attend the *école maternelle*, which currently receives almost 500,000 children from the age of two, and their number is still increasing. The per centage attending these schools increased from 40 to 55 between 1963 and 1964 and to 70 in 1974. In 1974, 40 per cent of children under the age of four were attending such schools.[29]

The way children were looked after varied according to social and professional categories. Women in higher management positions made use of paid help; clerical workers, midway between managers and manual workers, operated at an appropriately intermediate level, using either paid help or a member of their family. Female clerical workers married to middle managers or skilled workers most often used the kindergarten. In the United States, day-care centres are not as commonly used as in France. In 1973, 14.5 per cent of children aged three and 34.2 per cent of those aged four were enrolled in nursery schools, which are used almost exclusively by middle-class parents. As in France, the day-care centre movement was originally associated with philanthropic help for unmarried mothers, and they are still chiefly used by this group. American children with working mothers are usually looked after within the family. In the case of black or Hispanic ethnic groups, both parents manage to adjust their working hours to ensure that they can take turns to look after the children, with other relatives helping out occasionally. In the white middle classes, children are usually looked after at home by paid help.[30]

The provision for young children of working mothers is thus rather a hit-or-miss affair. Public institutions, which are quantitatively insufficient and qualitatively sometimes not all they might be, are often criticised. Asking rather incredulously whether a mother places her young child in the care of an institution is an insidious way of criticising her and making her feel inadequate. It is not the system itself which is harmful for young children, but the way in which it is organised (or not organised). An energetic policy for looking after young children would help to solve the problems of young mothers. If it is not too rigidly organised, public care offers a collective means of socialising young children in a way beneficial to their personalities.

It is not surprising to observe a correlation between the frequency with which married women are obliged to give up their job and the type of job itself (Tables 6.7 and 6.8). Given the fact that problems vary in different social categories, some women choose the most radical solution, that of stopping working. Workers in commerce, in manual jobs, in industry and service jobs are most often those who give up their work when the first or second child is born. The work done by female manual workers does not provide much job satisfaction and is badly paid. When it becomes difficult to put up with the loss of earnings following from stopping work, such women take up

Table 6.7. *Married women leaving paid employment after a birth, by educational level and socio-professional category* (in %)

Educational level	Leaving	Socio-professional category	Leaving
		Agricultural	
No qualifications	54.1	workers	34.4[a]
CEP (primary school certificate)	46.1	Higher managers	7.5
		Middle managers	
CAP (vocational certificate)	31.8	(office)	14.2
		Clerical	
BEPC (school certificate at age 15)	16.7	office	21.1
		commerce	48.5
		Manual workers	45.6
Baccalaureate or		Service jobs	
technical diploma	12.6	domestic service	
		and cleaning women	76.6

[a]No accurate figures available.

Table 6.8. *Mothers giving up their jobs, by sequence of birth and socio-professional category* (in %)

	Manual	Clerical	Higher or middle manager, liberal profession	All
First birth				
Number surveyed	151	272	161	673
Gave up job	67	71	86	73
Did not give up job	33	29	14	27
Second birth				
Number surveyed	76	112	94	356
Gave up job	39	71	88	70
Did not give up job	61	29	12	30

Source: Nadine Lefaucheur, *Jeunes couples ou nouveaux couples*, p. 27. From a survey by the *Institut National de Statistiques et d'Etudes Economiques*, 1977.

a job that can be fitted in with their family responsibilities such as work done at home or cleaning jobs. What is particularly striking overall, however, is the large number of women who manage to keep on working even after the birth of their second child.

These figures give some idea of the tensions to which mothers of young children are subjected. They are told mutually incompatible things. Psychologists say how important the mother–child relationship is, while at the same time, mothers are led to believe in the value of self-fulfilment and consequently wish to keep their jobs. In unfavourable economic circumstances, two incomes represent some sort of insurance if one of the spouses should become unemployed.

The mother–child relationship, which might be thought to be the most natural of all, is deeply marked by the social and cultural forces of every age. In the nineteenth century, with its belief in health and hygiene, children in certain families were taken away from their mothers for medical reasons and brought up under the supervision of experts in institutions. For their own sake, they were removed from a family environment that, as was discovered later, was better despite all its failings, than any institution for the latter could not provide rich affective relationships. Later, psychoanalysis too helped show the importance of the mother–child relationship.

At the moment, stressing its importance may seem suspect when the economic situation is bad, and when it has been over-emphasised, the favourable influence of a double environment has been neglected. We have recently begun to see again the importance for the child of development in a peer group and the role of the father. With regard to the latter, opinions and to a lesser extent practices have been changing. The father is being re-established. According to a public-opinion survey, 54 per cent of French women thought that bringing up a child during the first three years of its life should be the joint responsibility of the father and the mother. Thirty-one per cent thought that the mother should play the major part, helped by the father, and only 10 per cent thought it should be the mother's responsibility alone. And indeed, a number of young fathers do look after very young children. Seeing a man pushing a pram is no longer an amusing sight.[31]

The child from four to twelve

When they are not in kindergarten, children leave the immediate parental sphere at three or four and come into contact with other socialising factors such as the peer group and, in particular, school. From roughly four to twelve, they have certain dominant personality traits. This age-range is, of course, fairly wide but in comparison with adolescence it is a homogeneous period. Parents have to help children through certain stages that influence the development of their personality, for example progress towards autonomy, the control of aggression, sexual individuation and the shaping of identity.

In helping children become autonomous, parents have to help them cope with inevitable separations. Having some previous experience of collective institutions and being used to meeting people other than their mothers, even though the latter remains the central point of their existence, make such progress, and particularly beginning school, much less painful. Socialisation has most often been studied in terms of maternal relationships, which is inevitable given their apparently outstanding importance, and studies of children's relationships with their fathers and siblings are lacking.

Parental values, and hence the way children are brought up, vary from class to class and from culture to culture. The north of France is different from the south, and in the United States, white, black and Puerto Rican families are not the same. American studies of aggression in children of this age-group have shown that the degree of parental tolerance varies, with working-class parents, for example, having a lower threshold of intolerance than middle-class ones. Parent–child relationships are much more egalitarian in middle-class families. In working-class ones, parents expect a higher level of order and obedience. Parental roles also differ within couples according to social and cultural origins. It seems that in the United States, working-class fathers tend to leave all the responsibility for their children's education to the mother, and the general view is that maternal domination is a structural feature of the black American family.[32]

Another feature of the development of the child's personality is the need for sexual identity. But what roles should be assigned to the sexes? The allocation of roles based on sex seems to be shifting nowadays, and psychologists and sociologists are investigating the ways in which they are transmitted. Elina Gianini, for example, points out that babies are masculine or feminine even before birth, that girls are seen as inferior and that mothers and institutions (schools and illustrations in school-books in particular) help perpetuate outmoded sexual stereotypes.[33]

A high degree of institutionalised education isolates children and separates them from adults. Before education became compulsory, it was a secondary activity and children still lived in the adult world of the house, the workshop and the street. When it did become compulsory, even if there was no question of boarding-school, children were removed from that adult world and put into a separate one of their own. The complementary nature of family and school is evident in some, but not all, social categories. The educational system enables the middle classes to achieve their goal of social mobility and imposes the cultural values of the bourgeoisie that introduced it. Further down the social scale, congruence gradually gives way to contrast, but there is a complicity in a single system of social reproduction at the middle-class level and no trace of the hiatus between family and educational values that is so much a feature of working-class relationships with the educational system. The latter does not offer poorer families a way to social and economic improvement and simply delays their aim of getting their children out to work as soon as possible. By including technical education, the system offers a concrete response to deprived families, but its initial aim is doomed to failure since it blocks social mobility.

School and family are not the only areas governing the lives of children from four to twelve, a time when all their other potentialities – artistic, athletic and the like – have to be encouraged initially by the family. Out of school, the child may have judo or dancing lessons, learn to play the flute or to make pots, and it is the parents who have to organise all these activities. Nowadays schools, youth centres, music centres, sports clubs and similar institutions are overwhelmed by the demand from all social classes. In addition to all this, for a child in good health, there are occasional visits to the paediatrician, the speech therapist, the dentist and so on, and it is clear what a burden a child, and even more so several children, can put on parents.

Far from being eroded, as is often claimed, family functions in this area have multiplied, diversified and become more complex over the last ten years or so. As Noëlle Gérome says:

The responsibility for the child's education is divided amongst several kinds of bodies, amongst which the family group's particular role is to delegate its functions and to synthesise and supervise the provision of health care and education.[34]

Even if he does not object to changing nappies and feeding the baby, a young father is less in evidence at this stage of the child's life. Mothers have heavy responsibilities for this age-group and have consequently organised matters on a group basis, making use of neighbourhood, kinship and mutual-help networks.

In conclusion, it must be pointed out that there are few good studies of parent–child relationships at this age. Historians and anthropologists have been more particularly concerned with the infant, and Anglo-Saxon sociology is not often easy to adapt to French society. Also, things change quickly, and what was true ten years ago is no longer true today.

The child and the family

The adolescent

In addition to parents, grandparents, school, judo and dancing lessons, something new begins to loom on the child's horizon: the peer group, which, in the period we are about to examine, plays a major part.

The gang. Little is known about gangs apart from what the police and the courts are aware of, and that gives us a biased view of their activities, since it refers only to those punishable by law. Crubellier, surveying the literature on the subject, notes that the 'delinquency and violence of teenagers is a means of retaliation against adult society, which will not give them a status of their own'.[35] In pre-industrial society, the ways in which young people were organised were officially recognised, whereas today the gang is a more or less underground group, informally organised and opposed to the values of society (and seems, in France, however, to be less frequently organised by a boss or leader than those in the United States). As a phenomenon it transcends the parent–child relationship and is properly speaking a 'problem of society'. Gang or individual delinquency is also closely linked to social class. Maurice Cusson points out that teenagers from higher-income groups escape being labelled as delinquents because their parents are able to resolve the problems they raise without recourse to legal procedures by paying for damage and returning stolen money and persuading the victims not to go to the police.[36]

The gang has a socialising function that complements the functions of parents and of school, and plays an important part in everything to do with sexual information and growth. In pre-industrial society, sexual education was acquired by contact with nature, to some extent by observation of what was going on around the child, who had access to sexual games and symbols. In bourgeois society, the subject is still taboo, and even today the sexual information given by parents is minimal. Belonging to a gang means that sexual development is no longer a solitary and disturbing process at a time when the age of both puberty and the first sexual experience is lower than in the past. Permissiveness on the part of parents seems to be increasing as contraceptive information becomes more generally available. Sociologists therefore agree that gangs have a functional role, as their tension and rebellion integrate their members. They enable teenagers to leave the framework of the family and enter into society at large, where they can put into practice norms and values they have internalised despite their 'aggressive' behaviour within the family.

New kinds of parents and children?

Since the 1950s, parents have relaxed their control of their children's choice of friends. Other social mechanisms have come into operation, notably that of the principle of control by the environment, and in France the separation of residence and school has had a regulating effect. Indeed, it is parents living in large housing developments with a deliberate social mix who are most hesitant to let their children go out in case they meet children from other milieux. Parental attitudes towards freedom to go out are different with regard to boys and girls, particularly at this age. With girls, they are chiefly worried for reasons to do with sex and tend to be more rigid in their control. With boys, their main cause for concern is physical accidents or trouble of all kinds that they might encounter with friends of whom the parents disapprove.

Parental and teenage values: continuity or conflict? Parental attitudes often involve coming to some compromise with teenage children. From the point of view of the former, the problem can be formulated in terms of the latitude they give their children and where they draw the line. The latter see the problem as one of knowing just how far to go. What time they come home, whether they can use the moped, sexual relationships and smoking and drugs are all a matter for discussion.

Relationships between parents and teenage children also have to do with teenagers' participation in family life, their part in decisions about family holidays and helping at home and communication, with a reasonable balance between their private world and a reasonable amount of interaction. They can be all the more complex because by the time their children have reached adolescence parents are older, have spent fifteen or more years together, and their own relationship may be at a critical stage. They may indeed disagree about the models they would like to put into practice (which could be different or even contrary) as well as about the norms they have accepted and are obliged to formulate explicitly when it is time to hand them on to a child. Their values, which are a result of their own mode of socialisation, may at that point turn out to be more different than they had previously realised. The greater the difference in the social origins of husband and wife, the more violent the conflict is likely to be between one parent and another and between parents and children.

There is no simple reply to the question of whether adolescents accept or reject their parents' values. At the moment, the parents of teenagers are in a difficult phase. It is a commonplace to say that social values are changing, particularly in sexual matters. What the parents have received from their own childhood can no longer guide their children. In the United States, psychologists have noted the adverse effects of residential mobility, which necessitates a new psychological adjustment for the children each time the family moves. Bronfenbrenner has emphasised the isolation of the child and the teenager, which is perhaps an extreme effect of the American system. Teenagers, he writes, are deprived of their parents and society in general. The demarcation between residential and working zones, the disappearance of the neighbourhood, the influence of television, working mothers and specialists to look after children have all created a gap between the world of adults and that of children.[37] Edward Shorter in *The Making of the Modern Family* detects a lack of continuity in the values and opinions of children who refuse to act as guardians of family identity.

That is very far from certain. Children still learn to understand society in terms of relatively unchanged models. The myth of the generation gap is taking a long time to die.

Annick Percheron has shown that although the attitudes of young people are very much motivated by everything connected with personal freedom, they all have some conservative features with regard to values and norms.[38] Thus, basing her conclusions on a polling-institute survey that she directed in 1976, Percheron shows that the greatest differences of opinion between parents and children were those concerned with young people living together and the use of the pill, in other words things directly concerned with daily life and the peer group. On the other hand, most of them did not question the need for rules in the way society is organised or the social usefulness of a certain permanence of religion and the family (see Table 6.9).

At the political level, there is the same gap between parents and children as regards particular issues, but this becomes less marked with regard to major social problems.

These observations are valid for all social milieux and the consistent nature of parental and children's attitudes towards a specific problem such as continuing education. Parents in the upper and middle social categories see the educational system as a means of acquiring social status and a social image for their children, who share these views and go to university in large numbers. Similarly, in working-class milieux, parents and children both agree on the pointlessness of education and its inability to help them achieve the aim they both share, that of starting work and getting a wage as soon as possible. On this point, young people, their peer group and parents all think alike. The sixteen-year-olds are anxious to leave an institution that was not made for them.

New kinds of parents and children?

Table 6.9. *Opinion survey of parents and children.*

Questions	16–18s' replies %	Parents' replies %	Difference
More and more young people are living together without getting married (not shocking, not at all shocking)	76	41	35
Some people say that religion is an area where we shouldn't make too many changes (tend not to agree, totally disagree)	43	29	14
Some people say that keeping the family as it has always been is the most important thing (tend not to agree, totally disagree)	22	10	12

Source: Annick Percheron, *Se faire entendre: morale quotidienne et attitudes politiques des jeunes,* in Henri Mendras, ed., *La sagesse et le désordre* (Paris: Gallimard, 1980), pp. 144–5.

Youth's rebellions are directed against society rather than against the family, as J. R. Gillis points out in his *Youth in History:*

Nowhere in Europe or America is there very much evidence of a severe "generation gap," despite the student and worker upheavals of the 1960s and 1970s. Studies of "young rebels" indicate that, while there is a certain degree of child–parent tension, the major thrust of youthful discontent is directed not at family but outward, at social, political, and academic institutions that are only indirectly identified with the older generation. Young people and their parents are more likely to be united than divided on basic political and social issues, tensions arising over means rather than ends, a reflection of the normal pace of historical change rather than any intrafamilial disruption or severe hostility between groups on the basis of age alone. In many contemporary situations, the confrontation between young and old is actually conflict between persons of differing class position – students versus police, young workers versus employers. Therefore, we must be careful not to mistake these events as evidence of deep generational divisions.[39]

However, adolescents have their own culture. They are fascinated by television and its heroes and also have a culture based on sound. Rock, folk and new wave music is a means of private escape and of distancing themselves from their elders. Although parents have taken over certain emblems – jeans, physical exercise (sport, which was once an activity for young people, is now an adult one) – the music that they take so little interest in still helps create their own world for the young. There is the collective phenomenon of the concert, the hi-fi belting out unusual and exciting sounds and – the latest technical innovation – individual headphones creating a world of music that cuts the listener off from the real world and from other people.

In conclusion, it is important to stress that we have very few studies of parent–child relationships at various stages of the life cycle. Too little attention has been paid to the brother–sister relationship, for example, as if the parent–child relationship took no account of horizontal relationships between siblings or between siblings and parents. We have chosen to remain within the domestic group and to ignore the influence and role of members of the kinship group, which is important even if they are not co-resident (although it must be admitted that we know of virtually no studies of this topic). The study of parental and maternal attitudes should broaden to include those of grandparents and aunts, amongst whom can also be found behaviour patterns based on both authority and permissiveness.

The few models we have described, although they are certainly not complete, are also liable to change rapidly. In so far as there is a close connection between conjugal and parental roles, one might think that development and change in the latter might influence the former. If men devote more time to their homes and women to their jobs, sexual identification processes and the rigid sexual attribution of parental attitudes will also change.

But we must go beyond major, easy changes and reflect on deep and lasting trends. Crubellier, seeing children as being courted by the consumer society through advertising, show business, motor bikes and jeans, wonders whether they are not indirectly coming under the control of adults again.[40]

SUGGESTED READING

Basic works

Ariès, Philippe. *Histoire des populations françaises et de leurs attitudes devant la vie depuis le XVIIIe siècle.* 2d ed. Paris: Le Seuil, 1976.
  L'Enfant et la vie familiale sous l'Ancien Régime. 2d ed. Paris: Le Seuil, 1973. (The preface gives a descriptive bibliography of works on the subject since the first edition. Published in English as *Centuries of Childhood.* London: Penguin, 1973.)
Crubellier, Maurice. *L'Enfant et la jeunesse dans la société française.* Paris: Colin, 1979.

Suggested reading

De Mause, Lloyd, ed. *The History of Childhood*. New York: Harper & Row, 1974.

Gillis, John. *Youth and History*. New York and London: Academic Press, 1974.

Hunt, David. *Parents and Children in History: Psychology of Family Life in Early Modern France*. New York: Basic Books, 1970.

Laslett, Peter, et al., eds. *Bastardy and Its Comparative History*. London: Arnold, 1980.

Demographic change and contraception

Chaunu, Pierre. 'Malthusianisme démographique et malthusianisme économique'. *Annales Economies, Sociétés, Civilisations*, 1–2(1972): 1–9.

Dupâquier, Jacques, and Maurice Lachiver. 'Les Débuts de la contraception en France ou les deux malthusianismes'. *Annales Economies, Sociétés, Civilisations* 6(1969): 1391–1406.

'Enfants et sociétés'. *Annales de demographie historique*. Paris: Mouton, 1973.

The child in pre-industrial society

Gelis, Jacky, Mireille Laget and Marie-France Morel. *Entrer dans la vie*. Paris: Gallimard, 1978.

Knibiehler, Yvonne, and Catherine Fouquet. *L'Histoire des mères du Moyen Age à nos jours*. Paris: Montalba, 1980. (Also covers the present day.)

Lebrun, François. *La Vie conjugale sous l'Ancien Régime*. Paris: Colin, 1975.

Anthropological works on child–parent relationships

Loux, Françoise. *Le Jeune enfant et son corps dans la médecine traditionnelle*. Paris: Flammarion, 1978.

Pétonnet, Colette. *On est tous dans le brouillard*. Paris: Galilée, 1979.

Zonabend, Françoise. 'L'Enfance dans un village français'. *Revue internationale de Sciences Sociales* 31(1979): 534–49.

The Enduring Memory. Manchester: Manchester University Press, 1985.

The bourgeois family

Faÿ-Sallois, Fanny. *Les Nourrices à Paris au XIXᵉ siècle*. Paris: Payot, 1980.

The contemporary family

Boltanski, Luc. 'Prime education et morale de classe'. *Cahiers du Centre de Sociologie européenne*. Paris: Mouton, 1969.

Frischer, D. *Les Mères celibataires volontaires*. Paris: Nathan, 1981.

'La Famille, la crèche et l'école maternelle'. *Informations sociales* 1–2(1977).

'Les jeunes parents et la garde de leurs enfants'. *Informations sociales* 3(1980).

The child and the family

Percheron, Annick. 'Se faire entendre: morale quotidienne et attitudes politiques des jeunes'. In *La Sagesse et le désordre*. Ed. Henri Mendras. Paris: Gallimard, 1980.

Rapoport, Rhona, Robert Rapoport and Ziona Strelitz. *Fathers, Mothers and Society, towards New Alliances*. New York: Basic Books, 1977.

Psychoanalytic approaches

Bettelheim, Bruno. *La Forteresse vide*. Paris: Gallimard, 1969.

Dolto, Françoise. *Lorsque l'enfant parait*. Paris: Le Seuil, 1977.

Winnicott, D. W. *L'Enfant et sa famille, les premières relations*. Paris: Payot, 1978.

Psychosociological approaches

Bronfenbrenner, Urie. 'Socialization and Social Class through Time and Space'. In *Readings in Social Psychology*. Ed. Eleanor E. Maccoby, Theodore M. Newcomb and Eugene L. Hartley. New York: Holt, Rinehart & Winston, 1958.

Chombart de Lauwe, Marie-José. 'L'Image de l'enfant et sa signification personnelle et collective'. *Bulletin de psychologie* 4(1969): 614–20.

Un monde autre: l'enfance, de ses représentations au mythe. Paris: Payot, 1971.

Zazzo, Bianka. *Psychologie différentielle de l'adolescence*. Paris: PUF, 1972.

PART THREE

Domestic roles and activities

Chapter 7

〰〰〰

Roles within the couple in the nineteenth century

With household structures relatively unchanged, kin relationships still active, marriage still between partners of the same social origins and still combining love and freedom in its ideology, perhaps the family as an institution has not changed? Its structures may seem relatively stable, but behaviour and attitudes have not remained static.

A COMPLEX PROBLEM

The scarcity of sources and their unhelpful nature

It is no easy matter to study roles within the couple in bygone times. Our analysis of relationships between parents and children has given us some idea of the methodological difficulties encountered in studying attitudes, and the problem is even greater with a subject like the present one. We have no statistics comparable to figures for births and marriages to give a long-term overview of developments. Sources for different times and places are not identical and comparison is difficult. When we are dealing with questions of our own time, we can conduct surveys or ask couples about their opinions and their behaviour, but that is not possible when we are dealing with the past. This means that we have to consult literature, or works by experts in folklore, and may get a distorted picture. Historical and anthropological research also provides basic sources, but the approach of the two disciplines is not always exactly the same. There have been very few studies in the area we are now investigating, and up to a point we will have to dig around in research material, some of which deals principally with the organization of work and some with women. Other material less directly relevant to our

201

subject – such as research on prostitution – nevertheless provides a special perspective on what we are examining here.

The problems encountered with sources also arise from the fact that they have to be interpreted. Here, we are in the delicate area of attitudes and behaviour, and we have to be able to distinguish between rules, models and norms on the one hand and practices on the other, between what is said and what is actually done. We also have to reject the temptation to *judge*, to sort out what seems good from what does not. Certain propositions are tainted with an ethnocentric and markedly ideological bias. This means that it is easy to give a quick sketch of the situation in past times and produce a kind of horrifying but false picture of them for the contemporary couple. It is crudely simplistic to emphasise the improved situation of present-day women simply because it has become normal for them to go out to work. This is just another received idea about the family that one or two detailed studies now available have shown to be false or at least superficial. Where family change is concerned, nothing is simple.

Difficulties of this kind explain why there are at the moment very few sound theories about conjugal roles. The most articulate accounts of social change and developments in the model of the family have come basically from the Anglo-Saxon countries (see Chapter 8). In France, their theories have produced little response. Contemporary sociology in this area is making increasing use of psychological approaches, historical data and anthropological methods.

From role to status

By helping us to compare it with others, anthropology enables us to put our own culture in perspective, and this is particularly important where roles are concerned. In *The Family*, William Goode stresses that the sexual distribution of roles is basically a cultural matter and depends only to a small degree on biological considerations. A man cannot give birth to a child or suckle it. He is stronger and can run quicker than a woman, who might be temporarily handicapped by her periods or pregnancy. But women also have great physical stamina and enough speed to carry out a number of difficult tasks. What is seen as a male task in one society may be a female one in another, and any division is either culturally determined or based on a complex range of factors of which the least important are biological ones.

Carrying out a specific task also has symbolic meaning. Some carry greater honour than others and confer authority. In three quarters of primitive societies, women grind the grain, carry water, cook, make the clothes, weave, gather fruits and make pots. They can do all this near their homes and without leaving their children. In most societies, men watch the flocks, hunt, fish, cut wood, excavate ores, make musical instruments, build houses and so on. Some of these jobs demand a certain physical strength, others some movement away from the home. Others can be carried out with no expenditure of physical energy and near to home. Harvesting, on the other hand, calls for physical strength and in some societies is carried out by men and in others by women.

A study of the way tasks are divided in exotic societies shows that men could carry out all the female duties, but do not, and that the specifically male ones do not take up all their time. The same is true, as we will see, for peasant societies and present-day ones. The division of labour is based on neither biology nor equality. There is a further important factor involved, which underlies all societies: Whatever tasks men carry out are by definition the most honorific.

There is no society in which men and women are free to choose which tasks to carry out. Those involving control, management, decisions – those at the highest level and demanding no physical strength – are masculine ones. In both industrial and exotic societies, men are opposed to women carrying out such tasks and are themselves loath to carry out female ones. This can be seen in China, on the Israeli *kibbutzim* and in our own industrial societies, even if women have gained some sort of entry to the masculine world of work.

The distinction between role and status is sometimes vague, and we will take care to let each of the authors referred to keep his or her chosen titles. Nevertheless, we need a certain precision in the words we choose. Social psychologists define role as the behavioural response of an individual to social norms and cultural models. For an individual, a role means adopting concrete behaviour patterns that are expected, in our case within the couple, and more generally in society as a whole. It is merely the first stage in an organisational system that is interlocked with status in a very complex manner. In terms of the definition proposed by Henri Mendras in *Éléments de sociologie,* we can see status as the interplay of all the different social roles played by an individual or the reconstitution of his various positions. In the end, he is identified with his status that, in an industrial society, is defined in terms of job, income and life-style. Within the couple, roles and status are closely linked. The importance of the allocation of roles on a sex basis is made explicit by the fact that they determine the place of each person within the home and in society. The connotation attached to a role, however, can change. Thus the present low esteem in which domestic work is held is a recent phenomenon linked to the development of a society with values orientated towards productivity, efficiency, mechanisation and automation. In the past, work in the home, and hence a domestic role, conferred high status. Evelyne Sullerot, in her article 'Des Changements dans le partage des rôles', notes that in the past women often played down the importance of their own roles, emphasising their negative, demeaning or limiting character rather than seeking to make them the basis of conscious organised pov'er. Studies of attitudes often show that working women do not justify the fact by an apologia for work itself but by criticising staying at home, and women who stay at home explain their situation by describing how harshly alienated women are in the world of work, rather than by stressing the power of a wife and mother.

For these reasons, roles within the couple can be studied only within the overall framework of a society and its culture. The importance of economic and social change also makes it important to divide this analysis into two sections, one dealing with the period before the Industrial Revolution and the other the period after it.

Apart from noble and middle-class families, the population of France until 1850 was largely a peasant one. The model of the peasant household persisted well into the twentieth century, but new ones, emerging from the changes connected with the growth of mechanisation and urbanisation after the Industrial Revolution, created one type of relationship in middle-class couples and another in working-class ones.

PEASANT HOUSEHOLDS

An image of masculine authority

In the peasant household, domestic group and farm were not clearly distinguished. It was at once a place of residence and a place consuming its own products. Marriage, family and work were all linked in a particular form of economic organisation. If we accept the hypothesis that status is assigned as a result of the tasks and roles each person has within the household and that the relationships within the couple must be studied in conjunction with social organisation as a whole, the peasant household offers a model within which the sexes were relatively well balanced. However, the problem of the vesting of authority was central to the community's preoccupations, for the family cell, which was a microcosm of it, had to work according to the same principles. Consequently, masculine authority was publicly affirmed and, in appearance at least, had to be maintained within each household.

At the very time when the couple were being united, various items of peasant lore evident during the religious ceremonies emphasised the importance of who would wield authority. They were based on a symbolism that a shared cultural identity enabled the whole group to understand at once. If it was a struggle to get the ring on the bride's finger, or if the groom knelt on her apron, these were noticed and were so many signs of who would 'wear the trousers'. The couple in fact lived under the eye of the community and that outside influence worked in two ways. What we now see as being private matters, such as affective and sexual relationships, belonged to some extent to the public domain. The tension between husband and wife was reduced because social life was organised on a group basis. The local community did not tolerate wayward behaviour and controlled the image of the household by holding it up to public criticism if necessary. There are examples of social sanctions being imposed on widowers who married girls too young for them, or from too different a social group, and thus removing a possible spouse for a bachelor from the pool of marriageable women. Similarly, husbands who were beaten by their wives (and thus endangered the social order by accepting a reversal within their own private lives) were publicly stigmatised.

The organisation of tasks and areas

This depended, within marriage, on the complementary nature of men's and women's work, which were both part of a community-wide system of organisation. The allocation of areas within the household was akin to that at the village and extra-village level, and relationships between the sexes in the house and in the village were part of the same continuum.

Work in the household made women into social beings. Spinster sisters did not have the adult status that was the mistress's by right when she carried out a certain number of tasks that, although of a domestic nature, were not held in the low esteem we now grant them. To the woman fell the tasks of running the house, fetching water, preparing meals for the men, the farmer and the servants and getting the feed for the pigs and poultry. She would help to some extent in the fields, depending on the time of year, the type of economic organisation, the type of production and the number of paid hands. But even though the house was her symbolic domain, she was never shut up in it. Just as there was a female *house*, there was a male *outside*. When the woman went out, it was with other women, to carry out domestic tasks that could not be performed inside the house, such as washing the linen in the wash-house and baking bread in the village oven. The man's jobs were working in the fields and looking after the animals and crops. Male and female labour in any shared task was organised on a complementary basis, the man harvesting while the woman picked up the sheaves or ploughing while she led the team. Large-scale male tasks were organised on a community basis, with all neighbouring farmers helping each other.

This segregation was also a feature of the way in which the sale of farm produce was organised. The women sold the products of their farmyard at the local market and the men attended fairs. Their relationships with other men and women and the areas they circulated in were quite different.

Women's sociability was limited to the immediate area and closely linked to their work. There was little formal provision for it outside the women's religious organisations set up under church influence in the nineteenth century, and very little outside their area of work.

Men, on the other hand, might have a certain amount of leisure, and this is a constant feature of all societies. When they went to the blacksmith's to have a horse shod, it was also a time for exchanging news, but apart from such social occasions linked to work, men in some regions also had their guilds, *chambrettes*, clubs, musical or games associations and so on, for which there was no female equivalent.

Thus two patterns of social life, one for men and one for women, had grown up in peasant society. They were not equal, and female society was seen as inferior and second-rate by men. In this hierarchical arrangement, what was formal and public belonged in the masculine sphere. Men had their places on the local council and represented their households at the level of local authority. What was informal and private belonged to the world of women. Their domain was that of gossip, functionally similar to men's talk of politics and economics.

Recognised female status

By virtue of their work and the social relationships it entailed, women had considerable social status within the village community. On the whole, it was complementary to that of men, although there were regional differences. And yet the myth of male domination was part of the rural ideology,[1] perhaps working in counterpoint to the unspoken fear that the power of women evoked. The reputation their houses enjoyed arose from the image they created: thrifty, hard-working, hospitable to all and in particular to vagrants, marginal characters slightly feared by all. Of women, rural wisdom said that although they were not builders, they made or destroyed houses. A bad housewife brought ruin to her household. Men were also uneasy about the vague female powers women had and there were a number of prohibitions concerning women when they were menstruating.[2] They looked after the sick and produced new life, but also had something of the witch about them and could bring death. They were often thought to have violent sexual appetites, which gave them a certain power over men. Both sexes therefore seem to have maintained an image of male authority with the double aim of deceiving each other to some extent and exorcising the fear women aroused in all those matters never expressed in words.

Within the traditional organisation of husband and wife roles, women also controlled the household budget. The little ready cash coming in regularly was from the sale of farmyard or dairy produce, and it was wives who gave husbands their weekly money for tobacco or visits to the *bistrot*. When an item of livestock was sold at the fair, the woman of the house would settle the major bills for groceries and clothing. More generally, her function was to take the day's rations from the food stocks that the farm had provided – the wheat needed to make bread, the joints of pork in the salting tub. Thrift was a basic virtue. As the old proverb has it, a thrifty wife means a good home life.

Thus it was not so much mothers as working women that were esteemed in peasant societies, women in good health who could run the affairs of the household prudently and well. The work done by women on the farm was absolutely necessary, and until the middle of the nineteenth century, when middle-class ways were adopted on a very large scale, most women of all ages from little girls to grandmothers worked, according to their strength and their abilities. (The same was also true of small boys, of course.) It is important to remember that there is a very long tradition of women working, despite the fact that some maintain that the phenomenon is a recent one. There is, however, one basic characteristic that distinguishes older patterns from those operating today. In the past there was, relatively speaking, a greater harmonisation of productive and maternal tasks. Of course, it was not always easy to take a baby out into the fields, but if there was no other choice, mothers did so and put the cradle in one corner under a tree or a large umbrella. Otherwise the child was looked after at home by a grandmother, a servant or an older sister. In nineteenth-century peasant society then there was no contradiction – or at least no difficulty – in reconciling maternal duties and work, except of course for the fact that sheer exhaustion sent millions of women to an early grave.

The diversity of regional and cultural models

Within this overall pattern there were differences resulting from the way farms were worked, their size and what they produced. Over a single region assumed to be culturally homogeneous, the work done by women could cover a whole range of situations from working in the fields every day and in all weathers to supervising and controlling the farmyard and the vegetable garden and taking charge of the cooking. The variety of situations and attitudes can readily be seen in the differing degrees of fatigue and their implications for health and the serenity or anxiety at the prospect of a secure or precarious future.

The cultural norms proper to each region must also be taken into account and the reasons for these differences understood. We have a picture of the women of southern France as rather enclosed within the domestic interior and of those of the west – and Brittany in particular – as being more or less the equals of the men. The place of women in the social system in general and the practice of rules governing inheritance in particular were both the cause and the consequence of this situation.

In the west of France, women had equal rights to the family patrimony. In the south, the basically patrilineal system gave them a secondary place, and to some extent they were rejected by the paternal household and excluded, by their dowry, from the family patrimony. The small sum of money they received when they married deprived them of any rights to the property attached to the house. In addition, the rule of patrilocal residence (the bride went to live with her husband's parents) made them strangers in their own homes. They were subject to their mother-in-law and had to wait to become one in their turn before they had a say.

The way in which things private and things public were linked and the relationship between domestic matters and the farm in general also offer an explanation of the degree of authority women might have had. In Sicilian society, for example, women did not work in the fields, did not move outside their homes and had no public role. But this example does not imply that women who did work always had a major public role. They were generally seen as having authority in domestic matters and as their husbands' equals as far as the division of labour relating to the management of the farm was concerned, but their role outside these spheres depended to a large extent on the local culture. It was determined by the importance of the domestic domain, and if, as in Lorraine, Brittany and Burgundy, that aspect was a major one, they could establish their importance. When, however, it was the house and fields and its rights over common land that was the entity transmitted from generation, domestic matters were much less important, and in such cases women occupied a secondary place, really obeisant to the head of the household, the man in charge of the farm. The diverse nature of such regional models should not be underestimated, for it had cultural effects so powerful that their consequence for the status of women can still be seen.

What has been said so far has more to do with models or rules than with practice. It cannot be claimed that every couple behaved in such ways, but all behaviour was referrable to those rules and models; a couple could be punished by the younger generation if it departed seriously from them.

Profound changes

The peasant couple, like all others, was to become more private and was increasingly to see marital relations as of no concern to others. At the same time, relations were to be modified as a result of changes in agricultural work, despite the misleadingly timeless appearance of the countryside.

In the 1950s, the introduction of capitalism into the economy of agriculture meant that work had to be reorganised, and this deprived farmers' wives of an ever-increasing number of their responsibilities. Although they had often been the moving spirit behind progress on the farm and had encouraged their husbands to modernise, they were to see technical progress work against them and exclude them from productive tasks. They were entrusted with the accounts, which often simply meant sending out bills, lent a hand with various jobs and increasingly became indoor workers occupied with household tasks that took up more time than in the past. They had domestic appliances, but no-one to help them, and were subject to the influence of the mass media, which managed to play down the importance of domestic jobs and encourage housework at the same time. Countrywomen are concerned about their children's education and like their middle-class sisters are losing the status that goes with a job.

Conditions in the country, like those in the towns, now create a conflict between domestic and professional tasks. It is difficult to help the children with their homework when the cows have to be milked, and impossible to watch them whilst packing fruit to be shipped on a train that will not wait. Although a number of farmers' wives have their own jobs as social workers or teachers, it is sometimes hard for them not to give in to the demands of the farm.

ARTISANS' AND SHOPKEEPERS' HOUSEHOLDS

Rural communities were also made up of domestic groups whose major activity was not based on agriculture. The blacksmith, the cartwright, the potter and the clog-maker all worked for the village. Weavers and cutlers carried on family businesses working for a pre-capitalist outside market, or perhaps a capitalist one, which determined their standard of living to the extent that the law of supply and demand governed their income. They owned or rented a small plot of land and were thus agriculturalists to a small extent. Historians call such domestic groups 'protoindustrial' families.

The organisation of artisans' households offers an intermediate model between that of the peasant and the working-class household. Like the former, they had kinship links and shared values, and with the latter they provide a clue as to how roles were to be allocated. Wage earnings meant that the spouses could be much more independent of their parents, and the economic and social conditions of work prepared the ground for a relatively egalitarian allocation of roles. Men could stay at home and women go out. As Hans Medick writes:

Generally, however, the proto-industrial situation was characterized by a rather strong degree of assimilation between the production functions of men and women. Women in the roles of cutlers and nailers as well as organizers of the marketing of the industrial products were as common as men were in the roles of spinners and lacemakers. Occasionally this adaptation of familial work organization to the conditions of survival went beyond the disappearance of the traditional separation of labour between the sexes. It could lead to its reversal: where the necessities of production compelled women to neglect household 'duties', this 'loss of function' could be compensated for by the men assuming traditional women's roles. Behaviour which to contemporary observers from the middle and upper strata of society all too quickly appeared as a reversal of the 'natural order', posed no particular role problem to weavers or to specialized households of spinners. It was here that 'men . . . cook, sweep and milk the cows, in order never to disturb the good, diligent wife in her work'.

The distribution of family labour across the lines separating the labour between the sexes and age groups did not only determine the behaviour of family members in the sphere of production. Social behaviour and especially consumption and sexual activities were also influenced by the respective forms of co-operation between men and women and their outward constraints. As 'role functions' they were not separate from the process of production and reproduction, although in their symbolic, socio-cultural meaning they were more than mere extensions of that process.

Although precise investigations are lacking, there are indications that role behaviour of the sexes in consumption among the rural artisans was by no means constantly tied to a division of labour in which men would function as privileged consumers 'symbolising the role of breadwinner' (N. J. Smelser), and were thus entrusted with status consumption in public, whereas women would be restricted to householding, to caring and preparing for the necessities of life. It is precisely in status consumption that an egalitarian role of both sexes came to be symbolized. This happened within the boundaries of the house as well as in the wider community. In the 'plebeian public' of the rural artisans both sexes frequently articulated their needs by drinking and smoking in common. Their communality manifested itself not only by passive consumption, it showed itself also in the active defence of traditional norms of subsistence. During food riots and actions against unbearable price rises, women by no means withdrew from the public eye. Very often it was the women who were 'more disposed to be mutinous; . . . in all public tumults they are foremost in violence and ferocity'.[3]

Work within the artisan domestic group was perhaps even more closely based on the joint efforts of husband and wife (not to mention those of their children, whose important role in agricultural and artisanal production is well known). Husband and wife teams of weavers, with the former producing heavy woolen cloth and the latter cotton handkerchiefs on a lighter loom, as we have seen at Vraiville in the Eure department, and kinds of collaboration between cutlers and their wives and other artisanal groups, all depended on two sets of earnings to make sure the household would survive. Although in agricultural families the man–woman team could also be made up of mother and son, father and daughter or brother and sister, in the artisan family it could only be husband and wife since there was no patrimony to keep relatives together. Thus, the hypothesis that artisans remarried more rapidly than farmers can justifiably be put forward, since in their case the work of a wife was so indispensable. In addition, such couples were still subject to the rural community, sharing in its values and accepting its control, and in summer the men would abandon their looms and take part in harvesting as part of the traditional system of mutual help. During busy times in summer, the weavers of Avesnes-les-Aubert were obliged to leave their looms and hire themselves out in another

211

region. The whole domestic group would go with them, and this is the most extreme case of the proletarianisation of families in the traditional artisan framework. In Avesnes, there was also specialisation within the domestic group, with the women doing the winding for the weavers in the family.[4]

The work of women was also essential in small trading concerns in the towns. If we examine the professional path of those moving from Aubrac to Paris, we can see that the need for marriage and that for settling in a business coincided. The wife worked behind the café counter and the husband delivered wood and coal in winter and bread and ice in summer. As one of those surveyed said, in that job 'There have to be two of you and you have to be a real team.'[5] That remark was relevant to all trading in food in the nineteenth and twentieth centuries and to all artisanal undertakings in the *ancien régime* in villages or towns, as co-operation between husband and wife was vital. In the case of blacksmiths, the wife was at the counter and her complementary work with the cow or in the farmyard was essential if the household was to survive. Thus the whole of agricultural society was based on co-operation between the sexes, and protoindustrial society is characterised by a high degree of integration of the productive roles of men and women. Large-scale industrialisation did not destroy this general pattern, and a continuity in the work done by women could still be observed, whether it was carried out in a unit of production now separate from the family or within the conjugal cell in the form of domestic work.

WORKING-CLASS HOUSEHOLDS

Industrial society introduced a basically new separation between the place of residence and the place of work. As a result, in many families husbands and wives were apart for the greater part of each day and week. Wives did not know where their husbands were or what they earned, and children could no longer acquire technical knowledge by watching their fathers. The organisation of production left the hands of the domestic group and passed into those of the owners of capital and their agents. It seems accurate to say that the domestic group lost the productive and educational functions it had in former times.

Changes in women's work

In suggesting this kind of pattern of development of roles in the urban working-class household – which has the merit of proposing a general dynamic–we conceal a certain number of intermediate developments recently brought to light by a historical scholarship willing to analyse detailed urban censuses. By relating demography, economy and relationships within the household, it is possible to see how interdependent these levels are and how carefully one has to proceed when studying changes in the family, for relationships within the family and relationships between it and society take different forms according to the type of work involved.

The mistaken idea current in a certain kind of feminist ideology that sees working urban women as a purely contemporary phenomenon should be rejected at once. Women have contributed their labour throughout industrial development, and their per centage of the total working population has remained remarkably constant. As a per centage of the total female population, the figure for working women has fallen slightly.

That 'downward trend in the number of working women since the beginning of this century' has been accompanied by a shift in the types of jobs done. The number of women employed in industry fell by 0.3 million between 1906 and 1962 and the number of those in the tertiary sector has constantly increased. Not until 1962 did the number of women in employment begin to rise again.[6]

As Louise Tilly and Joan Scott have shown in their *Women, Work and Family*, working conditions for women and families varied considerably from one sector of industry to another, and this had a direct effect on tasks and the structure of roles within the household. For the most part, the female labour force consisted of young unmarried women, as factory work is difficult to fit in with family responsibilities of wives and mothers. Those working in factories did so if a second wage was absolutely necessary to make ends meet or if there was a family crisis such as the father falling ill.[7]

Combined wages in the working-class household

In the early stages of industrialisation the working-class family unit, like that of the bourgeoisie and the artisans, was an economically integrated one in which various wages had to be pooled. Husbands, wives, adolescents and children (when they were legally permitted to work) pooled their earnings. In this context, the work done by women was closely linked to the family life cycle (Fig. 7.1). After the early years of married life, with two wages coming in, factory work became difficult for mothers with young children. They could either give up their jobs, which clashed with their domestic responsibilities, and suffer a catastrophic fall in family income, or work in pre-

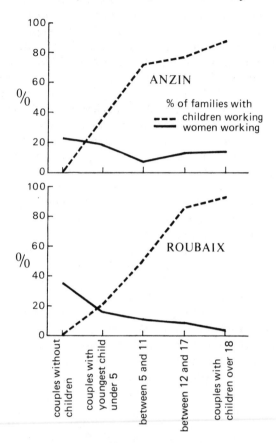

Fig. 7.1. Family life cycle. Employment model for women and children, Anzin and Roubaix, 1872. (From Louise Tilly and Joan Scott, *Women, Work and Family* [New York: Holt, Rinehart, & Winston, 1978], p. 135.)

carious conditions. A number of women adopted the first solution and stayed at home.

For the most part, textile mills employed young single women, but there were always a number of married women who could not survive without factory work. In 1872, 14.3 per cent and 19.3 per cent of women working in factories in Roubaix and Anzin, respectively, had at least one child under age five (Table 7.1).

When they were not working in factories, women sometimes sought other ways of increasing their income. In London, for example, they took in an increased number of lodgers, and in other industrial towns, married women often found work in non-industrial

Table 7.1. *Women and children working, by number and ages of children in the family, Roubaix and Anzin, 1872 (in %)*

	Women working	Children working
Roubaix		
Families with no children	34.1	–
Families with youngest child under 5	14.3	21.7
Families with youngest child between 5 and 11	10.6	51.5
Families with youngest child between 12 and 17	9.7	82.1
Families with youngest child over 18	4.3	89.9
Anzin		
Families with no children	22.0	–
Families with the youngest child under 5	19.3	36.8
Families with the youngest child between 5 and 11	7.3	69.1
Families with the youngest child between 12 and 17	13.7	75.8
Families with the youngest child over 18	14.3	85.7

Source: L. Tilly, 'Structure de l'emploi, travail des femmes et changement démographique dans deux villes industrielles: Anzin et Roubaix, 1872–1906', *Le Mouvement social* 105(1978): 45.

sectors, as washerwomen, manageresses in cafés, daily cleaning women or by taking in work at home.

Towards the end of the nineteenth century, the introduction of the sewing-machine brought an increase in this latter kind of work. This appliance may have been the handmaid of the middle-class housewife in her traditional tasks, but it was the instrument of external capitalism within the working-class home. For a meagre supplementary wage women who worked in this way were slaves to their sewing machines and regressed to the traditional position and function of their sex, establishing the symbolic image of women subject to discipline, which we still have in our own day in that of the typist glued to her typewriter. As the clothing industry grew, some domestic seamstresses managed to earn enough to pay for their machines and to supplement their husband's wage. To do so, they had to work throughout the day and often until late at night, which explains why at the beginning of the century many women went to work in factories again, as this seemed preferable to the torments of working at home. Later they were to swarm into war factories.[8]

When the children could work, their situation and that of the domestic group became less critical. From the age of eight, children had to contribute to household expenses.

The couple in the nineteenth century

The integral nature of the household sometimes extended into the the world of jobs, with parents and children working as a team in the same factory and workshop, as was the case in the French textile industry. We have the example of the Metigy family working at Tourcoing in 1853. The father, Joseph, aged forty-three, was a spinner and his three sons (sixteen, fourteen and thirteen) and daughter (twenty-one) binders. Their combined wages were 46.50 francs, which were handed over to the father.[9] The wife did not work. Girls with jobs lived with their parents, as their wages were not high enough to live apart from them and were in fact considered by employers to be supplementary income. Incorporation into the proletariat therefore temporarily strengthened the integration of the working-class domestic group.

The wife as the pivot of the working-class household

Whether she had a paid job or stayed at home, the wife's role in the working-class household was still a major one. In the economic poverty of the times, her traditional role as a good housewife and manager was at least as important as it had been in rural societies, since there was no longer any produce from the farmyard or the vegetable plot to help make ends meet. If, as was the case in certain working-class housing areas, there were gardens, looking after them and enjoying the social intercourse they provided were masculine privileges, whereas in the country they had been female ones. It was the wife's responsibility to maintain a balanced budget, to obtain credit from shopkeepers and to feed everyone, and all these tasks were particularly onerous as there was none of the help that there had been in country areas. In addition, teenage children lived at home until they married, and the mother also had to provide emotional support for the family. The father was now simply a wage-earner exerting no equivalent influence, unable to pass on to his children social possessions, technical knowledge or job security.

The decline in masculine status within the domestic group did not necessarily entail an improvement in the female one, however. Perhaps what happened was that the image of another man – an uncle or a grandfather – imposed itself on the family. We must also take care not to idealise the image of the working-class wife. In *Histoire des mères*, Yvonne Knibiehler and Catherine Fouquet stress the destructive effects of industrialisation on their traditional knowledge:

Industrialisation was to create, over whole groups, a new type of mother going out to work for twelve or fourteen hours a day and coming home exhausted, distraught, at the end of their tether and often incapable of performing the most basic domestic and maternal tasks. What was new was not that work took them from their children (which had often happened in country areas) but the overwhelming collective and large-scale nature of the phenomenon. Peasant women and farmers' wives often worked just as hard, but always at home, and very few people apart from a few doctors were aware of their common weariness. Factories and slums now concentrated these wretches into the same areas and gave a scandalous dimension to their wretchedness.[10]

The way in which female skills were passed on, namely the sociability of women, had been destroyed. They had had to do with the whole range of domestic life, involving cooking, housework, looking after children and so on. Although these practices had often been described as 'superstitious' by observers of the peasant milieu, they nevertheless continued to be passed on as self-evidently right and proper and of venerable and traditional origin. In the towns, where the contrast between working-class female behaviour and scientific and bourgeois knowledge was too great, the situation was quite different. Rather than laughing at them, observers were now openly hostile to working-class ways of doing things. It was all too clear that working-class women had lost their cultural birthright. By the end of the nineteenth century, criticism was rife:

Working-class women do no know how to sew, to mend or to make broth or how to bring up their children. It is not surprising that work in industry, which was certainly oppressive, destroyed the old female knowledge and housewifely virtues. The worst thing was that it put nothing in their place and left wives and mothers totally deprived and accused of negligence.[11]

A dual model

Faced with such a human and social muddle, philanthropists and doctors tried to get women back into their homes for good. A rise in living standards helped them to do so. Towards the end of the century the working class became more stable and better adapted to urban life as a result of the increased importance and normalisation of family life, as Alain Corbin writes in *Les Filles de noce*.

After half a century of rootlessness in which they were torn between a forgotten peasant culture and a bourgeois culture that they had not yet acquired, the working classes began to settle. Seen from the outside, their situation became more normal, their fertility fell and they began to aspire to an education for their children. The working-class woman, however, lost her status and with the growth of the consumer society finally withdrew from the labour market.

Within the household, tasks became clearly separated, with the man becoming the only bread-winner and the woman the mother of a small family, better educated and cared for than in the past and devoting herself to the home.

The husband alone assumed the full identity of the domestic group. The wife became the particular person the priest, the doctor and later the mass media addressed themselves to. It was perhaps at this time that the segregation of male and female roles was most marked. The husband did no jobs at home and spent the greater part of his free time in the bar or fishing. The wife often developed closer relations with her mother, whereas those between her and her husband became more distinct.

Given the present paucity of studies, we have been obliged to propose a contrasted image of the allocation of roles within the working-class domestic group. According to certain writers, 'equal' marriages in which both spouses had the same status came into being in the working-class family. Others, like Young and Wilmott in *Family and Kinship in East London*, maintain that the peasant family's myth of masculine authority became reality in the working-class family with its panorama of deviant social behaviour such as drunkenness and brutality on the part of husbands. Both images are probably relevant in different contexts.

BOURGEOIS HOUSEHOLDS

Accentuated separation of roles and status

The bourgeois husband either worked or managed capital, and social representation depended on him. Even if his wife had brought a large dowry – and bourgeois marriage, as we know, was a matter of interest, of establishment – the husband alone was responsible for material possessions. Legally and figuratively, the bourgeois wife was incompetent. She did not have to work in the home and her main task was to be mistress there, as Anne Martin-Fugier notes,[12] organising, giving orders to the servants, who were always there (in greater or lesser numbers depending on the social level of the couple) because they cost so little. She had none of the physical work that gave the peasant or working-class woman her dignity, and as a result such work was deemed of secondary importance, degrading and menial.

During the nineteenth century, the role of the middle-class wife became increasingly that of the mother looking after her children, as we saw in the last chapter. She did look after the very young children, but often with the help of a nurse, and in fact her role was primarily educational, in that it was she who formed their minds and hearts. This sublimation of her maternal quality meant that the bourgeois wife was a subsidiary figure in the conjugal couple. The mother was romantically idealised and hence untouchable. In his *Histoire des passions françaises*, Theodore Zeldin has this to say of these wives:

The cult of purity meant that they were inaccessible, and in such circumstances sexual pleasure with those consecrated to motherhood could not be envisaged.[13]

Bourgeois wives were the victims of religious views that saw chastity as the ideal state and sexuality as something of a lesser evil, to be tolerated if it led to procreation. In addition, as Zeldin points out,

The clergy described husbands as having sexual needs and wives as submitting to them. . . . Once children had arrived continence with the mutual consent of the spouses was desirable. . . . A woman was expected to be first and foremost a mother devoted to the Christian upbringing of her children.[14]

The church greatly helped to spread the sublimated image of motherhood. The nineteenth century was a time when the cult of the Virgin Mary flourished and with it religious organisations for women. Exalting Mary meant separating sexuality, which was harmful, from motherhood, which was good. From the time of the Restoration, the priests had made allies of the wife. Religious matters were often the source of dissension between husband and wife, and the latter alone was responsible for the religious upbringing of the children. As Zeldin goes on to point out, however, this association with religion was not always beneficial:

Women were seen as the instruments of clerical power, so much so in fact that the tendency to see them as an inferior species became more rather than less marked during the nineteenth century.[15]

Female sexuality, which was seen as a duty and also made impossible as a result of the cult of purity, was in addition constrained by birth control, achieved either by the frustrating practice of *coitus interruptus* or by abstinence. The ascetic attitude historians speak of when describing the sexual practices of the bourgeois couple seems to have been largely a female phenomenon, and studies of prostitution have shown the other side of the matter. Corbin illustrates changes in the demand for prostitutes. In the first half of the nineteenth century, it had come from working-class men, but as they adopted normal patterns of marriage they made less use of brothels.

After 1850, demand was increasingly from the bourgeois. The phrase 'the master's expenses' was used to designate payment for such services.[16]

Women as instruments of representation and social relationships

Recent studies have tended to reduce the role of the nineteenth-century bourgeois woman to a purely maternal one. She also organised social life, however, and that role was increasingly important towards the top of the social pyramid. She had an important social function, especially if her husband was professionally and socially ambitious. In taking a wife (something done with the greatest care), he had married into a network of connections and relationships, and his wife, freed from her domestic tasks by maids and her maternal ones by nurses, tutors and the educational system, played a major part in activating in-law, friendship and kinship networks. In the working classes, the wife who stayed at home ensured the reproduction of the labour force that her husband exchanged on the market for wages. In the better-off classes, the husband's career was in part built on the social and cultural direction established by his wife, who had the time for exchanging visits and giving dances and 'at homes' for her friends, who would be joined by their husbands. The necessity for a social life of this kind is partly explicable in terms of the social mobility specific to the nineteenth century, in which rapid upward movement had to be consolidated and the possibility of a decline guarded against. It is, of course, just as necessary in our own age, where the growth of the tertiary sector has meant that top management is recruited on the basis of ability. As Jane Marceau points out:

A manual worker's career does not depend on what happens in his family and outside work. In work of a purely productive nature, only criteria related to productivity are appropriate. At the management level, however, it is harder to judge productivity. The wife and the social and kinship network she can cultivate because she has the time are a considerable social guarantee for the husband.[17]

Social differences

The nineteenth-century bourgeoisie was not a homogeneous class. It was a vaguely defined, geographically and socially shifting category that included couples whose conjugal relationships were sometimes different from those just described, which are rather more typical of the middle and upper reaches of the middle classes.

Suggested reading

The fact that a wife did not have an occupation of her own did not always imply masculine domination. She could be the major partner in the domestic group even if her husband was the only one to go out into society and bring in an income. Richard Sennett, studying the middle classes in the Union Park district of Chicago in the 1880s, shows in *Families against the City* that withdrawal into the nuclear domestic group, what he calls the 'intensive family', coincided with the eclipse of the father, who, showing little energy in his professional life, was incapable of helping his children adapt to life in a town that became a large urban metropolis within a few decades. He was no more able than the worker to give his children the image of a father with a definite professional activity or a social identification. The wife once more assumed the major role in the domestic group, being a psychologically stable person who provided a model for reference. Sennett also shows that extended domestic groups that include several employed adults as well as parents are more able than nuclear domestic groups to give children the dynamic qualities necessary if they are to survive in a world undergoing major changes. This malfunction is perhaps explicable in terms of the structure of roles within the household, and a number of nineteenth-century literary examples portray colourless fathers and dominant mothers.

Thus professional activity is not necessary to establish female status. On the other hand, certain bourgeois women worked. In some of the great textile families of the north of France, for example, the women kept the firm's accounts and had a social image to protect in a society in which the working-classes and the bourgeoisie lived in immediate proximity.

SUGGESTED READING

The peasant family

In addition to the works by Philippe Ariès and Edward Shorter already mentioned:
Rogers, Susan. 'Les femmes et le pouvoir'. In *Paysans, femmes et citoyens*. Le Paradou: Actes Sud, 1980.
Segalen, Martine. *Mari et femme dans la société paysanne*. Paris: Flammarion, 1980. Published in English as *Love and Power in Peasant Society*. Oxford: Basil Blackwell; and Chicago: University of Chicago Press, 1983.
Verdier, Yvonne. *Façons de dire, façons de faire*. Paris: Gallimard, 1979.
Zonabend, Françoise. *The Enduring Memory*. Manchester: Manchester University Press, 1985.

The couple in the nineteenth century

The working class family

Chombard de Lauwe, Paul-Henri. *La Vie quotidienne des familles ouvrières.* Paris: Centre National de la Recherche Scientifique, 1956.

Corbin, Alain. *Les Filles de noce.* Paris: Aubier Montaigne, 1978.

Hoggart, Richard. *The Use of Literacy: Aspects of Working-Class Life with Special References to Publications and Entertainments.* London: Chatto & Windus, 1959.

Lequin, Yves. *Les ouvriers de la région lyonnaise, 1848–1914.* 2 vols. Lyon: Presses universitaires de Lyon, 1977.

Perrot, Michelle, ed. 'Travaux de femmes dans la France du XIXe siècle'. *Le Mouvement social*, Oct.–Dec. 1978: 105.

Pétonnet, Colette. *On est tous dans le brouillard.* Paris, Galilée, 1979, particularly pp. 127–57.

Pitrou, Agnès. *La Famille dans la vie de tous les jours.* Toulouse: Privat, 1972.

Portet, François. *L'Ouvrier, la terre, la petite propriété: jardins ouvriers. Logement social: 1850–1945.* Le Creusot: Ecomusée, 1978.

Thompson, Edward P. *The Making of the English Working Class.* London: Gollancz, 1963.

Tilly, Louise, and Joan W. Scott. *Women, Work and Family.* New York: Holt, Rinehart & Winston, 1978.

Verret, Michel. *L'Espace ouvrier,* chap. 16, 'L'Esprit de famille'. Paris: Colin, 1979.

Young, Michael, and Peter Wilmott. *Family and Kinship in East London.* London: Routledge & Kegan Paul, 1957.

The bourgeois family

Aron, Jean-Paul, ed. *Misérable et glorieuse, la femme du XIXe siècle.* Paris: Fayard, 1980.

Sennett, Richard. *Families against the City.* Cambridge, Mass.: Harvard University Press, 1970.

Smith, Bonnie G. *Ladies of the Leisure Class: The Bourgeoises of Northern France in the Nineteenth Century.* Princeton, N.J.: Princeton University Press, 1981.

Sullerot, Evelyne. 'Des Changements dans le partage des rôles'. *Informations sociales* 6–7(1977): 6–31.

Zeldin, Theodore. *Histoire des passions françaises. Ambition et Amour.* Paris: Encres, 1978.

222

vvv

Roles within the present-day couple

SOCIOLOGICAL ROLE THEORIES

Four theories, mostly Anglo-Saxon in origin and not directly trans-posable to French society, were very influential until history and social anthropology cast new light on studies of the family. They inspired a great deal of empirical research that provided the first corpus of quantitative data on these aspects of family life as well as material for current arguments about the development of intrafamil-ial roles in the context of the increasing numbers of women who work.

Parsons's theory of the separation of roles

This theory, which we have mentioned several times, is very useful in that it links family and social roles. That of the father is 'instru-mental'. He is responsible for contact with the outside world and is the economic provider. The mother's role is 'expressive', and she is responsible for all that is affective.

This model has only very infrequently corresponded to family practices. It has been violently criticised by feminists and recently destroyed by sociological analyses based on concrete cases, as Andrée Michel has shown in *Sociologie de la famille et du mariage*.

The network theory

The name of Elizabeth Bott is associated with the network theory, which she developed in *Family and Social Network*, linking the degree to which roles are separated to the density of the networks the spouses maintain outside the home. The closer their links with their networks of relatives, friends and neighbours and the denser these networks are, the more separate and hierarchical their relationship as a couple. The converse is also true: The less dense the networks, the less separate male and female roles will be.

Bott explains this in terms of cultural pressure. When the people an individual knows have an intense interaction with each other – when the network is dense – the members of the network tend to reach a consensus about norms and to exert informal social pressure to conform to them. They have numerous links with each other and engage in mutual help.

If husband and wife both belong to networks of this kind and the networks are maintained, marriage will simply be superimposed on existing relationships, with the spouses still drawn towards outside activities and people. A rigid separation of roles will be possible, since both spouses will be able to obtain support from outside.

On the other hand, if most of the people an individual knows do not know each other and the network is fairly loose, norms will probably vary to a greater extent within it, and social consensus and mutual help will be less strongly present. If the networks remain loose after marriage, husband and wife will carry out domestic tasks together and their roles will be less separate and more egalitarian.

'Bott's Law', as Henri Mendras calls it in *Éléments de sociologie,* enables us to analyse the structural relationships between the domestic group and conjugal roles and how they change. Thus, in peasant societies the kindred network was dense and roles therefore clearly more separate and differentiated. The flight from the land and settlement in towns meant that the networks became looser, with less differentiation and more complementarity in the roles. A similar change occurs when families living in shanty towns (where kinship and neighbourhood networks are close and effective) move to social housing developments and generally are separated from their relatives and friends.

The hypothesis of the dual-career family

In this situation, both husband and wife have jobs calling for high qualifications and a corresponding level of responsibility.[1] Robert and Rhona Rapoport have made a structural analysis of the constraints this kind of family experiences in adapting to social change. What compromise roles are assumed by each couple to reduce or meet in a different way the tensions and dilemmas encountered? The valuable feature of this hypothesis is that it sees the range of roles as an articulated rather than a distinct whole and considers both the domestic and the professional sphere.

Sociological role theories

To evaluate new behaviour patterns, the authors use a method of structural analysis based on the economic metaphor of profit and loss. Each domestic group decides whether, in its particular case, it is worthwhile to follow the changing course of the life of a dual-career family, given resultant tensions. The Rapoports distinguish five types of such tensions[2]:

1. *Overload:* The advantages of two careers are obtained at the cost of an excess of roles and the couple does not perform the least essential of their tasks.
2. *Environmental sanction:* Tensions arise from contrary norms, some indicating acceptance of women's work, others criticising it.
3. *Personal identity and self-esteem:* If husband and wife both have the same roles, it is hard for them to keep their own identities.
4. *Social network dilemmas:* What profits and losses are involved in relating to the spouse's network rather than to one's own when there is competition between them?
5. *Dilemmas of multiple role-cycling:* Both spouses are involved in three role systems – the professional system of the individual, that of his or her spouse, and the family system in which they both participate. Each has different demands following from his or her role position in the system and the demands of each role vary according to the stage of family life reached. At a given point in time, for example, one spouse may prefer to give more attention to his or her professional role, with the other delaying professional commitment to have more time for the family. Profits in the family area might mean professional losses, and vice versa. All kinds of combinations of roles in terms of the double cycle of professional and family life can be imagined.

This hypothesis is relevant only to couples who are both working and have equal status and salary, which is relatively uncommon. The authors maintain that it is a further refutation of Parsons, since there is a high degree of satisfaction in such couples. This is not simple to determine, however, as the divorce rate increases amongst professionally qualified women.

Economic role theories

The first approach here is to apply Ricardo's theory of international trade. B. Lemmenecier distinguishes two categories of goods,[3] those produced by the family and those produced on the market. Each member of a domestic group, by means of the income he can obtain, estimates the quantity of mercantile goods he is willing to do without, at the same rate of satisfaction, in order to produce an extra unit of non-mercantile goods at home. In this hypothesis, the separation of roles is ultimately explained by the difference between the capital investment of one spouse and the other if all their other characteristics are identical.

Lemmenecier then goes on to find the possible correlations between separation of roles and marital stability. He posits a previous hypothesis that in his view governs the allocation of roles between spouses, namely the difference in educational level. That difference, he maintains, affects that between the costs of making time available and of domestic productivity as between the spouses and leads to a new allocation of roles within the couple. Economists thus attempt to justify one of the two diametrically opposed views (i.e. those of Parsons on the one hand and those of the Rapoports on the other). The former view contends that there are more quarrels when the wife works, the latter that there are more when she stays at home. Lemmenecier constructs a table with two economic variables:

1. The 'ratio of costs of making time available' (the husband's salary divided by the wife's potential salary) deducted from the wife's cost of making time available when she is not working full time, assuming the salary she would receive on the labour market and the husband's salary.
2. The 'ratio of provision of human capital' (the number of years spent in full-time education by the husband and wife).

He also introduces variables of a more sociological nature such as the frequency of quarrels, family and social pressures and the status of the husband, as well as external variables such as the age of the wife, the number of children and the age of the youngest and the size of the town where the respondent lives.

By measuring the contribution made by each of these variables to the ways in which time is shared between domestic and professional tasks, Lemmenecier shows that the differences in the costs of making time available or in the provision of human capital for each of the spouses accounts for the separation of conjugal roles and the stability of marriage as well as, or perhaps better than, the hypotheses advanced by sociologists.

Gary Becker proposes an economic theory of marriage in which the allocation of roles is based on the maximum use of the abilities of each spouse. Men 'hire' women to produce children and take on domestic tasks because they cannot themselves perform the former function and their time is too valuable to carry out the latter, and women 'hire' men to earn the wages they otherwise cannot acquire. Each partner has something to gain from association with the other, and in this model male and female activities are complementary. The gains marriage brings then have to be compared with its costs.[4]

Research of this kind means that it is empirically possible to establish correlations between the stability of marriage and the extent to which wives are engaged on the labour market. Such hypotheses are important because they put in the place of the subjective aspects of human relationships a system of quantification as rigorous as that applied to the movements of international trade or the production of firms. This is a difficult proceeding, and the extent to which similar approaches can explain things is still limited because it is difficult to quantify roles and relationships. One can hardly construct an index of quarrels, or say what couples would call a quarrel, or measure their dissatisfaction in terms of just an index of quarrels (which may indeed also be sources of satisfaction). Evaluating what Becker calls 'full caring' also raises problems.

Economists need clear-cut categories, but reality is too complex to fit into them. They also see domestic and professional tasks as mutually exclusive, whereas practice shows that both spouses participate to a greater or lesser degree in the former.

FACTORS LEADING TO CHANGES IN ROLES

In the preceding chapter we stressed the importance of working conditions and social, economic and cultural contexts and implied some of the factors governing changes in roles. In a field as complicated as that of attitudes, it is hard to say which of these is of prime importance. They are all interlinked, and in the following list we certainly do not want to suggest that any particular one is more important than any other. Nor is it really possible to be exhaustive, and we will not return to certain phenomena such as declining fertility that have been dealt with elsewhere and that ultimately help to change relationships within the couple.

The factors that lead to changes in roles are not the same in every social milieu, nor are their effects felt at the same time. Birth control, for example, which changes the most intimate relationship a couple can have, was adopted at different times by the bourgeoisie and the working class. There have been no single, linear changes, and nowadays several norms coexist, even if the reference model is tending to become more uniform.

We can distinguish three types of factors leading to a couple in which roles tend to become shared to an ever-increasing extent.

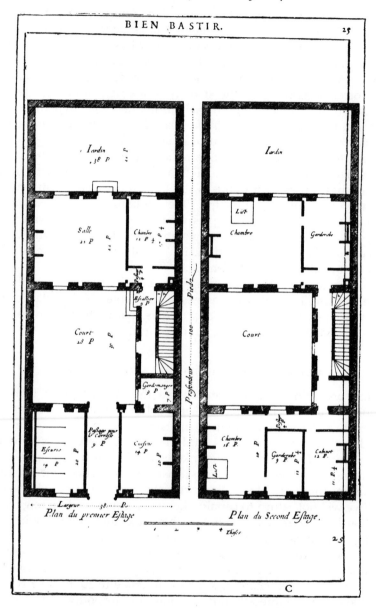

Fig. 8.1. Plan of a seventeenth-century town house, after Le Muet. (From G. Doyon and R. Hubrecht, *L'Architecture rurale et bourgeoise* [Paris: Vincent Freal, 1942], p. 69.)

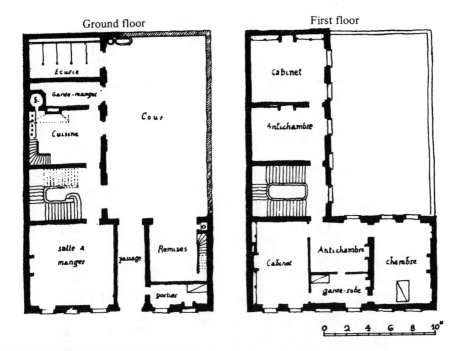

Fig. 8.2. Plan of an eighteenth-century private mansion by Brissard, published by Jonbert in 1728. (From G. Doyon and R. Hubrecht, *L'Architecture rurale et bourgeoisie* [Paris: Vincent Freal, 1942].)

The husband comes home again

Where people live changes them and is also changed by developments in the family. The inner space of a house is sensitive to the way people behave in it and reflects and reinforces the increase in family intimacy and the increasingly private life of the couple, first in the well-to-do classes, amongst the peasants at varying times, and much later in the working class. If we examine one or two house plans, this development can be seen clearly.

In the plan produced by Le Muet, the seventeenth-century architect, there is no dining room and the kitchen is not even next to the *salle*, the vague name of which underlines its multi-functional nature (Fig. 8.1). Eighteenth-century plans show a relative degree of specialisation of areas, but the public reception area and the private quarters are still not clearly separated; there is no isolating corridor, and to reach the bedroom one has to cross a succession of rooms, antechambers, and *cabinets* (Fig. 8.2). The nineteenth-century house,

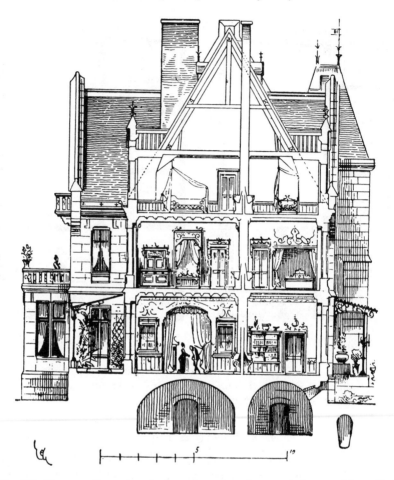

Fig. 8.3. Cross-section of a nineteenth-century bourgeois house. (From Viollet-le-Duc, *Histoire d'une maison* [Paris: Berger-Levrault, Reed, 1978; facsimile 1873], p. 182.)

as seen by Viollet-le-Duc and as it actually existed, has separate public and private areas and the various rooms fulfil special purposes (Fig. 8.3).

On the other hand, in peasant interiors even in the mid-twentieth century there are still several models. At Ploudalmezeau (Finistère), the communal hall was used for sleeping, eating, working and social life (Fig. 8.4). At Imbsheim in the Bas-Rhin department, however, a much richer peasant house is constructed on the bourgeois model, with the bedrooms mostly on the first floor and the room used for

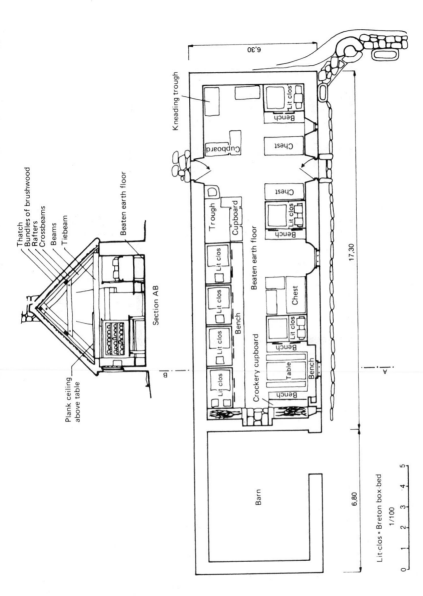

Thatch
Bundles of brushwood
Rafters
Crossbeams
Beams
Tiebeam

Beaten earth floor

Section AB

Plank ceiling
above table

Kneading trough

6,30

Cupboard

Chest

Bench
Lit clos

Trough

Cupboard

Chest

Lit clos
Bench

Lit clos

Lit clos

Lit clos

Lit clos

Bench

Chest

Lit clos
Bench

Beaten earth floor

Crockery cupboard

Table

Bench

Bench

17,30

Barn

6,80

Lit-clos = Breton box-bed

1/100

0   1   2   3   4   5

Fig. 8.4. Plan and section of a dwelling-house at Ploudalmezeau, Finistère. Several generations, many children, and servants occupied the same space. (From Martine Segalen, *Love and Power in Peasant Society* [Oxford: Basil Blackwell, 1983]. After the drawing by Jaegher Arts et traditions Populaires, no. 44.54.4.)

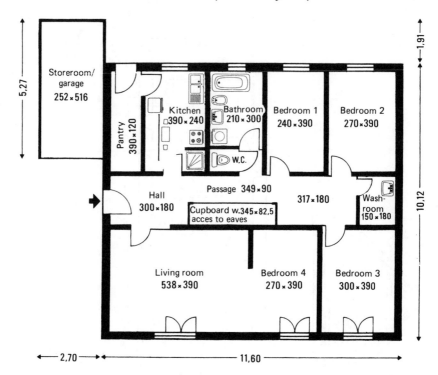

Fig. 8.5. Plan of a prefabricated concrete house. (From Pierre Piganiol, *Du nid à la cité* [Paris: Dunod, 1970].)

meals and relaxation separate from the rest. These two models of peasant houses have coexisted for a long time, and there have been farms with upstairs bedrooms since the seventeenth century in various parts of France.

In the twentieth century, public and private rooms in both houses and flats are seen as different and kept separate (Fig. 8.5).

Working-class housing was the last to be affected by these changes. Until the beginning of this century everything worked towards separating areas that reinforced the separation of roles. Small working-class dwellings were female areas, the domain of mothers, children and grandmothers, and husbands felt out of place there. When he had finished work, the only place where a man could relax with his friends was the café.

It became less necessary to rely on the kinship network as welfare laws came into force and, in an emergency, provided other channels of help than relatives. There was a comparative loosening of the mother–daughter tie as child health services developed and set up patterns of advice parallel to those handed on by grandmothers. Some women still listened to their mothers, but others, more anxious to be modern, paid no heed to their advice. With the sharp fall in infant mortality, young mothers had less cause for acute concern and had relatively less need for psychological support. The geographic and social mobility separating place of residence also helped temporarily to make relations between parents and children less close, particularly when cars came into widespread use.

Leisure was another area in which technical advances produced a major change in relationships between husband and wife. In working-class areas in the past, people had to go out for their amusements. Public festivities and games in towns, the café, the theatre and the cinema offered entertainment during the limited free time working-class people enjoyed. Their dark little houses were for eating and resting in. Electricity brightened them, and radio and television meant that people could entertain themselves at home. The small screen brought the world into everyone's living-room, a revolutionary development often wrongly seen as the cause of many of the evils in our society, but one that brought husbands and fathers back home and enabled them, their wives and their children to see and hear the same things. Television provides an opportunity of sharing things and is not necessarily, as is often claimed, a substitute for genuine conversation.

The husband gradually returned and shared with his wife a relationship now based on leisure activities rather than work, as had been the case with peasant and artisan domestic groups, and his return was further encouraged by improvements in the standard of living. He often invested time and money in improving the home and bought consumer goods of use to the whole family, and it has often been men who have decided to acquire washing-machines and dishwashers even if it has been women who have mostly used them. This allocation of resources is a new phenomenon. Instead of keeping a sum of money for their own purposes, husbands now use a larger proportion of their income to buy goods for the whole family, and the car of course comes into this category.

This increase in the amount of free time husbands spend at home is also due to the fact that many of them now spend endless weekends working on their own houses. No house, either the main one or a second home, is ever finished and can always be modified *ad infinitum.* There is always a wrought-iron grill to be put on the front porch or the garage or kitchen to be improved.

In the case of the middle- and working-classes, the new way in which roles are allocated has been linked to social and economic changes and the general improvement in living standards in Western societies over the last fifty years.

The trend has been the same in the bourgeois domestic group. In the nineteenth and early twentieth centuries, as we have seen, each sex had clearly differentiated roles. Even social life was compartmentalised, with women having their charitable institutions and men their clubs. Life in society, however, was shared, as were to an ever-increasing extent leisure-time, sports and holiday life. The relative levelling of incomes, the growth of the middle class, the increasing number of women working and the more or less total disappearance of servants has meant that the situation wealthy young couples now find themselves in is not markedly different from that of the least-privileged ones. With regard to this last point, the statistics speak volumes. Between 1896 and 1911, there were between 900,000 and 1,000,000 servants in all of France. In 1900, very wealthy households in Paris might employ a staff of thirty, and less rich ones around eighteen. Average bourgeois households would have three servants: chambermaid, cook and butler/valet, and most households had a general maid.[5] Around 1940, bourgeois married couples usually had a French maid. By 1960, it was a Spanish or Portuguese one. Since 1970, there has been a cleaning woman or au pair girl in less than 1 per cent of French households. In couples like this, the husband has to take on tasks that a generation earlier would have been specifically female ones.

The increase in the number of women working since 1962

At a certain point in time, women stopped going out to work and stayed at home to look after their children and their houses, and this was one stage on the way of improving their lot. The number of working women tended to fall from the beginning of the century to the 1960s. Since 1962, the situation has been changing and differential swings are becoming more marked. Changes have also occurred more rapidly since 1968. Between 1968 and 1975, the percentage of women aged between twenty-five and twenty-nine working rose from 50.2 to 62.7, and that of those aged between thirty and thirty-four from 42.4 to 54.6.[6] If the number of children is also taken into account, the percentage of women aged between twenty-five and twenty-nine with one young child who were in employment rose from 50.5 in 1968 to 66.6 in 1975. The corresponding figures for women aged thirty to thirty-four with two children including one very young one were 31.2 per cent and 47.9 per cent.[7] Overall, the number of women entering the labour market increased. Socio-economic analyses show the following characteristics:

1. There was an increase in the employment rate of the order of 16 or 17 per cent between 1968 and 1975 in the case of women aged from twenty-five to twenty-nine with a child under seven. This means that the increase occurred largely amongst young women.[8]
2. If all women under forty with one or two very young children are included, 37 per cent of married women were working in 1968, 40 per cent in 1975 and 44 per cent in 1980.
3. To a lesser extent, there has been an increase in the number of women over forty-five working.

The trend that became apparent between 1962 and 1968 has since become more marked and is expected to continue to do so until the mid-eighties. Increasing numbers of younger married women with children have jobs, and their numbers will go on rising. As Nadine Lefaucheur notes:

Amongst younger women, it is very rare to find any who have never worked. In addition, there is an increasing population of women who do not interrupt their careers although they have one or more children and of those going back to work at latest when their youngest child starts primary school.[9]

Although the total number of women working in 1980 was only 44 per cent of those of an age to do so (i.e. nine million women as compared with thirteen million men) it is more significant than its intrinsic value suggests, for two reasons. First, the number of women entering the labour market is increasing rapidly and they make a growing contribution to labour resources. Second, the new image of the working wife and mother is the accepted and encouraged model. The nineteenth century promoted the image of the mother, and the late twentieth century is promoting that of the working woman, even if views on working women are often contradictory.

Not only do more women have jobs, but overall they are working in different sectors. There has been a fall in self-employed categories such as independent farming and self-employed industrial and commercial activity and an expansion of salaried female workers in the liberal professions, in management and clerical work. The increase

Roles within the present-day couple

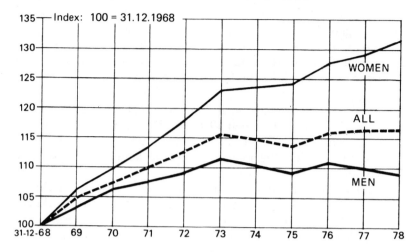

Fig. 8.6. Rate of changes in paid employment by sex. (From *L'Economie* no. 1445, 20 October 1980.)

has been particularly noticeable in middle-grade administrative posts, especially in education, the social and medical services and office jobs (Fig. 8.6, Table 8.1).

Of the white-collar jobs created between 1968 and 1972, 66 per cent were taken by women, in both service and management posts. The proportion of women engaged in manual work is decreasing slightly, however.

Assessing the place of women in the industrial sector is not an easy matter. On the one hand, more women were employed in it. From 1968 to 1972, they accounted for 38 per cent of the new waged jobs in industry (the figure for 1968 had been 29 per cent). On the other hand, there were increasing numbers of women amongst un-skilled production workers. Thus, although there were more women but fewer unskilled women in industry, they were increasingly nu-merous in fairly unskilled secretarial, data-processing and service posts.

Other data show considerable differences depending on socio-professional category, husband's profession and educational level. The greatest increase in employment was amongst the wives of higher managers. At the end of the 1970s, they were less likely to be employed than the wives of skilled workers or foremen, whereas nowadays they are more likely to be working.

In the case of women with young children, attitudes towards work vary from one socio-professional category to another, but the

236

Factors leading to changes in roles

Table 8.1. *Female working population with jobs, by socio-professional category, 1968 and 1973* (in %)

	Total female labour force		Feminisation of each category	
	1968	1973	1968	1973
Agriculture, self-employed	12.7	9.3	40.3	39.8
Agriculture, employed	0.9	0.5	12.4	11.4
Employers	11.4	9.9	38.8	39.2
Upper management and liberal profs.	2.6	3.7	18.2	21.3
Middle management	11.4	14.1	40.2	42.4
Office work	20.0	22.1	62.1	65.2
Commercial work	5.2	5.1	57.5	58.1
Skilled workers	4.7	4.8	12.8	12.0
Unskilled workers	17.3	17.9	27.2	31.2
Service personnel	13.6	12.2	79.4	79.2
Other services	0.3	0.4	6.8	8.1
All	100.0	100.0	36.5	37.9

Source: La Famille (Paris: Hachette, 1975), p. 145.

general trend in the allocation of roles within the couple is the same in all of them. Whether the wife is a manual worker or in management, there is always the same competition between domestic and professional roles. One cannot, of course, ignore the difference between social and professional categories, but as far as allocating tasks and status is concerned, they seem to be of a quantitative rather than a qualitative nature.

The phenomenon of an increase in the number of women working is not restricted to France. As in other areas connected with the family, such as a fall in fertility or an increase in the divorce rate, there have been rather similar developments in other European countries and the United States. In the United Kingdom, 56 per cent of married women and mothers were working between 1968 and 1973. The corresponding figures were 55 per cent for Sweden and 50 per cent for the United States. A longitudinal study conducted between 1968 and 1975 has shown that only 9 per cent of working mothers with children earned 20 per cent of the family income and 3 per cent one third of it. Only a minority of women seem to have seen their work as a major part of their identity.[10]

Roles within the present-day couple

Rapid changes in mentalities

We must consider the causes of this recent increase in the number of women working and its implications for the allocation of roles.

A comparison of the findings of a survey organised by the *Caisse nationale des allocations familiales* (CNAF, French National Family Allowances Office) in 1971 with those of more recent ones clearly reflects the rapid changes in mentalities. The CNAF survey covered 1,762 families living in towns with a population of 10,000 or more and receiving family allowances. Their views on working mothers were analysed. Amongst women, manual workers were the socio-professional category most opposed to working mothers, with attitudes becoming more favourable further up the social and professional goals. Men were in agreement, whatever social milieu they belonged to, whatever number of children they had, and whether their own wives worked or not, that women with children should not work. Even the youngest, both married and single, were less in favour of it than young women, as Nicole Tabard notes in *Besoins et aspirations des familles et des jeunes*. The survey also brought out the number of 'moderate' women respecting both the idea of wives staying at home and that of the work ethic and hence neither actively for or against the idea. These were middle-class women married to managers and in clerical and similar work themselves or women who had been in management. Men had the greatest say when women decided to give up work and if there was no agreement, it was usually their view that prevailed. It is possible that these apparently rather conservative ideas were the result of surveying particular social groups at a particular time.

It is difficult to make comparisons as questionnaires and the population surveyed are rarely identical. However, despite these reservations, the rapidity with which attitudes changed is striking if the CNAF findings are compared with those of a survey carried out by Louis Roussel in 1975 of a sample of young and older couples who answered the same questionnaire. Questions designed to assess the degree of cultural continuity between generations covered the division of roles and attitudes to women working. Both generations saw 'a fairly big change' of a rather beneficial nature (Table 8.2).

A specific question assessed the content of the new distribution of roles. The response to that concerning 'looking after the baby' showed a difference between the generations and a change in attitudes. Although 53 per cent of parents saw this as an exclusively maternal task, 57 per cent of the married children thought both parents should look after the infant. The gap was particularly wide

Table 8.2. *Question 1: 'Between your generation and that of your child, has there been a change in equality between men and women?' Question 2: 'If so, how do you see this change?'*

	Parents' survey			Children's survey		
	M	F	All	M	F	All
Question 1						
No	32	27	29	30	27	29
A little	23	18	20	21	18	19
Quite a lot	31	35	33	31	36	34
A great deal	13	20	17	17	17	17
Don't know	1	–	1	1	2	1
Question 2						
Very good	16	24	20	29	35	33
Good	60	59	59	61	57	59
Rather bad	8	8	8	5	2	2
Very bad	1	–	1	–	1	1
Don't know	15	9	12	5	5	5

Source: L. Roussel, *La Famille après le mariage des enfants.* Travaux and documents, cahier no. 78. (Paris: PUF, 1976), p. 121.

in the case of older parents, of whom 60 per cent saw this as the mother's specific task (Table 8.3).

The responses to the question concerning women working confirm the change in attitudes amongst the younger members of the community. From those over sixty-five to those under twenty-five, the percentage preferring mothers to stay at home decreases regularly, as Table 8.3 shows.

Roussel does point out, however, that the overwhelming majority of respondents are still opposed to the idea of both spouses having equally demanding jobs (Table 8.4). This clearly shows that women rather than men are still seen as responsible for running the home and in particular for looking after young children. Even if a differentiation of roles resulting from a social differentiation of male and female careers is becoming less of a major feature of our society, 'for the moment, the asymmetrical model is still the dominant one'.[11]

It is clear from these findings that there is not whole-hearted support for changes in roles. Even with major recent developments, the new model has not been unreservedly accepted.

These studies examined opinion and not behaviour, which we will look at in the next section. There is often a wide gap between the two, and although it is undeniable that opinions have changed, the

Table 8.3. *'Do you think it is preferable that only the mother should look after babies, or doesn't it matter whether it is the mother or the father?'* (responses reported in %)

	Parents' survey			Children's survey		
	Mother only	Both parents	Don't know	Mother only	Both parents	Don't know
Men	56	40	4	46	52	2
Women	51	45	4	35	62	3
All	53	43	4	40	57	3
Age						
Parents Children						
under 50 under 25	50	43	7	38	60	2
50–59 25–29	46	50	4	36	60	4
60–64 30–39	56	42	2	41	57	2
65 & over 40–49	60	35	5	46	51	3
Socio-professional category of respondent						
Agriculture	58	37	5	51	48	1
Manual	54	42	4	49	50	1

Clerical	52	46	2	40	55	5
Middle management	38	60	2	22	75	3
Traders	57	39	4	44	52	4
Upper management & professions	52	44	4	31	66	3
Size of commune						
Rural	55	40	5	46	52	2
Under 50,000	50	47	3	39	59	2
50,000–200,000	54	42	4	44	53	3
200,000 and over	55	42	3	39	59	2
Greater Paris	51	47	2	29	67	4
Religious practice						
No religion	56	41	3	35	63	2
Religious, not practising	54	44	2	42	56	2
Irregular practice	51	46	3	40	58	2
Regular practice	53	41	6	43	52	5
Educational level						
Primary	55	41	4	52	47	1
Technical & Commercial	45	51	4	43	55	2
Upper primary & secondary	50	47	3	33	63	4
Higher	51	45	4	26	70	4

Source: L. Roussel, *La Famille après le mariage des enfants*, p. 121.

Table 8.4. *'Which of these three models is nearest your own ideal of family life?'* (responses reported in %)

1. A family in which both husband and wife have equally demanding jobs?
2. A family in which the wife has a job, but a less demanding one than the husband's?
3. A family in which the wife stays at home?

		Parents' survey				Children's survey			
		1	2	3	Don't know	1	2	3	Don't know
Men		7	30	60	3	12	38	48	2
Women		7	34	55	4	14	46	37	3
All		7	32	57	4	13	42	42	3
Age									
Parents	Children								
under 50	under 25	6	39	49	6	17	46	36	1
50–59	25–29	7	33	56	4	17	44	36	3
60–65	30–39	8	35	55	2	12	42	44	2
65 & over	40–49	8	27	61	4	6	40	50	4
Socio-professional category of respondent									
Farmers		10	27	59	4	9	34	55	2

Ind./agri. workers	7	31	58	4	9	38	51	2
Clerical	4	32	60	4	14	43	39	4
Middle management	7	38	51	4	16	55	26	3
Traders	7	36	55	2	10	30	37	3
Upper management	7	31	58	4	20	44	31	5
Size of commune								
Rural	10	26	61	3	11	33	55	1
under 50,000	5	33	56	6	11	43	43	3
50,000–200,000	4	41	51	4	12	45	40	3
200,000 and over	5	34	58	3	12	47	39	2
Greater Paris	11	35	52	2	21	48	25	6
Religious practice								
No religion	10	38	48	4	25	41	29	5
Religion, not practising	8	34	55	3	13	43	43	1
Irregular practice	6	32	59	3	10	44	44	2
Regular practice	6	28	62	4	4	38	55	3
Educational level								
Primary	7	29	61	3	9	34	56	1
Technical & commercial	10	42	45	3	12	45	42	1
Upper primary & secondary	7	40	48	5	12	46	38	4
Higher	10	29	59	2	23	47	23	7

Source: Louis Roussel, *Le Famille après le mariage des enfants*, p. 125.

243

contemporary norm is ambiguous. Women who do not work feel that they are seen as inferior in certain milieux. On the other hand, the idea of women working might be accepted by an ever-increasing number of people, but only superficially and often with the proviso that domestic and maternal tasks should not suffer. It is too soon to talk of the emergence of a single norm that would facilitate changes in roles, and we are still at a transitional stage.

THE CONTEMPORARY COUPLE

Does our current practice really indicate an increasing movement towards a lack of differentiation between roles? What is happening to the respective status of husbands and wives? Does it bring about equality and a higher degree of satisfaction?

The new distribution of roles

A survey conducted in 1966 by Andrée Michel showed a correlation between women working and a more egalitarian distribution of roles and tasks.[12] Its findings, based on a comparison of the situation of wives who did not go out to work and those who did, were that unpaid work done by wives either in the form of domestic work or as shopkeepers or artisans did not in any way enhance their position or authority as women, as they had no wage or income of their own; that the more they worked in a prestigious sector and the better qualified they were within the manual-clerical worker group, the greater the improvement in the balance of power within the couple; and that the determining factor was the level of their earnings and in particular the difference between their own and those of their husbands.

By examining more closely the distribution of domestic tasks, which include household jobs and managing the budget, shopping, buying clothes, visits to shops and preparing tax returns, Michel has shown that they are shared more equally when the wife has a job (Table 8.5). By linking tasks and socio-professional category, she has established the degree of equality in the sharing of domestic tasks. Wives working in management received the greatest help from their husbands, with other socio-professional categories occupying intermediate positions between theirs and that of wives not going out to work, who received the least assistance.

We should note, however, that despite their increased workload, female manual workers most often carry out tasks such as shopping and buying clothes alone. They traditionally manage the

Table 8.5. *Individual score for completion of each domestic task, by nature of wife's employment*

	None	Trader, Artisan	Manual	Clerical, etc.	Management
Dishes	5.67	5.45	5.34	4.90	4.44
Shopping	5.70	4.90	5.67	5.14	4.91
Floor	5.50	5.20	5.30	4.72	4.95
Preps. for guests	5.28	5.00	5.23	5.01	5.37
Correspondence	4.67	4.57	4.62	4.75	4.33
Buying clothes	3.15	4.93	5.23	4.93	4.93
Managing budget	4.40	4.29	4.96	4.73	4.37
Taxes	2.67	3.47	2.85	3.47	3.26
Repairs	3.04	2.67	2.65	2.65	2.94
Total score	6.86	6.55	6.74	6.57	6.26

Note: The table shows the distribution of the score for female participation in each domestic task by the wife's employment. It should be borne in mind that it is a score for the *relative* contribution of husband and wife and that equal participation is indicated by a score of 4.
Source: Andrée Michel, *Activité professionnelle de la femme et vie conjugale*, p. 86.

family budget – a very tight one – and also wish to retain overall supervision of expenditure. But, as Michel points out:

With regard to the general score for domestic tasks, female manual workers may come close to those not going out to work, but that does not mean any real sharing of ideas and attitudes. The latter carry out most domestic tasks because they have a traditional idea of the woman's role, which has not been affected by going out to work. The latter, however, have overthrown certain traditionally male roles because most of them are considered by their husbands and by themselves to control the family purse-strings.[13]

The range of tasks used to establish the degree of authority and the extent to which tasks are shared can clearly be questioned. Why should polishing the floor be included, but not doing the washing and ironing? Nor does the responsibility for children appear in any clear form. It is not enough to subsume it under 'decisions concerning children'. We now know that the conflict between maternal and professional tasks is the hardest to resolve and the problems connected with education or looking after children are of a different nature from daily or weekly shopping. François de Singly also points out that it is not enough simply to take the level of wages into account, as what makes the real difference in 'the struggle within marriage for domestic power' is whether the wife's earnings are seen as indispensable income or merely as an extra wage.[14] In 1978, the *Fédération nationale des écoles de parents et des éducateurs* surveyed a representative sample of French families with children between the ages of seven and eleven. The parents had consequently been born during the war or just after it and were younger than those surveyed by Michel. In 1,300 families replying to the questionnaire, 37 per cent of the women had a full-time job.[15] The findings of this survey clashed with Roussel's. They did not perhaps contradict them, but simply showed the gap between what is said and what is done, what is wished for and what actually takes place in everyday life. For example, the mother prepared the meals in 82 per cent of the households and the father in 2 per cent. The figures for looking after children and caring for sick children were mothers, 81 per cent, fathers 1 per cent, and those for contacts with teachers 57 per cent and 9 per cent respectively. It was only in connection with play that the sexes participated to more or less the same extent: 15 per cent of fathers and 21 per cent of mothers. Thus, whether the mother worked or not, in practice there was less progress towards sharing than opinion polls might have led us to believe. In addition the social reproduction of roles was taking place within the families themselves, for girls (57 per cent) were expected to do the washing-up more often than boys (40 per cent) and also to clean the house (44 per cent as against 28 per cent) or look after a younger sibling (8 per cent as compared with 3 per cent). The only task boys were given more often than girls was running errands (23 per cent as against 15 per cent).

An egalitarian distribution of roles may be on its way to becoming the norm, but practice is changing slowly.

The pressure of domestic commitments

Studies of the conflict between maternal and professional tasks are most often concerned with the problem of looking after young children. This seems to presuppose that once the child starts school there is nothing else to do. We have, however, already mentioned tasks relating to health and out-of-school activities and the time spent with children of all ages in supervising homework or simply discussing things with them. Typically such jobs fall to the mother, as the father often stays later at work so as to further his career. Women's work is always seen as of secondary importance, and if a wife puts her job first she is usually given responsibility for her children's psychological problems.

In present-day society all things work together to increase the

Table 8.6. *Average daily timetable of married town dwellers with one or more children* (given in hours and minutes)[a]

	Men working	Women working	Women not working
Looking after children[b]	0 h 17	1 h 05	1 h 59
Other domestic activities[c]	1 h 13	3 h 53	5 h 53
Time at work (including travelling)	6 h 48	4 h 52	
Own time[d]	11 h 06	10 h 50	11 h 19
Free time[e]	3 h 52	2 h 39	3 h 52
Travelling not related to job	0 h 43	0 h 41	0 h 52
Total	24 h 00	24 h 00	24 h 00

[a] *Averages over seven days of the week, whether working days or not.*
[b] *Material care for infants and children, supervising homework and lessons, indoor and outdoor games, walks with children.*
[c] *Cooking, housework, washing, shopping, administrative formalities, etc.*
[d] *Sleep, meals at home and elsewhere, personal and medical care.*
[e] *Education, religion, associations, theatre and cinema, etc., receptions, sports, excursions, reading, television, music, repairs and improvements to the home, handicrafts, all other leisure activities.*
Source: Marie-Thérèse Huet, Yannick Lemel and Caroline Roy, *Les Emplois du temps des citadins*, Document 'rectangle', INSEE, Dec. 1978.

burden of responsibility on mothers, and the 'timetable' surveys conducted by the Institut National de la Statistique et des Etudes Economiques (INSEE) in 1974–75, covering around 7,000 people, show how overloaded a schedule they have (Table 8.6).

Table 8.6 very tellingly highlights the time devoted to children and domestic tasks by each sex. The facts are abundantly clear: Men who were working spent a mere fifteen minutes of their time on the former and one hour thirteen minutes on the latter each day, whereas working women daily spent over an hour and almost four hours respectively. They also cut down the time spent on cooking and housework and the like more than time spent on children.

It is true that if Table 8.6 is compared with the findings of the surveys conducted in the 1950s by Paul-Henri Chombart de Lauwe amongst working-class families, the increase in the standard of living is shown in the reduction in the number of hours spent in housework. Chombart de Lauwe reported that 55 per cent of women who were not working did more than twelve hours of

Table 8.7. *Husband's help in the home* (in %)

Reported help by husband at least once a week	Wife not working	Wife working part-time	Wife working full-time
No help	22	17	9
Washing-up only	14	15	12
Other tasks (cleaning, cooking, child care etc.) with or without washing-up	64	68	79
N	539	320	293

Source: Young and Wilmott, *The Symmetrical Family*, p. 115.

housework and 10 per cent over fourteen. The worst job was washing, as a number of dwellings had no running water.[16]

Wives still have heavy domestic commitments, however, and these increase with the number of children. A 1971 CNAF-(Centre de recherches et d'Etudes documentaires (CREDOC) survey showed that women with more than two children spent over one hour and twenty minutes more on housework than those with one or two children.

The temporal constraints within which roles are structured emerge clearly from surveys of budgets and timetables, and the roles themselves depend on social, economic and sexual factors. The surveys mean that it is possible to analyse how the twenty-four hours of each day are allocated to work, rest, leisure activities, free time and so on. With regard to the distinction between time at work and time spent attending to domestic obligations, it is remarkable how constant the gap between men and women remains irrespective of professional category.[17]

The variable nature of models

In France, we have no studies of the distribution of roles as detailed as certain Anglo-Saxon ones, and we will have to refer to the latter. As early as 1950, Bott was noting in her *Family and Social Network* that there was a double model of role distribution, with extremes that were perfectly polarised but quite accepted in the social circle under observation:

There was considerable variation in the way husbands and wives performed their conjugal roles. At one extreme was a family in which the husband and wife carried out as many tasks as possible separately and independently of

Table 8.8. *Choice between more pay and more time off (men and women working full-time) (in %)*

	Men		Women	
	Single	Married	Single	Married
More pay	57	49	51	22
More time off	37	47	44	75
Other answers	6	4	5	3
N	144	522	73	152

Source: Young and Wilmott, *The Symmetrical Family*, p. 115.

each other. There was a strict division of labour in the household, in which she had her tasks and he had his. He gave her a set amount of housekeeping money, and she had little idea of how much he earned or how he spent the money he kept for himself. In their leisure time, he went to cricket matches with his friends, whereas she visited her relatives and went to a cinema with a neighbour. With the exception of festivities with relatives, this husband and wife spent very little of their leisure time together. They did not consider that they were unusual in this respect. On the contrary, they felt their behaviour was typical of their social circle. At the other extreme was a family in which husband and wife shared as many activities and spent as much time together as possible. They stressed that husband and wife should be equals: all major decisions should be made together, and even in minor household matters they should help one another as much as possible. This norm was carried out in practice. In their division of labour, many tasks were shared or interchangeable. The husband often did the cooking and sometimes the washing and ironing. The wife did the gardening and often the household repairs as well. Much of their leisure time was spent together, and they shared similar interests in politics, music, literature, and in entertaining friends. Like the first couple, this husband and wife felt their behaviour was typical of their social circle.[18]

A survey of the middle classes carried out in the 1970s by Michael Young and Peter Wilmott in *The Symmetrical Family* shows that role-sharing tended to occur midway between these two extremes and establishes that even if the husband tended to do more if his wife was working (as was also the case in Michel's survey), the latter still lived in a state of permanent pressure (Table 8.7).

One question really brought out the sense of a hectic life. When those working full-time were asked whether, given the choice, they would prefer higher earnings or more free time, the men clearly preferred the former and the women the latter (Table 8.8). The difference between unmarried and married women was marked, the latter feeling themselves to be the persons ultimately responsible for home and family and wanting more time for their children and for running the house.

In present-day society, a job means a conflict that creates guilt feelings in the wife, who is torn between two roles. Those women who have one recognise its positive aspects, particularly in financial terms, and feel that it confers a certain status, but only at the cost of fatigue and a certain moral unease. Respondents to Young and Wilmott's questionnaires said that they had not enough time to look after their children properly and do all that needed doing in the home. Frenchwomen would give the same answer.

Managing the budget

When there are two wages coming in, the family budget is managed differently, and this is perhaps the role that has changed most. Even if it is lower than the husband's, a wife's wage cannot often be treated merely as 'extra' income. When a household is committed to hire-purchase agreements, to buying a house, a car or a domestic appliance, her wage is what pays the instalments.

In older types of working-class families, the husband usually gave the wife housekeeping money, with which she had to manage to feed the family and care for the children. This role did not always increase her standing. The husband kept back a fixed sum of pocket-money for drink and tobacco and the wife had to struggle to make ends meet if his wage fell. Chombart de Lauwe describes roles connected with the budget in the years following the Second World War:

The working-class man feels that it is his responsibility to keep his family. His domain is the work-place and not the home. He feels strongly that his world is that of work, the struggle of his class, and his comrades. A woman without a job sees it as her responsibility to keep the house in order and feed and clothe the family with the money her husband gives her. Their roles are clear-cut and often carried out with humour despite difficulties, and these exchanges between man and wife can be a source of relaxation and equilibrium. Nevertheless, women are often relegated to a lower rank and many of them want a different form of organisation that would enable them to go out to work.[19]

The bourgeois model, in which women did not work, was quite different. The husband gave his wife a personal allowance, but looked after expenditure and financed major purchases himself.

Table 8.9. *Budget management as between husband and wife (Paris sample) according to whether the latter has a paid job* (in %)

	Wife working	Wife not working
Mainly husband's task	24	9
Equally divided	33	42
Mainly wife's task	43	49
N	217	155

Source: Andrée Michel, *Activité professionnelle de la femme et vie conjugale,* p. 83.

First, the personal expenses of husband and wife decreased as a result of those cultural changes that had led the former to return to the home. Collective expenditure, however, increased correspondingly on such items as housing, equipment for the home, cars, family entertainment and holidays. Once expenditure became a family matter, there was no longer any point in making specific items either the husband's or the wife's particular responsibility. The latter's earnings also confirmed this tendency. If she allocated her income to items of collective expenditure, the husband would find it harder to keep his total earnings secret or to refuse to make a proper contribution. It would therefore seem that a change in roles in practice has less to do with the actual sharing of tasks, which indicates a high level of inertia, than with the ways in which the resources of the household are managed, which is important both symbolically and materially. The husband prefers to give his wife more prerogatives in an area that was traditionally his, particularly when she is still making a contribution to the budget. The survey conducted by Michel had already indicated this development.

There is another factor apart from roles that must be considered, and that is the sectors of responsibilities as internalised by both spouses, for this provides the key to current contradictions with regard to the status of women. The norm would be to accept the fact of women working provided that their homes do not suffer. Men have a job, women have two, the professional and the domestic, whatever they may actually do. There are certain great differences between the woman working in a factory and the woman who is an executive, but the general pattern of their lives is the same. The area in which shared roles is most concretely evident is that concerned with the family budget (Table 8.9), that of major decisions concerning life-styles and the future, holidays, expenditures and the ways in which the children are to be brought up and educated. Managing the budget and signing the tax form perhaps enhance the wife's status to some extent and may even look like social advancement, but husbands have no desire to load the dishwasher or cook the dinner every day. A husband might gladly cook on Sunday evening because it is something out of the ordinary or because he wants to make a special occasion of it, but putting the potatoes on to boil before he has even had time to take his coat off and answering the children, who are all talking at the same time and trying to get his attention, are jobs no man will deprive his wife of. It is clear why there is such a wide gap between opinions and practice and why the allocation of roles can only change slowly.

Male reluctance to share material tasks is due to the lowly status of these tasks, which can be related to their pre-industrial nature and mode of production. Such jobs cannot readily be standardised or rationalised or subjected to efficiency checks, all of which are attributes of industrial activity and have gradually become the values and myths of work and the whole of human activity. As Martha Reed Herbert has said, the industrial mentality systematically devalues any kind of work keeping its pre-industrial form, and it is the mode of production, not the product, which is seen as being of greater importance.[20]

An analysis of roles must take both domestic and professional ones into account. They must not be treated as separate and self-contained areas, as there is a constant process of mutual interference between them. A survey of households in Le Mirail, on the outskirts of Toulouse, considers their system of activity as a single whole.[21] In the case of each family, the observers note both the effects of professional life on family life and vice versa, seeing the domestic group as a place where resources (income, patrimony) are concentrated, where real work (housework) is carried out, where different networks (kinship, neighbourhood, affinity) are interconnected, where constraints can be regulated by a distribution of tasks amongst the members of the group, and decisions profoundly affecting the activity of everyone are taken.

Three models of life-styles emerge, which designate as many modes of role organisation and also link roles to the professional system and the system of social relationships; they also include visits to family and friends and activities with a rhythm and a timetable imposed from the outside, referred to as 'sociality' by the authors, such as sport and militancy, for example. The first of these models, the 'traditional' one, is characterised by a non-working wife, 'sociality' of a private type and an insistence on the traditional role of women. The second, or 'intermediate', model has an instrumental

252

type of relationship with professional work. Subjects in this group wanted to work more to earn more, and the wife's role was to devote herself to her husband's career. Here, 'sociality' was not a prominent feature. The third is 'egalitarian' or 'economic egalitarian', with the wife's job seen as important, or 'egalitarian exteriocentered', where the concern expressed about life-style was largely of a family nature.

Satisfaction within the couple

If it seems risky to speculate about the happiness of couples in past times, it might seem easy to discuss that of present-day ones, as we can always ask them whether they are happy. And yet this area is as difficult as power to analyse. Some studies are concerned with predicting the degree of conjugal harmony and try to put science at the service of family stability. If it is possible to establish what will make a successful or an unsuccessful couple, why not give those concerned the benefit of the information in advance?

Other research has treated the subject from the point of view of the family life cycle, in terms of the duration of the marriage and the number of children, concentrating on periods of tension.[22] When children are aged between six and fourteen, relationships between husband and wife change, even in the case of those couples who accept traditional roles. It is a period of economic, psychological and social constraints in which the wife is submerged by the multiplicity of demands made on her and the husband is absorbed by the preoccupations associated with his job. A number of studies have shown that satisfaction in marriage tends to decline once children are born, and much more so for women than for men. The inadequacy of the romantic idea of a love-match becomes clear in the practical situation in which the couple find themselves. The illusions of love are dispelled when husband and wife become aware of previously hidden differences of culture or education, or when two cultural traditions are in conflict over matters of hygiene or diet, when the in-laws are always intruding or when the arrival of children produces demands that cause the couple to split up.

The phase of the family life cycle in which several children make their rival – and considerable – claims to parental care and presence is a particularly critical one. The couple has to be able to adapt to anxiety-provoking situations for which there is no accepted behavioural framework, as present-day society has abolished those rituals that once offered means of coping with stress and worry. Parents have to adopt attitudes that they know to be of major importance and that could have irreversible effects on their children. In such a situation, each decision taken creates anxiety and could set off family conflicts that might even lead to divorce. A lack of agreement about bringing up children or about attitudes to be adopted with regard to their independence, their aggression or their educational progress sometimes reveals fundamental differences within the couple.

This tension seems to increase when the children reach their teens. Parents unconsciously compete with children developing sexually at puberty. The problems specific to that age – the rejection of parental values, the attempt to push parental permissiveness to its extreme limits, the first sexual experiences, drugs – all create a series of dilemmas for parents who have to face up to situations calling for a very high level of intuition and self-control. When their children are adolescents, parents are roughly half-way through their lives, at a critical point in their careers, and mothers are approaching the menopause. Present-day society imposes its cult of youth, which increases the difficulty of communicating with children.

In the latter hypothesis, the causes of the deterioration of understanding within the couple are linked to the increasing complexity of relationships entailed by the presence of children. Michel has tested a further variable, the external one of the wife's job. The fact that she has one might seem to guarantee the success of the marriage, but by revealing variations according to educational levels and socio-professional status, Michel shows that the correlation between the satisfaction of the wife and her job is by no means a straightforward one. We have already noted the relationship between her socio-professional status and the demand for divorce. Not only is the wife more often the partner instituting divorce proceedings when she has a job. The higher her socio-professional status is, the more likely she also is to be the initiator of such proceedings. Even though the opposite has not been shown, having a job does not guarantee that a woman will experience satisfaction and enjoy a lasting marriage.

Should the wife's job be seen as an 'external' variable of the couple's satisfaction? Very often, it is a cause of family dissension and becomes an issue. The jobs of husband and wife are no longer seen as complementary parts of a production activity, nor as based on a division of labour in which each partner carries out different but linked tasks for the sake of family unity. When there is competition between their careers, antagonism rather than an increased interdependence can result from it. The work of each spouse is no longer part of a common collective labour, as was the case in the peasant or working-class family of the past, but is based on an interdependence orientated towards the achievement of personal aims of a very varied nature. The work of each spouse could thus be seen as a potentially centrifugal force, and dual-career families offer an example of this.

Michel's research deals with the female side of such matters and is resolutely feminist in approach, implying perhaps that only women have suffered as a result of the traditional pattern of role structures. What happens in the male sphere when traditional models shift? There has been little work on this aspect apart from the first studies of divorced fathers claiming their paternity and the right to the custody of their children. Thus Yves Mamou's observations in *Le Monde* of 14 September 1980 suggest new approaches. He analyses the 'unease in the new man', who is confronted with a model that, although it is not always the operative one, profoundly questions his place in society. In supporting certain women's claims, which seem to them justifiable, such men suddenly discover that they are targets and victims. The male identity crisis is well explained: Women earn a wage, have a share in social representation, control their own fertility and achieve independence. Recognising that work is part of female identity and no longer a secondary activity is often a painful process for men. When there is a professional crisis in their lives, unemployment followed by a job outside the place of residence, tension may arise within the couple if the husband refuses to take his wife's professional situation into account. Men, who have been brought up to be the bulwark of the couple, find that they are vulnerable when they realise they are no longer indispensable. Mamou writes:

Upheavals in man–woman relationships force men to a new and profound reassessment for which nothing had prepared them, for the traditional conjugal relationship was part of the mother–son relationship. The traditional wife gave her husband the same services as his mother had given him, made him complete ('my better half') and reassured him. If the modern companion refuses that role, the man feels himself to be an orphan, with all the anxiety, distress and disorientation that the word implies.

SUGGESTED READING

The two works by Louis Roussel, *Le Mariage dans la société française contemporaine* and *La Famile après le mariage des enfants*, and *La Sociologie de la famille et du mariage* by Andrée Michel, which have already been mentioned, are the major references for this chapter.

Roles within the present-day couple

Bott, Elizabeth. *Family and Social Network.* 2d ed. London: Tavistock, 1971.

De Singly, François. 'La Lutte conjugale pour le pouvoir domestique'. *Revue française de sociologie* 17(1976): 81–100.

Fougeyrollas, Pierre. 'Prédominance du mari ou de femme dans le ménage'. *Population* 6(1951): 83–102.

'Masculin, feminin, pluriel. Les rôles au sein du couple. Les relations entre générations'. *Informations sociales* 6–7(1977): 1–99.

Michel, Andrée. *Activité professionelle de la femme et vie conjugale.* Paris: Centre National de la Recherche Scientifique, 1967.

Famille, industrialisation, logement. Paris: CNRS, 1967.

Parsons, Talcott. *Family, Socialization and Interaction Process.* Glencoe, Ill.: Free Press, 1955.

Rapoport, Robert and Rhona. *Dual Career Families Re-examined.* New York: Harper & Row, 1976.

Tabard, Nicole. *Besoins et aspirations des familles et des jeunes.* Paris: CREDOC and CNAF, 1974.

Touzard, Hubert. *Enquête psychologique sur les rôles conjugaux et la structure familiale.* Paris: Centre National de la Recherche Scientifique, 1967.

Young, Michael, and Peter Wilmott. *The Symmetrical Family. A Study of Work and Leisure in the London Region.* London: Routledge & Kegan Paul, 1973.

The psychotherapy of the family

Lemaire. J.-G. *Le Couple, sa vie, sa mort.* Paris: Payot, 1979.

Dialogue, Journal of the Association française des centres de consultations conjugales.

Roles and the cycle of family life

Rodgers, Roy. *Family Interaction and Transaction: The Developmental Approach.* Englewood Cliffs, N.J.: Prentice-Hall, 1973.

Hareven, Tamara K. 'The Family as a Process: The Historical Study of the Family's Cycle'. *Journal of Social History* 7(1974): 322–9.

Chapter 9

The domestic group and economic roles

Does the domestic group of our day still play a determining role? A reading of sociological studies might persuade us to think that it perhaps does not. The current view seems to be that it was once a unit of production but is now only a unit of consumption, and yet there is at the same time a view of society as a consumer society. This must mean that the domestic group tends to carry out a central function of a rapidly developing society. Consumption is not the minor factor that such a view might suggest. As a result of higher standards of living, it has become diversified and extended. Spending and consuming imply decisions made in terms of hierarchies of needs. The domestic group is becoming a unit of planning in areas that go beyond merely monetary matters, since every decision concerning expenditure has an affective aspect.

In the United States in particular, the 'new home planning' trend in research is rediscovering the family, and more especially domestic relationships in so far as they shape decisions about the allocation of time and goods. The household is becoming the directing factor in a complex economic organisation in which the process of consumption merits as formal a treatment as that of a commercial or industrial undertaking. Such research, however, does not take cognizance of the social, psychological and affective constraints that guide the choices made by households, seeing them simply as subject only to that of scarce resources. For sociologists, these investigations cannot be totally convincing.[1]

The economic function of the domestic group has another dimension, which is linked to inheritance and the transmission of goods. Every household transmits a patrimony, whether material, cultural or symbolic. That brings in once more a temporal dimension uniting the domestic group with past and future generations and containing the destiny of the family.

257

The domestic group and economic roles

THE DOMESTIC GROUP AS AN INCOME UNIT AND A CONSUMPTION UNIT

In examining family budgets, we will not attempt to determine who decides and authorises and carries out expenditures, as these are problems of power and authority of the kind examined in the last chapter, but rather to understand how domestic groups organise themselves with regard to their incomes and expenditures and subsequently to point out the importance of social inequalities and the redistribution of goods.

Here, the domestic group will often be called the household, following the definition and terminology suggested by the French system of national income accounting, even though these do not coincide exactly with historical and anthropological ones. The national system bases the household on its place of residence and is tightly defined in an attempt to observe its economic behaviour, its purchasing power and its budget. It is difficult to use the new system, however, as it includes individual undertakings amongst households and also uses consumption in a wider sense than is normally the case, to include rent, health care and so on.[2]

The domestic group as a productive cell and/or a unit of income

Some economists see the domestic group as a productive cell. Dominique Strauss-Kahn, for example, in his *Economie de la famille et accumulation patrimoniale*, does not consider the goods consumed so much as their functions: A vegetable is a good that makes it possible to prepare the commodity we call a meal, which corresponds to the 'feeding' function. Thus the household is seen as a small-scale undertaking whose consumption of foodstsuffs is organised on the basis of household time and goods purchased as a result of the sale of working time on the market. The labour force is a product of the household that is used for the transformation of foodstuffs, and whenever foodstuffs are utilised, the household will produce some labour force.

The idea of the household as a place of production has not yet been incorporated into the national system of income accounting (except in connection with the production from family gardens). It can be seen as such only if new economic models centred on the economic evaluation of housework are taken into consideration. Since the latter cannot be expressed in terms of money, it is not taken into account in the national system, unlike home consumption of farm produce or work done at home as part of a family business.

Tasks performed at home by women, however, have been estimated to account for between 25 and 30 per cent of national production,[3] which casts some doubt on the alleged loss of productive functions in the contemporary family. When there is production and home consumption domestic work remains to some degree an underground phenomenon, but the same is not true if instead of preparing our own dinner and eating it at home we go out to a restaurant, or if instead of washing our own shirts, we take them to the laundry, since such services come onto the market and give rise to a monetary exchange.

Classically, the household is the place where one or more incomes are brought in, where the resources each member can draw from his or her work are pooled, and where various types of financing not directly related to earnings from work are received.

Wages may be paid once a month or more frequently and be fixed or involve bonuses. The way they are broken down is not without interest here, since the husband often keeps bonuses and they do not become part of the joint budget. When there are two wages coming in, as is most often the case nowadays, the real part played by the second one in the income of the household is debatable, given the increase in taxation and the income lost when certain social security benefits are withdrawn. The INSEE (Institut National de Statistiques et d'Etudes Economiques) has therefore calculated the contribution made by a second wage after tax deductions, taking into account categories of income and whether or not the couple has a child (Tables 9.1, 9.2).

As well as one or more wages – the wages of children working and still living in the domestic group could be analysed in the same way – family allowances make a large contribution to incomes.

When large families are involved, such allowances often increase income considerably, especially when there are more than three children. Such families, in which it is very difficult for the mother to work, could not manage without these allowances, which sometimes amount to more than the father's wage. Their share of the total range of incomes, however, is still decreasing. According to a survey on the family conducted by the *Commissariat général au Plan*, it fell from 5.5 per cent in 1956 to 3.5 per cent in 1970.[4]

At the individual level, the allowances are paid directly to the mother and are quite different in nature from the father's wage.

Although it is not normal practice to do so in economics, perhaps all the credit commitments households take on should be added to the spectrum of family incomes. Payments in connection with hire-purchase agreements are spread over a number of years and enable

Table 9.1. *Wages and income available with one and two wages (reported in French francs) in 1978: couples with no children*

	Manual	Clerical	Middle management[b]	Upper management[c]
One wage				
Annual wage	35,540 F	41,800 F	66,600 F	128,040 F
Income tax	1,050 F	1,640 F	5,020 F	18,780 F
Family allowances[a]	440 F	210 F		
Available income	34,930 F	40,370 F	61,580 F	109,260 F
Two wages				
Annual wages	60,170 F	73,730 F	98,540 F	173,530 F
Wife's wage as % of same	41%	43%	32.5%	26%
Income tax	4,000 F	6,120 F	11,280 F	30,260 F
Family allowances				
Available income	56,170 F	67,610 F	87,260 F	143,270 F
From wife's job	38%	40%	29.5%	24%

[a] *Housing allowance and family supplement.*
[b] *Middle management and clerical in cases of two wages.*
[c] *Upper and middle management in cases of two wages.*
Source: F. Evrard, 'Travail des femmes et revenu familial', in *Ressources familiales types de salariés*. INSEE (Institut National de la Statistique et des Etudes Economiques), pp. 57–58.

the household to have the use of a car or a domestic appliance immediately. It may seem curious to include hire-purchase payments as income, but they are akin to it in that they represent a kind of enforced saving or reduced spending that contributes considerably to the resources of the household.

The domestic group as a unit of consumption

Economists recognise that overall, along with income and socioprofessional category, the make-up of the household and in particular its size and the age of its head is the major factor accounting for expenditure.[5] If we compare major items of consumption, we can see a disparity, especially with regard to those that are not strictly necessary, such as transport and leisure. Economists prefer to deal with budgetary weighting (a percentage share of total consumption in connection with various items of consumption) rather than the total level of expenditure, as the former provides a more precise measure enabling them to identify differences in behaviour

Table 9.2. *Wages and income available with one and two wages (reported in French francs) in 1978: couples with one child under three years of age*

	Manual	Clerical	Middle management[b]	Upper management[c]
One wage				
Annual wage	35,540 F	41,800 F	66,600 F	128,040 F
Income tax	460 F	1,040 F	3,810 F	15,220 F
Family allowances[a]	5,760 F	5,520 F		
Available income	40,840 F	46,280 F	62,790 F	112,820 F
Two wages				
Annual wages	60,170 F	73,730 F	98,540 F	173,530 F
Wife's wage as % of same	41%	43.5%	32.5%	26%
Income tax	2,990 F	4,690 F	8,950 F	26,680 F
Family allowances	4,160 F			
Available income	61,340 F	69,040 F	89,590 F	146,850 F
From wife's job	33.5%	33%	30%	23%

[a] *Housing allowance and family supplement.*
[b] *Middle management and clerical in cases of two wages.*
[c] *Upper and middle management in cases of two wages.*
Source: F. Evrard, 'Travail des femmes et revenu familial', in *Ressources familiales types de salariés*. INSEE (Institut National de la Statistique et des Etudes Economiques), pp. 57–58.

between households other than that brought about by income. The 'income effect' cannot, of course, be totally eliminated since according to Engels's law the bigger a budget, the smaller the proportion of it spent on necessary products. If, for example, income per unit of consumption increases by 5,000 francs to 20,000 francs, the budgetary weighting of food falls from 42 to 24 per cent.

It is clear from Tables 9.3–9.5 that expenditure on food and health increases with age, whereas young households spend more on transport, clothes and housing than older ones.

Households consume the equivalent of two thirds of the gross domestic product, either collectively in the form of household equipment and food or individually in that of clothing and leisure. It is also possible to distinguish between goods for immediate consumption and durable consumer goods, and this expenditure is closely watched by both statisticians and politicians (we all know the phrase 'the housewife's shopping-basket') and manufacturers seeking to increase their turnover and create new needs.

Household consumption has several aspects. Traditionally, expen-

Table 9.3. a. *Annual average household expenditure on clothing by age of head* (reported in French francs)

	Under 25		25–34		35–44		45–54		55–64		All age groups	
	F	%	F	%	F	%	F	%	F	%	F	%
Outer clothing	1,121	45.9	1,176	45.4	1,269	41.2	1,190	41.6	653	36.7	890	40.7
Underclothes, lingerie	629	25.8	692	26.7	903	29.3	859	30.0	618	34.7	664	30.3
Materials, haberdashery, baby clothes	203	8.3	160	6.2	228	7.4	232	8.1	135	7.6	166	7.6
Shoes, footwear	306	12.5	397	15.3	484	15.7	375	13.1	216	12.1	303	13.8
Repairs to clothes and shoes	39	1.6	45	1.8	63	2.1	73	2.6	35	2.0	50	2.3
Cleaning and dyeing	143	5.9	120	5.6	131	4.3	133	4.6	122	6.9	116	5.3
All	2,441	100.0	2,590	100.0	3,078	100.0	2,862	100.0	1,779	100.0	2,189	100.0

262

b. *Annual average household expenditure on clothing by type of household*

	Single person under 65		Single person over 65		Couple, no children under 65		Couple, no children over 65		Couple, 1 child		Couple, 2 children		Couple, 3 or more children		All types	
	F	%	F	%	F	%	F	%	F	%	F	%	F	%	F	%
Outer clothing	509	41.7	134	22.9	712	41.5	289	30.5	1,103	42.5	1,367	42.6	1,367	39.7	890	40.7
Underclothing, lingerie	306	25.1	234	40.0	511	29.7	350	37.0	775	29.9	1,004	31.3	1,031	30.0	664	30.3
Baby clothes	61	5.0	51	8.7	148	8.6	116	12.3	188	7.2	210	6.5	262	7.6	166	7.6
Shoes and footwear	146	12.0	68	11.6	207	12.0	87	9.2	359	13.9	444	13.8	583	17.0	303	13.8
Repairs to clothes, shoes	38	3.1	27	4.6	36	2.1	35	3.7	41	1.6	69	2.2	79	2.3	50	2.3
Cleaning and dyeing	160	13.1	71	12.2	104	6.1	69	7.3	127	4.9	116	3.6	118	3.4	116	5.3
All	1,220	100.0	585	100.0	1,718	100.0	946	100.0	2,593	100.0	3,210	100.0	3,440	100.0	2,189	100.0

Source: Georges Bigata and Bernard Bouvier, *Composition des ménages et structure de leur budget en 1971.* Collections de l'Institut National de la Statistique et des Etudes Economiques 115, no. 31. December 1973, p. 26.

Table 9.4. *Average relative importance of budget items by age of head of household (%)*

Age of head of household	Food	Food and drink outside home	Clothes	Housing	Hygiene, personal care	Transport, telecommunications	Culture and leisure	Miscellaneous	Total consumption (%)	Total consumption (francs)
Under 25	22.3	6.6	10.9	22.7	6.2	15.2	7.3	8.8	100.0	22,453
25–34	26.9	5.2	9.7	20.7	6.7	15.5	5.4	9.9	100.0	26,697
35–44	32.4	4.7	10.7	16.1	7.0	13.8	5.7	9.6	100.0	28,654
45–54	33.6	4.8	10.7	15.2	6.9	12.1	6.5	10.2	100.0	26,789
55–64	36.1	3.8	8.6	15.3	9.3	11.2	5.4	10.3	100.0	20,638
65–74	38.6	3.2	7.9	16.5	12.0	8.2	4.3	9.3	100.0	14,596
75 and over	39.4	2.8	6.0	17.9	14.4	6.0	3.9	9.6	100.0	10,488
All age groups	32.8	4.5	9.7	17.0	8.1	12.5	5.6	9.8	100.0	22,527

Source: Georges Bigata and Bernard Bouvier, *Composition des ménages et structure de leur budget en 1971.* Collections de l'Institut National de la Statistique et des Etudes Economiques 115, no. 31, December 1973, p. 20.

Table 9.5. *Average relative importance of budget items by type of household (%)*

Type of household	Food	Food and drink outside home	Clothes	Housing	Hygiene, personal care	Transport, telecommunications	Culture and leisure	Miscellaneous	Total consumption	Total consumption (francs)
Single person under 65	24.7	10.1	9.4	20.4	7.9	11.7	6.3	9.5	100.0	12,959
Single person over 65	38.4	2.6	7.3	22.7	13.2	3.9	3.8	8.1	100.0	8,027
Couple, no children under 65	27.5	4.7	8.6	21.8	6.9	15.5	5.5	9.5	100.0	23,077
Couple, no children, over 65	40.2	2.2	6.2	15.7	15.4	7.3	4.0	9.0	100.0	15,214
Couple, 1 child	30.5	4.5	9.9	16.8	7.3	14.3	5.9	10.8	100.0	26,090
Couple, 2 children	30.2	4.4	10.8	16.4	6.9	14.8	5.9	10.6	100.0	29,746
Couple, 3 or more children	34.7	4.3	10.7	15.5	7.2	11.9	6.4	9.3	100.0	32,046
Others	34.7	4.8	10.2	16.1	7.9	11.7	5.2	9.4	100.0	24,890
All types of households	32.8	4.5	9.7	17.0	8.1	12.5	5.6	9.8	100.0	22,527

Source: Georges Bigata and Bernard Bouvier, *Composition des ménages et structure de leur budget en 1971*. Collections de l'Institut National de la Statistique et des Etudes Economiques 115, no. 31, December 1973, p. 20.

diture can be classified under the headings of several major items such as housing, clothes, food, health, insurance, leisure, taxes and so on, which correspond to basic needs. Very soon, however, our classification must become a little more sophisticated. From a strictly physiological point of view, is a trendily decorated flat or an expensive meal really necessary?

Expenditure on clothes is a good example of the non-economic aspect of consumption. In 1971, it formed an important part (some 10 per cent) of household budgets, and there were great differences between age-groups, socio-professional categories and small and large families. The latter devoted a large share of their expenditure on clothes to buying shoes, whereas older households spent most of theirs on buying underclothes. Since they had retired, they had less need to dress well. Young households spent much more than the annual average, and this is linked both to the structure of the clothes trade (with fashions chiefly a matter for the young) and the fact that they live largely in towns.[6] Increased expenditure on clothes is particularly evident amongst adolescents, for whom they are so important as an expression of personality, status and age that expenditure has little to do with the simple fact of getting dressed and has an essential symbolic function.

The economic space connected with consumption also needs to be considered. Where are purchases made? In small local shops, in big stores, in the district the customer lives in, in the town centre or in the outer suburbs? All these questions are linked to the type and level of expenditure and the way in which the family organises its buying.

The organisation of the family budget is very revealing, but there have been no French anthropological studies of this particular area of daily life to cast light on the family behaviour patterns of interest to us here. We must therefore look to ones from abroad for our answers. Ann Grey, for example, has brought to light a real family budgetary system in her studies of working-class budgets in Edinburgh.[7] The husband's wage is divided into housekeeping money, which is handed over to his wife, and a sum he keeps for his personal expenses and to contribute to family expenditure. This he does either by giving his wife an extra amount, or by meeting specific expenses such as the heating bill or repaying loans. Thus family expenditure consists of the sum of the housekeeping money and the husband's extra contributions less what has been deducted for his own needs. The wife's wage generally goes in with the housekeeping money, and that of any employed child living at home goes straight to the mother, who returns some of it as pocket-money, or else it is kept by the child who then pays his or her board.

Table 9.6. *Who pays for different items in the household budget*

	No. of households[a] in which item is paid for by			
	Husband	Wife	Both	No expenditure
Paid for by wife in				
at least ⅔ of cases				
Rent	4	44	0	36
Rates	20	52	4	8
Coal	6	20	0	58
Electricity	13	68	1	2[b]
Gas	11	54	4	15
Hire-purchase				
payments	11	45	0	28
Wife's clothing	9	64	11	0
Insurance	13	59	10	2
TV Rental	6	47	2	29
Cigarettes for wife	2	38	0	44
Paid for by husband in				
at least ⅔ of cases				
Cigarettes for husband	43	0	5	36
Visits to pubs	57	0	3	24
Running of car	27	0	3	54
Paid for by either				
party or frequently				
shared				
Mortgage	12	14	5	53
Husband's clothing	35	39	10	0
Children's clothing	39	35	10	0
Repairs, decorating	26	37	18	3
Furniture paid for				
in cash	14	34	9	27
Saving, holidays	18	31	30	5
Children's pocket				
money	20	27	29	8

[a] *Total no. of households for which information available: 84.*
[b] *Two households paid all-inclusive 'board money' to relatives with whom they lived.*
Source: Ann Grey, 'The Working-class Family as an Economic Unit', in C. Harris, ed., *The Sociology of the Family: New Directions for Britain*, p. 197.

Grey's research reveals something quite different from the practices described so far in that it shows the flexible nature of the housekeeping allowance, for more than half the husbands interviewed also took charge of some collective expenditure. Table 9.6

indicates how the responsibility for expenditure was allocated in the domestic groups in question. The study demonstrates how important it is to analyse the budget as a whole. It is not enough to know the total of the major items in it.

Considering the budget as a whole also implies an interest in the rhythm of expenditure, whether it be daily, weekly, monthly or annual, and oscillations connected with the family life cycle in a household. Certain types of specific expenditure take shape according to income in the budget. Cycles appear and structure time in the family increasingly rigidly as one moves down the scale of incomes.

Paul-Henri Chombart de Lauwe has shown that the way the budget is organised in working-class domestic groups varies a great deal according to whether spending takes place the day after pay-day or at the end of a fortnight or a month.[8] Colette Pétonnet, describing subproletarians in her *On est tous dans le brouillard*, illustrates consumption patterns that, although seemingly economically irrational, are explicable in terms of penury followed by an influx of ready cash (in the form of family allowances, which are quickly spent on luxuries when essentials are lacking).

Depending on the family life cycle, some periods are more favourable for budgets than others. In the wealthier classes, earnings increase with age as a result of career structure, whereas in the most deprived categories they decrease, and the poorest people are found amongst the oldest. Chombart de Lauwe suggests a graph based on a diagram by Halbwachs that illustrates the different levels of balance during the existence of a working-class budget (Fig. 9.1).

Certain Marxist-inspired feminist currents of opinion are concerned with the political economy of domestic work and the relationships between productive and non-productive work and view women as perhaps occupying a secondary place in the household's consumption because they are seen as engaged in secondary work.

The bread-winner eats meat. Expressed as an aphorism, this statement cuts across a number of differential practices of consumption that symbolise the redistribution that takes place within a household. Christine Delphy, for example, shows that in agricultural households in south-western France the wife and children and old people come second with regard to food.[9] The head of the family gets the most meat and the best parts of it. This practice is, of course, linked to the image of meat giving the worker strength. The wife internalises the situation to such an extent that she no longer even has any needs to repress. She does not like meat, she is not

The domestic group as an income unit and a consumption unit

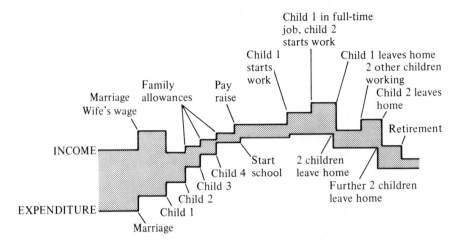

Fig. 9.1. Periods of income–expenditure convergence in a stabilized working-class budget.

hungry, and is not even aware that she is sacrificing herself. Chombart de Lauwe has described similar practices in working-class milieux. There would also be much to say about the mother in bourgeois households exercising her traditional right to save the scraps for herself.

Family budgets and social inequalities[10]

How the budget is managed is determined not only by the level of income and its internal organisation. Odile Benoit-Guilbot and Marie Moscovici have shown that it is managed differently by working-class households according to whether the place of work is a modern firm with an assured future or a traditional and less dynamic one.[11] In the first case, the basis for its management is a rational one involving security and foresight; in the second it is based on insecurity and lack of thought for the future. Families employed by the first type of firm plan their expenditures and save for specific purchases, whereas those in the second type do not think of the future and look out for further casual earnings. This is an interesting view that shows that how the firm works has some effect on the family's life-style as evidenced in its budget.

The financial inequalities between households are very clear.

269

Table 9.7. *Total average income (reported in French francs) per household by socio-professional category of head of household and number of dependent children, 1970*

	Number of dependent children[a]						
	0	1	2	3	4	5 and over	All
0. Agriculture, self-employed	10,229	11,555	12,871	11,673	13,359	12,439	11,339
1. Agriculture, employed	10,964	15,253	13,349	15,255	12,594	12,873	12,706
2. Professions	32,536	38,088	43,291	44,252	49,775	48,278	37,894
3. Upper management	53,948	54,803	57,540	59,121	73,692	71,493	57,229
4. Middle management	31,072	35,423	33,026	32,543	28,728	33,699	32,770
5. Clerical	20,827	25,381	24,278	22,544	20,429	20,844	22,546
6. Manual labourers	18,151	22,011	19,666	17,935	17,897	17,031	19,171
7. Not working	12,330	20,662	21,941	26,014	17,156	12,633	13,201
All	17,854	27,681	28,033	26,306	25,122	22,104	22,013
1965 average income (francs)	11,941	17,638	18,213	17,824	16,788	15,692	14,641
% increase 1965–70	49.5	56.9	53.9	47.6	49.6	40.9	50.4

[a] *As calculated for tax purposes.*
Source: *La Famille* (Paris: Hachette, 1975), p. 182, based on surveys of fiscal income of households in 1965 and 1970.

Table 9.8. *Average income (reported in French francs) per family[a] before and after family allowances,[b] by number of dependent children (fiscally), 1970*

	Number of families	Average fiscal income per family	Supplementary income from family allowances (%)	Average income per family with family allowances
No children	11,212	14,734	–	14,734
(where father employed)	(6,591)	(17,915)	–	(17 915)
One child	2,794	25,406	0.5	25,533
Two children	2,276	26,550	5.8	28,078
Three children	1,184	25,023	15.4	28,878
Four children	521	23,779	24.6	29,626
Five or more children	454	20,942	44.0	30,162
All	18,441	18,878	4.5	19,726

[a]*The survey covers families with a known fiscal income.*
[b]*Family allowances taken into account here include only family allowances in the strict sense of the term, the allowance for families with a single wage and that for a non-working mother.*
Source: *La Famille* (Paris: Hachette, 1975), p. 82, based on surveys of family fiscal incomes in 1965 and 1970.

Tables 9.7 and 9.8 give the average income in 1970 as reported on tax returns and also show how the number of children influences it. Depending on the socio-professsional category, the latter decreases after two, three or four children.

In order to have a more precise view of the situation one has to study the whole range of fiscal incomes of households to take into account income from children working and the extra financial burdens certain older members of the household might entail.

As Jean Stoetzel has shown, age also leads to an unequal distribution of income amongst the various social classes.[12] It goes hand in hand with the level of education, and almost without exception better education brings financial advantages. This peaks in the second (adult) age-cohort at every level. These two combined factors lead to extremes of minimum and maximum values in the distribution of incomes. Inequalities of this kind, which economists call primary inequalities, are to a greater or lesser extent corrected by various ways of trying to create a better distribution of wealth amongst families. There are several types of these, namely the setting up of collective facilities and services such as kindergartens, gymnasiums and the like, cutting down expenditures by reducing fares on public transport, providing health insurance and free education, and making money available for specific purposes such as housing allowances, scholarships, family allowances, single-wage supplements and family supplements for those working in government service.

How is aid of this kind seen at the level of the individual household? Do couples prefer help in kind or in cash? The *Caisse Nationale d'Allocations Familiales* (CNAF) set out to investigate these questions in Nicole Tabard's study of the needs and aspirations of families and young people:

Most people voted for cash allowances, and this trend was increasingly evident the further down the scale of incomes one went. The major role played by family allowances in particular for women with children overshadowed any other concern. At all levels of income a preference for help in the form of cash was associated with a dependence on social aid. The minority preference for help in kind was most marked in the case of young couples and families with a mother working. Here, the lower income groups favoured housing and the higher ones facilities (nurseries, etc.) for very young children.[13]

Policies aimed at redistributing income also achieve their purpose by means of family allowances and social security. Apart from help in kind or help specifically for the very poorest families in the form of holidays, the provision of home help and the services of social workers, etc., it seems that the social services are used most by families for whom they were not really intended. The CNAF survey showed that social centres, day nurseries, workshops and collective family holidays, children's holiday colonies and the like were increasingly used as both income and socio-professional category rose due to both the level of education and the professional status of parents and grandparents.

Tabard points out that differences in behaviour with regard to social provisions are closely linked to status, with the better-off classes benefiting from cultural, leisure or holiday activities and the least privileged using social workers, open-air centres and the like, which smack of public assistance. Thus not only are the compensatory effects of social action nil, but they consolidate inequalities by means of socio-cultural consumption that only the better-off classes can benefit from as a result of their level of education. The least-privileged families pay a double price because they both get little benefit from policies of this kind and find that when the policies are put into operation they themselves are institutionalized, controlled and supervised.

272

THE DOMESTIC GROUP AND INHERITANCE

The domestic group still has as one of its economic functions the transmission of a patrimony. Here we will examine inheritance practices; social reproduction as a whole, including the transmission of both material and cultural and symbolic goods, will be investigated in the next chapter.

If we compare peasant and present-day societies, for example, we can see that the importance of such practices is no longer the same. In the former, in which the ownership of land was the means of production, that land had to be handed on if the household was to survive. There have been a number of anthropological and historical studies of the ways in which that was done, and one can of course contrast systems entailing an equal division amongst all the heirs and those in which a single one was preferred. In practice, however, the distinction is too sharp, and there were various patterns that moved from one system to the other.[14]

Nowadays, with the growth of a wage-based economy (except, in France, in the case of the large number of farmers still working their own farms), an inheritance is not necessary for those wishing to set up house. The patrimony is transmitted in a much subtler way, by enabling children to study, for example, and many parents think that in giving their children a good education they are helping them more than they would by giving them tangible goods. As Louis Roussel says:

The first duty of parents is no longer to keep a patrimony in good order and pass it on to their children, but to enable them to become economically independent when they marry.[15]

The second feature of our present mode of transmitting goods comes from the increased life expectancy we enjoy. Whereas in the eighteenth century a son inherited from his father and was able to set himself up on a farm, the members of a young couple today typically do not lose their parents until they themselves are well on in years. The purpose of inheritance is simply to help parents get their own children established. In the first few years of their life together, parents enjoy a sort of usufruct of their own parents' goods, which their children will inherit. The inheritance skips a generation.

In a less obvious way and in complex circumstances, the transmission of goods still plays a part in French society.

The domestic group and economic roles

Patrimony and social inequalities

In concentrating on the couple as the means of transmitting an inheritance, we are following certain economists who use the unit of consumption as the basis of a model for the way in which the patrimony of households is accumulated. This model takes into consideration the income from work, the income and appreciation of capital, gifts, consumption and the size of the household.[16]

Linking the accumulation of the patrimony to the economy of the domestic groups is a new step for economists, who up to now have tended to consider the household in a context defined only by income, production, consumption and savings. Some distinguish between accumulated and inherited patrimony, human and non-human patrimony and the labour force sold on the labour market for different wages and cultural capital acquired within the family. When an individual dies, he leaves his heirs the non-human, inherited patrimony and its fruits and also the conversion and capitalisation of the human patrimony into a non-human one.[17] This new step provides a quasi-sociological link between the domestic group and the family, the diachronic and the synchronic. It also provides the tools for a better analysis of social inequalities.

What are the major elements of a patrimony, and what are the distinctions operating as a result of social category? Seventy per cent of the national patrimony consists of immovable goods (property in the form of buildings and income-yielding land) because of the more widespread ownership of property that access to credit brings. The average patrimony per household amounts to three times the annual income available (Fig. 9.2).

Patrimony is very unevenly distributed amongst the various social categories, even more so than income, in fact, and this phenomenon, far from becoming less marked during the family life cycle, becomes more so, as a result of both the differential rate at which savings are accumulated and unequal inheritance patterns.[18]

The level of personal wealth of clerical and manual workers scarcely makes them sufficiently credit-worthy to get beyond the stage of acquiring enough consumer durables and possibly owning their own homes, whereas managerial and professional workers soon move past that particular threshold and acquire considerable financial and property assets apart from the main home. Wage-earners gradually build up their patrimony throughout their lifetime. People of independent status do so immediately either by inheriting or by using credit, since the latter helps them establish themselves.

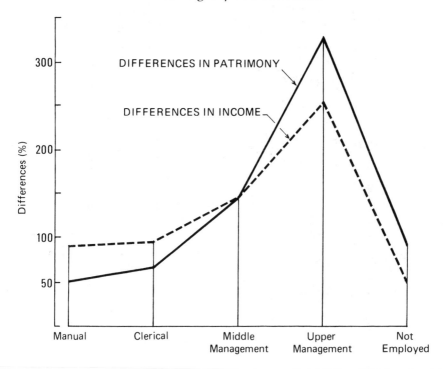

Fig. 9.2. Distribution of patrimony by social categories. (From *La Famille* [Paris: Hachette, 1975], p. 217.)

An analysis of the composition of the patrimony of households reveals considerable variations.[19] The average patrimony of an industrialist or large trader is twelve times larger than that of a manual worker, but the variations are even greater when inequalities within each category are taken into account (Table 9.9). The distinction between independents and those in paid work is also noticeable here. In the case of the former, the professional patrimony (half the total for farmers), that connected with the home and that in the form of investment property and financial assets together make up the whole. Amongst paid workers, those in higher management are distinguished by the importance they attach to transferable securities. Savings bank accounts are the chief form of savings for manual and clerical workers.

The patrimony may therefore seem less important now than in the past, as the number of those in paid employment has grown, but it is nevertheless a major asset for certain domestic groups and one of the factors perpetuating social inequalities.

275

Table 9.9. Composition of patrimony of households by socio-professional category of head (%) in 1975

Socio-professional category	Numbers in % N	Current account	Bank savings	Savings invested in building projects	Term bonds and deposits	Transferrable securities	Individual undertakings and businesses	Home	Second home	Investment property	Agricultural land and farms	Average total value (francs)
Agriculture	8.0	2	5	1	8	minimal	2	31	1	3	49	361,700
Industrialists, large traders	1.3	4	3	1	3	4	37	25	6	12	5	788,700
Small traders, artisans	6.7	5	5	2	2	2	34	35	6	8	2	328,100
Professionals	0.7	4	5	2	4	5	30	32	8	8	3	630,600
Higher management	4.3	5	9	2	2	10	1	44	14	9	4	291,100
Middle management	7.4	5	9	3	2	4	6	53	8	6	4	177,900
Clerical	7.4	6	12	2	2	3	1	54	5	14	2	100,600
Manual	32.6	6	14	2	2	1	1	62	6	3	4	66,900
Others employed	1.9	4	11	5	1	0	2	38	12	23	5	79,700
Not employed	29.4	5	10	1	7	11	4	42	9	7	4	217,000
With earnings *plus* unemployed	83.2	5	11	2	5	8	3	47	9	7	4	145,000
Independent	16.8	3	5	1	5	2	20	31	4	6	23	393,900
All	100.0	5	8	2	5	6	9	42	7	7	11	186,800

Source: André Babeau and Dominique Strauss-Kahn, *La Richesse des Français* (Paris: PUF, 1977), p. 134.

Table 9.10. *Frequency of a major gift to children on marriage, by socio-professional category of husband's father*

	Survey of parents[a]				Survey of married children[b]			
	Yes	No	No reply	Total	Yes	No	No reply	Total
All	42	56	2	100	41	57	2	100
Agriculture	43	55	2	100	46	52	2	100
Manual (agri./ind.)	32	67	1	100	27	71	2	100
Clerical	38	59	3	100	31	67	2	100
Middle management	42	56	2	100	38	59	3	100
Traders/artisans	50	48	2	100	46	52	2	100
Higher management/profs.	60	37	3	100	60	40	–	100

[a] *When your child married, did you give him a major gift (excluding outlay directly connected with the wedding)?*
[b] *When you married, did your father give you a major gift (excluding outlay directly connected with the wedding)?*

Source: Louis Roussel, *La famille après le mariage des enfants*, p. 49.

How goods are passed on

In the past, a patrimony was transmitted when there was a marriage or a death. This is no longer the case. The gifts children receive when they marry are no longer called dowries, and marriage contracts are almost a thing of the past. Sons and daughters receive quite large gifts to help them get established. Roussel has estimated that over 40 per cent of couples marrying receive a gift, varying in size according to socio-professional category, number of other children and so on. Such gifts may take the form of money or goods such as a house, a flat or a car. In one fifth of all cases, they come from both families. In two fifths, the couple receive them from only one side or not at all. The two sets of parents do not usually make a joint gift, preferring to make separate ones. Roussel's survey also shows that parental aid is not restricted to this specific occasion but continues, in the form of gifts or loans, throughout the whole cycle of family life. These may vary in size with different ages and standards of living (see Table 9.10), but loans are usually made on very advantageous terms for the children, to enable them to build up their own patrimony.

A second home should also be seen as a particular form of inheritance or indirect gift. If the parents live in the country, their children

Table 9.11. Frequency of gifts (in %)

		Survey of parents[a]					Survey of children[b]				
		Yes	No, not their way	No, not pos- sible	No reply	Total	Yes	No, not their way	No, not pos- sible	No reply	Total
Men		11	46	39	4	100	13	44	37	6	100
Women		12	40	43	5	100	12	42	37	9	100
All		12	43	41	4	100	12	43	37	8	100
Age Parents	Children										
under 60	under 25	3	50	44	3	100	5	46	40	9	100
50–59	25–29	6	43	42	4	100	8	43	41	8	100
60–64	30–39	14	45	41	5	100	12	45	36	7	100
65 & over	40–49	23	41	31	5	100	21	38	34	7	100

Socio-professional category (men)										
Agriculture	12	51	33	4	100	17	46	26	11	100
Manual	4	34	61	1	100	7	34	33	6	100
Clerical	7	35	55	3	100	3	45	46	6	100
Middle management	9	51	37	3	100	11	56	29	4	100
Traders	6	69	25	0	100	12	55	26	7	100
Upper management & professions	23	58	17	2	100	13	71	11	5	100
No. of children										
1	20	51	24	5	100					
More than 1	9	44	43	4	100					

[a] Since your child's marriage, have you given him large gifts, to some extent an advance on what he will inherit?
[b] Since your marriage have you received large gifts, to some extent an advance on your inheritance?
Source: Louis Roussel, La Famille après le mariage des enfants, p. 62.

Table 9.12. *Frequency of large gift from parents over sixty-five, by socio-economic category of father before retirement (in %)*

Survey of parents	Made gift	Not their way	Not possible	No reply	Total
Agriculture	38	34	20	8	100
Manual	13	34	50	3	100
Clerical, middle management	12	41	44	3	100
Traders	30	40	28	2	100
Upper management & professions	35	44	14	7	100
All	23	41	31	5	100

Source: Louis Roussel, *La Famille après le mariage des enfants*, p. 62.

and grandchildren come and stay with them for holidays. Those in the better-off classes buy a second home that their children can make use of without even having to pay the running costs. This is a considerable help and, in a more indirect way than loans or gifts, enables the young couple to enjoy a standard of living equal to that of the parents.

It can be seen that in our time a patrimony is handed on in very subtle ways that go beyond any attempt at quantification (Tables 9.11–9.13).

Family attitudes towards the transmission of a patrimony

Both sides maintain a front of strict independence, but behind that front there is an ambivalent situation. The chief wish of the children is to remain independent, and parents can show their affection by giving gifts only if they do so with great discretion, for they cannot afford to seem to be buying their children's love. This independence between the generations is confirmed by attitudes towards the legal provisions for inheritance, and the respondents to Roussel's survey were opposed to any right of usufruct, seeing it as a kind of dispossession. Roussel goes on to say that 'the corollary of the independence of married children is that they must not expect to receive from their parents, even by inheritance, the means of ensuring their social advancement or their wealth'. The inheritance must also be a means of removing certain inequalities between brothers and sisters, if, for instance, they are connected to infirmity. Attitudes towards the devolution of goods on marriage, when a parent dies or during

Table 9.13. *Frequency of large loan from parents to married children* (in %)

	Survey of parents[a]				Survey of children[b]			
	Yes	No	No reply	Total	Yes	No	No reply	Total
Men	19	80	1	100	17	82	1	100
Women	19	80	1	100	18	81	1	100
Total	19	80	1	100	18	81	1	100
Father's profession								
Agriculture	7	92	1	100	19	80	1	100
Manual	14	85	1	100	11	88	1	100
Clerical	23	76	1	100	18	81	1	100
Middle management	12	86	2	100	17	83	0	100
Traders	28	72	0	100	24	75	1	100
Upper management	29	69	2	100	29	71	0	100
Men[c]	12	78	10	100	16	74	10	100
Women	12	78	10	100	17	73	10	100
All	12	78	10	100	17	73	10	100
Men[d]	57	30	13	100	70	23	7	100
Women	52	35	13	100	65	25	10	100
All	54	33	13	100	67	24	9	100

[a] *Was such a loan made?*
[b] *Was such a loan received?*
[c] *If such a loan was made, did your parents want interest?*
[d] *Has the loan been repaid?*
Source: Louis Roussel, *La Famille après le mariage des enfants*, pp. 62–3.

the family life cycle fit in with the model of marriage characterised by juvenile cohabitation, separate residence and the independence of children. Does that mean that there is only one attitude towards the transmission of a patrimony? The whole destiny of a family, a whole image of the way in which generations follow each other beyond death, emerges from the ways in which it is carried out.

Using a factorial analysis of correspondence in the case of five hundred persons not receiving their income in the form of wages or salaries, Jacques Lautman has observed different attitudes connected to social criteria and the number of children,[20] distinguishing, for example, a range of factors in the industrialist and trader group denoting two contrasting attitudes (Table 9.14).

The left-hand column in Table 9.14 illustrates the family-centred view, devoted to the interests of the children and concerned for continuity; the right-hand column gives the short-term view of indi-

Table 9.14. *Contrasting attitudes towards the transmission of patrimony amongst industrialists and traders*

Child(ren) working in the business with or without the succession already decided on	No child(ren) working in the business
Financial interest for child(ren)	No family succession desired
Has already made limited gifts to child(ren)	Does not intend either to make a will or give child(ren) a share before his death
Division of estate in child(ren)'s interest, not that of his own retirement	Believes that child(ren) have no claim on family property

viduals who look no further into the future than their own lifetimes. Lautman observes that the latter are those who limit their offspring to single children, but not necessarily with a view to making their child their heir.

These self-made captains of commerce and industry are the kind of men who have not become bourgeois enough to think in terms of lines but have nevertheless broken with the generous emotional attitude towards children found in lower-class families, where a concern for their goods is a major characteristic. Such men are hard on themselves and on others and think that their children have no claims on their property. This view arises from a combination of a belief in getting on the hard way, an attachment to all that is associated with possession and possibly a taste for or a dream of selfish enjoyment. The small families they have might reflect a refusal to create burdens for themselves.[21]

Lautman selects seven variables for his factor analysis:

Profession and socio-professional group;
Social status of the respondent at birth;
Number of children;
Religion;
The manner of receiving the first gift; and
The reply to the question, 'Do you want one of your children to succeed you in your business or profession or do you intend to make a will or a donation during your lifetime?'

In a diagrammatic presentation of the analysis, agriculturalists stand out immediately because of the place and nature of the patrimony in

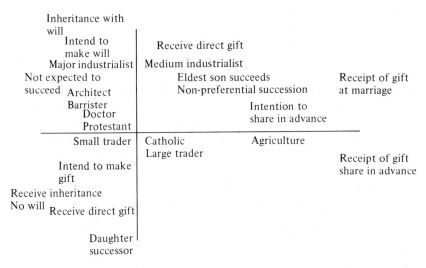

Fig. 9.3. Simplified diagram of factorial analysis of conformity. (From Jacques Lautman, 'Modèles familiaux de la transmission patrimoniale et théorie du cycle', in J. Cuisenier and M. Segalen, eds., *Le Cycle de la vie familiale dans le sociétés européennes* [Paris: Mouton, 1977], p. 461.)

their activity (Fig. 9.3). Traders are similar. In the case of the former, gifts on marriage are combined with gifts in the form of a share in the family property; in that of the latter, direct gifts are the most common practice. Industrialists and members of the liberal professions share similar attitudes, combining testamentary inheritance and the intention to make a will. There is also a striking correlation in each group between the manner of receipt of gifts and intentions with regard to transmission.

Those with earnings not in the form of wages or salaries therefore have a dual cultural model with regard to the future, a short-term one ending with their own death and a long-term one concerned with the family after it.

There are differing views about the effect of the number of children on the perspectives fathers adopt. There will be less division of the patrimony if there are few children, but a large number of offspring, particularly in families with a large patrimony, produces a dynastic effect and increases the number of interconnecting relationships in social life. Above a certain level of wealth, sharing out a patrimony does not seem to hinder the increase in the wealth of each child. This latter is often in the form of transferable industrial or financial shares that are the joint property of the family group in which each individual member owns a share and that bring in income. Dividends make up for, or perhaps more than make up for, reductions due to various inheritances.[22]

Inheriting and non-inheriting households can be contrasted in terms of their various strategies with regard to the patrimony.[23] One category includes those households benefiting from a major human and/or non-human patrimony, but patrimonies are heterogeneous and their human and non-human elements vary a great deal. If the most-favoured heirs in the system enjoy both, the less-favoured ones only have a minor non-human patrimony, and their strategy is based on a hereditary transmission largely consisting of non-human patrimony. As Strauss-Kahn writes:

That is the traditional behaviour in the middle reaches of society where the patrimony is all the smaller for having been spent on the children's education. These social groups (largely those comprising the various categories of clerical and related workers and 'junior management') lie on the border between heirs and non-heirs, where social mobility is at its greatest and where it is natural that one of the main aims should be to avoid letting children fall back into a lower category by providing them with the necessary minimum of education.[24]

On the other hand, non-inheriting households come into the cycle of their family life with a minimal human and virtually non-existent non-human patrimony. What they manage to accumulate during their existence is not enough to be transmitted and is simply a means of ensuring a reasonable retirement for the parents.

Only those who truly inherit can afford to rationalize their behaviour, which simultaneously involves strategies concerned with the patrimony, marriage and fertility, and those who do not do so feel incapable of shaping the future. Thus both advantages and disadvantages are cumulative and, as Strauss-Kahn observes, the distinction between couples who inherit and couples who do not illuminates social inequalities:

The benefits of growth are unequally distributed, but although the middle sections of society have perhaps not received the share that was due to them, the real losers here have been the 25–30% of households in the non-inheriting category.[25]

Patrimony thus continues to play a considerable part in the practice of family relationships, within the framework of trades and professions and, in a more general way, in 'placing' couples in the social constellation. The fact that for many social categories it is a cultural rather than a material matter makes this role even more important. Indeed, the two aspects go together and provide the means of functioning for social reproduction, which will be examined in the next chapter. At the level of the domestic group, the accumulation, management and transmission of a patrimony are important facets of its economic role. Managing the budget is a routine matter, on the whole, and belongs to daily life in the here and now, whereas thinking in terms of a patrimony gives the couple a long-term view and function and places it in an intermediate position between what Lautman calls 'past determination and looking forward to the future'.

SUGGESTED READING

Commissariat général au Plan. *La Famille.* Paris: Hachette, 1975, particularly pp. 175–236.

Cuisenier, Jean. 'Accumulation du capital et défense du patrimoine'. in *Le Partage des bénéfices.* Paris: Editions de Minuit, 1966.

Lautman, Jacques. 'Modèles familiaux de la transmission patrimoniale et théorie du cycle'. In *Le Cycle de la vie familiale dans les sociétés européennes.* Ed. Jean Cuisenier and Martine Segalen. Paris: Mouton, 1977.

Presvelou, Clio. *Sociologie de la consommation familiale.* Brussels: Vie Ouvrière, 1968.

Strauss-Kahn, Dominique. *Economie de la famille et accumulation patrimoniale.* Paris: Centre de Recherche et d'Etudes du Patrimoine, 1977.

Concerning the 'new home economics'

Becker, Gary. *The Economic Approach to Human Behavior.* Chicago: University of Chicago Press, 1976.

Easterlin, R. A. *Birth and Fortune: The Impact of Numbers on Personal Welfare.* New York: Basic Books, 1980.

Theodore W. Schultz, ed., *Economics of the Family: Marriage, Children, and Human Capital.* Chicago: University of Chicago Press, 1974.

Chapter 10

vwvwvwvwvwvwvwvwvwvwvwvwvwvwvwvwvwvwvwvwvwvwvwvwvwvwvwvwvwvwvwvwv

Family and society

Some time ago, a small but rather disturbing item of news was reported in the French press. Tourists and art-lovers could not visit certain galleries in the Louvre on Saturdays and Sundays. Why? Because there had been a strike, and as a result the attendants, who are mostly women, had gained the right to spend every other week-end at home with their families. As there had been no increase in staff, half the galleries were closed because there was no-one to look after them. This is an example of the constant interplay between family and society, complicated in this case by the twofold role and recommendations of the state. As an employer, the state has to work within the constraints of its budget. As custodian of the nation's future, it purports to urge mothers to look after their children on weekends.

The complex relationships between the family (and it is quite in order to use the general term here) and society are more than simply those between the family and the state. In this work, we have frequently raised the question of the interlinked effects of family and social change, of whether the family is modified by the influence of migration, urbanisation and industrialisation. We first established that changes are not unilinear and do not take place in the same way or at the same rate in different social classes. It is only possible to speak of industrialisation in very general terms given the very varied ways in which work is organised and the wide range of technical contexts, the importance of which has emerged from our study of family structures and relationships. In establishing the increasingly 'private' nature of the latter and noting a trend towards greater intimacy within the family, we have seen just how ambiguous such formulas are. Now as in the past, relationships between parents and children and between spouses are the link between private and public behavior.

The family and social control

Using the examples examined in earlier chapters, we should now try to take our analysis of that relationship further. Is the family a static structure that society frames and shapes according to its own needs, or is it the scene of resistance and of an alternative kind of power that puts obstacles in the way of social change?

THE FAMILY AND SOCIAL CONTROL

Like individuals, domestic groups are subject to the constraints of a range of laws and rules that limit their freedom. They are the target of family policies, government action and administrative measures imposing guidelines they are supposed to follow. They are also subject to the pressure of frequently tacit and contradictory norms, and if they do not adapt to them, they are watched and punished by various institutions seeking to control their degree of departure from them.

From constraints to control

In an article on family power, Agnès Pitrou lists the main constraints affecting the family.[1] The first is law, which defines the make-up of the couple and the rights and duties of members of the family. Then there is social legislation, which extends the area covered by law, and economic decisions concerning everyday working conditions and standards of living and hence the decisions the couple make. There are also measures covering the status of women, constraints regarding the education of children and their future, such as the school guidance system and medical examinations, and those determining life-styles by providing housing and encouraging home ownership. Large-scale social housing shapes a whole way of living. The media are powerful, and present a certain image of the family, and all sorts of controls permanently affect the pattern of family life.

Whatever its social level, every family is subject to overall control. Some, however, are more rigorously supervised than others because they do not conform to the norm. In such cases, the state assumes the right to intervene in the way such families are run, and constraints become controls. On the pretext of improving its understanding of them and the help it gives them, the state is promulgating a norm and attempting to make families conform to it. But what could such a norm be, and what is a normal family? We can see it negatively, so to speak, in the norm implicitly suggested by those families that are the object of public aid described by Pitrou:

Family and society

'Problem' families are above all those that cannot adapt to the habits of their social context. They have no regular employment, they are in debt and cannot control their children. These are systematic criteria, for without exception the social welfare system takes over in the case of families low on the socio-economic scale and in particular circumstances: unpaid rent, complaints from neighbours about disturbances, children often absent from school, ill-treated or engaged in petty crime.[2]

This normative attitude on the part of the state is not peculiar to our own times. Once again, a retrospective examination of how institutions for controlling the family came into being will provide a better understanding of our aims today and what is involved.

The family as an instrument of social control

A few years ago, several works dealing with the increasing control exerted on and by families appeared almost simultaneously. Using sources such as medical literature and speeches by philanthropists, legislators and administrators that had previously been little exploited, Jacques Donzelot, Isaac Joseph, Philippe Fritsch and Philippe Meyer showed the major concerns that highlighted the contrast between the working-class family with its range of deviant behaviour (common-law unions, high rates of infant mortality, abandoned children, juvenile delinquency and so on) with the bourgeois family in the nineteenth century and described the action taken to eliminate deviations of this kind.

The growth of the sociology of the family illuminates the history of family control. In his *De la famille-cible à l'objet famille*, Fritsch traces the ideological ancestry of the identification of problem families, covering a range of investigations from the works of Auguste Comte and Frederic Le Play, the surveys of the *Economie et Humanisme* group (1943) and, in our own time, allocation-of-time studies. Fritsch analyses texts by nineteenth-century administrators seeking to eradicate working-class pauperism and poverty. The normalisation of the family was a means rather than an end in itself, and the result was that the household became a unit of investigation, a situation perpetuated in the surveys carried out in our own age (see Chapters 8 and 9).

Many institutions were concerned with the nineteenth-century working-class family. The *Société de St François Régis*, for example, helped to regularise the matrimonial situation of couples who wanted to achieve this but could not afford to do so. In particular, Donzelot shows that the strategy of 'familialisation' was based on women receiving help from doctors and priests and from social measures such as housing aid, instruction in domestic science and so on.

Women were the internal means by which the normalisation of the family was to be achieved.

Means of controlling the family grew up around the problem of the endangered or dangerous child. It would be useful to outline the genealogy of these controls, as Isaac Joseph does in his *Tactiques et figures disciplinaires,* following the work of Michel Foucault.

In the first place, school took the place of parents incapable of bringing up their children, and the teacher became 'a counsellor on how children should be brought up at home and the governor of the family'. During the nineteenth century, school became increasingly important for the family, and the old relationship, in which it had been an extension of the education given by the family, was reversed. The school became the place where the family was produced. The child became a kind of hostage, an excuse for visits to the home whose real aim was to ensure that educative relationships there were of a normal kind. Then the doctor intruded, addressing himself primarily to the mother. Childhood became a medical speciality and the family was incorporated into the domain of that profession. The homes of poor families also gradually became the objects of expert scrutiny, and the domestic group was hedged in from all sides in all its relationships and areas of operation. Philanthropists and charitable societies discovered working-class poverty and sought to eradicate it, and means that were often mutually contradictory were proposed to this end. Perhaps such families should be 'normalised' by being put into the ghettos of working-class housing developments that created their own collective facilities (kindergartens, schools and shelters) and tended to weaken family ties and clash with traditional patterns of help from charitable associations? Or should the working class be set in a network of social relationships dense enough to provide it with models and guides to control its tendency towards revolt and resistance? Should it live cheek by jowl with bourgeois families who would provide it with an exemplary model? Isaac Joseph shows how between 1860 and 1880 the state tried to inculcate habits of obedience and thought for the future and to orientate working-class families toward the home. The ranks of schoolmasters, doctors, architects and philanthropists were gradually swelled by the addition of children's judges, social workers and psychologists. The family, that dangerous entity, was placed in care and the father's authority taken from him.

Nowadays, the social control of the family is more discreet and less coercive but probably more extensive and insidious as a result of the growth of popular psychoanalysis, which makes no judgements and always lets subjects have their way. These techniques are all the more powerful in that they apparently impose neither social norms nor moral rules. No-one is either innocent or guilty, but despite this aspect of the psychological approach, contemporary social endeavour imputes guilt. In his *L'Enfant et la raison d'Etat*, Meyer analyses consultations in an education centre for delinquent minors and shows the detailed examination the family has to undergo. Two things – the minor and the family environment – are discredited. The way the family is classified – which is always negative – is based on the twin criteria of over-protection or rejection.

Before the divorce laws were reformed, couples were subject to the same type of inquisition, ostensibly to protect the children. In divorce proceedings, the court was an agency of control, punishing what it saw as unsatisfactory behaviour. The criticism of the spouses was stereotyped and non-egalitarian: The husband was blamed for ineptitude in connection with his job, for drunkenness, for not providing for his family, and the wife for being a bad wife, a bad mother and a bad manager, and wrongs were pronounced as such on the basis of an implicit ideology of the family. Divorce based on the notion of guilty parties and penalties meant the humiliation of touting for evidence and undergoing inquiries and being compared to the implicit model in the minds of judges. The link between the court and the social services was also a major aspect of divorce proceedings, especially when they made financial difficulties worse. It is because it is now much more common that divorce is tending to become acceptable and to lose the stigma associated with it. The research of Fritsch, Joseph and Meyer shows that our present-day restrictive attitudes towards the family can be traced back to the middle of the eighteenth century and that the resulting norm has been produced by controlling people of marginal status. But the state itself, with the best intentions in the world, creates deviant behaviour. In seeking to control families it removes them from, for example, shanty towns and puts them into social housing, where the dwellings are too small for them to 'contain' their young people or look after their elderly parents. It breaks up their sense of community and traditional neighbourhood.

In the next section, an analysis of views relating to the present-day crisis in fertility will help us to see the complexity of the problem of the confrontation of social and family power.

The present-day problem of fertility

The children for whose sake the state, administration, political power and middle-class 'normality' penetrated the working-class family in the nineteenth century are disappearing, for we no longer produce them in sufficient numbers. At all levels from the biological to the national, the most intimate act of every couple now has social, economic and political consequences.

The demographic situation of France is serious. The public authorities are aware of this, and the government has recently proposed a series of measures to help large families, and this strategy will be pursued in all sectorial policies likely to have a favourable effect on our demography. But family size is a matter for couples themselves to decide. All the state can do is ensure that the choices expressing their wishes and their freedom are more real and more responsible, in particular by providing better information about their consequences for the nation as a whole. The people of France must understand and choose.[3]

This is how a government report summarising the powers of the state and their limits reads. The right to intervene is clear. The state, which represents the community, cannot take a neutral attitude towards a situation that has such serious medium-term implications. Various states, when they are confronted with the opposite problem, that of over-population, impose sterilisation or forbid abortion when the birth rate falls. Between total neutrality and authoritarianism, there is a place for gently persuasive action. Is it not simply a question of shifting the emphasis in family policy?

Public discourse on the matter is sometimes riddled with contradictions. In overall terms, fertility, apparently analysed objectively, is related to every possible variable, and particularly that of women working. Implicitly, that analysis becomes distorted, ceases to be neutral, and the idea of a norm comes to the surface. The 'freedom of couples', which is the 'best guarantee of a satisfactory increase in population',[4] receives great lip-service, but family policies intrude into private life and the sheer scope of the provisions embraces all aspects of the family. The following are the proposals of the *Haut Comité de la Population* as given in a report dated June 1980:

1. A policy aimed at raising the birth rate must deal with all the factors adversely affecting this aim and cannot be exclusively based on an increase in financial aid to families. . . . [We must bring about] a fundamental change in the living conditions of families . . . a general climate of opinion favourable to welcoming children.
2. There is a need to make the parents' work and the presence of children in the home compatible. The report sees the working wife as a datum for the future.

3. In the case of families of more than three children, there are special rights that must be recognised.
4. Family allowances must take into account the real costs a child involves.

These aims are followed by a number of concrete proposals concerning information, policies about living conditions, town planning, the arrangement of working time, housing policy, national and regional development and so on.

The report says, for example, that small and medium-sized towns are more favourable to a high fertility rate and should be developed, as should space for families, and urban areas should be geared to families' and children's needs. Housing policy should be re-examined with a view to increasing the stock of bigger houses and flats, and working time should be organised to give a shorter working day and an increase in part-time work opportunities.

It can be seen that every aspect of everyday life is gradually being taken into account and that families are hemmed in on every side by projects that highlight the permanent contradiction in public action illustrated by the example of the museum attendants. The state does not admit its own responsibility in the matter, but does say that it has built houses and flats that are too small, that allowances have not kept up with increases in the cost of living and that town planners have created areas in which there is no place for children.

Finally – and this is not the least of the paradoxes involved here – family policies have shown that they have only a limited ability to change attitudes to fertility. Couples are often ill informed and like to think that a decrease in the population, and in particular a smaller number of young people arriving on the labour market, could make it easier to find employment and would bring about an improvement in living standards, and these are frequently heard arguments. Any policy encouraging a greater number of children can succeed only if it is supported by couples themselves. This may seem painfully obvious, but it needs to be said. Demographic policies are not like agricultural or transport policies, and in this respect, the experience of the countries of Eastern Europe is enlightening.[5] The effectiveness of the measures that some of them introduced in an attempt to encourage high birth rates and halt the fall in fertility is at once unmistakable, ambiguous and limited. It is unmistakable because an increase in current fertility followed measures aimed at that end. (In Romania, for example, abortion was made illegal, and for several months the number of births trebled.) It is ambiguous because it is difficult to estimate the extent to which changes are due to various measures such as reducing abortion or encouraging procreation. It is limited, because after an initial phase when the number of births increases, fertility drops once more, which perhaps indicates that some couples have an earlier pregnancy than originally intended in order to take advantage of available benefits, but do not increase their final number of children.

The fertility crisis in our own times shows the ambiguities and difficulties inherent in policies aimed at exerting control over the family and the complex nature of the relationships between family and society, family and social or state power.

THE FAMILY AND SOCIAL POWER

There is a permanence about the family, and it seems to offer many forms of resistance to social change. To express this in another way, it seems, in Pierre Bourdieu's phrase, to have a power to *reproduce.*

It occupies a mediatory position between the generations and ensures continuity at a point where macrosocietal changes and changes within family life converge.

The power of the family is not simply passive. It is active and, as we have seen, implies strategies connected with marriage and social advancement. Through its transmission of a material, cultural, social and symbolic heritage, it conserves social and cultural inequalities, lurks within them and perpetuates them. What in the case of the most-favoured classes is a 'power' turns against the least-favoured ones, who can reproduce only their wretchedness. If we take this line of argument to its extremes, the family can be seen as having the power to block the structures society sets up.

The family and unequal opportunities

A democratic society sees as one of its functions the reduction of inequalities between social groups and in particular between families. That was the particular task entrusted to secular, republican education. In the nineteenth century, the education system had a disciplinary mission, as we have seen: that of providing for the most deprived children and turning them into good workers. When it was concerned with all social categories and with girls as well as boys, its mission was to make them equal in the sense that they would all have a scholastic capital acquired within the system. It must be admitted that this aim has not been achieved. Not only do children not receive an education that would wipe out differences, but the school system, which transmits dominant values, compounds social

293

Table 10.1. *Academic achievement at the end of primary education* (in %)

	Excellent or good	Average	Mediocre or poor	Total
Agri. labourers	33	37	30	100
Farmers	43	37	20	100
Manual workers	35	35	30	100
Traders, artisans	44	34	22	100
Clerical	45	34	21	100
Middle management	64	25	11	100
Industrialists, liberal professions	56	33	11	100
Higher management	62	28	10	100
All	41	33	26	100

Source: Raymond Boudon, *L'Inégalité des chances*, p. 59.

and cultural inequalities and helps to maintain the position of the dominant classes.

In the early years of childhood in particular, academic success, given equal parental income, varies with the parental level of education, as measured by the highest qualification held by either parent. This finding clearly indicates the influence of the cultural heritage (Table 10.1).[6] The influence of a child's surroundings also seems crucial. The greater the degree of encouragement and stimulation of young children in a culturally favoured environment, the better their chances of academic attainment and success in life. Alain Girard has demonstrated the connection between academic performance and the number of children in the family. Children from large families do less well.

The determining influence of socio-professional category can be observed by following the school careers of a group of children.

The general progress of a year-group does not occur at the same rate in different social groups. . . . The social origin of the children has been an important element in their school careers from the very first time they were separated, when they went into the first form of the *lycée*. During subsequent years, that element remains present, but does not exercise so great an influence, as the first option has been the decisive one. Later orientation always moves, however, in the direction of a more rigorous social selection.[7]

In his introduction to *Population et L'Enseignement*, Girard concludes that disregarding the influence of heredity, which cannot of course be denied, that of the family is determining, since what the school does can only be done in close liaison with the family milieu. Two children, hypothetically of equal intelligence, but one the son of a farm-worker or a labourer and the other of a teacher, a doctor or an engineer, do not develop at the same rate. One has no advantages, the other has them all: the material surroundings of course, but also cultural surroundings, good toys, family conversations, connections, help with school work, parental aspirations. It is not simply a question of money, and financial capital, if there is any, is not everything. As is their social duty, parents bequeath to their children the intellectual capital they themselves have acquired.[8]

What can be done to provide a balance? The widespread introduction of kindergartens and day-care centres is aimed at giving every child equal educational opportunities by means of socialisation at an early age. Since it tries to compensate for social inequalities, such a system should be the strongest adversary of family power. But the aim is foiled by the fact that the children attending such schools are segregated at home, as children from different social classes hardly live in the same areas. In addition, by insisting that their children 'work' rather than 'waste their time' drawing, parents bring in again the means of distinguishing between privileged children and others.

Pierre Bourdieu and Jean-Claude Passeron note the same combined effect of social position and cultural heritage in access to university education. Their survey of the social origins of students, conducted in 1961–62, shows a real process of elimination: The son of an upper manager was eighty times as likely to go to university as the son of an agricultural worker, forty times as likely as the son of an industrial worker and twice as likely as the son of a man in middle management.[9] Between 1961 and 1980, the number of university students increased tenfold, from 80,000 to 800,000, but to see this bigger intake as a more democratic one is simply an illusion.

Reproduction and social mobility

Scholastic inequality thus acts as a brake on social mobility. In his *L'Inégalité des chances*, Raymond Boudon notes that

unequal opportunities of an educational and a socio-professional nature thus seem to be the only form of inequality not seriously affected by the growth of industrial societies. A worker's son will certainly have a higher standard of living than his father's, but his chance of receiving higher education will not be much greater than those of his father's generation and his chance of reaching a higher social category than his father's will be much

Table 10.2. *Socio-professional category of married children by that of father (survey of parents; in %)*

	Father's socio-professional category						
	Farmer	Manual	Clerical	Middle managem.	Traders	Upper management professions	All
Son's category							
Farmer	39	–	–	–	–	–	7
Manual	25	47	28	11	26	–	22
Clerical	17	15	27	9	14	20	27
Middle management	4	21	26	30	18	15	19
Trader, artisan	9	7	6	4	24	–	7
Upper management, professions	6	10	13	46	18	65	18
Total	100	100	100	100	100	100	100

Distribution of fathers by their own category	15	34	14	13	13	11	100
Daughter's category							
Farmer	27	–	–	–	–	–	5
Manual	6	14	9	–	5	–	7
Clerical	22	36	37	23	31	17	28
Middle management	6	12	12	17	15	17	12
Trader, artisan	1	3	4	2	9	2	4
Upper management, professions	3	1	7	24	10	26	10
Not working	35	34	31	34	30	38	34
Total	100	100	100	100	100	100	100

Source: Louis Roussel, *La Famille après le mariage des enfants*, p. 108.

the same as his father's was. Nor will he be sure that the difference between his income and that of someone in higher management will be any less than in his father's generation.[10]

Is it possible that the family has the immense power necessary to block social mobility?

History shows that in democratic societies, both generally and with regard to the family, there is upward social mobility. Every genealogy shows that from a common ancestor, the various lines have different social fates, some remaining locally rooted in the traditional family profession and others going off to take their chances successfully in quite a different sector.

Louis Roussel's study also shows significant mobility over the span of two generations only (Tables 10.2 and 10.3).[11]

It is true that this phenomenon does not affect every social milieu in an identical way, and there is still the inertia of social reproduction. A son is more likely to move into management, for example, the closer his father is to that socio-professional category. But mobility over two generations is undeniable and is characterised by improvements that are particularly evident in intermediate groups. From one generation to the next there has usually been an improvement in the level of education, and the middle classes are characterised by a fairly high degree of upward mobility in the socio-professional sphere. Those who take a pessimistic view of the possibility of a freezing of the social system will retort that social mobility and social reproduction are not mutually incompatible. Social mobility is necessary in a changing society demanding new knowledge and new qualifications, but it does not affect every social category in the same way.

Bourdieu has this to say:

The controlled social mobility of a category of individuals selected and modified by and for upward social mobility on an individual basis is not incompatible with permanent structures and can even contribute, in the only conceivable way in societies claiming to be democratic in ideals, to social stability and hence to the perpetuation of the class structure.[12]

The family is the agent of a phenomenon that contradicts it and goes beyond it, that of social reproduction, but also that of mobility. Its power, after three generations, melts into the dynamics of the whole social body.

WOMEN IN THE FAMILY AND IN SOCIETY

The change in the status of women provides a good example of the complex nature of the relationships between the family and society, which are not to be seen simply in terms of power or resistance. Women are the link between the two entities, and the situation has changed both within the family and in opposition to it. It is clear that the new social and family models the twenty-first century will produce will depend on their status in the years to come.

Changes in the status of women

The status of women has changed much more rapidly than social and economic structures. At its base is the new complex of physiological facts illustrated in Table 10.4, and change has been particularly rapid over the last ten years. The phenomenon is a major and recent one.

Following the victories women have won in the political and educational spheres, society is now slowly maturing. Women are better educated than their mothers were and are seeking to define their new social roles. In *Le Fait féminin*, Evelyne Sullerot analyses the social changes that have paved the way for this situation. As early as the immediate post-war years, the powerful pressure of the idea of equal rights for all citizens brought about considerable changes in legislation. Even though practice sometimes lagged behind, a number of laws were passed establishing the equality of the sexes in education, the handling of property, wages and social rights.

Second, the industrial and technical revolution produced an upheaval in domestic roles, not so much in connection with the material conditions in which work was done as with its economic and ideological value. In 1950 it was more profitable to make one's own clothes and preserves than to buy them. By the late 1970s, all the budget calculations show that it was more profitable to work and buy mass-produced goods and services. The economic value of work done at home fell, and as a result its status was lower. Third, progress in medicine has meant a considerably greater life expectancy, the risks associated with pregnancy and birth have been significantly reduced and the widespread use of baby foods has freed women from the constraints of breast-feeding. In theory at least, it has given fathers and mothers equal status with regard to the newborn child. Improved birth control has enabled women to take the enormous step of adapting the number and frequency of their children to their job, a complete reversal of the former situation.[13] Last, a massive movement to towns has helped separate couples physically during the daytime and to bring them together for leisure and relaxation.

During the 1960s, Western societies were faced with these pro-

Table 10.3. *Educational level of married children, by that of parents* (survey of parents, in %)[a]

Educational level of child	Educational level of son/father					Educational level of daughter/father				
	Primary	Tech and comm.	Secondary	Higher	All	Primary	Tech and comm.	Secondary	Higher	All
Primary	37	[b]	6	–	24	41	–	–	–	25
Technical, commerc.	36		26	–	32	29	29	21	16	26
Secondary	18		28	14	19	21	58	44	36	30
Higher	9		40	86	25	9	13	35	48	19
Total	100	100	100	100	100	100	100	100	100	100
Distribution by level of father	61	8	21	10	100	60	5	25	10	100

Educational level of child	Educational level of son/mother					Educational level daughter/mother				
Primary	33	b	b	5	22	35	b	3	b	24
Technical, commerc.	43			30	37	35		18		30
Secondary	15			23	19	22		47		28
Higher	9			42	22	8		32		18
Total	100			100	100	100		100		100
Distribution by level of mother	57	9	2	32		63	5	28	4	

[a] The 'higher primary' level is included in 'Secondary'.

[b] Insufficient numbers.

Source: Louis Roussel, La Famille après le mariage des enfants, p. 109.

Table 10.4. *'Old' and 'new' demographic patterns with regard to women in years*

	Old	New
No. of children born alive	6	2
Age at birth of last child	40	30
Age at marriage	18	23
Life expectancy at onset of menstruation	37	64
Life expectancy at marriage	35	54
Life expectancy at onset of puberty of last child	14	33
Time between marriage and birth of last child	22	7
Total period of breast-feeding (months)	72	5
Total period of pregnancy and breast-feeding	13.5	1.9
Couples surviving at time of wife's 50th birthday (in %)	18	88

Source: Population et Sociétés, Oct. 1979, no. 128.

found changes and forced to reconsider the justification for the traditional allocation of roles, which had been the cause of so much discrimination. Women sought to use the skills that improved education had given them and hoped to achieve personal fulfilment at work and within a family life restructured in such a way as to avoid the double burden of a job and domestic tasks. If the new legislation providing the first steps towards a new definition of the status of women was to be implemented, the feminist movements, whose only weapons were their radicalism and their humour, had their part to play. They were not the only factor, clearly, but they were both catalysts and transmitters. The laws on contraception, abortion and divorce were simply legal measures reflecting the acceptance of long-standing practices. Women had the force of law behind them, and new ways of seeing and acting became generally acceptable. Various trends have since appeared in these movements. Some feminists are seeking a specifically feminine role in tune with their bodies and their rhythms and others are deeply concerned with sexual questions such as the recognition of homosexuality and anti-rape measures, all of which affect society as a whole. In some cases, reflection is centred on ways of achieving true sexual equality in professional and domestic life. These divergent trends lead to incompatible courses of action, with some claiming total equality and others the right to be different. Both feminist movements in particular and women and society in general are still reflecting on ways of achieving real equality in the family and in society.

Such ways to some extent coincide with and support a policy of the family, but they are also more widely related to every sphere of social organisation.

Changes in the situation of women and social innovations

We should mention some of the other legal inequalities that still make women inferior beings in relation to their husbands in the field of marriage laws, taxation and other areas that might seem marginal but that nonetheless indicate that men and women are not equal. This is blindingly evident in sport. Why are men's and women's age-groups not identical in athletic events? It was not until 1980 that women were officially classified when they ran a marathon (42 km, 26 miles). Before that, they had to be content to run in men's events without a number and without having their running time considered, even if they beat their male competitors.

Inequalities are still obvious where jobs are concerned. Wages are lower, and women are the first to go in a recession (60 per cent of those seeking work in 1981 were women). Their career paths are slower and harder than men's. Discrimination against women when recruiting for jobs and unequal pay are only two elements of the problem.

Rather than introducing part-time work for women, which would penalise them even more, it would be better to restructure and reduce working hours for everyone. The environment should also no longer be a factor hindering women who want to go out to work. The great distance they often have to travel from home to place of work means that more time has to be spent out of the house. Architects' ideas of homes could also perhaps change. They might have direct experience of the function of space rather than simply shape it. If so, there would be more storage space, bigger kitchens and so on. Everything to do with the status of women thus affects social organisation to an increasing degree. And yet the question arises as to whether it is society alone that alienates them.

The family, in which women are second and which obliges them to choose between being overburdened by domestic and outside work or giving up their jobs, still plays a part in it.

How can the model of the reproduction of roles still operative within the family be dismantled? Some projects that at first seem to help the situation of women are not without risks. An example of this is the maternal wage, which Yvonne Knibiehler and Catherine Fouquet describe in thier *L'Histoire des mères* as an obstacle to advancement in this area:

303

The suggested maternal wage, which makes it into paid work like any other, with a right to training, social security benefits, holidays and retirement, seems conservative but is really revolutionary, as it tends to split the parental couple and overthrow the traditional way the family works. . . . It follows the logic of a mercantile society that evaluates everything in money terms and sees children as a product like any other.[14]

Instead of a maternal wage, some feminists suggest a reassessment of housework, a proposal that, pushed to extremes, would have many consequences for society. Andrée Michel and the researchers associated with her have reflected on why housework is still classified as unproductive, both within the home and at the social level.

Thus national accounting ignores it, and yet American studies have shown that the American male (the reasoning also applies to his European counterpart) saves, if he marries, 218 hours of housework a year. If we multiply this by 44, the average length of marriages in years, we get a total of 9,592 hours, which he is free to devote to his career, leisure interests and so on. If he had to pay for this service instead of getting it done for nothing, his family would have a much lower standard of living and his own career would be more difficult. If housework were included in national income accounting, we would have a better idea of what it entails, but that would be a social innovation that might meet resistance from the state, producers, and trade unions, as has been the case so far.

As Michel writes in her *Les Femmes dans la société marchande*:

Excluding the domestic production of families from the indicators of production and consumption means that women are devalued economically and socially. Since they are not 'producers' in a society that is proud of its indicators of mercantile growth and consumption, they can only be an inferior and devalued sex. Hiding the productive tasks women perform thus devalues them in the family, in the economy, in society and in their own idea of their importance.[15]

THE FAMILY AND SOCIAL DESTINY

William Goode shows in his *The Family* the influence of different family systems on industrial development. He contrasts Japan and China, two countries that reacted quite differently to the possibilities of industrialisation occurring for both in the late nineteenth century, when they became open to Western influence.

The two countries shared some social and economic characteristics. Both had an agrarian economy, rapid population growth, an extensive but corrupt and inefficient bureaucracy, an emphasis on individualism and the family, tension between town and country

304

and a merchant class without prestige that could have played an important part in the modernisation process. Goode contrasts the Chinese failure with the success enjoyed by Japan, which, in a half-century, had managed with very little outside capital to set up heavy industries and change its distribution system. Several characteristics of the family system, and in particular that of the system of inheritance, explain the difference. In China, it was an egalitarian one; in Japan, a single child inherited all the property, which made it possible to accumulate capital. The most striking difference concerned the links between the family and the state. In China, loyalty was to the family and nepotism a duty, so that if there was upward social movement every member of the line would benefit from it. In Japan, ties were of a more feudal kind, and within the family a father could disinherit his own son and adopt a young man who seemed more worthy. The Chinese system allowed for some degree of social mobility, and merchants occupying a lowly position might rise socially if they stopped being traders. Japanese merchants, on the other hand, were restricted to a narrower type of mobility, that depending on financial success. Since they had no means of rising in the social scale, bankers and merchants developed considerable technical expertise and were much better placed to deal with the complex problems raised by industrialisation. Goode is careful not to attribute Japanese success and Chinese stagnation solely to family structure, but he does draw attention to its influence, which has often been underestimated.

Our social destiny depends on the future structure of the domestic group and the relationships that will be established between the family and society. Will we see, for example, communes like those invented by the youngsters of the 1960s flourishing once more? They rejected the family, urban life and work styles and went 'back to nature'. Perhaps all the land in the Pyrénées and the Cévennes deserted by those who once lived there will be worked again. The creed of the young of those days was very explicit:

We have to build on the ruins of the Family. Once the foundations have been undermined, great principles collapse. The sense of property disappears when goods are shared, authority becomes a ridiculous idea and competition is pointless once the members of the commune find that they are complementary to each other and try to resolve their differences peacefully.[16]

After some years of struggle, the commune experiment seems to have collapsed. In the Cévennes, Danièle Léger and Bertrand Hervieu have noted that the symbolism of the old-fashioned family and an aggressive utopianism have made a strong come-back. People have invented grandparents so that families can consist of three generations, as they perhaps never did in the past. The traditional allocation of roles is returning rapidly and patriarchal authority is stronger, being based on a desire to pass on a certain mode of relationships to children.

Gérard Mauger, who studied a commune in the suburbs of Paris for a long period, also reports that the relationships between the various couples there, which were based on a desire for sexual freedom and the exchange of partners, are literally and metaphorically dramatic.[17] At the tragic level, he compares the situation to that of Racine's *Andromaque* and at a less exalted level to that of a Feydeau farce. Jealousy, a bourgeois emotion that the new vocabulary has not managed to hold in check, soon poisons all relationships.

Today family structures are tending to diversify. The number of divorced persons who remarry is increasing, but so too is the number who do not remarry. The figure was 461,000 men and 684,000 women in early 1979 as against 352,00 and 558,000 in early 1975. This population is also getting younger. The number of men and women in the twenty-five to thirty-five age-group who divorced almost trebled between 1968 and 1979.[18] The domestic groups of these divorced people are made up of a parent (most often the mother) and her children. The new spouse or partner is usually more or less stable. This gives a new matrifocally based structural model, and it is remarkable that the social norm now accepts this along with that of the classical nuclear domestic group.

SUGGESTED READING

Relationships between families and power

'Famille, pouvoirs et changement social'. *Economie et Humanisme* 251 (Jan.–Feb. 1980).
'Familles et pouvoirs'. *Informations sociales*, 4–5(1980).
'Familles et pouvoirs'. *Sociologie du Sud-Est*. 21 (July–Sept. 1979).
These three issues contain papers from a colloquium on this topic organized by Yvonne Knibiehler and Emile Temime.

The family and social control

Donzelot, Jacques. *The Policing of Families*. London, 1979.
Joseph, Isaac, and Philippe Fritsch. *Disciplines à domicile, l'édification de la famille*. Recherches no. 28, Nov. 1977.
Katz, Michael B. *The people of Hamilton, Canada West. Family and Class in a Mid-Nineteenth Century City*. Cambridge, Mass.: Harvard University Press, 1975.

Suggested reading

Levine, David, ed. *Proletarianization and Family History*. Orlando: Academic Press, 1984.

Meyer, Philippe. *L'Enfant et la raison d'Etat*. Paris: Le Seuil, 1977.

Ryan, Mary P. *Cradle of the Middle Class. The Family in Oneida County*. First published New York 1970; Cambridge, Mass.: Cambridge University Press, 1981.

Pitrou, Agnès. *La Vie précaire. Des familles face à leurs difficultés*. Paris: Caisse National d'Allocations Familiales, 1978.

The family and unequal opportunities

Boudon, Raymond. *L'Inégalité des chances, la mobilité sociale dans les sociétés industrielles*. Paris: Colin, 1973.

Bourdieu, Pierre, and Jean-Claude Passeron. *La Reproduction. Eléments pour une théorie du système d'enseignement*. Paris: Editions de Minuit, 1970.

Girard, Alain, and Henri Bastide. 'La Stratification sociale et la démocratisation de l'enseignement'. *Population* 3(1963): 435–58.

'Population' et l'enseignement. Paris: PUF, 1970.

Women

Among the wealth of literature are the following:

Bonte, Pierre, and Nicole Echard. 'La condition féminine'. In *Anthropologie et sexualite*. Paris: Editions sociales, 1978.

Boserup, Ester. *Women's Role in Economic Development*. New York: Allen & Unwin, 1970.

Chafe, W. H. *The American Woman: Her Changing Social, Economic and Political Roles, 1920–1970*. Oxford: Oxford University Press, 1972.

Flexner, Eleanor. *Century of Struggle: The Women's Rights Movement in the United States*. Cambridge, Mass.: Belknap Press, 1959.

Herbert, Martha Reed. 'La libération des femmes et la production industrielle'. *Esprit* 7–8(1973): 85–94.

Hufton, Olwen, and Joan Wallach Scott. 'Survey Articles: Women in History. I. Early Modern Europe. II. The Modern Period'. *Past and Present* 101(1983): 125–57.

Lloyd, Cynthia B., et al., eds. *Women in the Labor Market*. New York: Columbia University Press, 1977.

Michel, Andrée, ed. *Les femmes dans la société marchande*. Paris: PUF, 1978.

Rogers, Susan Carol. 'Woman's Place: A Critical Review of Anthropological Theory'. *Comparative Studies in Society and History* 1(1978): 123–62.

Rosaldo Zimbalist, Michelle, and Louise Lamphere, eds. *Woman, Culture and Society*. Stanford, Calif.: Stanford University Press, 1974.

Shorter, Edward. *A History of Women's Bodies*. New York: Basic Books, 1982.

Sullerot, Evelyne. *Histoire et sociologie du travail féminin*. Paris: Denoël, 1968.

ed. *Le Fait féminin*. Paris: Fayard, 1978.

307

Notes

Chapter 1. The domestic group

1. Henriette Dussourd, *Les Communautés familiales agricoles du centre de la France* (Paris: Maisonneuve et Larose, 1978), p. 18.
2. Lutz Berkner and John Schaffer, 'The Joint Family in the Nivernais', *Journal of Family History* 3(1978): 102.
3. Frédéric Le Play, *Organisation de la famille* (Tours: Mame, 1971), p. 8.
4. Jean-Louis Flandrin, *Families in Former Times* (Cambridge: Cambridge University Press, 1979), p. 60, quoting Gérard Bouchard, *Sennely en Sologne* (Paris: Plon, 1972).
5. Myfanwy Morgan and Hilda H. Golden, 'Immigrant Families in an Industrial City: A Study of Households in Holyoke, 1880', *Journal of Family History* 4(1979): 59–68.
6. William Goode, *The Family* (Englewood Cliffs, N.J.: Prentice-Hall, 1964), pp. 44–5.
7. Agnes Fine-Souriac, 'La Famille-souche pyrénéenne au XIXe siècle', *Annales Economiés, Sociétés, Civilisations* 3(1977): 481.
8. Martine Segalen, 'Cycle de vie familiale et transmission du patrimoine en Bretagne. Analyse d'un cas', *Ethnologie Française* 4(1978): 271–8.
9. Lutz Berkner, 'The Stem Family and the Development Cycle of the Peasant Household: An Eighteenth-Century Austrian Example', *American Historical Review* 77(1972): 398–418.
10. E. A. Hammel, 'The Zagruda as a Process', in P. Laslett and R. Wall, eds., *Household and Family in Past Time* (Cambridge: Cambridge University Press, 1972), p. 370.
11. Christane Klapisch, 'Household and Family in Tuscany in 1427', in Laslett and Wall, eds., *Household and Family in Past Time*, p. 279.
12. Hans Medick,'The Proto-Industrial Family Economy: The Structural Function of Household and Family during the Transition from Peasant Society to Industrial Capitalism', *Social History* 3(1976): 291–315.
13. John Modell and Tamara K. Hareven. 'Urbanization and the Malleable Household'. *Journal of Marriage and the Family* 35(1973): 467–79.

14. M. Baulant, 'La famille, en miettes', *Annales Economies, Sociétés, Civilsations* 4–5(1972): 959–68.
15. Jean Ganiage, *Trois villages d'Ile-de-France* (Paris: PUF, 1963).
16. Alain Corbin, *Archaisme et modernité en Limousin au XIXe siècle* (Paris: Marcel Rivière, 1975). The diaspora in the Limousin region is analysed on pp. 204–25 and 283.
17. *La Famille* (Paris: Hachette, 1975), pp. 77–84; D. Marchand and G. Ballard, *Ménages, Familles, résultats du sondage au 1/20e*, no. 120 des collections de l'INSEE (Paris: Institut National de Statistiques et d'Etudes Economiques, 1974).
18. Dominique Maison and Elisabeth Millet, 'La Nuptialité', *Population*, June 1974, p.49.
19. Jack Goody, 'Domestic Groups', *Anthropology*. Addison-Wesley module 28 (Reading, Mass.: Addison-Wesley, 1972), pp. 28–4 .
20. Jack Goody, 'The Evolution of the Family', in Laslett and Wall, eds., *Household and Family in Past Time*, pp. 107–8.

Chapter 2. Kinship and kinship groups

1. Robin Fox, *Kinship and Marriage: An Anthropological Perspective* (London: Penguin, 1967).
2. A. R. Radcliffe-Brown and Daryl Forde, *African Systems of Kinship and Marriage* (Oxford: Oxford University Press, 1950), pp. 27–8.
3. David Schneider, *American Kinship: A Cultural Account* (Englewood Cliffs, N.J.: Prentice-Hall, 1968), pp. 25–9.
4. Alice Rossi, 'Naming Children in Middle-Class Families', *American Sociological Review* 30(1965): 503.
5. Fox, *Kinship and Marriage*, pp. 88–9.
6. Ibid., p. 115.
7. Ibid., pp. 135–6.
8. Ibid., pp. 137–8.
9. Meyer Fortes, 'The Structure of Unilinear Descent Groups', *American Anthropologist* 1953–1(1953): 17–41 (pp. 28–9).
10. Robin Fox, *The Tory Islanders: A People of the Celtic Fringe* (Cambridge: Cambridge University Press, 1978), p. 159.
11. J. D. Freeman, 'On the Concept of Kindred', *Journal of the Royal Anthropological Institute* 91(1961: 192–220). (p. 211).
12. Claude Lévi-Strauss, *The Elementary Structures of Kinship* (Boston: Beacon Press, 1959), p. 115.
13. Ibid., p. 116.
14. Fox, *Kinship and Marriage,* p. 224.
15. Louis Dumont, *Introduction à deux théories d'anthropologie sociale* (Paris: Mouton, 1971), p. 92.
16. Ibid., p. 114.
17. Fox, *Kinship and Marriage*, p. 262.
18. Emile Benveniste, *Le Vocabulaire des institutions indo-européennes*, vol. 1 (Paris: Editions de Minuit, 1969), p. 223.

19. Isac Chiva, *La Parenté dans les sociétés paysannes* (in press).
20. Pierre Lamaison, 'Les stratégies matrimoniales dans un système complexe de parenté: Ribennes en Gévaudan (1650–1830)', *Annales Economies, Societés, Civilisations* 4(1979): 721–43.
21. Marie-Claude Pingaud, *Paysans en Bourgogne. Les gens de Minot* (Paris: Mouton, 1970), p. 133.
22. Marie-Claude Pingaud, 'Chronologie et formes du pouvoir à Minot', *Etudes rurales* (July–Dec. 1976): 63–64, 205.
23. Martine Segalen, 'Cycle de la vie familiale et transmission du patrimoine: Analyse d'un cas', *Ethnologie Française* 1–2(1978).
24. Michèle Dion-Salitot, 'Strategies de reproduction et accumulation des patrimoines fonciers', *Etudes rurales* (Jan.–March 1977): 31–48.
25. Tina Jolas and Françoise Zonabend, 'Cousinage et voisinage', *Mélanges offerts a Claude Lévi-Strauss à l'occasion de son 60e anniversaire. Echanges et communications* (Paris: Mouton, 1970), p. 172.
26. Tina Jolas, Françoise Zonabend and Y. Verdier, 'Parler Famille', *L'homme* 10(1970): 5–26.
27. Laurent Lévi-Strauss, 'Pouvoir municipal et parenté dans un village bourguignon', *Annales Economies, Sociétés, Civilisations* 1(1975): 149–59 (p. 158).

Chapter 3. Kin relationships in urban society

1. Talcott Parsons, 'The Kinship System of the Contemporary United States', *American Anthropologist* 45(1943): 22–38. A French translation appeared in François Bourricauld, *Eléments pour une sociologie de l'action* (Paris: Plon, 1955).
2. Talcott Parsons, 'The Normal American Family', in S. M. Farber, (ed.), *Man and Civilization: The Family's Search for Survival* (New York: McGraw-Hill, 1965), pp. 34–6.
3. John Mogey, 'Residence, Family and Kinship: Some Recent Research', *Journal of Family History* 1(1979): 95–105 (p. 96).
4. Edward Thompson, *The Making of the English Working Class* (London: Gollancz, 1963), p. 416.
5. 'Provinciaux et Provinces à Paris', *Ethnologie Française* 10(1980), ed. Guy Barbichon.
6. Eric Wolf, 'Kinship, Friendship and Patron-Client Relations in Complex Societies', in Michael Banton, ed., *The Social Anthropology of Complex Societies* (London: Tavistock, 1966), pp. 14–15.
7. Tamara Hareven, 'Family Time and Industrial Time: Family and Work in a Planned Corporation Town', in Hareven, ed., *Family and Kin in Urban Communities, 1700–1930* (New York, London: New Viewpoints, 1977), pp. 187–208.
8. Tamara Hareven, 'The Dynamics of Kin in an Industrial Community', in *Turning Points* 84(1978): S151–82. Supplement of *American Journal of Sociology*.
9. Marie-Hélène Zylberberg-Hocquard, 'Les Ouvrières d'Etat dans les dernières années du XIXe siècle', *Le Mouvement social* 105(1978): 87–107.

10. Michael Young and Peter Wilmott, *Family and Kinship in East London* (London: Routledge & Kegan Paul, 1957), p. 101.
11. Peter Dobkin Hall, 'Family Structure and Economic Organisation', in Hareven, ed., *Family and Kin in Urban Societies*, p. 44.
12. Yvonne Knibiehler and Emile Temime, 'Présentation du colloque Famille et Pouvoir', (Aix, June 1979), *Informations sociales* 4–5(1980): 3–10.
13. Sylvain Maresca, Grandeur et permanence des grandes familles paysannes. L'essor des organisations agricoles en Meurthe-et-Moselle', *Actes de la Recherche en Sciences Sociales* 31(1980): 35–61.
14. Monique de Saint-Martin, 'Une grande famille', *Actes de la Recherche en Sciences Sociales* 31(1980): 4–21.
15. Louis Roussel, *Le Mariage dans la société française* (Paris: PUF, 1975), pp. 352–75.
16. Andrée Michel, 'La Famille urbaine et la parenté en France', in Reuben Hill and René König, eds., *Families in East and West* (The Hague: Mouton, 1970), pp. 436–7.
17. Catherine Gokalp, 'Le Réseau familial', *Population* 6(1978): 1077–94.
18. Ibid., pp. 1088–9.
19. Françoise Cribier, 'Les Parisiens et leur famille à l'âge de la retraite', *Gérontologie* 30(1979): 20–30.
20. Roussel, *Le Mariage dans la société française*, p. 146.
21. Odile Bourguignon, in Louis Roussel, ed., *La Famille après le mariage des enfants* (Paris: PUF, 1976), p. 175.
22. Ibid., pp. 195, 237.
23. Ibid., p. 244.
24. Roussel, *La Famille après le mariage des enfants*, p. 105.
25. Agnès Pitrou, 'Le Soutien familial dans la société urbaine', *Revue française de Sociologie* 18(1977): 80–3.
26. Young and Wilmott, *Family and Kinship in East London*, p. 61.
27. Michael Young and Peter Wilmott, *Family and Class in a London Suburb* (London: Routledge & Kegan Paul, 1968), p. 76.
28. Marvin Sussman, 'The Help Pattern in the Middle-Class Family', *American Sociological Review* 18(1953): 22–8; Ethel Shanas, *Family Relationships of Older People* (New York: Health Information Foundation, 1961); Sylvia Junko Yanagisako, 'Women-Centered Kin Networks in Urban Bilateral Kinship', *American Ethnologist* 4(1977): 220.
29. Yanagisako, 'Women-Centered Kin Networks in Urban Bilateral Kinship', p. 220.
30. Gokalp, 'Le Réseau familial', p. 1088.
31. Raymond Firth, ed., *Two Studies of Kinship in London* (London: Athlone Press, 1956), p. 38. (*Ego* is the person whose genealogy is being constructed and who is at the centre of the pattern, below ascendants and above descendants.)
32. Firth, *Two Sides of Kinship*, pp. 40–5.
33. Guy de Maupassant, *Pierre et Jean* (Paris: Gallimard, 1982 [1888]), p. 49.

34. H. Leichter and W. Mitchell, *Kinship and Casework* (New York: Russell Sage Foundation, 1967), p. 90.
35. Gokalp, 'Le Résau familial', pp. 1079–81.
36. Elizabeth Bott, *Family and Social Network*, 2d ed. (London: Tavistock, 1971), p. 121.
37. Christopher Turner, *Family and Kinship in Modern Britain* (London: Routledge & Kegan Paul, 1969), pp. 18–19.
38. C. C. Rosser and C. Harris, *The Family and Social Change* (London: Routledge & Kegan Paul, 1968), p. 229.
39. W. E. Mitchell, 'Descent Groups among New York City Jews', *Jewish Journal of Sociology* 3(1961): 121–8.
40. E. Leyton, 'Composite Descent Groups in Canada', quoted by C. C. Harris, *Readings in Urban Kinship* (Oxford: Pergamon Press, 1970), pp. 179–86.
41. P. Garigue and R. Firth, 'Kinship and Organisation of Italianates in London', *Two Studies of Kinship*, pp. 67–93.
42. Ibid., p. 70.
43. Marvin B. Sussman, 'The Urban Kin Network in the Formulation of Family Theory', in Hill and König, eds., *Families in East and West*, p. 495.
44. Marvin B. Sussman, 'Relationships of Adult Children with their Parents', in Ethel Shanas and Gordon F. Streib, eds., *Social Structure and the Family* (Englewood Cliffs, N.J.: Prentice-Hall, 1965).
45. Danièle Auffray, Thierry Baudoin, Michèle Collin and Alain Guillerm, *Feux et lieux, histoire d'une famille et d'un pays face à la société industrielle* (Paris: Galilée, 1980).
46. Ibid., p. 197.
47. Martine Segalen, 'Faire construire. Résistances et pouvoirs familiaux en Bretagne', *Economie et Humanisme* 251(1980): 40–50.
48. Pitrou, 'Le Soutien familial dans la société urbaine', pp. 54–5.
49. Béatrix Le Wita 'La mémoire familiale des Parisiens des classes moyennes', *Ethnologie Française* 1(1984): 57–66.
50. Michel, 'La Famille urbaine et la parenté en France', in Hill and König, eds., *Families in East and West*, p. 436.
51. Pitrou, 'Le Soutien familial dans la société urbaine, p. 59.
52. Young and Wilmott, *Family and Kinship in East London;* R. Firth, J. Hubert and A. Forge, *Families and Their Relatives;* Rosser and Harris, *Family and Social Change.*
53. Young and Wilmott, *Family and Kinship in East London,* p. 98.

Chapter 4. The historical sociology of marriage

1. André Armengaud, *La famille et l'enfance en France et en Angleterre du XVIe au XVIIIe siècle* (Paris: Société d'Edition d'Enseignement Supérieur, 1975), p. 28.
2. Jean Boissière, 'Us et coutumes du mariage dans l'ancienne France, les

unions à Fontainebleau dans la première moitié du XVIIIe siècle', *Ethnologie Française* 4(1974): 261.

3. Armengaud, *La famille et l'enfance*, p. 24.
4. Pierre Goubert, *Beauvais et le Beauvisis de 1600 à 1730* (Paris: Société d'éditions et de vente des publications de l'Education Nationale, 1960), pp. 47–8.
5. 'Situation démographique de la France', *Population* (March–April 1978): 305–6.
6. Jean Bourgeois-Pichat, 'Le mariage, coutume saisonnière', *Population* 4(1946): 623–42; for symbolic aspects and prohibition in May see Nicole Belmont, 'Le joli mois de mai', *L'histoire* 1(1978): 16–26.
7. Jean Boissière, 'Nuptialité et union à Fontainebleau', *Mémoires publiés par la Fédération des sociétés historiques et archéologiques de Paris et de l'Ile de France*, vols. 26, 27 (Paris: 1975–6), pp. 300–1.
8. Henri Polge, 'Cycles saisonniers et hebdomadaires de la nuptialité gersoise sous l'Ancien Régime', *Bulletin de la Société Archéologique, Historique, Littéraire et Scientifique du Gers* 2(1958): 438–45.
9. Not all demographers are in agreement about these findings. Etienne de Walle sees a slow fall in the number of unmarried women until the Revolution, followed by a rise. 'La Nuptialité des Françaises avant 1851, d'après l'état-civil des décédées', *Population*, no. spécial (Sept. 1977): 454.
10. Louis Henry and Jacques Houdaille, 'Célibat et âge au mariage aux XVIIIe et XIXe siècles en France, I. Célibat', *Population* (Jan.–Feb. 1978): 43.
11. 'Situation démographique de la France', pp. 306–8.
12. Maurice Garden, *Lyon et les Lyonnais au XVIIe siècle* (Paris: Les Belles Lettres, 1970), p. 165.
13. John Knodel and Mary Jo Baynes, 'Urban and Rural Marriage Patterns in Imperial Germany', *Journal of Family History* 1(1976): 129–61.
14. Louis Roussel, *Le Mariage dans la société française contemporaire* (Paris: PUF, 1975), p. 98.
15. John Hajnal, 'European Marriage Patterns in Perspective', B. V. Glass and D. E. C. Eversley, eds., *Population in History* (London: Arnold, 1965).
16. 'Situation démographique de la France', p. 309.
17. François Lebrun, *La Vie conjugale sous l'Ancien Régime* (Paris: Colin, 1975).
18. Alain Collomp, 'Alliance et filiation en Haute Provence au XVIIIe siècle', *Annales Economies, Sociétés, Civilisations* 3(1977): 469.
19. Lebrun, *La Vie conjugale*, pp. 28–9.
20. According to canon law reckoning; the civil administration adds the degree of both lines finishing in a common ancestor.
21. Jean-Louis Flandrin, *Les Amours paysannes* (Paris: Gallimard-Julliard, 1975).
22. Albert Jacquard and Martine Segalen, 'Isolement sociologique et isolement génétique', *Population* 3(1973): 506.

23. Pierre Bourdieu, 'Célibat et condition paysanne', *Etudes rurales* 5–6(1962): 33–135 (pp. 33–4).
24. Pierre Bourdieu, 'Les stratégies matrimoniales dans le système de reproduction', *Annales Economies, Sociétés, Civilisations* 4–5(1972): 1125.
25. Pierre Lamaison, 'Les stratégies matrimoniales dans un système complete de parenté: Ribennes en Gévaudan (1650–1830)', *Annales Economies, Sociétés, Civilisations* 4(1979): 121–43.
26. Martine Segalen, 'L'Espace matrimonial dans le sud du pays bigouden au XIXᵉ siècle', *Gwechall* 1(1978): 109–22.
27. Jacqueline Vu Tien Khang and André Sevin, *Choix du conjoint et patrimoine génétique. Etude de quatre villages du Pays de Sault de 1740 à nos jours* (Paris: Centre National de la Recherche Scientifique, 1977), p. 102.
28. Peter Dobkin Hall, 'Family Structure and Economic Organization: Massachusetts Merchants 1700–1850', in Tamara K. Hareven, ed., *Family and Kin in Urban Communities 1700–1930* (New York: New Viewpoints, 1977), pp. 42–3.
29. Nicole Belmont, 'La Fonction symbolique du cortège dans les rituels populaires du mariage', *Annales Economies, Sociétés, Civilisations* 3(1978): 650–5.
30. Jean-Marie Gouesse, 'Parents, famille et mariage en Normandie au XVIIᵉ et XVIIIᵉ siècles', *Annales Economies, Sociétés, Civilisations* 4–5(1972): 1144.
31. Jean-Louis Flandrin, 'Repression and Change in the Sexual Life of Young People in Medieval and Modern Times', *Journal of Family History* 2–3(1977): 202.
32. Arnold Van Gennep, *Manuel du folklore français contemporain*, vol. I, 1 and 2 (Paris: Picard, 1943–6), p. 264.
33. Pierre Caspar, 'Conceptions prénuptiales et développement du capitalisme dans la principauté de Neuchâtel (1678–1820)', *Annales Economies, Sociétés, Civilisations* 4–5(1974): 989–1009.
34. Caspar, 'Conceptions prénuptiales', p. 1007.
35. Yves Lequin, *Les Ouvriers de la région lyonnaise (1848–1914)*, vol. 1 (Lyon: Presses Universitaires de Lyon, 1977), pp. 205–69.
36. D. E. C. Eversley, 'Population, Economy and Society', in B. V. Glass and D. E. C. Eversley, eds., *Population in History* (London: Edward Arnold, 1965).
37. This phenomenon has already been observed in the case of village communities undergoing industrialisation in the eighteenth century. Cf. David Levine, *Family Formation in an Age of Nascent Capitalism* (New York: Academic Press, 1977). See in particular 'Illegitimacy: Marriage frustrated, not Promiscuity Rampant'.
38. Michel Frey, 'Du mariage et du concubinage dans les classes populaires à Paris, 1846–1847', *Annales Economies, Sociétés, Civilisations* 4(1978): 803–29.
39. Charles Benoist, *Les Ouvrières de l'aiguille à Paris* (Paris: Leon Chailly, 1895).

40. Alain Corbin, *Les Filles de noce. Misère sexuelle et prostitution (XIXe et XXe siècles)* (Paris: Aubier-Montaigne, 1978). On prostitution of female textile workers, see. pp. 308–9.
41. Corbin, *Les Filles de noce*, pp. 278–9.
42. Frey, 'Du mariage et du concubinage'.

Chapter 5. Marriage and divorce in contemporary society

1. Louis Roussel, *Le Mariage dans la société française contemporaine* (Paris: PUF, 1975), p. 37.
2. Michel Louis Lévy, 'La Démographie française en 1978', *Population et sociétés* 122(1979), and 'La population de la France en 1980', *Population et sociétés* 145(1981).
3. Gerard Calot and J. C. Deville, 'Nuptialité et fécondité selon le milieu socio-culturel', *Economie et Statistique*, 27 October 1971, pp. 3–42.
4. Roussel, *Le Mariage*, pp. 66–7.
5. Ibid., p. 105.
6. Ibid., p. 109.
7. Tamara K. Hareven, 'Family Time and Historical Time', *Daedalus* 106(1977): 60.
8. W. R. Catton and R. J. Smircich, 'A Comparison of Mathematical Models for the Effect of Residential Propinquity on Mate Selection', *American Sociological Review* 29(1964): 522–9.
9. Alain Girard, *Le Choix du conjoint*, 2d ed. INED, Travaux et documents, cahier no. 70. (Paris: PUF, 1974), p. 188.
10. Catherine Gokalp, 'Le Réseau familial', *Population* 6(1978): 1089–90.
11. A. D. Hollingshead, 'Cultural Factors in the Selection of Marriage Mates', *American Sociological Review* 16(1950): 619–27. A. C. Kerchoff and K. E. Davis, 'Value Consensus and Need Complementarity in Mate Selection', *American Sociological Review* 27(1962): 295–303.
12. Girard, *Le Choix du conjoint*, pp. 75–6.
13. Ibid., p. 198.
14. François de Singly, 'Mobilité féminine par le mariage et dot scolaire: l'exemple nantais', *Economie et Statistique* 91(1977): 33–4.
15. De Singly, 'Mobilité féminine', p. 40.
16. Alain Desrosières, 'Marché matrimonial et classes sociales', *Actes de la Recherche en Sciences Sociales* 20–1(1978): 97.
17. Girard, *Le Choix du conjoint*, p. 45.
18. William Goode, 'The Theoretical Importance of Love', *American Sociological Review* 24(1959): 32–47.
19. Ibid., p. 45.
20. Goode, *The Family* (Englewood Cliffs, N.J.: Prentice-Hall, 1964), p. 39.
21. Roussel, *Le Mariage*, pp. 236–365.
22. Louis Roussel, 'La Cohabitation juvénile en France', *Population* 1(1978): 15–42.
23. Girard, preface to the second edition of *Le Choix du conjoint*.

24. Louis Roussel, 'Démographie et mode de vie conjugale au Danemark', *Population* 2(1977): 339–59.
25. France Prioux-Marchall, 'Le Mariage en Suède', *Population* 4–5(1974): 825–53.
26. Roussel, 'La Cohabitation juvénile en France'; Patrick Festy, 'Fécondité hors mariage et cohabitation: tendances récentes en Europe occidentale', Communication to the Seminar on Fertility in Europe, Paris, 1979.
27. Patrick Festy, 'Le Nouveau contexte du mariage', *Population et Sociétés* 131(1980): 1–3.
28. Desrosières, 'Marché matrimonial', p. 106.
29. Jacques Commaille, 'Le Divorce en France', *La Documentation Française* (1975): 75.
30. Michel Louis Lévy, 'Divorces et divorcés', *Population et Sociétés* 144(1981).

Chapter 6. The child and the family

1. Roland Pressat, 'La Population française: mortalité, natalité, immigration, vieillissement', *Actes du Colloque National sur la démographie française*, June 1980 (Paris: PUF, 1981), pp. 6–27.
2. Ibid., pp. 10–12.
3. Henri Léridon, 'La Maîtrise de la fécondité: ses motifs et ses moyens', *Colloque national sur la démographie française*, June 1980, pp. 49–50.
4. André Burguière, 'De Malthus à Max Weber; le mariage tardif et l'esprit d'entreprise', *Annales Economies, Sociétés, Civilisations* 4–5(1972): 1121.
5. Gérard Calot, *Le Monde*, 2 Oct. 1979.
6. Gérard Calot, 'Le Baisse de la fécondité depuis 15 ans', *Colloque national sur la démographie française*, June 1980, pp. 29–39.
7. Léridon, 'La Maîtrise de la fécondité', p. 56.
8. Léridon, 'La Maîtrise de la fécondité', p. 56.
9. *Populations et Sociétés* 128(1979).
10. Chantal Blayo, 'Les Interruptions volontaires de grossesse en 1976', *Population* 2(1979): 307–42, and *9e rapport sur la situation démographique de la France*, Ministère du travail et de la participation, 1980, pp. 21–40.
11. Pierre Chaunu, 'Analyse historique du présent', *Histoire* 3(1978): 21–40.
12. Calot, 'La Baisse de la fécondité depuis 15 ans', p. 33.
13. Alain Girard and Louis Roussel, 'Fécondité et conjoncture. Une enquête d'opinion sur la politique démographique', *Population* 3(1979): 567–88.
14. Chaunu, 'Analyse historique du présent', p. 66.
15. J.-C. Chesnais, B. Marchal and C. Quoniam, 'Dossier pour la préparation du VIIIe plan', *Le Monde* 29 Nov. 1979.
16. Margaret Mead, 'Adolescence in Primitive and Modern Society', *Readings in Social Psychology* (New York: Holt, 1947), pp. 6–14.
17. Margaret Mead, *Culture and Commitment: A Study of the Generation Gap* (New York: Doubleday, 1970).
18. As developed by Elizabeth Badinter in *L'Amour en plus* (Paris: Flammarion, 1980).

19. Philippe Ariès, preface to second edition of *L'Enfant et la vie familiale sous l'Ancien Régime* (Paris: Le Seuil, 1973), p. 7.
20. Maurice Crubellier, *L'Enfance et la jeunesse dans la société française* (Paris: Colin, 1979), p. 59.
21. Natalie Z. Davis, *'La règle a l'envers'*, *Les Cultures du peuple* (Paris: Aubier-Montaigne, 1979), p. 171.
22. Fanny Faÿ-Sallois, *Les Nourrices à Paris au XIXe siècle* (Paris: Payot, 1980), p. 244.
23. Philippe Ariès, *Histoire des populations françaises et de leurs attitudes devant la vie depuis le XVIIIe siècle*, 2d ed. (Paris: Le Seuil, 1976), p. 166.
24. Tamara Hareven, 'The Family Life Cycle in Historical Perspective', in J. Cuisenier and M. Segalen, eds., *Le Cycle de la vie familiale dans les sociétés européennes* (Paris: Mouton, 1977), p. 345.
25. Jean Cuisenier, 'Type d'organisation familiale et cycle: changement ou mutation dans les sociétés européennes', *Le Cycle de la vie familiale dans les sociétés européennes*, pp. 488–9.
26. Henri Bastide and Alain Girard, 'Attitudes des Français sur la conjoncture démographique, la natalité, la politique familiale à la fin de 1976', *Population* 3(1977): 519–44; Alain Monnier, *La Naissance d'un enfant: incidences sur les conditions de vie des familles* (Paris: PUF, 1981).
27. Anne-Marie Coutrot, 'L'Illusion du choix', *Informations Sociales* 3(1980): 10–12.
28. Martine Lévy, 'La Mère qui travaille en dehors', *Informations Sociales* 3(1980): 45–6.
29. Nadine Lefaucheur, 'Jeunes couples ou nouveaux couples', *Informations Sociales* 3(1980): 25.
30. Suzanne H. Woolsey, 'Pied Piper Politics and the Child Care Debate', *Daedalus* 106(1977): 129–30.
31. Lévy, 'La Mère qui travaille en dehors', p. 44, quoting a *Société Française d'Etudes et de Sondages* survey of June 1979.
32. Melvin L. Kohn, 'The Effects of Social Class on Parental Values and Practices', in David Reiss and Howard A. Hoffman, eds., *The American Family, Dying or Developing?* (New York and London: Plenum Press, 1978).
33. Elina Gianini, *Du côté des petites filles* (Paris: Des Femmes, 1974).
34. Noëlle Gérome, 'Les formules du bonheur: "Parents" 1969–1976; l'information des familles par la grande presse', *Le Mouvement Social* 129(1984): 89–115.
35. Crubellier, *L'Enfance et la jeunesse dans la société française*, pp. 315–24.
36. Maurice Cusson, *Délinquants, pourquoi?* (Paris: Armand Colin, 1981), p. 36.
37. Robert and Rhona Rapoport and Ziona Strelitz, *Fathers, Mothers, and Society* (New York: Basic Books, 1977).
38. Annick Percheron, 'Se faire entendre: morale quotidienne et attitudes politiques des jeunes', in Henri Mendras, ed., *La Sagesse et le désordre*, (Paris: Gallimard, 1980), p. 143.

39. John R. Gillis, *Youth in History* (New York and London: Academic Press, 1974), pp. 205–6.
40. Crubellier, *L'Enfance et la jeunesse dans la société française*, p. 374.

Chapter 7. Roles within the couple in the nineteenth century

1. Susan Rogers, 'Les Femmes et le pouvoir', *Paysans, Femmes et citoyens* (Le Paradou: Actes Sud, 1980), pp. 59–138.
2. Yvonne Verdier, 'Les Femmes et le saloir', *Ethnologie Française* 6(1976): 349–64.
3. Hans Medick, 'The Proto-Industrial Family Economy: The Structural Function of Household and Family during the Transition from Peasant Society to Industrial Capitalism', *Social History* 3(1976): 291–315 (pp. 312–13).
4. Louise Tilly, 'Vies individuelles et stratégies familiales', *Bulletin de la Société d'Ethnologie Française* 7(1979): 349–64.
5. Jean-Luc Chodkiewicz, 'L'Aubrac à Paris', *L'Aubrac*, IV (Paris: Centre National de la Recherche Scientifique, 1978), p. 226.
6. *La Famille* (Paris: Hachette, 1975), pp. 111–13.
7. Louise Tilly and Joan Scott, *Women, Work and Family* (New York: Holt, Rinehart & Winston, 1978), p. 125.
8. Michèle Perrot, 'De la nourrice à l'employée', and 'Machine à coudre et travail à domicile', *Le mouvement social* (Oct.–Dec. 1978): 5, 161–6, respectively.
9. Tilly and Scott, *Women, Work and Family*, p. 113.
10. Yvonne Knibiehler and Catherine Fouquet, *Histoire des mères* (Paris: Montalba, 1980), p. 245.
11. Ibid., p. 254.
12. Anne Martin-Fugier, 'La Maîtresse de maison', in Jean-Paul Aron, ed., *Misérable et glorieuse, la femme du XIXe siècle* (Paris: Fayard, 1980), pp. 116–34.
13. Theodore Zeldin, *Histoire des passions françaises. Ambition et Amour* (Paris: Encres, 1978), p. 340.
14. Ibid., p. 347.
15. Ibid., p. 341.
16. Ibid., p. 287.
17. Jane Marceau, 'Le Rôle des femmes dans les familles du monde des affaires', in Andrée Michel, ed., *Les Femmes dans la société marchande* (Paris: PUF, 1978), pp. 113–24.

Chapter 8. Roles within the present-day couple

1. Robert and Rhona Rapoport, *Dual-Career Families Re-examined* (New York: Harper & Row, 1976).
2. Robert and Rhona Rapoport, 'Problèmes de recherche dans les familles

à double carrière', in Andrée Michel, ed., *Sociologie de la famille* (Paris: Mouton, 1970), pp. 231–40.

3. B. Lemmenecier, 'The Economics of Conjugal Roles', in Louis Lévy-Garboua, ed., *Sociological Economics* (London: Sage, 1978).
4. Gary Becker, 'A Theory of Allocations of Time', *Economic Journal* 75(1965): 512.
5. Anne Martin-Fugier, *La Place des bonnes. La domesticité féminine à Paris en 1900* (Paris; Grasset, 1979), p. 35.
6. L. Thévenot, 'Les Catégories sociales en 1975: l'extension du salariat', *Économie et statistique* 91(1977): 7.
7. Martine Lévy, 'La Mère qui travaille au dehors', *Informations sociales* 3(1980): 44.
8. Nadine Lefaucheur, 'Jeunes couples ou nouveaux couples', *Informations sociales* 3(1980): 25.
9. Ibid., p. 25.
10. Lee Rainwater, 'Mother's Contribution to the Family Money Economy in Europe and in the United States', *Journal of Family History* 4(1979): 198–211.
11. Louis Roussel, *La Famille après le mariage des enfants* (Paris: PUF, 1976), p. 126.
12. Andrée Michel, *Activité professionnelle de la femme et vie conjugale* (Paris: Centre National de la Recherche Scientifique, 1967).
13. Ibid., p. 89.
14. François de Singly, 'La Lutte conjugale pour le pouvoir domestique', *Revue française de sociologie* 17 (1976): 81–100.
15. *Le Groupe familial* 83(1979), special issue.
16. Paul-Henri Chombart de Lauwe, *La Vie quotidienne des familles ouvrières* (Paris: Centre National de la Recherche Scientifique, 1956), pp. 44–5.
17. Yannick Lemel, *Les Budgets-temps des citadins*, l'INSEE, ser. M, no. 33, March 1974, p. 39, as had already been noted in 1963 by Madeleine Guilbert, 'Enquête Budgets-temps', *Revue Française de Sociologie* 6(1965): 325–35, 487–512.
18. Elizabeth Bott, *Family and Social Network*, 2d ed. (London: Tavistock, 1971), pp. 52–3.
19. Paul-Henri Chombart de Lauwe, *La Vie quotidienne*, p. 138.
20. Martha Reed Herbert, 'La Libération des femmes et la production industrielle', *Esprit* 7–8(1973): 85–94.
21. Equipe de Toulouse, 'Le Système des activités des ménages au Mirail', ATP *Observation du changement social et culturel*, December 1980, cyclostyled.
22. Robert and Rhona Rapoport, *Fathers, Mothers and Others*, pp. 229–30.

Chapter 9. The domestic group and economic roles

1. Isabel J. Sawhill, 'Economic Perspectives on the Family', *Daedalus* 106(1977): 115–25.

2. Bernard Brunhes, *Présentation de la comptabilité nationale française*. Institut National de la Statistique et des Etudes Economiques, Dec. 1976, no. 216, pp. 32–5.
3. Françoise Evrard,' 'Travail des femmes et revenu familial', *Informations sociales* 3(1980): 55.
4. Commissariat général au Plan, *La Famille* (Paris: Hachette, 1975), pp. 40–3.
5. Georges Bigata and Bernard Bouvier, *Composition des ménages et structure de leur budget en 1971*, INSEE, Dec. 1973, no. 31, pp. 11–30.
6. Ibid., pp. 21–2.
7. Ann Grey, 'The Working-Class Family as an Economic Unit', in C. Harris, ed., *Sociology of the Family: New Directions for Britain* (Keele: University of Keele, 1979), pp. 187–213.
8. Paul-Henri Chombart de Lauwe, *La Vie quotidienne des familles ouvrières* (Paris: Centre National de la Recherche Scientifique, 1956), p. 135.
9. Christine Delphy, 'La Fonction de consommation et la famille', *Cahiers internationaux de sociologie* 58 (1975): 23–41.
10. Commissariat général au Plan, *La Famille*, pp. 176–211.
11. Odile Benoit-Guilbot and Marie Moscovici, 'Consommation moderne, gestion du budget et perspectives d'avenir', in Jean-Daniel Reynaud, ed., *Tendances et volontés de la société française* (Paris: Société d'Edition d'Enseignement Supérieur, Futuribles, 1966), pp. 148–66.
12. Jean Stoetzel, 'La Distribution des revenus en France', *Mélanges en l'honneur de Raymond Aron*, vol. 2 (Paris: Calmann-Lévy, 1971), p. 118.
13. Nicole Tabard. *Besoins et aspirations des familles et des jeunes* (Paris: Centre de recherches et d'études documentaires and Caisse Nationale d'Allocations Familiales, 1974), p. 205.
14. Jack Goody, Joan Thirsk and Edward P. Thompson, eds., *Family and Inheritance* (Cambridge: Cambridge University Press, 1976).
15. Louis Roussel, *La Famille après le mariage des enfants* (Paris: PUF, 1976), p. 73.
16. André Babeau, *Un Essai de modélisation retrospective de l'accumulation patrimoniale*, Centre de recherches en épargne, Université de Paris X, offset, 1974.
17. Dominique Strauss-Kahn, *Economie de la famille et accumulation patrimoniale* (Paris: Centre de recherches et d'études du patrimoine, 1977), pp. 36–41.
18. Commissariat général au Plan, *La Famille*, pp. 215–226.
19. André Babeau and Dominique Strauss-Kahn, *La Richesse des Français* (Paris: PUF, 1977), pp. 134–8.
20. Jacques Lautman, 'Modèles familiaux de la transmission du patrimoine et théorie du cycle', in J. Cuisenier and M. Segalen, eds., *Le Cycle de vie familiale dans les sociétés européennes* (Paris: Mouton, 1977), pp. 452–66.
21. Ibid., p. 459.
22. Commissariat général au Plan, *La Famille*, p. 227.
23. Strauss-Kahn, *Economie de la famille*, pp. 44–48.

24. Ibid., p. 45.
25. Ibid., p. 52.

Chapter 10. Family and society

1. Agnès Pitrou, 'Pouvoir familial et changement social', *Economie et humanisme* 251(1980): 17.
2. Agnès Pitrou, *La Vie précaire. Des familles face à leurs difficultés* (Paris: Caisse Nationale des Allocations familiales, 1978), pp. 217–18.
3. *Présentation du rapport général sur la situation démographique de la France*, p. IX, 1980, report no. 9, Ministère du Travail et de la Participation.
4. Paul Boyer, 'Critique du natalisme', *Le Monde*, 2 Oct. 1980.
5. Michel Louis Lévy, 'Préoccupations natalistes en Europe de l'Est', *Population et sociétés* 143(1981): 1–4.
6. Articles reprinted in *Population et L'Enseignement* (Paris: PUF, 1980).
7. Alain Girard and Henri Bastide, 'Orientation et sélection scolaires', *Population* 1(1964): 9–46; 2(1964): 195–261.
8. Alain Girard, *Population et l'Enseignement*, p. xxvi.
9. Pierre Bourdieu and Jean-Claude Passeron, *Les Héritiers, les étudiants et la culture* (Paris: Editions de minuit, 1964).
10. Raymond Boudon, *L'Inégalité des chances, la mobilité sociale dans les sociétés industrielles* (Paris: Colin, 1973).
11. Louis Roussel, *La Famille après le mariage des enfants*, chap. 5, 'Reproduction sociale et continuité culturelle'.
12. Pierre Bourdieu, 'Reproduction culturelle et reproduction sociale', *Informations sur les sciences sociales* 10(1971): 45–75.
13. Michel Louis Lévy, 'La Carrière des femmes', *Population et sociétés* 146(1981): 1–4.
14. Yvonne Knibiehler and Catherine Fouquet, *L'Histoire des mères du Moyen Age à nos jours* (Paris: Montalba, 1980).
15. Andrée Michel, ed., *Les Femmes dans la société marchande* (Paris: PUF, 1978), p. 71.
16. Danièle Léger and Bertrand Hervieu, *Le Retour à la nature. Au fond de la forêt, l'Etat* (Paris: Seuil, 1979).
17. Gérard Mauger, 'Tragédie, vaudeville et communautés', *Autrement* 3(1975): 52–66.
18. Michel Louis Lévy, 'Divorces et divorcés', *Population et Sociétés* 144(1981): 1–4.

Index

aborigines (Australian), 44
adultery: as grounds for divorce, 152
affrairement, 14
Africa, North, 37
America, *see* United States of America
Amoskeag Manufacturing Company, 76–7
Anderson, Michael, *Household and Family in Past Time*, 31
anthropology: and sociology of the family, 3–6
Anzin, 214
Ariès, Philippe, 4, 164, 175–7, 180
Aubrac, 212
Aude region, 27
Auffray, Danièle, 96
Australia, 44
Austria, 28; *see also individual towns and regions*
Auvergne, 75
Avesnes-les-Aubert, 211–12

Bas-Quercy, 35
Bas-Rhin, the, 230
Baulant, M., 32
Béarn, 35, 123
Beauvais, 111
Becker, Gary, 226–7
Belgium, 81, 139
Belgrade, 24–5
Benoit-Guilbot, Odile, and Marie Moscovici, 269
Benveniste, Emile, 61
Berkner, Lutz, *Population Patterns in the Past*, 30
Bessède, 27
Bethmale Valley, 130
Bethnal Green, 88, 98–9, 101
Bigouden, the region, 126

Bilhères d'Ossau, 35
birth rate *see* children
Bordeaux, 81–2
Borneo, 56
Bott, Elizabeth, *Family and Social Network*, 91, 223–4, 248–9
Boudon, *L'Inégalité des chances*, 295–8
Boulay, 35
Bourdieu, Pierre, 293, 295, 298; 'Célibat et condition paysanne', 123
Bourricaud, François, 73
Brie, 34
Bristol (USA), 24–5
Britain, Great: kinship relations in, 88, 92; *see also* England; Wales
Brittany, 32–3, 97, 130, 208–9
Bugey, 120
Bulan, 26
Burchinal, Lee, 92
Burguière, André, 165
Burgundy, 69, 209

Caisse nationale des allocations familiales (CNAF), 238, 248, 272
Calenberg, 30
Calot, Gérard, 165–6
Cambridge Group for the History of Population and Social Structure, 23–4
Canada, 23, 75, 94
Canevet, Yves, 69
Cantal, 75
Caspar, Pierre, 130–2
Centre de recherches et d'études documentaires (CREDOC), 248
Cevennes, the 305
Chailly, 34
Chaunu, Pierre, 116, 169
Chesnais, Jean-Claude, 172

Index

Chicago, 47

children: studies of, 159–60; birth rate, 160–4; contraception and, 164–72; changing parental relationships, 173–4, 183–5; in pre-industrial societies, 174–7; in nineteenth century, 177–9; in the peasant family, 179; in the working-class family, 179–81; in family life cycle, 181–3; young, 185–9; from four to twelve, 189–91; in adolescence, 192–6

China, 203, 304–5

Chiva, Isac, 62

Chombart de Lauwe, Paul-Henri, 247, 250, 268–9

clans: organisation of, 55; see also filiation

Cleveland, 96

CNAF, see Caisse nationale des allocations familiales

cohabitation, 148–51; see also marriage

Collomp, Alain, 119

Commaille, Jacques, 152, 155

communities: tacit, 14–17

Comte, Auguste, 288

contraception: and demographic changes, 117, 164–72

Corbin, Alain, 136, 219; Les Filles de noces, 217

Cornouaille, 97, 130

Coulommiers, 34

Coutrot, Anne-Marie, 186

CREDOC, see Centre de recherches et d'études documentaires

Creuse, 75

Cribier, Françoise, 84

Crubellier, Maurice, 175–8, 180, 192, 196

Crulai, 33–4

Cuisenier, Jean, 182

Cusson, Maurice, 192

Dauphiné, 120

Davis, Natalie Z., 176

de Singly, François, 146, 245

Delphy, Christine, 268

Denmark, 150

Desrosières, Alain, 147, 153

Deyon, Pierre, Colloque de l'histoire de la famille, 78

divorce, 139–43, 151–7; see also adultery; marriage

Dolto, Françoise, 182

domestic groups: definitions, 13–40; size, 20–2; structure, 22–4; dynamics, 24–31; instability, 31–7; recent developments in, 37–9; and kin relationships, 39–40

Donzelot, Jacques, 288

Dussourd, Henriette, 15

Dyaks, 39–40

Ealing, 24–5

Economie et Humanisme (1943 survey), 288

Edinburgh, 266

emigration, 36–7

Engels, Frederick, 261

England: households in, 24–5; industrialisation in, 132; nuptiality rate in, 139; birth rate in, 160; working women in, 237; see also Britain, Great; individual towns and regions

Eskimos, 61

Eure, 34, 120, 126, 211

family: 'in crisis', 1–3; past studies of, 3–6; definitions of, 7–8; 'extended', 17; stem, 18–20; relationship with society, 286–7; and social control, 287–90; and fertility, 290–3; and social power, 293–5; and social mobility, 295–8; women in, 298–304; and social destiny, 304–6

Faÿ-Sallois, Fanny, Les Nourrices à Paris au XIXᵉ siècle, 178

Féderation nationale des écoles de parents et des éducateurs (1978 survey), 246

fiche de famille, 4

filiation: concepts of, 46–52; bilineal and complementary, 52–4; undifferentiated (cognatic), 54–5; see also kinship

Fine-Souriac, Agnès, 27–8

Finistère, 34, 230

Firth, Raymond, 91–2, 94; Two Studies of Kinship in London, 88, 90

Flandrin, Jean-Louis, 164; Amours paysannes, 122, 129, 131; Families in Former Times, 24

Fortes, Meyer, 54

Foucault, Michel, 289

Fox, Robin, 51, 53–4, 60; Kinship and Marriage, 44, 48; The Tory Islanders, a People of the Celtic Fringe, 67–9

France: households in, 24–6, 28, 38; emigration in, 37; family as repository for cultural tradition, 75; agricultural restructuring in, 79; kinship relations in, 81, 89, 96; marriage in, 110; birth control in, 117; premarital chastity in, 129; illegitimacy in, 131; industrialisation in, 132; nuptiality rate in, 139, 141–3; patterns of cohabitation in, 151; divorce in, 151–2; remarriage in, 157;

Index

birth rate in, 160; contraception in, 164, 169; day-care centres in, 187; upbringing of small children in, 189; differing parental attitudes in, 190; peasant population in, 204; regional diversity of women's roles in, 208; female professional activity in, 221; servants in, 234; working women in, 237; distribution of roles in, 248; importance of inheritance in, 273; *see also individual towns and regions*

Freeman, J.D., 56

Frey, Michel, 135

Fritsch, Philippe, 290; *De la famille-cible à l'objet famille*, 288

gangs, 192–3; *see also* children

Germany, 115, 139

Gérome, Noëlle, 191

Gianini, Elina, 190

Gillis, J.R., *Youth in History*, 195

Girard, Alain, 149–50, 171; *Le Choix du conjoint*, 143–7; *Population et enseignement*, 294–5

Gokalp, Catherine, 82–4, 89, 144–5

Goode, William, 3, 147; *The Family*, 22, 148, 202, 304; *World Revolution and Family Patterns*, 103

Goody, Jack, 'Domestic Groups', 39

Gossiaux, Jean-François, *Famille et tradition communautaire en Yougoslavie*, 17

Göttingen, 30

Goubert, Pierre, 111

Gouesse, Jean-Marie, 129

Grey, Ann, 266–7

group, domestic: and inheritance, 273–85; as unit of consumption, 257–69

Halbwachs, Maurice, 268

Hall, Peter Dobkin, 78, 127

Hammel, E.A., *Household and Families in Past Times*, 28

Hareven, Tamara, 75–6

Haut Comité de la Population (1980 report), 291–2

Haut-Gévaudan, 124

Hautes-Pyrénées, 26

Heidenreichsstein, 28

Henri III, King of France, 110

Henry, Louis, 4

Herbert, Martha Reed, 252

history: and sociology of the family, 3–6

Holyoke, 21

Hopi Indians, 49, 55

Iban people, 56

Ile-de-France, 33, 35

Imbsheim, 230

INED, *see* Institut National d'Etudes Démographiques

inheritance: and marriage strategies, 124–8; *see also* group, domestic

INSEE, *see* Institut National de la Statistique et des Etudes Economiques

Institut National d'Etudes Démographiques (INED), 4, 91, 140, 186

Institut National de la Statistique et des Etudes Economiques (INSEE), 38, 118, 247, 259

Ireland, 23

Iroquois, 39–40, 45

Israel, 203

Italy, 95

Jacquard, Albert, 122

Japan, 25, 304–5; *see also individual towns and areas*

Jolas, Tina, 126

Joseph, Isaac, 288, 290; *Tactiques et figures disciplinaires*, 289

kinship: and industrialisation, 5; and domestic group, 13–40; concept of, 43–5; terminology of, 45–6; filiation, 46–55; kindred, 55–6; marriage and, 56–61; lineage and, 61–2; and peasant societies, 62–71; in urban society, 73–103

Klapisch, Christiane, *Household and Family in Past Time*, 29

Knibiehler, Yvonne, and Catherine Fouquet, *L'Histoire des mères du Moyen Âge à nos jours*, 178, 216–7, 303–4

Lafiteau, *Moeurs des sauvages américains*, 45

Laguiole, 26

Lamaison, Pierre, 64, 124

Landes, 37

large peasant family, 14–20; *see also* zadruga

Laslett, Peter, 23; *Household and Family in Past Time*, 22

Lautman, Jacques, 281–2, 285

Laval, 96

Lavedan, 18–19

Le Mirail, 252

Le Muet (17th century architect), 229

Le Play, Frédéric, 288; *Organisation de la famille*, 18–20

Index

Le Wita, Beatrix, *La mémoire familiale des Parisiens des classes moyennes*, 99–100

Lebrun, François, 120; *La Vie conjugale sous l'Ancien Régime*, 116

Lefaucheur, Nadine, 235

Léger, Danièle, and Bertrand Hervieu, 305

Lemmenecier, B., 225–6

Liberté 81 (survey), 184–5

Limoges, 116

Limousin, 16, 37

Litwak, Eugene, 92

London, 94, 214

Longuenesse, 24–5

Lorraine, 209

Lower Saxony, 30

Lyon, 115, 120, 132–3

Lyonnais, 120

Mamou, Yves, 255

Manche, 34

Manchester (USA), 75

Marceau, Jane, 220

marriage: and kinship, 56–7; elementary systems of, 57–60; complex systems of, 60–61; concept of, 107; religious framework for, 108–10; nuptiality rate, 110–16, 139–43; age of, 116–19; homogamy, 119–23; strategies, 123–8; and love, 128–32, 147–8; in proto-industrial society, 132–4; working-class, 134–6; bourgeois, 136–7; and choice of partner, 143–7; *see also* cohabitation; divorce

Martin-Fugier, Anne, 218

Massachusetts, 21

Mauger, Gérard, 306

Maupassant, Guy de, *Pierre et Jean*, 91

Maurienne, 130

Mayenne, 96

Mead, Margaret, 173–4

Medick, Hans, 210–11; 'The Proto-Industrial Family Economy', 31

men: and division of tasks, 203, 205–6; and masculine authority, 204–5; within artisans' households, 210–11; in bourgeois households, 218–20; and separation of roles, 223; in network theory, 223–4; in working-class households, 232; and masculine authority, 204–5; *see also* roles

Menangkabao, 50

Mendras, Henri, *Eléments de sociologie*, 203, 224

Meulan, 34

Meurthe-et-Moselle, 79

Meyer, Philippe, 288

Meyer, *L'Enfant et la raison d'Etat*, 290

Michel, Andrée, 81–2, 244–6, 249, 251, 254; *Families in East and West*, 100; *Les Femmes dans les sociétés marchandes*, 304; *Sociologie de la famille et du mariage*, 223

Middle Ages: tacit communities in, 15–17

Midi, the, 116

Mirabeau, 26

Monde, Le (newspaper), 184, 255

Monot, 69

Montplaisant, 26

Morgan, *Systems of Consanguinity and Affinity in the Human Family*, 44–5

mortality rate: and marriage, 111; in children, 163

Moselle, 35

Mostuéjouls, 26

Nantes, 97, 146

Netherlands, the, 139, 166

Neuchâtel, 130, 132, 135

New England, 78

New Hampshire, 75

Nice, 26

Nigeria, 53–4

Nishinomiya, 25

Normandy, 33, 122, 126, 129, 132

Norway, 150

Ordinance of Blois, 110

Orne, 34

parental relationships, *see* children

Paris, 82, 84, 99–100, 135, 180, 212, 306

Parsons, Talcott, 73–5, 80–1, 86, 181

Passeron, Jean-Claude, 295

patrimony, *see* inheritance

Pays de Sault, 34, 127

Péone, 26

Percheron, Annick, 194

Périgord, 26

Pétonnet, Colette, 180; *On est tous dans le brouillard*, 100, 268

Pingaud, Marie-Claude, *Paysans en Bourgogne*, 64

Pitrou, Agnès, 87, 89, 99–100, 287–8

Ploudalmezeau, 230

Pont-l'Abbé, 69

Portugal, 37

Provence, 26

Pyrénées, the, 27, 305

Quittard-Pinon, 52

326

Index

Radcliffe-Brown and Forde, *African Systems of Kinship and Marriage*, 45
Rapoport, Robert and Rhona, 224–5
religion: and the institution of marriage, 108–10
remarriages: and structure of domestic group, 32–6
Ribennes, 124
Ricardo, David, 225
roles: difficulties of studying, 201–2; and status, 202–4, 206–8; and authority, 204–5; and tasks, 205–6; cultural differences in, 208–9; changes in, 209–10, 227–44; within artisans' households, 210–12; within working-class households, 212–18; within bourgeois households, 218–21; separation of, 223; and network theory, 223–4; and dual-career family, 224–5; economic, 225–7, 257–84; within contemporary couples, 244–55;
Romania, 292
Rosser and Harris, 93
Roubaix, 76, 214
Rouergue, 26
Roussel, Louis, 85–7, 141, 149–50, 171, 238–9, 246, 273, 277, 280, 298; *La Famille après le mariage des enfants*, 82; *Le Mariage dans la société française contemporaine*, 139; *Le mariage dans la société française*, 80–1

Saint-André-d'Hébertot, 34
Saint-André-les-Alpes, 29
Saint-Etienne, 133
Saint-Jean-Trolimon, 34
Saint-Malo, 120
Saint-Martin, Monique de, 80
Saint-Martin-de Vésubie, 26
Savoie, 75, 130
Schneider, David, *American Kinship, ι Cultural Account*, 46
schooling: and family relationships, 190–1
Seattle, 143
Second World War, 4
Segalen, Martine, *Nuptialité et alliance*, 126
Seine Valley, 67
Sennely-en-Sologne, 21, 33–4
Sennett, Richard, *Families against the City*, 221
Serbia, *see* Yugoslavia
sexuality: premarital, 128–9
Shorter, Edward, 3, 164; *The Making of the Modern Family*, 129, 194
Shoshone Indians, 55

Sicily, 208
Sologne, 21
Spain, 37
status, *see* roles
Stoetzel, Jean, 271
Strauss-Kahn, Dominique, 284; *Economie de la famille et accumulation patrimoniale*, 258
Sullerot, Evelyne, 'Des Changements dans le partage des rôles', 204; *Le Fait féminin*, 299
Sumatra, 50
Sussman, Marvin, 92
Swansea, 88, 93, 139, 150, 160, 237
Sweden, 160
Switzerland, 132

Tabard, Nicole, 272; *Besoins et aspirations des familles et des jeunes*, 238
tacit communities *see* communities
tasks, *see* roles
Thiers, 52
Thompson, E.P., *The Making of the English Working Class*, 74–5
Tilly, Louise, and Joan Scott, *Women, Work and Family*, 213
Tonnerois, 34
Tory Island, 67–9
Toulouse, 252
Tourcoing, 216
trades: passed on within domestic groups, 67
Turner, Christopher, *Family and Kinship in Modern Britain*, 92

United States of America: households in, 23–5, 31; emigrants in, 75; kinship relations in, 81, 89, 94, 96; nuptiality rate in, 142; incidence of divorce in, 152; children's upbringing in, 183; day-care centres in, 187; differing parental attitudes in, 190; adolescent gangs in, 192; working women in, 237; *see also individual states and towns*

Van Gennep, Arnold, 130; *Manuel du folklore français contemporain*, 127
Vendée, the 129
Vienne, 133
Villedieu-les-Poëles, 34
Violet-le-Duc (19th century architect), 230
Vraiville, 34, 120, 126, 211

wages: and organisation of artisans' households, 210; in working-class households, 213–16

327

Index

Wales, 160
Winnicott, D.W., 182
women: and biological determination, 202; and division of tasks, 203, 205–6; status, 206–8; within artisans' households, 210–11; in working-class households, 212–13, 216–18, 232; in bourgeois households, 218–21; and separation of roles, 223; in network theory, 223–4; working, 234–46
Woodford, 101
World War II, *see* Second World War

Yako people, 53–4
Yanagisako, Sylvia, 89

Young, Michael, and Peter Wilmott, *Family and Class in a London Suburb*, 98–9; *Family and Kinship in East London*, 77, 88, 98, 218; *The Symmetrical Family*, 249–50
Yugoslavia, 17–18, 24–5; *see also individual towns and regions*

zadruga, 17–18, 28; *see also* large peasant family
Zeldin, Theodore, *Histoire des passions françaises*, 219
Zimmerman, Fred, *La Parenté*, 45
Zonabend, Françoise, 126